THE GIFTED AND THE TALENTED:
THEIR EDUCATION AND DEVELOPMENT

THE GIFTED AND THE TALENTED:
THEIR EDUCATION AND DEVELOPMENT

The Seventy-eighth Yearbook of the
National Society for the Study of Education

PART I

By

THE YEARBOOK COMMITTEE

and

ASSOCIATED CONTRIBUTORS

Edited by

A. HARRY PASSOW

Editor for the Society

KENNETH J. REHAGE

1 9 NSSE 79

Distributed by THE UNIVERSITY OF CHICAGO PRESS • CHICAGO, ILLINOIS

The National Society for the Study of Education

The purposes of the Society are to carry on investigations of educational problems and to publish the results of these investigations as a means of promoting informed discussion of important educational issues.

The two volumes of the seventy-eighth yearbook (Part I: *The Gifted and the Talented: Their Education and Development*, and Part II: *Class-Management*) continue the well-established tradition, now in its seventy-eighth year, of serious effort to provide scholarly and readable materials for those interested in the thoughtful study of educational matters. The yearbook series is planned to include at least one volume each year of general interest to all educators, while the second volume tends to be somewhat more specialized.

A complete list of the Society's past publications, including the yearbooks and the recently inaugurated series of paperbacks on Contemporary Educational Issues, will be found in the back pages of this volume.

It is the responsibility of the Board of Directors of the Society to select the subjects to be treated in the yearbooks, to appoint committees whose personnel are expected to insure consideration of all significant points of view, to provide for necessary expenses in connection with the preparation of the yearbooks, to publish and distribute the committees' reports, and to arrange for their discussion at the annual meeting. The editor for the Society is responsible for preparing the submitted manuscripts for publication in accordance with the principles and regulations approved by the Board of Directors.

Neither the Board of Directors, nor the Society's editor, nor the Society is responsible for the conclusions reached or the opinions expressed by the Society's yearbook committees.

All persons sharing an interest in the Society's purposes are invited to join. Regular members receive both volumes of the current yearbook. Those taking out the "comprehensive" membership receive the yearbook volumes and the volumes in the current series of paperbacks. Inquiries regarding membership may be addressed to the Secretary, NSSE, 5835 Kimbark Avenue, Chicago, Illinois 60637.

Library of Congress Catalog Number: 78-66031
ISSN 0077-5762

Published 1979 by
THE NATIONAL SOCIETY FOR THE STUDY OF EDUCATION

5835 Kimbark Avenue, Chicago, Illinois 60637

First Printing, 9,000 Copies

Printed in the United States of America

Officers of the Society

1978-79

(Term of office expires March 1 of the year indicated.)

JEANNE CHALL

(1981)

Harvard University, Cambridge, Massachusetts

N. L. GAGE

(1979)

Stanford University, Stanford, California

JOHN I. GOODLAD

(1980)

University of California, Los Angeles, California

A. HARRY PASSOW

(1981)

Teachers College, Columbia University, New York, New York

KENNETH J. REHAGE

(Ex-officio)

University of Chicago, Chicago, Illinois

HAROLD G. SHANE

(1979)

Indiana University, Bloomington, Indiana

RALPH W. TYLER

(1980)

Doctor Emeritus, Center for Advanced Study in the Behavioral Sciences
Stanford, California

Secretary-Treasurer

KENNETH J. REHAGE
5835 Kimbark Avenue, Chicago, Illinois 60637

v

The Society's Committee on
The Education of the Gifted and the Talented

Associated Contributors

ALEXINIA Y. BALDWIN

Assistant Professor of Education
State University of New York
Albany, New York

ERNEST M. BERNAL, JR.

Professional Associate
Southwestern Regional Office, Educational Testing Service
Austin, Texas

WILLIAM W. BRICKMAN

Professor of Education
Graduate School of Education, University of Pennsylvania
Philadelphia, Pennsylvania

CAROLYN M. CALLAHAN

Associate Professor of Education
University of Virginia
Charlottesville, Virginia

GWENDOLYN J. COOKE

Coordinator, Office of Gifted and Talented Programs and Services
Baltimore Public Schools
Baltimore, Maryland

JUNE COX

Academic Director
Gifted Students Institute
Arlington, Texas

DAVID FELDMAN

Associate Professor of Child Study
Tufts University
Medford, Massachusetts

JACOB W. GETZELS

Professor of Education and Behavioral Sciences
University of Chicago
Chicago, Illinois

MARVIN J. GOLD

Coordinator, Programs for the Gifted
University of South Alabama
Mobile, Alabama

MILTON J. GOLD

Dean Emeritus of Programs in Education
Hunter College
New York, New York

NANCY E. JACKSON

Research Assistant Professor
Child Development Research Group
University of Washington
Seattle, Washington

SANDRA N. KAPLAN

Assistant Director, National/State Leadership Training Institute
on the Gifted and the Talented
Los Angeles, California

DANIEL P. KEATING

Associate Professor
Institute of Child Development
University of Minnesota
Minneapolis, Minnesota

BRUCE G. MILNE

Director, Educational Research and Service Center
School of Education
University of South Dakota
Vermillion, South Dakota

CAROL N. NATHAN

Editor, DIALOGUE
Kensington, California

HALBERT B. ROBINSON

Professor of Psychology and Chairperson,
Child Development Research Group
University of Washington
Seattle, Washington

WENDY C. ROEDELL

Research Assistant Professor
Child Development Research Group
University of Washington
Seattle, Washington

MARSHALL P. SANBORN

Professor of Education
University of Wisconsin
Madison, Wisconsin

PAULINE S. SEARS

Professor Emeritus of Education
Stanford University
Stanford, California

LINDA H. SMITH

Instructor and Research Associate
Department of Educational Psychology
University of Connecticut
Storrs, Connecticut

JULIAN C. STANLEY

Professor of Psychology
Director, Study of Mathematically Precocious Youth
The Johns Hopkins University
Baltimore, Maryland

E. JEAN THOM

Supervisor, Division of Major Work Classes
Cleveland Public Schools
Cleveland, Ohio

E. PAUL TORRANCE

Professor of Educational Psychology
University of Georgia
Athens, Georgia

VIRGIL S. WARD

Professor of Education
University of Virginia
Charlottesville, Virginia

JEFFREY J. ZETTEL

Specialist for Policy Implementation
Council for Exceptional Children
Reston, Virginia

Acknowledgments

The National Society for the Study of Education is deeply grateful to Professor A. Harry Passow, to members of the committee on the Education of the Gifted and the Talented, and to the several authors whose collaboration has made possible this comprehensive review of a very important aspect of the contemporary educational scene. We are also greatly indebted to Professor Herman G. Richey, formerly Secretary-Treasurer of the Society, for preparing the index. The Society is proud to present this volume as Part I of its Seventy-eighth Yearbook.

KENNETH J. REHAGE
Editor for the Society

Table of Contents

Perspective on the Study and Education of the Gifted and Talented

A. HARRY PASSOW

Almost six decades ago, the National Society for the Study of Education published the first of three yearbooks dealing with the education of the gifted. That volume, entitled *Classroom Problems in the Education of the Gifted*, was published in 1920. The considerable interest in the subject was probably responsible for the appearance only four years later of a second yearbook, *The Education of the Gifted*, which was concerned more broadly with the subject. Guy M. Whipple, chairman of the Committee of the Society that was responsible for this second volume, provided a brief historical summary of the interest in and concern for the education of gifted individuals, observing that perhaps the first systematic approach to providing for "bright pupils" was developed by the Superintendent of Schools in St. Louis, Dr. William T. Harris. In his reports for 1868-69 and for 1871-73, Harris commented on the advantages of promoting pupils at short intervals, as short as five weeks in the lower grades, and of accelerating gifted pupils through the grades. He noted that the plan provided gifted pupils with more challenging work and prevented them from acquiring habits of laziness.

Whipple prefaced this Twenty-third Yearbook, *The Education of the Gifted*, with the note that "despite extended correspondence and two sessions for the personal interchange of views, the Committee has not found itself in agreement upon some of the fundamental principles involved in the education of gifted children" (p. vi). The lack of consensus among committee members centered on different evaluations of the various methods presented "for the selection of gifted pupils or the administration of their training" (p. 24). Whipple reported that the Committee had agreed to disagree and would leave it to the proponents of the various approaches to the handling of gifted children to prove their respective cases.

Some idea of the body of literature already extant by 1924 is found in the final section of the Twenty-third Yearbook, which contains an annotated bibliography consisting of no fewer than 453 entries. One of the earliest entries was a 1906 article by Lewis M. Terman on "Genius and Stupidity."

In 1958, a third yearbook appeared. Also entitled *Education of the Gifted*, it dealt with "the desirability of providing opportunities for reasonable adaptations of curriculums and procedures of formal education to the extraordinary capacities and interests of the gifted segments of school populations" (p. vii). Planning for that yearbook was begun prior to the launching of the Russian Sputnik, which proved to be a powerful stimulus to efforts to provide for the gifted and talented. Once again the question was raised as to "whether or not all members of the present yearbook committee would subscribe to all of the pronouncements of the several contributors to the volume " (p. vii). Nevertheless, the yearbook was seen as stimulating "further advances in the improvement of educational opportunities for the superior students in all types of educational institutions" (p. viii).

In 1975, the Board of Directors of the Society authorized the preparation and publication of the present volume, which looks at the problem of educating the gifted and the talented in the light of significant developments that have taken place in the past two decades. In the first chapter, the five years following Sputnik and the years following Watergate are viewed by Abraham J. Tannenbaum as "twin peaks of interest in the gifted and talented," separated by a period of neglect in which schools and the public were concerned with other populations in the schools. Tannenbaum reviews the cyclical nature of interest in the gifted, observing that no other group has experienced such treatment. Focusing particularly on the "turmoil of the 1960s," he examines the focus on the disadvantaged and minorities, the effects of the Vietnam war and youth dissent, and the devaluation of science as they affected educational provisions for the gifted and talented. The brief historical review is concluded with a discussion of the resurgence of interest in the gifted and speculation that provisions for the gifted may "rescue" public education by altering the total school atmosphere.

Unresolved issues and the "misguided efforts" of current educators are examined by James J. Gallagher. The issues are grouped into three categories: the gifted individual, special educational programming, and the future of educational programs for the gifted. Pointing to the influence of early research that regarded giftedness as being created entirely by genetic forces, Gallagher suggests that the implications of developmental data that support a paradigm of interaction between environment and genetic ability have not yet been fully grasped. He sees the inadequacies of our definitions as symptoms of our incomplete knowledge about relevant concepts. Gallagher sees programmatic efforts for the gifted as focusing on three dimensions—the content, special skills, and a modified learning environment. Practitioners are faced, however, with a dearth of curricular resources for implementing plans. Gallagher discusses issues connected with such concepts as creativity, underachievement, and the culturally different, as well as the cost benefits of special programming. He concludes with a discussion of some of the components of an effective support system for quality education for the gifted.

The emergence of national and state concern for the education of the gifted and talented is discussed by David M. Jackson. Beginning with the fulfillment of a congressional mandate in 1971 by the report of the then United States Commissioner of Education, Sidney P. Marland, Jackson traces the move from advocacy to categorized funding by the federal government. In Jackson's view, this funding for gifted and talented at the federal level "is as much a consequence of emerging concerns at the state and local levels as it has been a stimulus to that concern," with the possible result that the cyclical interest and neglect of the gifted may be at an end. Jackson also reports on two other major developments: The ERIC Clearinghouse on Handicapped and Gifted Children and the National/State Leadership Training Institute on the Gifted and Talented. Finally, he discusses five major developments at the state level affecting activities for the gifted and talented.

The current status and delivery of services to gifted and talented children and youth by the states are reported by Jeffrey Zettel. The data were compiled from a nationwide survey of state education agencies. Statutory provisions, procedures for screening and identification, state-level coordinators, preservice and in-service training programs, and parent advocacy groups are described by Zettel.

In the final chapter of Section One, Pauline S. Sears provides an update on Terman's *Genetic Studies of Genius*. Terman's studies of more than 1,000 California children scoring in the top 1 percent of tested intelligence were begun in 1922 with assessments of their physical, intellectual, and personal-social qualities, which were then compared to measures of the "generality" or a nonselected group. In the intervening years, further data have been collected on the "Terman children," the last follow-up having taken place in 1972. Sears presents some of the findings from the fifty-year follow-up, dealing primarily with life-cycle satisfactions, with work patterns and occupational satisfaction, and with family life, and reports on male-female differences in each case. As she points out, the "Terman children" are now moving "toward later maturity" (they are now in their sixties) and represent a unique population of highly productive individuals who can now be studied gerontologically.

CHAPTER I

Pre-Sputnik to Post-Watergate Concern about the Gifted

ABRAHAM J. TANNENBAUM

The half-decade following Sputnik in 1957 and the last half-decade of the 1970s may be viewed as twin peak periods of interest in gifted and talented children. Separating the peaks was a deep valley of neglect in which the public fixed its attention more eagerly on the low functioning, poorly motivated, and socially handicapped children in our schools. It was not simply a case of bemoaning the plight of able and then disadvantaged learners, with each population taking turns as the pitied underdog or the victim of unfair play. Rather than *transferring* the same sentiments from one undereducated group to another, the nation found itself *transforming* its mood from intense anxiety to equally profound indignation: anxiety lest our protective shield of brainpower became weaker, rendering us vulnerable to challenge from without, followed by indignation over social injustice in the land, which could tear us apart from within. Now we are experiencing a revival of earlier sensitivities to the needs of the gifted. Judging from these vacillations in national temperament, it seems as if we have not yet succeeded in paying equal attention simultaneously to our most and least successful achievers at school.

The cyclical nature of interest in the gifted is probably unique in American education. No other special group of children has been alternately embraced and repelled with so much vigor by educators and laymen alike. Gardner saw signs of public dilemma rather than fickleness when he commented that "the critical lines of tension in our society are between *emphasis on individual performance and restraints on individual performance.*"[1] Such conflict would arise

1. John Gardner, *Excellence: Can We Be Equal and Excellent Too?* (New York: Harper and Row, 1961), p. 33 (italics in original).

logically from a failure to reconcile our commitments to excellence and to equality in public education. Fostering excellence means recognizing the right of gifted children to realize their potential, but it also suggests something uncomfortably close to encouraging elitism if the ablest are privy to educational experiences that are denied all other children. On the other hand, promoting egalitarianism will guarantee increased attention to children from lower-status environments who are failing at school. As we concentrate more exclusively on raising the performance levels of these minorities, however, there is danger of discriminating against the minority of gifted students by denying their right to be challenged adequately on grounds that they are advantaged. Perhaps because we cannot live exclusively with excellence or egalitarianism for any length of time and tend to counterpose rather than reconcile them, we seem fated to drift from one to the other indefinitely.

The 1950s: Pre-Sputnik and Post-Sputnik

From the current perspective, the 1950s are viewed as sedate, conservative years, at least in contrast to the convulsive 1960s. But this kind of hindsight is fairly myopic. While it is true that America was spared too much internal dissension, except for McCarthyism and some grumbling about our involvement in Korea, still it was the age of cold warfare at its worst and its threat to the psyche seemed lethal. Two superpowers, determined to undo each other's political systems, possessed the ultimate weapon of destruction, and each feared that the other would use that weapon as a deterrent if it imagined itself about to be attacked.

Unlocking secrets of the atom to produce the bomb represented a scientific as well as a military breakthrough, increasing the dependency of armed power on the innovativeness of the scientist. Americans had grown confident that our country's leadership in science and technology was unchallengeable. We expected ourselves to be always the first in creating new gadgetry to make life and death easier, whether through sophisticated home appliances, computer systems, communications equipment, or explosives with the power of megatons of TNT. Image the shock, then, when this illusion was shattered by the successful launching of Sputnik by none other than our arch enemy in the midst of a cold war that at any moment could turn hotter than any conflict in history. Sputnik was not simply a demoralizing technological feat; it had potential military applications as well. Suddenly, the prestige and survival of a nation were jeopardized because the enemy's greatest minds of the day had outperformed ours, and the Russians capitalized on this coup by broadcasting to every nation on earth its success, at long last, in reducing America to a second-class power.

Although the shock of Sputnik in 1957 triggered unprecedented action on behalf of the gifted, educators had already expressed their lament over public indifference to these children much earlier in that decade. In 1950, for example, the Educational Policies Commission decried the school's neglect of mentally superior children and the resulting shrinking of manpower in the sciences, arts, and professions.[2] A year later, the Ohio Commission on Children and Youth revealed that only 2 percent of the schools in that state had special classes for the gifted and a mere 9 percent reported any kind of enrichment in the regular classroom.[3]

Criticism of the elementary and high schools eventually came also from the academic community. In 1953, Bestor, an academician, published a sensational indictment of public education for practicing what he considered its special brand of fraudulence on America's children.[4] Because of what he regarded as a misplacement of power in the hands of know-nothing "educationists," Bestor was convinced that schools provided meager intellectual nourishment or inspiration, especially for the gifted who often marked time in their studies until graduation released them from boredom and euphoria.

To some extent, the eagerness among educators to increase the nation's talent supply was inspired by politicians and economists who had worried about our diminishing reservoir of high-level manpower in science and technology even before Sputnik dramatized the problem. For example, Wolfle, Director of the Commission on

2. Educational Policies Commission, *Education of the Gifted* (Washington, D.C.: National Education Association, 1950).

3. Ohio Commission on Children and Youth, *The Status of the Gifted in Ohio* (Columbus: Ohio Department of Education, 1951).

4. Arthur E. Bestor, *Educational Wastelands* (Urbana, Ill.: University of Illinois Press, 1953).

Human Resources and Advanced Training, asserted that the United States failed to prepare enough men and women in the natural sciences, the health fields, teaching, and engineering.[5] Only six of ten in the top 5 percent and only half of the top 25 percent of high school graduates went on to earn college diplomas. At the more advanced levels, a mere 3 percent of those capable of earning the Ph.D. actually did so. What made matters worse were expectations that the shortages would become even more acute in the late 1950s unless the schools succeeded in encouraging gifted students to continue on to advanced studies.

Manpower statistics confirmed the existence of shortages in key professions. Again, the cause of this alarming situation was attributed to the commitment of the schools to deal with mediocrity rather than superiority. Allegedly, teachers were geared to work with average or even below average students, with the result that the ablest were often disregarded. Many dropped out of school before graduation or refused to go on to college after four years of high school.

Aside from the exhortative statements and surveys dramatizing the failure to educate gifted children, there is also evidence of scholarly activity in the early part of the decade. Few people could forecast the impact of Guilford's paper on creativity on the subsequent research pertaining to the nature and measurement of productive thinking.[6] That paper encouraged psychometrists to abandon the assumption that tests of general intelligence, such as those developed in the early part of the century by Lewis Terman, could be used to locate the pool of children out of which virtually all of the gifted would probably emerge. Rather, Guilford's model brought attention to multiple aptitudes, including divergent production or "creativity," as it is sometimes called. His ideas about creativity and its measurement were later adapted by Getzels and Jackson in their comparison of "high creative-low IQ" and "high IQ-low creative" students at the University of Chicago High

5. Dael Wolfle, *America's Resources of Specialized Talent* (New York: Harper and Row, 1954).

6. Joy P. Guilford, "Creativity," *American Psychologist* 5 (1950): 444-54.

School.[7] This study had a stunning influence on educational researchers because it announced a breakthrough in the use of so-called "creativity" measures to identify a talent resource that would be overlooked by tests of general intelligence. The question of whether instruments for assessing creativity can locate otherwise undiscoverable talent has never been fully settled,[8] but protagonists for the use of such tests have inspired the kind of general enthusiasm that today would greet an announcement of new sources of energy.

Much of the work in the early 1950s was codified in *Education for the Gifted*, the fifty-seventh yearbook of the National Society for the Study of Education. Published in 1958, it was the first yearbook of the Society on the topic since 1924.

Despite the work of specialists on the gifted and the portents and premonitions concerning Russia's strides in building its talent reservoir, there was no serious action in America's schools until Sputnik was launched in 1957. At that time, the rhetoric started to become more strident and the research more abundant, and together they either produced or accompanied radical changes in public education. We were convinced that the Russians slipped ahead of us in space technology because we had insufficient manpower to advance the sciences. Predictably, the schools were singled out as scapegoats.

While the nation kept careful watch on scientific developments in the Soviet Union, it also monitored the rate at which Soviet education was producing new scientists and the kind of training they received in the process. Invariably, invidious comparisons were made between the enemy's system and ours. One report claimed that before graduating from a Russian high school, a student had to complete five years of physics, biology, and a foreign language, four years of chemistry, one year of astronomy, and as many as

7. Jacob W. Getzels and Philip W. Jackson, "The Meaning of 'Giftedness': An Examination of an Expanding Concept," *Phi Delta Kappan* 40 (1958): 75-77.

8. Susan B. Crockenberg, "Creativity Tests: A Boon or Boondoggle for Education?" *Review of Educational Research* 42 (1972): 27-45.

ten years of mathematics.[9] Our own graduates were woefully under-educated by comparison. Worse than that, the young people in American colleges earning science degrees and committing their talents to defense-related professions did not compare in number with their counterparts in the Soviet Union.

It was essential to build up our supply of high-level human resources quickly or else risk seeing a national emergency deteriorate into a national catastrophe. In time, school officials began to acknowledge that something was wrong with public education and that there was much overhauling to be done. It was probably the mounting exposés of malpractice in the schools, capped by Sputnik and its ominous implications, that moved them out of their complacency and made them more reform-minded. Indeed, the reaction to Sputnik might not have been so swift and strong if the critics' cries for change in our schools had not had a cumulative effect.

When the educational community finally took action on behalf of the gifted, it did so with alacrity. Public and private funds became available to assist in the pursuit of excellence, primarily in the fields of science and technology. Academic coursework was telescoped and stiffened to test the brainpower of the gifted. Courses that had been offered only at the college level began to find their way into special enrichment programs in high school and subsequently in elementary school. Even the self-contained classroom, which had been a tradition in elementary education, briefly gave way to limited departmental instruction in a few localities. Attempts were made to introduce foreign languages in the elementary schools, but that too did not last long after an auspicious beginning. Also making short-lived appearances were courses with such attractive titles as the Mathematics of Science, Opera Production, Seminar in the Humanities, Integration of the Arts, World Affairs, Structural Linguistics, and Critical Thinking. There were even special efforts made to locate and nurture giftedness among the socially disadvantaged, most notably through the P.S. 43 Project in

9. *Soviet Commitment to Education*, Report of the First Official U.S. Education Mission to the USSR, Bulletin 1959, No. 16, Office of Education, U.S. Department of Health, Education, and Welfare (Washington, D.C.: U.S. Government Printing Office, 1959).

New York City, which later became the widely heralded but eventually ill-fated Higher Horizons Program. Interest spread also to school systems in rural areas and to colleges and universities where the gifted were provided with enrichment experiences never before extended to them.

There is no way of knowing precisely what percentage of our schools offered something special to the gifted in the years immediately after Sputnik. Many of the crash programs were never taken seriously enough by their sponsoring institutions to last long. But there were prominent exceptions that started out as enrichment experiences for the gifted only and later changed the curriculum for all children. Much of what is taught today in the mathematics and sciences, for example, is a legacy of post-Sputnik designs in gifted education. Similar influences can be felt in current secondary school programs that are comprehensive enough to accommodate human diversity without shortchanging the gifted. Conant expressed the sentiment of the late 1950s in a report entitled *The American High School Today*.[10] He offered a broad, twenty-one step plan for changing secondary education with special emphasis on core courses that were challenging in content and required of all students regardless of their career plans. His proposals took special note of the academically gifted (the upper 15 percent) and the highly gifted (the upper 3 percent). The tougher standards he suggested for them were far more acceptable to school officials than were those recommended by Bestor and his fellow critics.

In addition to the plethora of special enrichment activities initiated in the schools during the late 1950s and early 1960s, there was an upsurge in research activity dealing with the characteristics and education of gifted children. Investigations in vogue at the time focused primarily on such topics as the relative effectiveness of different administrative designs (for example, ability grouping, enrichment in regular classes, and acceleration); the social status of the gifted at school and its effect on their motivation to learn; the causes and treatment of scholastic underachievement among children with high potential; achievement motivation and other non-

10. James B. Conant, *The American High School Today* (New York: McGraw Hill, 1959).

intellective factors in high-level learning; and the psychosocial correlates of divergent thinking processes. Professional journals were
deluged with research reports and with exhortations to do something special for the gifted. So rapid was the buildup of literature
in the field that one writer claimed there were more articles published in the three-year period from 1956 to 1959 than in the
previous thirty years.[11]

High scholastic standards and standing, academic advancement,
studiousness, and career-mindedness were conspicuous themes in
our schools. It became virtually unthinkable for a gifted child to
bypass the tougher courses in favor of the less demanding ones.
It certainly was no time for youth to do their own thing or to
enjoy the privilege of doing nothing. Instead, they were brought
up in a period of total talent mobilization, requiring the most able-
minded to fulfill their potentials and submit their developed abilities
for service to the nation.

The 1960s: A Decade of Turmoil

The 1960s opened with John F. Kennedy's election to the presidency amid promises and dreams of a modern utopia. There was
excitement in the air as the nation prepared itself to sweep away the
stodginess of the 1950s and create a new age of excellence. Kennedy's earliest presidential messages made it clear that brains and
loyalty to the flag were among our most precious assets. He
announced boldly his intention to put a man on the moon by 1970,
a clear sign that we were accepting Russia's challenge for suprem-
acy in space exploration and that the most brilliant scientists would
be called upon to make such a feat feasible. This meant encouraging the largest possible number of able students to enroll in science
programs that offered them the best possible special education. For
who else but the gifted could yield from their ranks a cadre of
scientists qualified to honor the President's commitment?

There were other hints of meritocracy in the air. Kennedy
gathered around him some of the most precocious men (although
few women) of his generation to advise him on governmental mat-

11. Joseph L. French, ed., *Educating the Gifted* (New York: Henry Holt,
1959).

ters. Known then as the "Whiz Kids," some had earned their rep-
utations as scholars at leading universities and others as promising
idea men in industry. All of them projected an image of braininess
with a zest for unraveling the chief executive's knottiest problems.
They were gifted children grown up and enjoying the glamor of
fame and power rather than living in relative obscurity as so many
other gifted people must do, even in their most productive years.
At last, able children had their own celebrity role models to
emulate, much as budding athletes and entertainers have theirs.

It would, of course, be naive to suggest that we had reached a
point in history when the brilliant student was taking his place
alongside the sports star as a hero on campus. Far from it. Research
by Coleman[12] and Tannenbaum[13] demonstrated that acclaim among
peers was far more easily achieved on the athletic field than on the
honor roll. Still, the Kennedy years were making good on promises
of social and economic rewards for those willing to cultivate their
superior scholastic abilities despite the lack of enthusiastic cheering
from schoolmates.

The bids were high for brains in the early 1960s, but there was
a string attached. President Kennedy himself expressed it best in
his immortal admonition to his countrymen: "Ask not what your
country can do for you—ask what you can do for your country."
It was a call for unselfish accomplishment, to dedicate the work of
our citizens to the greater glory of the nation. Those with higher
abilities had more to contribute and were therefore under pressure
not to bury their talents or even to indulge in creative productivity
that was impractical. The feeling during that cold war period was
that the scientist could better serve the nation than the poet.

Judging from the career plans of gifted children in the late
1950s and early 1960s, they evidently believed that the nation was
worth serving. By far the largest number of students with high
tested intelligence majored in the sciences, and many of them
aspired to enter fields of technology that could somehow help the
defense effort. The lure of employment opportunities in these in-

12. James S. Coleman, *The Adolescent Society* (Glencoe, Ill.: The Free
Press, 1962).

13. Abraham J. Tannenbaum, *Adolescent Attitudes toward Academic Brilliance* (New York: Teachers College Press, 1962).

dustries and professions was reinforced by the glamorization of science as man's most exciting modern frontier.

Yet, the flurry of activity on behalf of the gifted has left some unfinished business to haunt us. Even the threat of Sputnik and the indulgence of excellence during the Kennedy era were not enough to guarantee that the needs of the gifted would be cared for perpetually at school. Instead, enrichment was considered a curricular ornament to be detached and discarded when the cost of upkeep became prohibitive. Moreover, the fervor with which guidance counselors ushered gifted youths into science programs backfired to some degree as large numbers of these students switched their academic majors by the time they reached their sophomore year in college,[14] and many who did stay on to pursue the careers mapped out for them became victims of the shaky fortunes of the aerospace industry. On the other hand, little more than lip service was paid to the needs of a special breed of students not gifted academically but possessing exceptional talent in the arts, mechanics, and social leadership. Also, whatever work was done in defining and measuring divergent productivity remained in the research laboratory. Few people attempted to develop ways of cultivating this kind of intellective functioning and translating it into curriculum sequences. Finally, the national talent hunt failed to penetrate the socially disadvantaged minorities whose records of school achievement were well below national norms and whose children with high potential were much harder to locate because their environments provided too little of the requisite encouragement and opportunity to fulfill whatever promise they might have shown under other circumstances. A notable exception to this general neglect of talent among the underprivileged was the aforementioned P.S. 43 project in New York City, which was then modified to become the Higher Horizons Program.[15] But these efforts were shortlived, coming to an end when a subsequent evaluation revealed no special accomplishments of the program, perhaps due to an underestimate of costs, personnel, curriculum plan-

14. Donivan J. Watley, *Stability of Career Choices of Talented Youth* (Evanston, Ill.: National Merit Scholarship Corp., 1968).

15. Jacob Landers, *Higher Horizons Progress Report* (New York: Board of Education of the City of New York, 1963).

ning, and just plain hard work needed to duplicate on a much larger scale the earlier successes at P.S. 43.[16]

Focus on Underprivileged Minorities

The 1954 Supreme Court decision to desegregate public schools set off an inexorable movement toward updating the Constitution and the Bill of Rights. Once again, education became the linchpin of a national priority, this time for social justice, as it had formerly been for the Great Talent Hunt. Separatism and equality were declared an impossible combination and therefore unconstitutional. Educators and social and behavioral scientists placed the cause of disadvantaged children at the top of their priority list, even ahead of the gifted. We were now more concerned with bolstering freedom and equality within our borders than with playing the lead on the world stage despite the unabated pressures of cold warfare that brought confrontations between East and West in Europe, Southeast Asia, and the Middle East.

In addition to diverting interest away from the gifted, the advocacy movement for the socially disadvantaged actually contested at least two features of special programs for the ablest: (a) the use of intelligence tests and other conventional measures of aptitude as a means of determining who deserves to be called gifted; and (b) grouping children in special classes for the gifted on the basis of their performance on these kinds of assessments. The intelligence test, a major instrument for determining academic potential ever since Terman initiated his monumental studies of genius in the early part of the century, came under heavy attack for being biased against some racial minorities and the socioeconomically depressed. It was charged that the problem-solving tasks, which are mostly verbal, favor children with experience in higher-status environments. Consequently, these children obtain higher scores, thus creating the delusion that they are basically more intelligent and perhaps even born with superior intellect. As a result of these charges, some urban centers with large racial minorities, notably New York and Los Angeles, discontinued the use of such tests.

16. J. Wayne Wrightstone et al., *Evaluation of the Higher Horizons Program for Underprivileged Children* (New York: Board of Education of the City of New York, 1964).

The push toward greater egalitarianism aggravated a mild distrust of intelligence testing that had always existed in this country. Many suspected that it is vaguely antidemocratic to declare, on the basis of a test score, that a child is fated to become an achiever or a failure, economically comfortable or uncomfortable, and a high- or a low-status person, even if such forecasts allowed broad limits of error. Such an idea did not square with our traditional faith in this country that one is given the freedom and opportunity to make of himself what he will. The residual aversion to testing intelligence on grounds that it predestines inequality among *individuals* was compounded by charges that the measures discriminate against racial and socioeconomic *groups* as well. It was enough to threaten the use of mainstay instruments for identifying gifted children.

Since racial minorities, such as Hispanics, Blacks, Chicanos, and Native Americans, traditionally performed less well at school than did white majorities, it was logical to regard ability grouping for the gifted as de facto racial segregation. Critics argued that schools were practicing blatant favoritism by creating separate classes for children who rated superior on conventional measures of intellect and also by offering those chosen few a kind of enrichment in their curriculum that was denied everyone else. The objections were not against special ability grouping per se for the gifted, or even the unique educational experience reserved for them because of their ability. What created the furor was the practice of denying enough children from disadvantaged subpopulations their rightful access to these classes. There was an overwhelming sentiment favoring the idea that high potential is equitably distributed among all races, privileged and underprivileged, but that life's circumstances in some groups are oppressive enough to cast a shadow over their innate competencies.

Thus we see that American education was not able to reconcile its interest in the gifted with its concern about the disadvantaged, nor could it design a satisfactory methodology for locating and cultivating giftedness among these minority groups. The dilemma was easy to resolve inasmuch as it reduced itself to a choice between battling for social justice or pursuing excellence, and there was no doubt as to which of the two would better fit the mood of the 1960s.

VIET NAM AND DISSENTING YOUTH

During the brief Kennedy era, the United States faced the communist world in several near-conflicts. In each instance, we emerged with our self-image intact as the champions of the free world against forces of darkness. The subsequent adventure in Viet Nam turned out to be disastrously different, despite the fact that President Johnson justified our entanglement on the same grounds that his predecessor defended his risks of war in Berlin and Cuba. Eventually, the nation grew tired of the war, suspicious of politicians' promises of a quick victory, and increasingly convinced that our country was meddling in affairs of other nations rather than serving as a judge and enforcer of what was morally right in the world.

Among the many casualties of the Viet Nam conflict was our perception of giftedness in political leadership. The Whiz Kids of the Kennedy years, many of whom had stayed on in the Johnson era to help formulate strategy for the war effort, rapidly lost their image as people who could become heroes in public life by virtue of their brainpower alone. In fact, their sad history seemed to prove that being supersmart in the scholastic sense of the term was no guarantee of superunderstanding of man's most serious problems and how to solve them. Gifted youth on campuses throughout the country learned to despise them for their role in the Viet Nam debacle rather than revere them as graduated honors students distinguishing themselves as national leaders.[17]

A far more serious by-product of Viet Nam was a growing unrest among students in the colleges. Kenneth Keniston, who studied these young people in great detail, made it quite clear that a complex mix of personal attributes, familial influences, peer associations, and school environments set them apart from their more conforming age-mates.[18] It is noteworthy, however, that a disproportionate number of disaffected youth on campus distinguished themselves in their studies at school and were frequently enrolled in some of the more enriched and prestigious programs. Their im-

17. David Halberstam, *The Best and the Brightest* (Westminster, Md.: Random House, 1972).

18. Kenneth Keniston, *Youth and Dissent: The Role of a New Opposition* (New York: Harcourt, Brace, Jovanovich, 1971).

mediate targets were the colleges they were attending, which represented to them an establishment with archaic standards for success and unreasonable controls over their lives. Yet these same gadflies in centers of learning were themselves described in one study as possessing high degrees of intellectualism.[19]

The unrest on campus underwent some dramatic changes over a relatively short period of time. As one observer remarked, "The key difference between the Berkeley riots of 1964 and the Columbia crisis of May, 1969 is that in the pre-Columbian case the major impetus for unrest stemmed from the perceived abuse or misuse of authority ('Do not bend, fold, or mutilate'), whereas the later protest denied the legitimacy of authority."[20] The revolt was not only against institutions (educational or otherwise) and their leaders; it was also against a tradition of rationalism that sanctified ivory-tower scholarship. When Columbia rioters willfully destroyed a professor's research files, the act may have carried a message that goes beyond ordinary vandalism. It seemed to imply that all the work invested in accumulating those files was a waste of the professor's talent, which ought to have been dedicated to building a better society rather than dabbling in trivia and esoterica. And to make matters worse, the educational establishment expected its brightest students to follow in the footsteps of professors like him.

Many questions were raised among gifted college students as to whether they ought to funnel their psychic energies into a life of the mind. Many were attracted to the sensitivity training movements, which told them that "talking is usually good for intellectual understanding of personal experience, but it is often not effective for helping a person *to experience*—to feel."[21] Accordingly, man should not be seen simply, as though he were a machine, but rather as a complex biological, psychological, and social organism who can fulfill himself through all of these dimensions of his being. Every part of the body has to be exercised to its fullest potential, which

19. Richard Flacks, "The Liberated Generation: An Exploration of the Roots of Student Protest," *Journal of Social Issues* 23, no. 3 (1967): 52–75.

20. Warren G. Bennis, "A Funny Thing Happened on the Way to the Future," *American Psychologist* 25 (1970): 595–608.

21. William C. Schutz, *Joy: Expanding Human Awareness* (New York: Grove Press, 1967), p. 11 (italics in original).

means building up the strength and stamina of its muscles, its sensory awareness and aesthetic appreciation, its motor control, and the gamut of its emotional and social feelings. Inhibiting other aspects of self for the sake of the intellect amounts to robbing life of its multidimensionality, so the task of the individual is to make something of all his capacities, even if in so doing he cannot make the most of any of them.

Significantly, a new utopia emerged in the form of Consciousness III, depicted by Reich in his best seller, *The Greening of America*. One of the postulates of this new world was described by Reich as follows:

Consciousness III rejects the whole concept of excellence and comparative merit. . . . It refuses to evaluate people by general standards, it refuses to classify people, or analyze them. Each person has his own individuality, not to be compared to that of anyone else. Someone may be a brilliant thinker, but he is not "better" at thinking than anyone else, he simply possesses his own excellence. A person who thinks very poorly is still excellent in his own way. Therefore people are in no hurry to find out another person's background, schools, achievements, as a means of knowing him; they regard all of that as secondary, preferring to know him unadorned. Because there are no governing standards, no one is rejected. Everyone is entitled to pride in himself, and no one should act in a way that is servile, or feel inferior, or allow himself to be treated as if he were inferior.[22]

Thus we see how life for campus dissidents became strangely paradoxical. Many of them espoused the habits of intellectualism generally associated with gifted students. At the same time they rejected excellence and its trappings as violations of democracy and too stultifying to the attainment of total joy and liberation. Even those consenting to live the life of the mind learned an unforgettable lesson from the events in Viet Nam. No longer could they be adjured to cultivate their talents for the sake of their country's prestige and need for survival. The immoral war in Southeast Asia tarnished the nation's image enough to discourage such commitments among many who could potentially be counted among our high-level human resources. Besides, some may have felt it faintly

22. Charles A. Reich, *The Greening of America* (New York: Random House, 1970), pp. 226-27.

dehumanizing to be treated like natural resources; it simply did not fit well with the new spirit of selfhood and individuality.

THE DEVALUATION OF SCIENCE

For many years, consuming or producing scientific knowledge was regarded as a human virtue, particularly if it helped conquer nature in order to make man's life more comfortable. There was hardly much doubt that gifted children would derive great personal satisfaction and a certain measure of power and freedom if they became highly informed about the secrets of the universe or contributed significantly to unraveling some of these mysteries. In the 1960s, however, serious doubts were raised about the value of scholarship as it had been traditionally transacted in the schools. Significant segments of campus youth began to sour on knowledge factories, and Herbert Marcuse, one of their most influential spokesmen, warned about the mechanizing, denaturalizing, and subjugating impact of knowledge.[23]

Gifted youth in the age of Sputnik were bombarded with the message that a lifetime devotion to achievement in science was not only in the interests of the state, but of mankind in general. Such pursuits have their own built-in ethic, that any efforts at pushing back the frontiers of theory and research deserve the highest commendation because they attest to man's divine-like power of mastering his environment and creating his own brand of miracles in it. Suddenly the nation was told that man's science is as fallible as he is himself. Among the most vocal critics were the environment-minded scientists who warned that, in our enthusiasm for conquering nature, we may be destroying ourselves in the process unless we impose restraints on such activity.[24] Perhaps the best-known writer to forecast doom if science were to continue on its conventional course was the biologist Commoner, whose book, *Science and Survival*, enjoyed wide circulation and influence. Commoner took the ecological point of view that the elements of nature are in-

23. Herbert Marcuse, *One-Dimensional Man* (Boston: Beacon Press, 1964).

24. Philip L. Bereano, "The Scientific Community and the Crisis of Belief," *American Scientist* 57 (1969): 484-501.

tegrated but our knowledge of these elements is so limited that we do not see their connectedness. Expressing deep concern about the preoccupation of science with the elegance of its methods rather than the danger of its products, he directed much of his fire at the polluting effects of such symbols of technological giantism as nuclear testing and industrial waste. He acknowledged the need for brainpower to enrich scientific thinking, but he also warned that "no scientific principle can tell us how to make the choice, which may sometimes be forced upon us by the insecticide problem, between the shade of the elm tree and the song of the robin." [25] With such caveats, it became more difficult to convince gifted children that a life dedicated to science is the kind of high calling it once was unless closer links were made between the intellect and the conscience.

Besides being tarnished because they failed to take account of their human consequences, careers in science lost more of their glitter when the job market in various related fields began to tighten. The manpower crisis dramatized by Sputnik gradually calmed down when we began to overtake the Russians in the technology race and achieved a victory of sorts by transporting the first man to the moon in 1969. Manpower shortages in the various fields of science were no longer critical, partly because the flood of graduates in the early 1960s had filled available jobs, and also because the cold war was not considered serious enough to create new jobs through lucrative defense contracts. In fact, by the late 1960s, many Americans were suspicious of the so-called "military-industrial complex" for carving too much out of the tax dollar to support projects that were wasteful in times of peace. The primary need was to solve the problems of social unrest rather than to prop up our defense technology. Many would-be scientists and engineers began to realize that these professions attracted neither the prestige nor occupational rewards that would have been guaranteed only a few years earlier. Unfortunately, however, the supply of scientific talent did not slow down in accordance with the reduced demand, and as a result of the imbalance, many highly

25. Barry Commoner, *Science and Survival* (New York: The Viking Press, 1966), p. 104.

trained personnel found themselves either unemployed or working at unskilled jobs outside their fields.

The 1970s: A Renewed Interest

The decline of attention to the gifted in the 1960s is evident in the contrasting number of professional publications on that subject at the beginning and end of the decade. The number of entries under "Gifted Children" in the 1970 volume of *Education Index* was less than half the number in the 1960 volume. Nevertheless, by the outset of the present decade, there were unmistakable signs of a revival of interest. Probably the biggest boost came from a 1970 congressional mandate that added Section 806, "Provisions Related to Gifted and Talented Children," to the Elementary and Secondary Education Amendments of 1969 (Public Law 91-230). This document expressed a legislative interest in the gifted that eventually led to federal support of program initiatives throughout the country.

As a result of federal encouragement and some public and private initiative, the gifted have been exposed to an increasing number of special educational experiences in the 1970s. While as late as 1973 fewer than 4 percent of the nation's gifted children were receiving satisfactory attention at school, and most of the fortunate ones were concentrated in ten states, by 1977 every state in the union demonstrated at least some interest in the ablest.

Leadership at the federal level also grew much stronger in the first half of the decade. After being in existence for a brief three-year period as an understaffed, temporary unit in the U.S. Office of Education, Bureau of the Handicapped, the Office of the Gifted and Talented was given official status by legislation in 1974. The Special Projects Act resulted in a 1976 appropriation of $2.56 million for developing professional and program resources in the field. That allocation was renewed for 1977, and there is every reason to expect that federal support will be sustained at least for the years immediately ahead. There are also proposals for legislation that would change the Bureau of the Handicapped to the Bureau of Exceptional Persons, thus including gifted and talented individuals as eligible for sustained support of their education, along with the handicapped. If passed, such federal legislation will go a long way toward erasing the image of education for the gifted as being only a periodic fad in the schools. It is admittedly a way of forcing attention on the ablest by tying their fortunes to those of the handicapped, for whom funding rarely abates appreciably. The public may never feel equally sympathetic to both groups, but it could be forced to reduce some of its favoritism toward one over the other if they are combined rather than separate recipients of support through legislation.

The thrust of recent activity for the gifted has been mostly programmatic and promotional, with relatively little emphasis on research. Funding at all levels is invested in curriculum enrichment, teacher education, and training for leadership in the field. As part of their work on curriculum, many educators are designing or adapting special instructional systems in order to offer the ablest students experiences that are uniquely appropriate for them, not just promising practices from which all children can derive benefits.

Present-day efforts to design distinctive curricula for the gifted may result in some lasting contributions to the field. Products that have already been developed and distributed in many localities incorporate large numbers of exercises in divergent thinking. This trend reflects the foundational work of several prolific educators whose writings fairly dominated the field during the 1960s. Among the most widely influential persons has been E. Paul Torrance, who alone and with the help of occasional collaborators was responsible for at least seven major books and monographs as well as a large number of professional papers on the subject of creativity from 1960 to 1970. The popularity of research and materials development pertaining to divergent thinking is also having its impact on the classroom more than ever before. "Values clarification" has made its debut in recent years and is gradually spreading in classes for the gifted. It introduced a new dimension in the curriculum by stimulating children to understand themselves better and to develop belief systems and behavior codes that they can justify as bases for some of the most important decisions of their lives.

Again, as in the post-Sputnik period, interest has been expressed in gifted children who have high social intelligence and in those especially talented in the visual and performing arts. It is hard to say whether educators today are paying more attention to the needs of such children than their predecessors did two decades ago. From all indications, it would seem that they are not as yet far beyond the lip-service level of commitment. Even less fortunate are the gifted among underprivileged minority populations who still remain largely neglected, except in the arts, but not deliberately so. There is no doubt that many educators would gladly initiate enrichment experiences for these children and that support could be obtained for such plans if they stood a chance of success. Yet, the profession is still stymied in its efforts to find a way of discerning high-level academic potential that is buried under a thick overlay of social and economic handicaps. In fact, it is no less difficult today than ever before to tease out and inspire the fulfillment of scholarly talent in the nation's underprivileged classes.

Generally, the enrichment programs initiated in the present decade have been impressive in their variety, inventiveness, the extent of their dissemination, and in the spirit and proficiency with which they are being implemented. The same cannot be said for research productivity. A review of the state of research for the years 1969-1974 revealed a fairly bleak picture;[26] only thirty-nine reports on the gifted and talented had been published in that period. Today, these efforts continue to be limited, but there are several major projects now underway that deal with the nature and nurture of talent at all age levels.

What prompted the resurgence of activity in gifted education after nearly a decade of quiescence? A full answer probably will not come until future historians can view the 1970s in a proper time perspective. But the explanation that seems most obvious right now is America's backlash against awareness-oriented youth who turned excessively self-indulgent, and against campus revolutionaries who trashed some sacred scholarly traditions. Geoffrey Wagner has recently published a scathing indictment of universities for compromising academic standards, inflating grades, and diluting degree requirements in order to fend off unrest among students.[27] Perhaps these are signs that the pendulum is inevitably swinging

26. R. L. Spaulding, "Summary Report of Issues and Trends in Research on the Gifted and Talented," (undated manuscript).

27. Geoffrey Wagner, *The End of Education* (South Brunswick, N.J.: A. S. Barnes, 1976).

away from extreme egalitarianism in the direction of excellence. It is hard to imagine that there would be a popular acceptance of the Consciousness III notion about brilliant minds not being better at thinking than anyone else and poor thinkers necessarily being excellent in their own ways. This kind of argument is too fantasy-ridden to flourish successfully even in an egalitarian-minded society. There are, however, legacies of the 1960s that are volatile enough today to have prevented the gifted from making a comeback. They include the following realities:

1. Few manpower shortages exist at the high-skill levels. The job market is glutted with Ph.D.'s who cannot find work in their fields of training. In 1976, the starting salary of college graduates was only 6 percent above that of the average American worker, whereas in 1969, a person with a college diploma could earn 24 percent more than the national mean.[28]

2. The cold war, while relentless, does not threaten any new surprises to shake our confidence in the nation's talent reservoir. There is even talk of moderating the confrontation between East and West through policies of detente and the SALT talks.

3. It is not much easier today than in the late 1960s to persuade our ablest students that they have to work hard at school in order to serve their country in ways that only they can. National policies in Viet Nam and in the civil rights movement had persuaded too many of them that the country was not worthy of such dedication. When the Viet Nam war came to an end, Watergate emerged to reinforce the cynicism and alienation of youth, including many gifted individuals among them.

4. Quality, integrated education is as much a dream today as it has ever been. A prodigious amount of work yet remains to be done before underprivileged children can begin to derive their rightful benefits from experiences at school. That kind of investment of effort in compensatory programs usually draws attention away from curricular enrichment for the gifted.

5. Science and scientists are still monitored critically for possible moral lapses. The most recent controversy concerning value judgments in the scientific community has revolved around experiments

28. *Newsweek*, April 26, 1976.

in genetic engineering. Some gifted children may choose to avoid fields of science in order to keep their consciences clear about possibly opening any kind of Pandora's box in scientific discovery.

6. The 1970s have experienced hard times and drastic cutbacks in expenditures for education. Programs for the gifted are usually the most expendable ones when budgetary considerations force cutbacks in services to children.

Despite the aforementioned lingering influences of the 1960s, we are experiencing a drift toward excellence after indulging egalitarianism for awhile. This revival of interest, however, is no more a sign of pure historical inevitability than was its decline a decade ago. It is rather, in part at least, a sign of initiatives taken by people who believe in differentiated education at every ability level and who are participating in vigorous campaigns to save the schools.

Attention to individual competencies among the handicapped has dramatized the need to individualize education, with every child receiving a fair share of what is uniquely appropriate for him, regardless of how deficient or proficient he is in mastering curriculum content. It is logical, then, that the gifted also receive special attention to accommodate their unique learning strengths and thereby demonstrate the educator's attention to human differences. Eventually, PL 94-142 may include the gifted, which would take us a long way toward actualizing the belief that democracy in education means recognizing how children are unlike each other, and doing something about it. Protagonists for the gifted argue that the more sophisticated we become in discerning human individuality and the more inventive we are in providing for individual needs of the ablest, the more likely we are to achieve equality in the schools.

THE ROLE OF THE GIFTED IN "RESCUING" PUBLIC EDUCATION

It is no secret that educators are searching desperately for ways to maintain order in thousands of classrooms. This is especially true in big-city schools where more than 10 percent of the nation's pupil population is enrolled. The dismal picture is a familiar one: scholastic achievement levels are three, four, and even five years below norms; drugs, violence, vandalism, and truancy have reached epidemic proportions; and costs are climbing to such a height that there may soon be insufficient funds to pay the bills while main-

taining an adequately staffed program.[29] Many middle-class families
have fled the inner city or sought help from private schools in order
to provide a meaningful educational experience for their children.
This has further aggravated the situation in urban centers.

School administrators are aware that one way to bring back the
middle classes to the schools is to initiate special programs for the
gifted. They are, therefore, opening so-called "magnet schools" that
offer enrichment activities in particular subject matter areas and are
luring back to their classrooms sizable numbers of children who
would otherwise be studying elsewhere. The presence of the ablest
is beginning to make a difference in the total school atmosphere,
which demonstrates that they are capable of enhancing all of education if their learning capacities are properly respected. This
truism may turn out to be the most important lesson learned from
our experience with gifted and talented children in the 1970s.

29. *Ibid.*, September 12, 1977.

CHAPTER II

Issues in Education for the Gifted

JAMES J. GALLAGHER

In every field of endeavor each generation leaves a mixed legacy to the next. Along with the hard-won wisdom that comes from experience and the progressive accumulation of knowledge, collections of misinformation and misjudgments that can only be explained by understanding the temper and biases of the times are also passed along. As an antidote to any misplaced confidence that we at last have the tiger of education for the gifted by the tail, it may be useful to catalogue some unsolved issues or misguided efforts that have been created or accepted by the present generation and which we are in danger of turning over to the next generation.

A Definition of Giftedness

One splendid example of how the incorrect assumptions of past generations influence us today involves the acceptance of the concept that giftedness is entirely created by genetic forces. The early influential research by Terman et al. was based on this assumption.[1] Until the last decade, our major identification techniques and much of our program design have also been based on this assumption.

For example, a single intelligence test score was usually considered sufficient to define giftedness, thus implying that we did not expect major changes or modifications in measured ability in the child as a result of environmental intervention, except in the most seriously deprived situations. If changes in intelligence test scores occurred, they were accounted for on the basis that the children were finally free to show their "true" ability. The earlier

---

1. Lewis Terman et al., *Genetic Studies of Genius*, vol. 1, *Mental and Physical Traits of a Thousand Gifted Children* (Stanford, Calif.: Stanford University Press, 1926).

score could then be dismissed as invalid because of the special conditions of the earlier examination.

Other variations in measured ability were explained as due to faults in the testing instrument or to errors in measurement. Few people suggested that those children who failed to achieve the cutoff scores required for eligibility for a gifted program should be retested, because few believed that the children could progress enough intellectually to meet the standards of eligibility for the program at some future time.

The acceptance of the purely genetic nature of intelligence led to some embarrassing and troubling results, such as the consistent racial and ethnic differences found in the proportions of children testing as gifted. Such results were not widely quoted or displayed, although there have been clear and consistent findings on the question.[2]

The accumulation of evidence from studies in child development suggests that there is a subtle and complex interaction between environment and native ability, the result of which is what is measured by a score on an intelligence test.[3] The full range of implications of this fact has not been fully grasped or acted upon by educators of the gifted, although some initial steps have been taken. These steps include the use of many different techniques to identify gifted children in minority groups. But we still have not fully accepted the interaction concept—the concept that we can create giftedness through designing enriched environments and opportunities, or that we can destroy it by failing to create those environments and opportunities. We have lived for so long with the single-dimension concept that genetic forces totally control intelligence (or with some disbelievers, that environment totally controls intelligence) that we have not yet adjusted to all the implications of the interaction paradigm.

A broadened concept of giftedness, designed to include more

2. Mortimer Adler, "A Study of the Effects of Ethnic Origin on Giftedness," *Gifted Child Quarterly* 7 (1963): 98-101; Walter Barbe, "Characteristics of Gifted Children," *Education Administration and Supervision* 41 (1955): 207-17.

3. Helen L. Bee, "A Developmental Psychologist Looks at Educational Policy," (Paper given at the Aspen Institute Program on Education for a Changing Society, Aspen, Colo., 1976.

than those characteristics measured by intelligence tests, was given additional impetus by the extraordinarily influential study by Getzels and Jackson,[4] who attempted to differentiate between gifted and creative children, and by a decade of work by Torrance[5] focusing on the distinctive characteristics of creative children. Once the magic aura of the intelligence quotient was broken, it became possible to think of other dimensions that should be included in a general definition of giftedness. In addition, the increasing emphasis on the culturally different gifted children spurred the search for other valuable talents beyond the purely academic.

The effort to identify a variety of talents led to a broadened definition of the gifted child that appeared in a report on the status of the gifted child in the United States. That report, prepared for the U.S. Congress by Sidney P. Marland, Jr., then commissioner of education, provided a definition that was included in subsequently enacted federal legislation. The definition represented the first formal recognition, by name, at the federal level of the problems of education for gifted children. Since this definition has been so widely used, it is probably the one that should be discussed in terms of its virtues and faults. The definition reads as follows:

Gifted and talented children are those identified by professionally qualified persons [and] who by virtue of outstanding abilities are capable of high performance. These are children who require differentiated educational programs and services beyond those normally provided by the regular school program in order to realize their contribution to self and society.

Children capable of high performance include those with demonstrated achievement and/or potential ability in any of the following areas: (a) general intellectual ability, (b) specific academic aptitude, (c) creative or productive thinking, (d) leadership ability, (e) visual and performing arts, (f) psychomotor ability.[6]

Stating a definition is one thing and making it operational in an

4. Jacob Getzels and Philip Jackson, *Creativity and Intelligence* (New York: Wiley, 1962).

5. E. Paul Torrance, *Creativity* (Belmont, Calif.: Dimensions Publishing Co., 1969).

6. Sidney P. Marland, Jr., *Education of the Gifted and Talented*, vol. 1 Report to the Congress of the United States by the U.S. Commissioner of Education (Washington, D.C.: U.S. Government Printing Office, 1972), p. 2.

educational sense is quite another. What is leadership ability? Is it the same whether we think of the captain of a football team, of the leader of a debate team, or of the leader of a student protest movement? What is the test or means for identifying such leadership characteristics? If this trait can be trained, can we "create" gifted leaders with an appropriate educational program?

If we measure for general intellect and ability, how many who are gifted academically and in leadership will be intellectually gifted? There is now some suspicion that in our eagerness to specify these new dimensions we may have overestimated their separateness from high intellectual ability.[7] For example, the "High Creative—Low IQ" syndrome made popular by Getzels and Jackson was based on research on a group with extremely high IQs. The "Low IQ" students turned out to be "low" only relative to their comparison group. The "High Creative—Low IQ" group obtained a mean intelligence score of 127, a score that would qualify most of them for educational programs for the academically gifted in many cities and states.

What is psychomotor ability? If it includes basketball and football players, then we have had many more sophisticated talent searches and special programs for the gifted than most of us have realized. Do those who use the term "psychomotor ability" have in mind ballet dancers? If so, what is the link to the visual and performing arts? Who are included in the visual and performing arts anyway, and how are *they* identified?

In education, it is natural for us to respond to the question "Who are you talking about?" by trying to state a definition. Scientists know that the definition of a concept is not the first thing to be completed, but quite literally the last. We will not have a better definition until we find out more than we now know about the questions posed above. The inadequacies of the definition are merely symptoms pointing to our incomplete knowledge about the relevant concepts. If we are to pass along a more coherent statement to the next generation, then we will need not only better rhetoric but more sustained research and development as well.

There is also an increasing tendency to focus attention on spe-

7. Michael Wallach, "Creativity," in *Carmichael's Manual of Child Psychology*, 3d ed. Paul H. Mussen (New York: John Wiley, 1970), vol. 1, pp. 1211-1272.

cial subgroups within the gifted category (for example, gifted women). Some of these subgroups are touched upon in other parts of this volume and will not be dealt with here.

Educational Programming for the Gifted

Attempts to modify the school program for gifted students must focus on one or a combination of three major dimensions: (a) the content, (b) special skills, and (c) a modified learning environment.[8]

CONTENT

By far the most common discussion of special programming for gifted children has focused upon possible changes in setting or learning environment. The literature is cluttered with discussions of acceleration, of whether special classes are better than regular classes, or of whether resource room programs are as effective as other models of program design. Relatively little attention has been paid to the actual content that would make up the heart of any differentiated program, regardless of the particular learning environment in which it was delivered.

Renzulli has commented as follows on the lack of systematic and sophisticated content in programs for the gifted:

In conducting evaluative studies, I have witnessed far too many programs for the gifted that are essentially collections of fun-and-games activities; such activities lack continuity and show little evidence of developing in a systematic fashion the mental processes that led these children to be identified as gifted.[9]

Elsewhere I have urged the development of more complex curriculum units and materials for the gifted based upon advanced conceptualization of a subject, to which Bruner has referred as the "structure of the discipline."[10] Such coordinated curriculum or self-contained units, however, are more easily discussed than cre-

8. James J. Gallagher, *Teaching the Gifted Child*, 2d ed. (Boston: Allyn and Bacon, 1975).

9. Joseph S. Renzulli, *New Directions in Creativity* (New York: Harper and Row, 1973).

10. Jerome S. Bruner, *Toward a Theory of Instruction* (Cambridge, Mass.: Belknap Press, 1966).

ated, and at the present time there are few visible attempts to generate differentiated curriculum in the content fields. It would be
useful to develop curriculum units around central seminal ideas in
a fashion similar to that used in Bronowski's television series, "The
Ascent of Man." For example, Bronowski dealt with the concept of
war as follows:

War, organized war, is not a human instinct. It is a highly planned and
cooperative theft. And that form of theft began ten thousand years ago
when the harvesters of wheat accumulated a surplus and the nomads
rose out of the desert to rob them of what they themselves could not
provide.[11]

Kaplan has emphasized the importance of integrating content
with additional attention to the learning process.[12] She stressed the
use of topics that stimulate thinking, are action-oriented, and provide options for individual differences among gifted students.
Renzulli recommended that one side of his "enrichment triad
model" (individual and small-group investigations of real problems)
was particularly relevant for gifted students, and developed ideas on
how to stimulate such investigations.[13] Despite these and other suggestions, it is clear that the educational practitioner who must
provide direct service to gifted students is essentially entering a
difficult instructional situation almost totally unarmed because there
are few, if any, organized curriculum resources to draw upon.

SPECIAL SKILLS: CREATIVITY

Over the past decade, there has been no single topic that has
been so well discussed and researched as the dimension of "creativity." [14] The reason for such interest is clear. In a rapidly chang-

11. Jacob Bronowski, *The Ascent of Man* (Boston: Little, Brown and Co.,
1973), p. 88.

12. Sandra Kaplan, *Providing Programs for the Gifted and Talented: A
Handbook* (Ventura, Calif.: Office of the Ventura County Superintendent of
Schools, June, 1974).

13. Joseph S. Renzulli, *The Enrichment Triad Model: A Guide for Developing Defensible Programs for the Gifted and Talented* (Wethersfield,
Conn.: Creative Learning Press, 1977).

14. John C. Gowan, *Development of the Creative Individual* (San Diego,
Calif.: Robert Knapp, 1972); Torrance, *Creativity.*

ing and developing modern society, it is foolish to prepare students for the world of their parents. Gifted first graders today may not leave their advanced graduate programs or professional schools until the year 2000. How do we prepare those students for the year 2001?

As Silberman put it:

> To be practical, an education should prepare a man for work that doesn't yet exist and whose nature cannot even be imagined. This can be done only by teaching children how to learn, and by giving them the kind of intellectual discipline that will enable them to apply man's accumulated wisdom to new problems.[15]

There are two dramatically different views of the fundamental nature of creativity itself. On one hand, it may be approached as if it were a set of teachable cognitive skills, and cognitive models, such as Bloom's taxonomy of objectives for the cognitive domain[16] or Guilford's "structure of intellect," [17] are seen as ways of providing an analytic approach to creativity. There are key dimensions in each of these models that are especially concerned with creativity. In the Guilford model, for example, divergent production has been identified by a number of writers as closely equivalent to creativity. Many exercises and activities that would enhance these skills have been produced in the last decade.[18]

On the other hand, one school of thought suggests that creativity is associated with a distinctive set of personality traits that sets some individuals apart from their more unimaginative peers. Such a finding would result in some educational strategies very different from the cognitive exercises noted above. In reviewing the litera-

15. Charles Silberman, *Crisis in the Classroom* (New York: Random House, 1970), p. 114.

16. Benjamin Bloom, *Taxonomy of Educational Objectives: The Classification of Educational Goals, Handbook I: Cognitive Domain* (New York: Longman, 1956).

17. Joy P. Guilford, *The Nature of Human Intelligence* (New York, McGraw-Hill, 1967).

18. Mary N. Meeker, *The Structure of Intellect: Its Interpretation and Uses* (Columbus, Ohio: Charles Merrill, 1969).

ture, Dellas and Gaier[19] and Dewing[20] suggested that an openness to stimuli, whether the stimuli were taboo in the society or not, is one of the key characteristics of the creative mind. Part of the reputation of creative persons for bizarre or unusual behavior undoubtedly stems from their ignoring taboos with regard to violence, sex, and so forth.[21] Another strong and consistent finding is that gifted individuals are independent in attitude and social behavior.[22] They neither follow nor are swayed by the crowd. They have a strong self-concept and sense of personal identity. In this sense, they are sometimes viewed as unusual in a group, since they neither follow the social path set by the group nor do they repress antisocial or asocial feelings.

Torrance explored teacher attitudes toward the most desirable student characteristics.[23] In reviewing the attitudes of over a thousand teachers, he identified those characteristics that seemed most ideal to teachers in the United States. Among these were: consideration for others, determination, industriousness, sincerity, courtesy, doing work on time, and so forth. When these qualities were compared with a list of characteristics most highly rated by a panel of experts as important components of the productive and creative person, there were only two characteristics found in common—curiosity and independence in thinking.

Missing from the teachers' list were such creativity-related factors as intellectual courage, independence in judgment, being absorbed or preoccupied with tasks, intuitiveness, persistence, the willingness to take risks, and the unwillingness to accept the judgment of authorities. It should be obvious that characteristics widely

19. Marie Dellas and Eugene Gaier, "Identification of Creativity: The Individual," *Psychological Bulletin* 73 (1970): 55-73.

20. Kathleen Dewing, "Family Influences on Creativity: A Review and Discussion," *Journal of Special Education* 4 (1970): 399-404.

21. Donald W. MacKinnon, "The Nature and Nurture of Creative Talent," *American Psychologist* 17 (1962): 484-95.

22. Frank Barron, *Creative Person and Creative Process* (New York: Holt, Rinehart and Winston, 1969).

23. E. Paul Torrance, *Rewarding Creative Behavior* (Englewood Cliffs, N.J.: Prentice-Hall, 1965).

desired as socially conforming may be antithetical to creative production. The paradox with which the educators must come to grips is that there are competing positive characteristics, all valued by our society, which may predispose the child to shun a life of creativity.

SPECIAL CASES: THE UNDERACHIEVERS AND THE
CULTURALLY DIFFERENT

There are two groups of children about whom our knowledge has substantially increased over the last decade, but for whom that increase in knowledge has not been matched by appropriate modifications in the educational environment. These are the gifted underachievers and the gifted who are culturally different.

For gifted underachievers. There have been a variety of devices used to define the underachiever in terms of the gap between potential and performance. Some programs use the gap between achievement test scores and intelligence test scores for defining purposes. Others use the gap between academic grades and intelligence test scores. Regardless of the device used, the general portrait of the underachiever seems fairly consistent from study to study. A composite portrait of the gifted underachievers reveals a lack of self-confidence, the inability to persevere, a lack of a sense of purpose or drive, the presence of feelings of inferiority, and family conflict.[24]

A chicken-egg problem seems to be involved here. That is, are the children underachieving because of a low self-concept, or is their low self-concept the result of their chronic underachievement? By the time the school becomes concerned with these issues in the upper-elementary school, the interactions have become so intertwined that they have to be dealt with as a combination of effects.

In the past, two different strategies have been used in attempts to eliminate or reduce the problems of underachievement. The first of these was personal counseling based upon the research findings of a low self-image and of feelings of inferiority among underachievers. The second strategy has been a shift in educational environment to create either a more permissive or a more demanding

---

24. Lewis Terman and Melita Oden, *Genetic Studies of Genius*, vol. 4, *The Gifted Child Grows Up: Twenty-five Years' Follow-up of a Superior Group* (Stanford, Calif.: Stanford University Press, 1947).

environment, either of which might tend to modify the destructive patterns of response of the underachievers. Raph, Goldberg, and Passow reported the experimental findings from both of these approaches and commented upon the lack of positive results in both instances.[25] Because the counseling that has been described in such evaluation studies has often been limited and short-term, it has apparently not had outstanding impact. The modifications in educational environment likewise appear to have had little effect.

It may well be that the schools have underestimated the powerful effects of the personality patterns involved and thus underrate the amount of modification required to make a major impact. At any rate, we currently seem to be waiting for the next generation to emerge with better and more effective techniques to deal with these underachieving children.

For the culturally different gifted. Another group consists of those children referred to as the "culturally different gifted." We can anticipate special educational problems for children who come from the multitude of diverse ethnic and racial backgrounds that comprise American society. Increasing attention has been paid to these children over the past decade. Unfortunately, attention appears to be focused more on how to identify and recognize outstanding talent from cultural subgroups rather than on the more educationally fruitful discussion of what special experiences, content, or skills should be provided for them.[26]

One of our incorrect assumptions has been that talent is essentially indestructable. This concept relates to the idea noted earlier that ability is entirely genetically determined. Following that assumption, we have tried to find methods to uncover the talent that would always be there, just as one would lift up a basket and find a lantern shining beneath it. An alternative explanation, however, is more in line with known facts. Since ability in young children is the product of an interaction of the environment and native ability, then a very bad environment, experienced over an extended

25. Jane B. Raph, Miriam L. Goldberg, and A. Harry Passow, *Bright Underachievers* (New York: Teachers College Press, 1966).

26. Ruth Martinson, "The Identification of the Gifted and Talented," (Ventura, Calif.: National/State Leadership Training Institute on the Gifted and Talented, 1974).

period of time, can be expected to reduce substantially or even eliminate the high talent and ability that might have been present originally. The notion that superior talent can in fact be suppressed or destroyed should lend additional urgency to our attempts to provide stimulating and exciting educational experiences for the culturally different gifted.

Torrance and Torrance, as well as other authors, have emphasized that the culturally different child may come to school with a number of advantages as well as disadvantages, and that those advantages might provide the base for special educational programming.[27] Such advantages could be more freedom to explore, less inhibition, less commitment to established norms—all of which could provide a foundation for special program opportunities.

Gallagher and Kinney reported on a conference oriented to the culturally different gifted in which there was major participation of persons from a variety of culturally different backgrounds. Four major recommendations emerged from the conference:

1. The need for a curriculum stressing cultural pluralism;
2. Full use of community resources to supplement the school program;
3. The importance of recruitment and training of personnel who understand cultural pluralism and who may be members of the culturally different group themselves; and,
4. The need to impress on public decision makers at the state and federal levels that resources are needed to produce model programs and demonstrations that would illustrate good practices with the culturally different groups.[28]

It is clear that we have no organized strategy to deal with the diversity of needs and interests. As one thinks of the American Indian in the desert, the inner-city Puerto Ricans in New York, blacks living in poverty in the rural south, and the Chicanos in southern California, one realizes the foolishness of designing *one* alternative program to meet the needs of all these special groups. One of the major unsolved issues of our day, therefore, is that of

27. E. Paul Torrance and Pansy Torrance, "Combining Creative Problem Solving with Creative Expressive Activities in the Education of Disadvantaged Young People," *Journal of Creative Behavior* 6 (1972): 1-10.

28. *Talent Delayed—Talent Denied: A Conference Report*, ed. James Gallagher and Lucretia Kinney (Reston, Va.: Foundation for Exceptional Children, 1974).

determining the strategy for effective programming in these varied situations.

One of the strongest and most influential movements in the past decade in American education has been the development of systematic program planning and evaluation.[29] Planning is an increasingly used device, if not a popular one, as resources become limited and problems intractable. The related issue of cost benefits has emerged, placing the educator under pressure to demonstrate that the extra cost of any special program is compensated for by the greater range of benefits that the program produces. These benefits are often defined by student output or other associated benefits. A compelling case can be made for the cost benefits of gifted programs. Even if we assume only modest benefits resulting from additional assistance to the gifted and the talented, the potential future impact of these students on the society makes any gains of substantial importance.

Nevertheless, we should be about the business of developing a systematic methodology that can weigh the benefits of the programs for the gifted, even as procedures have been devised to provide similar evidence for the programs for the mentally retarded. The economic costs of a total educational program should include the cost of *not* having a special program for the gifted. Here the results could become dramatic. What is the cost of the medical discovery never made? Of the political compromise never reached to head off a war? Of the sonata that was never written?

The story of unrealized potential has been and will continue to be a strong, dramatic theme. Since all of us realize less than our own potential, it is easy for us to identify with such stories. In the field of medicine there have been startling new discoveries in immunization and in antibiotics, new and dramatic surgical techniques, and a wide variety of other contributions to better health. Who made these discoveries? It is clear that they were made by *gifted* scientists in various biomedical fields. What is the cost effectiveness of a special program for gifted students who may become, among

29. *School Evaluation: The Politics and Process*, ed. Ernest R. House (Berkeley, Calif.: McCutchan Publishing Corp., 1973).

many other possibilities, medical scientists and researchers? The cost of *not* having them is obviously a cause of grief.

The Future of Educational Programs for the Gifted

AMERICA'S LOVE-HATE RELATIONSHIP WITH THE GIFTED

The gifted scholars of tender years are often told by their elders that they are the future of the nation and that we are delighted with their academic performance and look eagerly to their forthcoming contributions to the society. These gifted students might well be confused by the conflicting messages they receive because even the most perceptive of them has a difficult time grasping the fundamental point that we adults do not say everything we mean, nor do we mean everything we say, about their talent.

A strong case can be made for the presence in the American society of a love-hate relationship with giftedness and talent. On one hand, we revere the gifted individual who has risen from humble background. We are proud to live in a society where talent can triumph over environment or family status. At the same time, since our origins came from battling an aristocratic elite, we are suspicious of attempts to subvert our commitment to egalitarianism. We do not wish a new elite class to develop, and as a result we seem to waver in our attitudes. We design our elementary and secondary programs for gifted students in ways that can be defended by careful administrators as giving no special favors, no tipping the scales in favor of the socially powerful or the specially endowed.[30]

Sometimes satire is the best way to illustrate the ambiguous positions in which we find ourselves. Kurt Vonnegut, Jr. has carried one of the common feelings about the gifted in our society to a logical conclusion in a short story entitled *Harrison Bergeron*, set in some future society:

The year was 2081, and everybody was finally equal. They weren't only equal before God and the law, they were equal in every which way.

30. John Gardner, *Excellence: Can We Be Equal and Excellent Too?* (New York: Harper and Row, 1961).

Nobody was smarter than anybody. No one was better looking than anybody else.[31]

The reason for this enforced equality was that people who were outstanding in various ways were given handicaps. Those that could dance well had to wear sandbags on their feet, those who were strikingly good looking would have to wear a mask so as not to embarrass those who did not have those characteristics. And those with high intellectual ability?

George, while his intelligence was way above normal, had a little mental handicap radio in his ear. He was required by law to wear it at all times. He was tuned into a government transmitter. Every twenty seconds or so, the transmitter would send out some noise to keep people like George from taking unfair advantage of their brains.[32]

The essentially destructive approach to "equality" does not really pass until we reach higher education when a miraculous transformation takes place. The United States has created the most complex and extensive higher education and professional school establishment in the world. We do not call the Stanford Medical School or the Harvard Law School a program for gifted students, but we know that they are and no apologies are made that only the "best" students should be allowed to attend. After all, some of us may need a good lawyer from time to time, others may need an excellent surgeon, and others would like to get some good advice from a competent psychiatrist.

As we view the needs of the society, the agenda of unsolved problems such as pollution, population, energy, and a lacking sense of national purpose, we feel the need for the best and the brightest to be well prepared and well motivated, not only to achieve their individual destiny, but also to aid the society as a whole.

At the local, state, and federal levels we vacillate in our public school program between the need to be "fair" and the need to be "effective." At times when the society seems to be threatened, such as in the Sputnik era and recently with the variety of problems surrounding energy shortages, we lean toward the productive use

31. Kurt Vonnegut, Jr., *Welcome to the Monkey House* (New York: Dell, 1950), p. 7.

32. Ibid.

of all talent. In more placid eras such as the early 1950s, the post-World War II decade, when there seemed to be little to worry and threaten us, we sought "equality" as a more appropriate goal. At the very least, we need to make these conflicting values visible so that a more mature societal decision can be made.

Requirements of quality programs for the gifted. Since the bulk of education for the gifted will inevitably be focused on public education, which is funded and supported in part through legislative bodies, attention must be turned toward legislative action at both the state and federal levels to support innovative programs. It is this route that would provide the resources for the development of new programs, for training, and for innovation. But such action is quite recent. It was in the 1950s and 1960s that a number of states became specifically involved. It was only in 1974 that the gifted were first mentioned in federal legislation in P.L. 93-380.

Rossmiller, Hale, and Frohreich have catalogued the relative expenditures of programs for exceptional children from five states.[33] The excess cost, over and above the normal cost of schooling, ranges from $92 per child for the intellectually gifted to $1,729 per child for the physically and multiply handicapped. Of all exceptional children, the programs for the gifted cost the least, but these costs are often enough above the average to be significant in hindering the development of special programs.

There is no conceivable way in which the number of specialists needed for the gifted could be trained by existing training institutions under current assumptions and models for delivery of services.[34] Experimentation with a variety of other models that lie within the bounds of possibility is obviously called for.

MAJOR COMPONENTS OF AN EFFECTIVE SUPPORT SYSTEM

There are major components of an effective support system that would bring quality education to the gifted. These components could be provided by legislation not now on the books. As I have

33. Richard A. Rossmiller, J. Hale, and L. Frohreich, *Educational Programs for Exceptional Children: Resource Configurations and Cost* (Washington, D.C.: National Education Finance Project, 1970).

34. James J. Gallagher, "Technical Assistance—A New Device for Quality Educational Services for the Gifted," *TAG Newsletter* 16 (1974): 5-8.

indicated elsewhere, the following components are essential elements in a support system for educational programs for the gifted:

1. *Continuous in-service training.* It is important that any such programmatic effort involve a continuous and systematic effort to upgrade the skills and knowledge of the teachers directly involved in the program. Workshops and institutes in content areas such as mathematics or social studies, or in stimulating productive thinking, would be examples of such training efforts.

2. *Leadership training.* It is important that a program of any considerable size have a staff person in a leadership position who has responsibility for systematic program development. Leadership personnel would organize and participate in in-service programs, coordinate content fields, bring in the best of what we know in fields such as mathematics or art from the rest of the educational staff or the community, and provide the administrative leadership for the program within the school system.

3. *Research and development.* There is a natural assumption that somewhere in some secluded laboratory or research center important research is being done that will produce new curriculum adventures for the gifted. Unfortunately, this is not true. What is urgently needed, particularly by those resource teachers who are working with the gifted children, is the development of self-contained units that have conceptual validity and that provide the kind of specialized experience and insight to the gifted students that they would not be capable of obtaining through the regular program.

4. *Technical assistance and communication.* It is important to establish a continuing program of technical assistance that would be available for program consultation to a school system that might wish specialized and individual help on its own program development. Such a unit would provide help on a variety of needs, such as special curricula and the design and execution of evaluation programs, so that the local school system could assure itself that it is doing a creditable job.[35]

In education generally, state funds have traditionally been spent

35. James J. Gallagher, "Educational Support Systems for Gifted Students," *North Carolina Association for the Gifted and Talented Quarterly Journal* 1 (1975): 10-11.

on activities in programs of direct service, with very limited funds set aside for research, demonstration, leadership training, or technical assistance. It therefore seems appropriate that some type of federal legislation could be developed to extend the current section in the Elementary and Secondary Education Act to provide resources for these support functions that are catalytic to good program development.

Summary

The field of gifted education has many unresolved issues that will be passed along to the next generation for more adequate resolution. Among the most important are the comprehension of the full implications of giftedness that is created by a mix of genetics and environment and of the broadened definition that is still far from operational.

In the special education dimension, there is a particular need for major curriculum materials to meet the needs of gifted students and of special educational adaptations proved successful for the gifted underachiever or the culturally different gifted.

Finally, we have yet to come to grips with the ambivalent feelings about giftedness that are abroad in modern American society. These feelings of pride and envy, of security and anxiety, of achievement and competition, shade all of the public actions related to education for the gifted and we have yet to be able to adapt our own planning and educational programs to that fundamental ambivalence.

CHAPTER III

The Emerging National and State Concern

DAVID M. JACKSON

A slow but steady development has characterized the federal concern for the gifted and talented since the late 1960s. This effort has coalesced with the diffused efforts of several pioneering states to produce what can now be viewed as an initial effort of truly national dimensions. While the most recent attention on the part of federal and state governments is best viewed as continuous with earlier attempts, current federal activity springs most directly from the Education Amendments of 1969, and specifically from an amendment offered by Congressman John Erlenborn of Illinois.

Erlenborn had been impressed with the efforts made on behalf of the gifted and talented by the Illinois Department of Public Instruction, particularly by its efforts to provide a comprehensive identification program, by the variety of programs offered, and by the quality of in-service education for teachers available through the state's network of resource centers. Moreover, he had been convinced of the critical needs of gifted and talented children for differentiated educational experiences. His amendment voiced a congressional intent that gifted and talented children should benefit from federal legislation, particularly from Titles III and V of the Elementary and Secondary Education Act, as well as from the teacher education provisions of the Higher Education Act of 1965.

Most significantly, however, the amendment directed the U.S. Commissioner of Education to launch a study that was to have four basic objectives: (a) to discover the extent to which special education provisions were necessary to meet the needs of gifted

I wish to acknowledge the assistance of Dr. Bruce O. Boston in the preparation of this paper.

and talented children, (b) to discover whether any existing federal programs were currently meeting some of those needs, (c) to evaluate how programs of federal educational assistance could become more effective in meeting these needs, and (d) to recommend what new programs were needed to meet them.

The congressional mandate was fulfilled on October 6, 1971, when Commissioner Sidney P. Marland submitted to the Congress a document that can be viewed as the embryo of recent developments in gifted child education.[1] Its recommendations and consequences have been more far-reaching than one might ordinarily expect from yet another report from the U.S. Office of Education. The Marland report offered recommendations for eleven actions to be taken under then existing legislative authority (P.L. 91-230, Sec. 806). The recommendations called for (a) a planning report on implementing a federal role in educating the gifted and talented; (b) the establishment of a staff within USOE for gifted education; (c) a national survey of programs to find costs, evaluation procedures, and model programs and to develop a clearinghouse on gifted/talented education; (d) the utilization of Title V of the Elementary and Secondary Education Act to strengthen capabilities for gifted/talented education; (e) two national summer leadership training institutes to upgrade supervisory personnel in state education agencies; (f) program and research support for institutions interested in gifted children in minority groups; (g) program activities specific to career education for the gifted and talented; (h) special attention in one experimental school to project the relation between gifted and talented education and comprehensive school reform; (i) cooperation with Title III programs; (j) one staff member for each of the ten regional Offices of Education to be assigned to gifted and talented education; and (k) the study of Office of Education programs relating to higher education to optimize their potential for the gifted and talented.

The record of the Office of Education in fully or partially implementing most of these recommendations is impressive, especially

---

1. Sidney P. Marland, Jr., *Education of the Gifted and Talented*, vol. 1, Report to the Congress of the United States by the U.S. Commissioner of Education (Washington, D.C.: U.S. Government Printing Office, 1972).

in view of the normal organizational and policy fluctuations within the agency that caused some programs to disappear, the reassignment of personnel, and the reevaluation of policy goals.

Beyond its recommendations, Commissioner Marland's report provided some notable "firsts" for a serious federal involvement in the education of the gifted and talented. Specifically, the following steps were taken for the first time:

1. Gifted and talented children were attended to as a specific population with special educational needs. Thus a crippling assumption, that these children could somehow "make it on their own," was officially undercut. Previous efforts benefitting gifted and talented children had entered the school house via the back door, through programs under the National Defense Education Act, the National Science Foundation, and others. Now gifted and talented children were seen as worthy of assistance in their own right—a significant step forward.

2. A definition of "gifted and talented" was attempted for purposes of identifying this population. Significantly, the definition was a broad one and not circumscribed by a view of giftedness that focused on cognitive superstars. The new definition sought to encompass not only generalized intellectual ability, but also specific academic aptitude, original and creative abilities, leadership abilities, talent in the visual and performing arts, and psychomotor abilities.

3. Staff attention within USOE was to be directed toward improving the educational lot of gifted and talented children.

4. Elements of a national strategy for the education of the gifted and talented began to take shape.

The Role of the Office of Education: From Advocacy to Categorical Funding

The rudiments of what eventually became the Office of Gifted and Talented (OGT) in the U.S. Office of Education were already present in the staff that gathered the material, conducted the regional hearings, and prepared the final draft of the Marland report. The recommendation that such an office be established was very quickly implemented.

The Office of the Gifted and Talented faced the immediate

problem of how to foster a truly national effort without program funds. By dint of circumstance, the new office was in a position where it could not attempt to develop, or even coordinate, a national program nor promulgate a national policy for educating the gifted. In the absence of programmatic clout, a pluralistic tack was taken in which OGT tried to stimulate activity at several levels simultaneously. The strategy was one of identifying when and where interesting and productive things were happening, to call attention to them, to persuade, to advocate, and to bear witness. This stance of persuasive advocacy was manifested in different but related strands of activity.

First, in order best to fulfill the advocacy role for the gifted and talented, OGT had to know what was in fact happening. This investigative task had already been accomplished in some measure by the needs assessment survey completed for the Marland report. The survey results were not encouraging, but they did provide OGT with an agenda for advocacy. Among the findings were the following:

1. Differential educational provisions for the gifted and talented had an extremely low priority in the competition for the federal, state, and local educational dollar. Programmatic concern was found to be "miniscule."

2. Minority and culturally different gifted and talented children were scarcely being reached.

3. While twenty-one states made some legislative or regulatory provisions for these children, more often than not such provisions represented mere intent. Only ten states had full-time personnel in their state education agencies concerned with gifted child education. There was a gap between what should be and what actually was.

4. Gifted and talented children, contrary to myth, were *not* succeeding on their own. In fact, the reverse was true. Research had convincingly demonstrated that they required specialized educational programs to live up to their potential.

5. Identification of the gifted and talented suffered woefully from lack of adequate testing procedures, inadequate funds, and in some cases from apathy and downright hostility to their educational needs on the part of teachers and administrators.

6. When differentiated programs for the gifted and talented were implemented, the effects were measurable.

7. Perhaps most disturbing of all, from the point of view of OGT, was the finding that while people tended to look to the federal government for help for the gifted and talented, the federal role in the delivery of services to these children was for all practical purposes nonexistent.

Clearly the job to be done was enormous and the resources for doing it meagre. But the Marland report did provide the context for significant opportunity. It scarcely mattered where one began since so little was being done. The needs assessment survey provided a justification for a pluralistic approach to problems; the lack of federal funds precluded throwing money at the situation and pointed to a strategy of sustained advocacy.

Second, while casting about for a way to make a demonstrable impact on the gifted scene nationally, OGT resorted to the time-honored American approach of federalism. A leadership training effort at the state level was mounted in order to (a) shore up already existing support among those in the field who had long been committed to gifted child education, (b) reach key educators, opinion shapers, and legislators, and to begin to develop the potential parent constituency, and (c) provide concrete skills in planning and program building at the state level. Because no specifically earmarked funds were available for leadership training in the gifted and talented area, OGT turned to the funding possibilities contained in the Education Professions Development Act. This initiative is discussed below.

Third, in pursuit of more effective advocacy for the gifted, and in order to focus national attention on the problems brought to light by the needs assessment, a number of other initiatives were taken. Official federal and state inattention could be remediated in part by calling on private foundations, business, industry, and community groups to invest in programming and support for the gifted and talented.[2] An extensive national travel and speaking schedule, numerous network and local TV and radio appearances, and a lengthening series of articles in popular and professional journals,

2. Jane Case Williams, *The Gifted and Talented: A Role for the Private Sector* (Washington, D.C.: U.S. Office of Education, 1972).

newspapers, and magazines were undertaken. Greater visibility for the gifted and talented was gained through programs like Exploration Scholarships, a national symposium for gifted high school students, jointly sponsored with the American Association for Gifted Children. OGT also took over administrative responsibility for the Presidential Scholars Program initiated by President Lyndon B. Johnson in 1964. Local and state education agencies were alerted to the funding possibilities for programs for gifted students that could be developed by applying the techniques of creative grantsmanship to various Titles (for example, Titles I, II, V, IX) of the Elementary and Secondary Education Act and its amendments. Vocational and career education funds were also tapped for the gifted and talented. Other sources within the federal education establishment were also sought out, such as the National Endowment for the Arts and the Humanities, the National Science Foundation, and others. Little by little the needs of gifted children and existing resources were brought together. Applications were made for funds, programs were initiated, interest was stimulated, and results were generated.

In 1975 a breakthrough occurred. Under the provisions of the Special Projects Act of P.L. 93-380, Section 404, categorical funds were for the first time made available for the education of the gifted and talented. The hopes of OGT and the gifted education community had come to fruition. Appropriations for gifted child education were set at $2.56 million, to be apportioned as shown in table 1.

Three points may be made about these funds and the uses to which they were put. First, the categorical funding was a cause for both rejoicing and dismay: rejoicing because the gifted and talented children had emerged from the welter of 50 million American school children as worthy of attention in their own right, and dismay because the amount appropriated was so disproportionate to the need.[3] Nonetheless, it was a beginning.

---

3. Congress had originally authorized $12.25 million for the gifted and talented, but had later accepted the administration's figure of $2.56 million. The larger figure had been arrived at through prolonged consultation with leaders in the field and had been considered a bare minimum for effective action nationwide.

TABLE 1

APPROPRIATIONS FOR GIFTED CHILD EDUCATION FOR 1976 IN THE
SPECIAL PROJECTS ACT OF P.L. 93-380, SECTION 404

PURPOSE	NUMBER OF GRANTS	APPROPRIATION (IN DOLLARS)
Information services	1	$ 125,000
Grants to state education agencies	26	1,500,000
Local projects grants	18	260,000
Graduate training for leadership personnel	1	190,000
Inservice training and technical assistance	1	165,000
Internships to train leaders	1	70,000
Research, research training, surveys, dissemination of findings	0	0
Model projects for special categories: early childhood, community-based mentor programs, visual and performing arts, exceptionally disadvantaged, creativity, sparsely populated areas	6*	260,000

* One grant made in each of the special categories.

Second, the uses to which the funds were put indicate two wagers that are mutually reinforcing. One took seriously the success of the strategy adopted by the National/State Leadership Training Institute on the Gifted and Talented as well as a significant finding of the Marland report that a commitment to gifted and talented education on the part of professionals at the state level was the most determinative factor in the development of strong programming. This had certainly been the experience of those states that were already leaders in the field long before federal interest was manifested. Therefore, fully half of the available funds were channeled into state education agencies for professional staff development.

The other wager was a commitment to the "ripple effect" that could be generated from local levels outward and upward. Thus, a total of $520,000 was awarded to proposals for local projects and model programs that had a built-in replicability factor. The overall effect of concentrating funds in state capitals and in selected geographical and project areas would be to create wave and splash at the same time—a combination of sustained activity and raised visibility for experimental approaches in targeted program areas.

Finally, a look at the history of the OGT reveals that categorical funding for gifted and talented education at the federal level is as much a consequence of emerging concern at state and local levels as it has been a stimulus to that concern. In other words, the traditional federal function of pump priming has now met the water table of local concerns and activities that have been very quietly percolating beneath the surface for many years. To alter the metaphor, this federal/local encounter over the needs of our nation's gifted and talented students is fast approaching a critical mass, indicating that the encounter now has the definite potential for breaking out of the cyclicism which has plagued that concern over the last two generations and for becoming a continuing priority over the long term.

The major lacuna of the federal effort has been the lack of funding for research. Federal support in this area has been negligible, and such activity as has occurred has resulted from the individual interests of leading educators in the field who have managed to capture foundation, departmental, or private funds to sponsor research in which they have personally been interested. This state of affairs is likely to continue for the foreseeable future, casting a baleful influence over the entire effort.

A further cause for concern is the fact that categorical funding for gifted and talented education has emerged in the context of "Special Projects," on a par with and tied to metric education, educational programs related to women's rights, and the like. The congressional intent regarding all these programs is that they be phased out once the need for them is mitigated. Federal appropriations were continued for the gifted and talented until 1978 as a kind of "extra." While it is possible to believe that once American school children have been taught to "think metric" they will continue to do so without a further infusion of federal funding, and that textbook and curriculum publishers will sustain initial efforts in this area, it is unlikely that the parents of the United States will cease producing gifted and talented children for whom special educational provisions must be made. A post-1978 strategy was needed to assure continued attention to the needs of these children.

Gathering and Disseminating Information: The ERIC Clearinghouse

While not self-consciously a part of an overall federal strategy, the ERIC Clearinghouse on Handicapped and Gifted Children nevertheless functions as an active component of the federal effort. One of a number of such clearinghouses funded by the ERIC (Education Resources and Information Center) subdivision of the National Institute of Education, it has been operated by the Council for Exceptional Children since its official inception in 1972.[4] With respect to the education of gifted children, the Clearinghouse performs five main functions:

1. Gathers, evaluates, abstracts, and disseminates information on all aspects of gifted child education on an ongoing basis. Dissemination generally occurs by way of regularly published bibliographies of abstracted documents that are grouped generically (for example, "Identification of the Gifted and Talented," "Creativity," "Programming for the Gifted and Talented," "Mathematics and Science for the Gifted and Talented," and so forth);

2. Sponsors and publishes "information analysis products" in the form of published monographs, studies, manuals, and reports;

3. Conducts a computer search service on specialized topics;

4. Sponsors workshops for potential users of the ERIC system;

5. Responds to client requests for information on all aspects of gifted child education.

The most important function performed by the Clearinghouse is its role as a repository and dissemination center for a national data base on the entire gamut of information available on the education of gifted and talented children. The growth of this data base in the last several years has been little short of phenomenal. Thousands of abstracts of documents on gifted child education are

4. The Council for Exceptional Children began data gathering and information dissemination activities some three years prior to 1972 and functioned as an ERIC Clearinghouse without being officially designated or funded as such.

accessible in the DIALOG computer system. Since 1972, the Clearinghouse has published bibliographies and information analysis products related to the education of the gifted and talented. While the greatest volume of the activity in information gathering and dissemination relates to various handicapping conditions, it is significant to note that a full 15 percent of its client services relates to information requests on gifted child education, as much as for any other single need in special education.

Bridge to the States: The National/State Leadership Training Institute

In August of 1972, some five months after the appearance of the Marland report, the National/State Leadership Training Institute on the Gifted and Talented (LTI) was formed. It was funded primarily through a grant released under the authority of the Education Professions Development Act and administered under the fiscal aegis of the Ventura County (California) Superintendent of Schools. Perhaps more than any other actor in the field, the LTI has directed its efforts to changes at the state level, translating a federally articulated vision into planning and program activity by state and local education agencies.

The basic rationale for the LTI has always been that in order for gifted and talented students to achieve the instructional benefits that would best develop their abilities and talents, and in order for gifted child education to achieve the level of presence and recognition called for at the federal level, decision makers had to be involved at both state and local levels at the crucial points where educational policy is made.

Accordingly, the early goals of the LTI have remained in effect over the long term. These goals may be expressed as follows: (a) to formulate and initiate activities to be carried out by uniquely constituted state-level planning teams; (b) to establish a working communications network among USOE/OGT, regional offices of education, the states, and local education agencies; (c) to specify measurable objectives that can be met in identifiable time periods for implementing the national commitment to the education of the gifted and talented called for in the Marland report; (d) to develop training modules for regional offices, states, local education agencies, schools, and parent groups, which would suggest action steps to be taken in the development of a gifted and talented program at state and local levels; (e) to provide technical assistance in adapting these training modules to the unique circumstances of the above-named groups; (f) to develop and disseminate effective publications and media resources on the problems and promise of the gifted and talented; (g) to create a clearinghouse for the gifted and talented that would identify, analyze, and disseminate information on ongoing programs for this population.

This diversity of goals was focused fundamentally on bringing about the policy changes necessary for successful programming for the gifted and talented at state and local levels. These changes have run the gamut from legislation and funding to in-service and curriculum development.

The overall LTI goal of policy change has taken shape around three strategies: (a) developing awareness of the educational needs of gifted and talented children; (b) training educational leaders in appropriate pedagogical strategies for thtse children; and, most importantly, (c) planning for the educational needs of gifted and talented children at state and local levels.

In pursuit of these goals the LTI held three national and nine regional conferences between 1973 and 1976. Five-member teams were recruited and invited for training in educational planning. Teams were comprised of one representative each from the decision-making level and one from the operating level of the state agency; one representative from local education agencies; and two or more representatives chosen from among teachers of the gifted and talented, parents, the academic community, a local school board, and the private sector. One noneducator was to be represented on each team.

In the three-year period during which the LTI conducted its national institutes, a total of forty-eight state teams received training and developed state plans. Teams from the New York City and from the Los Angeles schools were also trained. Literally hundreds of educators, administrators, parents, and other policy makers participated in the institutes.

The training sessions took as their major objective the writing of a long-range plan for the development of strategy and programming for gifted and talented children in each participating state. State-level goals, objectives, and strategies were delineated. Responsibilities were assigned, time frames established, and points of impact and leverage identified. Upon returning to their states, the teams sought to implement their state plans in a variety of ways. Team members pushed for enabling legislation and for categorical funds, and lobbied in state and local education agencies for both policy and personnel support for gifted and talented education. Sometimes the private sector was approached. Media attention was sought. Participants and teams also worked to organize programs and advocacy support.

A second objective of the LTI was the development of what amounted to a national network of persons and agencies committed to gifted and talented education. Several strategies were undertaken in the service of network development, including the following: (a) follow-up visits by national LTI staff members; (b) the forging of linkages at and across local, state, and federal levels; (c) the publication of a monthly newsletter providing information regarding national developments, changes in state policies, innovative practices and programs instituted in local school districts, the activities of parent groups, news of local, state, and regional conferences on the gifted and talented, and the like; (d) on-site technical assistance; (e) recruitment and deployment of consultant assistance across local, state, and regional lines; (f) the organization of topical regional conferences on appropriate strategies for teaching the gifted, on the problems of disadvantaged gifted children, and on culturally different gifted children; and (g) the "recycling" of both knowledge and personnel from previous regional and national institutes and conferences into the ongoing activities of the LTI in other locations.

A third long-range objective of the LTI has been the establishment of a continuing publication program designed to meet the policy-making and instructional needs of those involved in or advocating gifted child education. As a consequence of a sustained effort, more than ten major publications have been developed covering such diverse topics as "Developing a Written Plan for the Education of the Gifted and Talented," "The Identification of the Gifted and Talented," "Providing Programs for the Gifted and

Talented," "Parentspeak," and "Evaluating Programs for the Gifted and Talented."

According to one study, the policy impact of the LTI on the states has been significant.[5] Of the top twenty-five states with which the LTI has had the greatest amount of interaction since 1972, sixteen (64 percent) ranked among the states having the highest percentage of policy changes most often mentioned in connection with LTI activity. These policies include: (a) the utilization of LTI methods, including a broadening of the terms used, for identifying gifted and talented children; (b) higher priority rankings for services to gifted and talented children within the state; (c) the increased representation of minority and female students within the ranks of those identified as gifted and talented; and (d) the establishment and broadening of channels of communication between and among states as they relate to the needs of the gifted and talented.

Other changes noted include an increased level of national public awareness, an increase in the numbers of students and programs for the gifted and talented, and an upsurge in in-service programs devoted to gifted child education. To take but one finding of the evaluation report, 52 percent of those policy makers, administrators, and staff persons in state and local education agencies who were polled indicated that since 1972 gifted and talented programming has received a higher priority in policy and planning as a result of LTI efforts.

Activities at the State Level

Until the 1960s, activity at the state level was more or less limited to the developments occurring in California, Connecticut, Florida, Georgia, Illinois, and North Carolina. In these states either a legislative definition of "gifted" was enacted or categorical funds were authorized for the education of the gifted, or both. State-sponsored in-service programs both stimulated, and were stimulated by, local interest.

Today, there are at least thirty-eight states that make provision

5. Elsbery Systems Analysis, *Evaluation Summary: National/State Leadership Institute for the Gifted and Talented, 1972-1976* (New York: Elsbery Systems Analysis, 1975).

for the gifted and talented in their legislation, in the regulations of the state education agency, or both. In some cases the legislation expresses intent only, without specific financial provisions. In a growing number of states (sixteen at last count), funding is available to *every* local education agency in the state to provide program support. Only since 1971 have eight of these states instituted their policies of funding local programs. Only about one-fifth of the states had full-time coordinators for gifted education in 1971 but by 1977 this proportion had risen to about one-half of the states.

Since the states and local education agencies bear 92 percent of all educational costs, it is to the state and local levels that we must look for continued development of programming, despite the significant advances that have been made at the federal level since 1972. Clear evidence of this point is seen in the fact that in any given year such states as California, Florida, Illinois, and Pennsylvania devote more funds to gifted and talented education than does the federal government. Approximately one-third of the states fund programs statewide, another third are beginning to show interest in and support for planning, in-service training, and special projects, and the remaining third lack any significant involvement on behalf of their gifted and talented, with the possible exception of some outstanding local programs. In view of these facts, it is fortunate that the categorical funds contained in P.L. 93-380 (Section 404) will probably touch every state in some way, whether directly or indirectly.

An overview of the activities for gifted and talented students at the state level over the past several years reveals five major developments:

1. There has been an increase in both the number and the quality of personnel at the state level devoting professional attention to the educational needs of the gifted and talented. Beyond the administrative attention of full- and part-time personnel, the emerging quality factor entering upon the state scene has probably been the most significant advance for both the short- and long-term future. Increasingly, the professionals emerging at state and local levels have specialized academic training in gifted education (often

with masters degrees or doctorates in the field). They also count among their number many who have labored long in the vineyards, and who now feel that their time has come. Thus, at both the state and local level, there are more and more teachers and administrators who are not only highly qualified and willing to take advantage of recent developments across the country, but who are also equipped to bring pressure to bear on local school boards and state education agencies to assure gifted and talented children their rightful place in the educational sun.

2. There have been significant policy changes at the state level associated with legislative advances and developments within state departments of education. These advances have been of two basic kinds. First, state legislatures, as they respond to both congressional and state initiatives, are slowly undertaking to provide legislative definitions of all manner of exceptional children—the mentally retarded, the handicapped, the learning disabled, and the gifted and talented. Thus, gifted and talented children are reaping the benefit of legislative attention directed at other forms of exceptionality. Their visibility as a "special" population is being more sharply focused. If the historical pattern continues to hold, and program funding follows recognition and legislative or regulatory definition, the outlook is for more rather than less state involvement in the education of the gifted and talented.

Second, state education agencies have taken a different tack with regard to gifted and talented children over the last half decade. Prior to the most recent surge of activity, gifted child education was viewed in most state agencies as an "educational fringe." Such activity and attention as did occur usually came about because of the personal interests and predelictions of a particular state-level bureaucrat. State education agencies are currently faced, however, with two developments that are sure to bring about policy change: a federal initiative and an organized parent and teacher pressure for special programming for these children. In some states this pressure has been exerted through the courts (for example, in Pennsylvania) in due process proceedings. In others, organized local pressure has reached the point where it warrants attention by state administrators with respect to policy.

3. The third significant development in the states has been the

shift away from the dominance of cognitively oriented programs toward a massive diversification in programming. The root of this development has been an increasing sophistication on the part of educators, which has led them away from the narrow perspective that the gifted child is basically a cognitive "superstar" with a very high IQ. The six dimensions of giftedness/talent delineated in the Marland report have contributed significantly to broadcasting this academic consensus to an ever-widening audience of parents, teachers, and local program administrators. As a consequence programmatic attention has been construed along a wide variety of lines. Diversification has also been encouraged in state and local education agencies through grants offered by the Office of Gifted and Talented for model projects in 1976. As noted above, proposals were requested in the areas of the visual and performing arts, creativity, early childhood programs for the gifted, the exceptionally disadvantaged gifted, innovative rural programs, and community-based mentor programs. At state and local levels, increasing attention has also been given to career education for the gifted and talented, as well as to vocational education, and to the gifted handicapped.

4. Following this diversification, the states have also been making significant inroads into the development of different pedagogical styles for gifted and talented children. The educational basis for such a movement is not difficult to discern, for it is clear that different kinds of giftedness require different instructional modes. A child who flourishes in a resource room environment or in an independent study program may not get the same educational benefit from an accelerated program or from one based on an intensive relationship with a mentor. While the debate between acceleration and enrichment has not ceased among educators of the gifted and talented, the ground for the discussion has recently begun to shift from a discussion of teaching styles to an exploration of various learning styles. This shift has opened up a variety of programming options. It is worth noting in this regard that one listing of program options for the gifted and talented from a Pennsylvania intermediate unit lists over fifty kinds of program options. Thus, not only is programming being diversified to meet the needs of different

gifts and talents, but different modes of working with these children are emerging within program types.

5. A fifth and final factor of significance in state-level development of programming for the gifted and talented is the propensity to "piggyback" on community and private sector resources. This strategy has been found to be effective for the gifted and talented. Pupils like it because it brings them into direct contact with more people and resources that can both stimulate and direct their interests. Teachers like it because it provides an alternative to what is offered in the classroom and hence an educational environment that can be brought into a truly dialectical tension with classroom instruction and independent study. Administrators like it because it brings down per pupil expenditures.

Involvement of the community and of the private sector in the education of the gifted and talented has gone far beyond the restricted perspective of attempting to secure private funding for public education. The most significant developments include the enlistment of skilled persons from the private sector (for example, business, the professions, artists, artisans, industry) as both a support system for and a complement to what goes on in the public schools. Typical examples of public school/private sector cooperation in support of gifted education would be the seminars in probability theory for gifted inner-city mathematics students conducted by an insurance company actuary in the northeast, or the internships in city management conducted by a west coast city manager for a small coterie of gifted social science students.

Beyond the involvement of competent community-based persons, gifted and talented programs have also made effective use of a wide variety of community resources such as museums, libraries, theaters, laboratories, hospitals, clinics, recreation programs, and the like.

Since 1972, then, there has been a notable resurgence of interest in and attention to gifted and talented children at both federal and state levels. Federal leadership has been significant symbolically, even if not financially determinative. State-level advances have tended in two basic directions: toward policy development and toward the expenditure of administrative energy. These, combined with the diversification in program development, tend to inspire an attitude of cautious optimism on the part of those who have long considered the gifted and talented as the neglected stepchildren of our educational system. What remains clear is that the competition for federal funds for gifted and talented children remains fierce. The line at the federal fiscal window will continue to lengthen because it moves slowly. The educational future of these children will more likely be determined by what happens in the administrative and legislative branches of state governments. Prospects remain bright, even though the gap from the Cleveland Major Work Program to a program for the gifted and talented in every school district still remains very considerable. But it is not the gap that it once was. State laws are changing. Policies of state education agencies are changing. More teachers are being trained. Experienced professionals are seeking graduate degrees in gifted child education. More programs are underway, both in number and in diversity. The end is not yet in sight, but the emerging national and state concern for the gifted and talented is encouraging enough to prompt the wager that an ineluctable beginning has been made.

CHAPTER IV

State Provisions for Educating the Gifted and Talented

JEFFREY ZETTEL

The Council for Exceptional Children, under a grant from the Office of the Gifted and Talented of the U.S. Office of Education, undertook a nationwide survey of state education agencies in 1977 to ascertain the current status of services to gifted and talented children and youth. This chapter is a summary of the findings and presents a picture of educational provisions for this population from the perspective of the states.

Statutory Descriptions of Gifted and Talented Children

There are four principal ways in which states describe gifted and talented children in their laws and statutes. The first, and perhaps the most explicit, occurs when a state specifically mentions or defines an individual as being "gifted or talented." Nine states describe this population in such a manner. Delaware, for example, uses the following statutory description of gifted and talented individuals:

"Gifted children" means children between the chronological ages of four and twenty-one who are endowed by nature with high intellectual capacity and who have a native capacity for high potential intellectual attainment and scholastic achievement.
"Talented children" means children between the chronological ages of four and twenty-one who have demonstrated superior talents, aptitudes, or abilities, outstanding leadership qualities and abilities, or consistently remarkable performance in the mechanics, manipulative skills, the art of expression of ideas, oral or written, music, art, human relations or any other worthwhile line of human achievement.[1]

---

1. *Delaware State Code*, Article 14, Section 3162, 1953.

Sixteen states, on the other hand, mention gifted and talented children under the broad, general rubric of exceptional children. Alabama, for instance, defines its exceptional children to include:

persons between the ages of six and twenty-one who have been certified under regulations of the State Board of Education by specialists as being unsuited for enrollment in regular classes of the public schools or who are unable to be educated or trained adequately in such regular programs, including but not limited to the mild and moderately to severely retarded, but not including the profoundly retarded; the speech impaired; the deaf and hearing impaired; the blind and vision impaired; the crippled and those having other physical handicaps not otherwise specifically mentioned herein; the emotionally conflicted; the socially maladjusted; those with special learning disabilities; the multiply handicapped; *and the intellectually gifted.*[2]

Similarly, there are seven additional states which, although they do not specifically mention the words "gifted and talented" in their definition of "exceptionality," use language such that gifted and talented children could be easily construed as being a portion of this population. In New Mexico the definition of exceptionality lends itself to such an interpretation:

"Exceptional children" means the children whose abilities render regular services of the public school to be inconsistent with their educational needs.[3]

Four states, as exemplified by the following Tennessee statute, describe their gifted and talented children in terms of their being "handicapped":

"Handicapped child" means handicapped children and youth between the ages of four (4) and twenty-one (21) years inclusive who have been certified under regulations of the State Board of Education by a specialist as being unsuited for enrollment in regular classes of the public schools or who are unable to be educated or trained adequately in such regular programs without the provision of special classes, instruction, facilities or related services, or a combination thereof. This term includes the educable, trainable, and profoundly retarded; the speech and/or language impaired; the deaf and hearing impaired; the blind and visually limited; the physically handicapped and/or other health impairments including homebound, hospitalized, and pregnancy; the learning disabled including perceptually handicapped, emotionally conflicted,

---

2. *Code of Alabama*, Section 1, Act 106, Laws of 1971, p. 375. Italics added.

3. New Mexico Special Act, Section 77-11-3-1, 1972.

functionally retarded, and socially maladjusted; the multiply handicapped; *and the intellectually gifted;* and any other child whose needs and abilities cannot be served in a regular classroom setting.[4]

Finally, there are fourteen states that make no reference at all to gifted and talented children in their state codes or statutory language.

Screening and Identifying Gifted and Talented Children

For the purposes of federal education programs, a suggested definition regarding the identification of gifted and talented children was proposed in 1971 by the report on the education of the gifted and talented prepared by the U.S. Commissioner of Education.[5] According to this report, gifted and talented children should be selected from those capable of high performance in six areas: (a) general intellectual ability, (b) specific academic aptitude, (c) creative or productive thinking, (d) leadership ability, (e) visual and performing arts, and, (f) psychomotor ability.

At present there are twenty states that have adopted a similar if not identical definition suggesting that their gifted and talented population be representative of all six performance areas mentioned above. Two states, Alaska and Iowa, use a similar yet slightly different six-category definition in that they substitute the category "manipulative skills" in place of "psychomotor ability."

The majority of the states, however, do not use such a broad definition to identify their potentially gifted and talented children. In fact, there appears to be considerable disagreement among the states not only as to which, but also as to how many, of these particular performance areas should be used as potential pools for the selection of gifted and talented individuals.

THE IDENTIFICATION OF INDIVIDUALS WITH HIGH GENERAL INTELLECTUAL ABILITY

Thirty-eight states include individuals capable of high performance in general intellectual ability as a part of their gifted and

4. *Tennessee Code Annotated*, Section 49-2914, chapter 29, 1972. Italics added.

5. Sidney P. Marland, Jr., *Education of the Gifted and Talented*, vol. 1, Report to the Congress of the United States by the U.S. Commissioner of Education (Washington, D.C.: U.S. Government Printing Office, 1972), p. 2.

talented definition. The methods and procedures used to identify these children vary from state to state. There are a number of states that use broad, somewhat nonrestrictive definitions to identify children capable of high intellectual performance. Illinois, for example, describes these children as "consistently superior to . . . other children in the school to the extent that [they] need and can profit from specially planned educational services beyond those normally provided by the standard school program." [6] The responsibility for the development of specific identification criteria, therefore, is left largely to the discretion of the local school districts.

Other states provide their local education agencies with very specific identification procedures and criteria. California, for instance, not only mandates that these children need to demonstrate a "general intellectual capacity as to place [them] within the top 2 percent of all students having achieved [their] school grade throughout the state." It further stipulates who should be involved in the screening process, as well as suggesting specific tests and attainment scores needed to qualify a child as a "mentally gifted minor." [7]

There are also differences among the states as to which, if any, minimum attainment score should be required on a standardized measure. Alaska stipulates that a child capable of high intellectual performance must place at least two and one-third standard deviations above the norm on an individualized intelligence test. New Mexico, at the other extreme, endorses a minimum score of 115 on a group intelligence test for screening purposes.

The most common standard among states using intelligence tests, however, appears to be a minimum intelligence score of 130 or the attainment of at least two standard deviations above the norm on an individual intelligence measure.

SPECIFIC ACADEMIC APTITUDES

Currently thirty-four states define the gifted and talented so as to include individuals capable of high performance in specific

6. Illinois State Board of Education, *Rules and Regulations to Govern the Administration and Operation of Gifted Education Reimbursement Programs* (Springfield, Ill.: State Board of Education, 1976), p. 1.

7. *California Administrative Code*, Chap. 6 Article 14, Section 6421 (Sacramento, Calif.: Department of Education, 1971).

academic aptitudes. As is largely the case with the identification of the intellectually gifted, the methods and procedures used to determine individuals capable of high academic performance likewise differ dramatically from state to state. Many states use fairly simplistic regulatory procedures to help them identify their academically able. Oregon, for example, defines these children as those "who have demonstrated or show potential of a very high level of academic or creative aptitude."[8] States using these simplistic definitions rely quite heavily, for the most part, upon local school districts to develop specific methods and criteria for the identification of their academically able children.

Some states use more precise and definitive descriptions. In Idaho, the definition of the academically able leaves very little room for interpretation by the local school district:

A specific academic aptitude can be measured by aptitude or achievement tests [CAT, DAT, SRA, Stanford, Iowa Test of Basic Skills, ITPA, Metropolitan, and so forth]. Eligibility can be determined by achievement levels at the 98th percentile or above on verbal and/or performance scores. Subtests are (also) valuable indicators.[9]

The majority of the states suggest the use of a standardized aptitude or achievement test as a means for identifying these particular children. Suggested minimum eligibility levels range from a required score at the 98th percentile or above in California and Idaho to a score at least one standard deviation above the national norm on a standardized achievement or aptitude test, as in Mississippi. The most common performance level required by the states to identify children with high academic aptitude, however, appears to be a score at least at the 95th percentile on a standardized measure.

CREATIVE AND PRODUCTIVE THINKING

At present, thirty-two states include individuals capable of high performance in creative and productive thinking as a part of their definition of the gifted and talented. According to guidelines used in South Carolina, creative and productive thinking refers to "those

8. *Oregon State Statutes*, Section 343.395, 1971.

9. Idaho State Department of Education, *Guidelines for Gifted/Talented Programs* (Boise, Idaho: State Department of Education, 1975), Setcion 3.1.2, p. 5.

students who have advanced insight, outstanding imagination, intense interest in one or more fields of achievement, innovative or creative reasoning ability, ability in problem solving, and high attainment in original or creative thinking."[10]

Maryland suggests specific precedures to help screen and identify students capable of creative and productive thinking. Screening may be accomplished (a) by recommendations from staff, parent, peers, and others; (b) by performance that demonstrates creative productivity such as contributions to school newspapers, science fairs, essay and art expositions, dramatic productions, concerts, and related community activities; and (c) by a behavioral checklist. Identification procedures include (a) judgment of a submitted creative product; (b) high performance on a test of creativity such as the *Torrance Tests of Creative Thinking*; and (c) high creativity that in conjunction with other demonstrated talents might lead to a placement in special classes such as creative problem solving as well as working with tutors and mentors who would supervise special projects.[11]

LEADERSHIP ABILITY

In twenty-six states gifted and talented children are defined so as to include individuals capable of high performance in leadership ability. A child who possesses leadership ability, according to a South Dakota position statement, is one "who not only assumes leadership roles, but also is accepted by others as a leader to the extent that he needs and can profit from specially planned educational services beyond those normally provided by the standard school program."[12]

Idaho suggests the use of the following four measures to identify individuals with high leadership ability: the *Barclay Classroom Climate Inventory;* the *Bonney-Fessondon Sociogram;* the *Junior-*

10. South Carolina Department of Education, *State Guidelines—Gifted and Talented* (Columbia, S.C.: South Carolina Department of Education, 1977-78), Section 2.1.

11. Maryland State Department of Education, *Maryland Guidelines for Gifted and Talented* (Annapolis, Md.: Maryland State Department of Education, undated), Section 2.3, p. 3.

12. South Dakota National/State Leadership Training Institute Team, "Who Are the Gifted and Talented? A Position Statement," 1973.

Senior High School Personality Questionnaire (for grades seven through twelve; and the *Vineland Social Maturity Scale* (all ages).[13]

VISUAL AND PERFORMING ARTS

Twenty-eight states include individuals capable of high performance in the visual and performing arts in their definition of gifted and talented. Missouri defines visual and performing arts to include such areas as: "art, music, drama, speech, and language ability—debate, oratory, writing, poetry, and plays—[in which talent can be] demonstrated or indicated through affective as well as cognitive performance."[14]

To identify individuals suspected of having talent in this area, Idaho recommends the use of one of the following four measures: the *Barren Welsh Art Scale;* the *Graves Design Judgment Test* (grades seven through twelve); the *Music Aptitude Profile* (grades four through twelve); the *Seashore Measures of Musical Talents* (grades four through twelve).[15]

On the other hand, Maryland suggests an initial screening and a final selection process to identify such children. For the initial screening the following are proposed: (a) recommendations by self, staff, parent, peer, and others; (b) nominations by specialists in the visual and performing arts within and outside the schools; and (c) a behavioral checklist. For final screening a panel of experts will judge submitted projects, auditions, and/or interviews. Behavioral checklists and standardized aptitude tests should be used by experts to look for children with potential but undemonstrated talent. The appropriate placement of students selected for programs in the visual and performing arts should be based on their potential as well as their demonstrated proficiency in their area of talent.[16]

13. Idaho State Department of Education, *Guidelines for Gifted/Talented Programs,* Appendix A, p. 16.

14. Missouri Department of Elementary and Secondary Education, *Program Development Regulations and Guidelines for Services for the Gifted and Talented* (Jefferson City, Mo.: Department of Elementary and Secondary Education, 1975), p. 3.

15. Idaho State Department of Education, *Guidelines for Gifted/Talented Programs,* Appendix A, p. 16.

16. Maryland State Department of Education, *Maryland Guidelines for Gifted and Talented,* Section 2.5, p. 4.

PSYCHOMOTOR ABILITY

Only twenty-three states include individuals capable of high performance in psychomotor ability as a part of their definition of gifted and talented. South Carolina defines this subpopulation to include "those students who have demonstrated high ability or attainment in either gross or fine motor coordination manifesting itself in areas such as sculpturing, mechanics, surgical medicine, athletics, and so forth.[17] Many states, possibly fearing public reaction over the inclusion of athletes within this particular talent category, have purposely deemphasized or excluded their participation. Missouri, for example, limits this population to include persons capable of "high ability or attainment in either gross or fine manipulative activities, including disciplines such as sculpturing and mechanics."[18]

Idaho suggests that individuals capable of high performance in "manipulative skills" can be identified through the use of: the *Arthur Point Scale* (Leiter adaptation); the *Bennett Hand Tool Dexterity Test* (grades seven through twelve); the *Crawford Small Parts Dexterity Test* (grades seven through twelve); the *D.A.T. Mechanical Reasoning Test* (grades seven through twelve); the *MacQuarrie Tests of Motor Proficiency;* and the *Oseretsky Tests of Motor Proficiency* (kindergarten through grade eleven).[19]

At present, there appear to be only two states that are providing specialized instruction for individuals who demonstrate high performance in psychomotor ability or manipulative skills. Idaho reported serving fifty students and Utah indicated it had funded three projects placing "great" or "considerable" emphasis in this area.

Figure 1 shows the percentage of states in which identification procedures for various categories of giftedness and talent have been adopted or suggested by state departments of education.

17. South Carolina Department of Education, *State Guidelines—Gifted and Talented.*

18. Missouri Department of Elementary and Secondary Education, *Program Development Regulations and Guidelines for Services for the Gifted and Talented,* p. 8.

19. Idaho State Department of Education, *Guidelines for Gifted/Talented Programs,* Appendix A, p. 16.

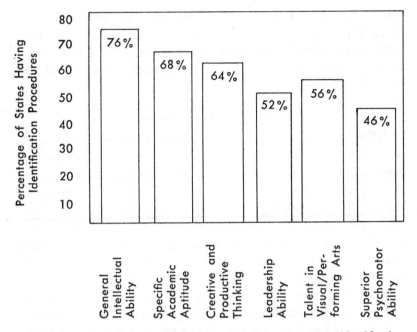

Fɪɢ. 1. Percentage of states having adopted or suggesting identification procedures for specific categories of gifted and talented children.

State Activities in Support of Education for the Gifted and Talented

Twenty-one states have an "approved state plan" regarding the education of their gifted and talented children, the majority having been approved since 1974. Another twenty-one states are currently in the process of either writing or submitting such plans for state approval.

STATE LEVEL PERSONNEL

Over half the states employ a full-time individual at the state level to help them initiate and coordinate educational programs and services for the gifted and talented. Nineteen of these states use state-generated appropriations to support this full-time position, seven use federal entitlements, and one uses a combination of federal and state funds.

An additional nine states employ individuals at the state level who devote from three-fourths to half of their professional time to activities related to the gifted and talented; eleven states have such persons devoting less than half time; and three states do not employ anyone at the state level to coordinate their gifted and talented activities.

STATE FINANCIAL SUPPORT

Thirty-one states presently appropriate state-generated funds to provide specialized educational services for their gifted and talented populations. Eight states appropriate annually between $5,000 and $75,000; fourteen appropriate between $100,000 and $950,000; and another nine appropriate between $1 million and $20 million. Moreover, twelve states indicated they did not allocate any funds to this specific population and seven reported they were unable to provide accurate information on the exact amount of funds actually spent on this group.

Thirty-seven states, on the other hand, reported receiving federal appropriations to help them provide adequate services for their gifted and talented populations. Six states indicated they received between $11,000 and $41,000; nine between $51,000 and $63,000; three between $70,000 and $99,000; and eighteen states reported receiving federal appropriations of between $100,000 to $813,000. Ten states reported receiving no federal financial assistance to help them in meeting the needs of their gifted and talented children.

STATE PRESERVICE AND IN-SERVICE TRAINING

Forty-five states have at least one university or college within their boundaries that offers a regularly scheduled course in gifted and talented education. Furthermore, there are at least twenty-seven universities and colleges that presently offer Master's degrees and certification programs in education for the gifted and talented and at least twelve that offer the doctorate.

There are thirty state education agencies that conduct local in-service training for groups that include regular classroom teachers, teachers who have special responsibilities for the education of the gifted and talented, support and administrative personnel, and parents and interested citizens.

Thirty-six states report state and/or local parent advocacy groups for the gifted and talented. Twenty-one states have at least one active parent group; ten states have two or three of these groups; three states have four or five; and one state—California— has at least forty active parent groups working on behalf of the gifted and talented.

A Free Appropriate Public Education

During the past decade, the handicapped have made rather remarkable progress in winning the right to an education, largely through federal and state judicial and legislative mandates. Public Law 94-142 in essence established the right to a free appropriate public education for all of the nation's handicapped children.

Even though they do not yet have the same powerful and unified advocacy base that education for the handicapped has had, supporters of the gifted and talented have also begun to make some important strides toward winning the right to a free appropriate public education.

On June 16, 1975, the parents of Christopher Fisher, brought suit against the Franklin County School System in Tennessee on the grounds that "educational services were denied because no suitable program of education or related services was maintained" for their gifted son. The parents won the right to be present at a new "multi-assessment conference," which was to determine the appropriate educational program and placement for their son.[20]

On October 21, 1975, gifted and talented students were included as plaintiffs in the class action case involving the right to education —*New Mexico Association for Retarded Citizens* v. *State of New Mexico*.[21]

20. *Mr. and Mrs. David Fisher for Christopher Fisher* v. *Franklin County School System*, Due Process Hearing Decree, Tennessee State Department of Education, July 10, 1975.

21. *New Mexico Association for Retarded Citizens* v. *State of New Mexico*, U.S. District Court, Albuquerque, N.M., Civil action 75-633M, October 1, 1976.

There are presently nine states (Idaho, Georgia, Louisiana, Missouri, North Carolina, Pennsylvania, Tennessee, Utah, and West Virginia) that mandate the provision of services for gifted and talented children due to their "exceptional child" terminology.

The states of Pennsylvania and North Carolina, in preparing for the requirements of Public Law 94-142, have mandated that individualized education programs must also be developed for their gifted and talented students as well.

At least thirteen national organizations and over thirty-eight state and local gifted and handicapped parent and advocacy groups have suggested that the present general definition of "handicapped" be changed to "exceptional" so as to include the gifted and talented within its scope. These groups have likewise suggested that the present name of the Bureau for the Education of the Handicapped of the U.S. Office of Education be changed to the Bureau for the Education of Exceptional Persons and that gifted and talented children become a targeted population within that Bureau.

It is only through the often difficult and tedious efforts of individuals and organizations such as those mentioned above that the fight for a free appropriate public education for all of the nation's gifted and talented children will be conducted and hopefully carried through to a speedy and successful conclusion.

CHAPTER V

The Terman Genetic Studies of Genius, 1922-1972

PAULINE SNEDDEN SEARS

Introduction

By 1916, Lewis M. Terman had completed his comprehensive American revision of the Binet-Simon scale, the Stanford-Binet Intelligence Test.[1] Measurement of large populations with this scale provided normal distributions of intelligence quotients (mental age/chronological age × 100), with a population mean of 100 and as many children scoring above average as below.

Terman's famous study of gifted children, started soon after his return from test construction duties during World War I, reflected his great interest in children who scored at the extremely high end of the scale, the upper 1 to 2 percent. He was confident that they were a very able and potentially productive part of the population, and was concerned that common "myths" about them were injuring their development. Folklore had it that "Early ripe, early rot." Similarly, it was thought by some that precocious children were more prone than the average to insanity, were weaker physically, undersized, unduly specialized or one-sided in their abilities, and without play interests normal for their age. To test the truth of these assertions, Terman selected a group of 1,000 California children scoring in the top 1 percent of tested intelligence, and measured them on a host of physical, intellectual, and social qualities. He then compared the means of these measures from the gifted group with similar measures from groups of children who had not been selected for high IQs. Neither his gifted nor his unselected groups were random samples of the American population. All the

1. Lewis M. Terman, *The Measurement of Intelligence* (Boston: Houghton Mifflin, 1916).

gifted, and most of the unselected, children were from California, chiefly from urban centers.

Not surprisingly, but unhappily for those who wish to untangle the effects of heredity and environment on child IQ, the parents of the gifted group were better educated than the general population. More were born in this country. The fathers were more likely to work in high-status occupations. For ethnic origin, the gifted sample, compared to estimates of frequency of occurrence in the large cities of California, shows fewer Negro parents (which group constituted only 2 percent of the adult population of California at the time) and fewer parents from Mexico. There were twice as many children as expected of Jewish descent. The limitation of the search to California's large cities brought in factors of selective parental migration, parental and child education in this or other countries, language of origin, and many other influences. Children of Chinese descent were not sampled, since at the time they were attending special schools for Orientals. Terman was meticulous in reporting these deviations from a normative group, although he occasionally got carried away in his generalizations by his own hereditarian bias. The data available are less useful for study of group differences than for examination of the fifty-year development of a group of IQ-talented, environmentally advantaged children.

Terman found the "myths" mentioned above to be false. Within the gifted group of children, however, there was wide variability on the many obtained measures, and the same was true of the unselected groups. His results disproved the folk tales in terms of *averages*, with the gifted surpassing the unselected children in almost all respects, but for an individual child in either the gifted or unselected group, the IQ was often not a strong predictor of other qualities. The initial selection of the gifted group, and the many measurements obtained on the members, are reported in Volume I of *Genetic Studies of Genius*.[2]

This cross-sectional account of young children (average age, twelve years) was only the beginning. Terman wished to monitor

2. Lewis M. Terman et al., *Genetic Studies of Genius*, vol. 1, *Mental and Physical Traits of a Thousand Gifted Children* (Stanford, Calif.: Stanford University Press, 1925).

their development over the periods of their growing up into adolescence, adulthood, and later maturity. By 1928, he had added another 528 cases to the gifted group, and with a series of tests, questionnaires, and interviews over succeeding decades, he created a truly life-cycle study of human development.

Contacts with the original children, with their parents and teachers, and later with their spouses (and in a few cases with their children) were begun in 1922, and many additional data were collected in 1927-28, 1936, 1939-40, 1945, 1950, and 1955. Lewis Terman died in 1956, having completed the 1955 follow-up and having started planning for 1960. Oden completed that follow-up, and in 1972 Robert Sears and Lee Cronbach, serving as Terman's scientific executors, secured another set of responses with the most recent questionnaire. Thus, there have been nine major contacts with the subjects over a period of fifty years and, of course, many additional data have been contributed to the files by many of the subjects, by letters or clippings, in the periods between formal follow-ups. The results of these studies have been reported in four volumes.[3] The most recent studies, some published and some not yet published, are summarized here.

In any longitudinal study, attrition of the sample population is a serious problem. When members of the sample do not respond to requests for information, the nagging question arises: Are they different in some systematic way from those who do respond? In this study, the attrition over the fifty years has been less than in many studies, even though there has been considerable mobility in the group.

Responses to the 1972 mailing were obtained from 64 percent of the women in the original 1928 sample, constituting 75 percent of the women believed to be living. In 1960, 80 percent had re-

3. Barbara Burks, Dortha Jensen, and Lewis M. Terman, *Genetic Studies of Genius*, vol. 3, *The Promise of Youth: Follow-up Studies of a Thousand Gifted Children* (Stanford, Calif.: Stanford University Press, 1930); Lewis M. Terman and Melita Oden, *Genetic Studies of Genius*, vol. 4, *The Gifted Child Grows Up: Twenty-five Years' Follow-up of a Superior Group* (Stanford, Calif.: Stanford University Press, 1947); idem, *Genetic Studies of Genius*, vol. 5, *The Gifted Group at Mid-life: Thirty-five Years' Follow-up of the Superior Child* (Stanford, Calif.: Stanford University Press, 1959); Melita Oden, "The Fulfillment of Promise: Forty-year Follow-up of the Terman Gifted Group," *Genetic Psychology Monographs* 77 (1968): 9-93.

sponded. As a check on possible biased selection, data were used from the 1960 follow-up to compare those respondents who did with those who did not respond in 1972. Six variables were compared: occupation, family income, marital status, health, general adjustment, and feelings of having lived up to their intellectual ability. While there were some average differences between those who responded in 1972 and those who did not, they were minimal, ranging from 1 to 5 percent. Those who had given complete cooperation in the past continued to do so. The "dropouts" came largely from those subjects for whom data in 1960 were also sketchy.

Earlier Studies on Special Aspects of Subsamples

The bulk of published reports on the gifted group is essentially normative. The four volumes of *Genetic Studies of Genius* and the Oden monograph are chronologies of the group's development and status reports on a great number of variables measured at successive ages in the life cycles of the group members. Most of the reported data are in the form of averages and measures of group variability. Where possible, Terman gave comparisons of this group's performance with the performance of the "generality," sometimes by using U.S. Census data and sometimes data from other normative samples. Mainly, his purpose was to document the development and accomplishments of this intellectually gifted part of the larger society.

As early as the 1940s, however, some use was made of the data for the study of differentiable subsamples within the group. These are worth mention here, for they represent a style of data analysis that will undoubtedly become increasingly profitable with improving theory in economics, psychology, and sociology, and with the development of more sensitive statistical devices for isolating causal sequences in personality development or other aspects of change with time.

Two published studies were concerned with marital happiness.[4] Terman had originally become interested in marital adjustment in

4. Lewis M. Terman and Paul Wallin, "The Validity of Marriage Prediction and Marital Adjustment Tests," *American Sociological Review* 14 (1949): 497-504; Lewis M. Terman, "Predicting Marriage Failure from Test Scores," *Marriage and Family Living* 12 (1950): 51-54.

connection with the gifted group, but he pursued that interest also with unselected samples. He was also interested in background correlates of entry into a scientific or humanistic field of work. For this study, the sample of gifted men was used.[5] Success in occupational achievement was studied at two points in time, 1940 and 1960, when the men averaged twenty-eight and forty-eight years of age.[6]

Present Status of the Material on the Gifted Sample

The raw data of the gifted study consist of the original test forms; interview notes; parent, teacher, subject questionnaires and rating scales; medical reports and anthropometric records—all collected between 1922 and 1972. These materials are essentially the same for each subject during the period the subject remained active, although there are missing data for each at some point in the half century of data collection.

With the single exception of the test forms for the marital happiness and aptitude study, which were destroyed after being coded, this entire set of data sources is maintained in closed files at Stanford University. Nearly all the objectively codable responses were coded on the documents themselves, as they were received, but many questionnaire items that permitted open-ended answers have never been coded. Probably less than half the coded responses have ever been transferred to tabulation sheets. The ones that were tabulated provided the statistical summaries—mainly normative findings—that were published by Terman, Oden, and others prior to 1972. Not surprisingly, the untabulated responses constitute the richest source of data for subsample analyses and longitudinal study of social, intellectual, and personality development. When (and if) financial support can be obtained, the trustees of the study have expressed their intention to transfer all codable data from the original protocols to computer tape for storage.

Terman and his successors have been most meticulous in keeping the promise of confidentiality for the filed protocols. Access to them is limited to the professional staff. The tabulation sheets

5. Lewis M. Terman, "Scientists and Nonscientists in a Group of 800 Gifted Men," *Psychological Monographs* 68 (1954): 44.

6. Oden, "The Fulfillment of Promise."

present data in anonymous form, of course, and hence are available for within-office use by responsible investigators. From time to time since the 1972 follow-up, economists, clinical psychologists, anthropometricians, and educators have made use of these materials for a variety of problems. Their reports are summarized here in order to bring up to date the diverse findings that have been obtained from the gifted group data, and to give a current perspective on how the material may be used in the future.

Life-Cycle Satisfactions

SEX DIFFERENCES

Method of measurement. In the 1972 questionnaire, both men and women were asked an identical and rather complex series of questions about areas in which they had sought and experienced life-satisfaction. Thus the data are suitable for comparing the ways in which satisfaction was or was not achieved by the two sexes. On the average, these subjects were born in 1910, and doubtless younger cohorts would respond differently. The present data are useful to show how bright people of that generation viewed the satisfactions that came to them as they worked out their lives.

The first question was: "How important was each of these goals in life, in the plans you made for yourself in early adulthood?" There were six areas to be judged by the respondents: occupational success, family life, friendships, richness of cultural life, total service to society, and joy in living. Second, for the same areas, they were asked: "How satisfied are you with your experience in each of these respects?"

Importance. The six areas were clearly not of equal importance as channels for life satisfaction.[7] (See figure 1.) On five of them there were significant sex differences ($p < .05$); only for service to society was the sex difference nonsignificant. Men were higher

---

7. These and following summaries of life satisfaction in 1972 are abstracted from the following: Pauline S. Sears and Ann H. Barbee, "Career and Life Satisfaction among Terman's Gifted Women," in *The Gifted and the Creative: Fifty-year Perspective*, ed. Julian Stanley, William C. George, and Cecilia H. Solano (Baltimore: Johns Hopkins University Press, 1977), pp. 28-65; Robert R. Sears, "Sources of Life Satisfactions of the Terman Gifted Men," *American Psychologist* 32 (1977): 119-28.

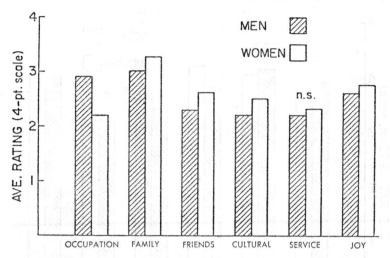

FIG. 1. Importance of six areas for life satisfaction in young adulthood, viewed retrospectively in 1972. N = 486 men, 430 women; n.s. indicates no significant difference.

only on occupational importance. Women evidently planned in early adulthood for a more varied or multi-faceted type of life, at least as viewed retrospectively when they were in their sixties. For both sexes, family life was judged the most important area for achieving life satisfaction.

Satisfaction, success. Figure 2 shows the average rating of satisfaction or success actually achieved by both sexes in the six areas. Men and women did not differ with respect to success in their family life, their service to society, or their joy of living. But again, the men had significantly higher ratings with respect to occupation.

Final satisfaction formula. Since "importance" of the various areas differed for individuals, a life-satisfaction score was devised to give success in important areas more weight than success in less-valued areas. A "general life-satisfaction" score was computed for each area by multiplying the success score by the importance score. A subtractive element was necessary to take account of the direction of any difference between importance and success. The formula used provided a scale of possible scores ranging from 1 to 21 for life satisfaction in each of the six areas. Figure 3 shows the average scores for men and women in the six areas.

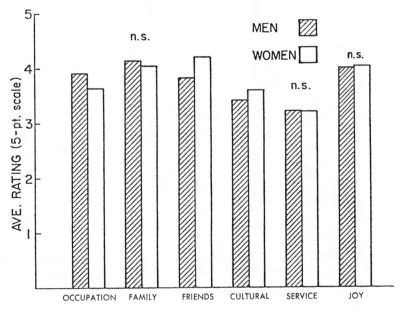

Fɪɢ. 2. Success achieved in each of six areas over a lifetime (1972). N = 486 men, 430 women; n.s. indicates no significant difference.

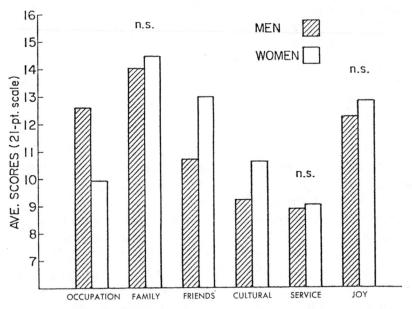

Fɪɢ. 3. Satisfaction scores for six areas, as judged in 1972. N = 486 men, 430 women; n.s. indicates no significant difference.

Again occupational satisfaction was clearly greater for the men than for the women, friends and cultural activities more for the women than for the men, while satisfaction with family life was the highest of all for both sexes and without significant sex difference.

Women "income workers" and working men compared. All but a tiny fraction of the Terman men were employed or recently retired. Of the Terman women, 43 percent were "income workers" according to the criterion of having had steady income-producing work for four of six half-decade periods, 1941-1972. Figure 4 compares these working women with the working men with respect

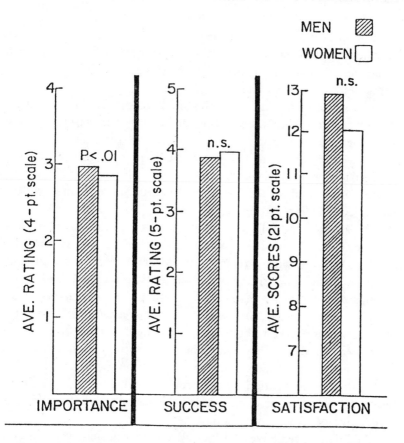

Fig. 4. Importance, Success, and Satisfaction in Occupation for Men and Income Worker Women. N = 461-473 men, 170 women; n.s. indicates no significant difference.

to the three measures in the occupational sphere: importance, success, and life satisfaction.

Early judgments, made retrospectively, of the importance of occupation as a goal in life, show the expected sex difference, with men ascribing greater importance to it. On reported success and satisfaction with occupation, however, the working women are as pleased with their situation as are the men. The 1972 questionnaire did not ask directly if employed women had suffered discrimination on account of their sex, but these data give indirect evidence against this. Most of the women acknowledged considerable success at their work and found satisfaction in it.

EARLIER PREDICTORS OF LIFE SATISFACTION FOR WOMEN

For an overall measure of the degree of life satisfaction obtained by the women so far, the life-satisfaction scores of five of the areas were combined, omitting the joy in living, and a "General Satisfaction 5" score was obtained.

In the choice of variables to be tested as contributing to general life satisfaction when the woman was in her sixties, various specific hypotheses as to antecedents or processes of personality development were formulated and tested. Such predictions were tested against the target variable "General Satisfaction 5." By a one-way classification analysis of variance for each of 158 independent variables (obtained from the files for 1922-1972) that related to the hypotheses, the following results were obtained: (a) there was little evidence of modeling on parents' education and career; (b) positive relations with parents in early years were strong predictors of later satisfaction (the measures of relationship came both from ratings *of* subjects *by* parents, and from ratings *of* parents' qualities *by* the subjects); (c) self-confidence, feelings of inferiority, and persistence were rather highly correlated over the years (1940 and 1950) in which they were obtained as self-ratings, and favorable self-ratings predicted general satisfaction with life in 1972; (d) subject's occupation in the professional-managerial-arts fields, as contrasted with the clerical-sales fields or being a housewife, was predictive of general satisfaction.

Additional predictive variables were not surprising: good health, level of education, and occupation of husband, subject's opinion of the vocational success of her father, time devoted to volunteer work, and a staff rating on general adjustment.

Scores for the area labelled "joy in living" were based on the five-point scale for successful experience in that area. The antecedents among the 158 variables obtained earlier were examined by chi-square analysis. "Joy" scores correlated +.51 with "General Satisfaction 5" scores, and many of the early predictors were the same. For "joy," however, there was additional predictive value from stable income-producing work, and from self-ratings on ambition for excellence in work, both in early and later adulthood.

Work Patterns and Occupational Satisfaction

Because the occupational roles of the two sexes differed radically, the men and women of the sample were considered separately.

MEN

Employment and retirement. Since the men of this sample were in their early sixties in 1972, on the average, it was of interest to see how they were handling their occupational life. This area had been reported as extremely important to them. Now the time of retirement—mandatory or voluntary—was approaching. A measure of "work persistence" was devised to permit a study of factors leading to early work reduction or retirement. Work persistence was defined as "to how late an age the man continued to work." "Work" was defined in several ways: a continuing law practice with pay, or a continuation of previous work but without pay (for example, a scientist's research), or significant volunteer service (for example, as a trustee for a community organization).

There was a steady decrease in fully employed men from 97 percent at ages fifty-one to fifty-five to 60 percent at ages sixty-one to sixty-five. The analysis stops at age sixty-five, when mandatory retirement confounds the variable as a measure of voluntary choice. A work persistence index could be calculated for only 324 of the 486 men who responded in 1972; the remainder had not yet reached age sixty-one. These 324 men could be defined as either continuing full-time work into the sixty-one to sixty-five age period or reducing their work load before then. Since the correlation between this index and occupational life satisfaction was +.17, the two variables are apparently largely independent.

Predictors of work persistence. The men who continued their full time employment were better educated, had higher occupational status, and had been more successful in their careers from age thirty to age fifty. Three decades before 1972, they had judged themselves to be more persistent and better integrated in their work than other men. Twelve years before, in 1960, they had described themselves as more ambitious than other men. They had liked their work better in mid-life and had gotten special satisfaction from it. Now, in 1972, they reported themselves as having higher vitality than did their work-reduced comparison group. As for income, of course, the full-time employed were making more money in 1972 than the semiretired or fully retired. But, curiously, group comparisons show that there had been no difference between the groups before actual retirement started. Income has been a nonsignificant predictor of satisfaction in most instances.

Earlier predictors of occupational satisfaction. A path analysis provided information on the life history variables from 1940 to 1972 that predicted occupational satisfaction reported in 1972.[8] High satisfaction was predicted quite well by several measures of feelings the men had expressed in earlier years. At average age thirty, these included (a) a high self-rating on persistence and planfulness about work activities, and (b) a statement that the current occupation had been chosen and not just drifted into. In the next two decades a liking for the work chosen, reported superior health, a belief that potential had been lived up to, and a self-rating of having higher ambition than other men were also predictive. Interestingly enough, there was no predictive value from such objective measures of success as occupational status, income, or education.

WOMEN

Method of measurement. The 1972 questionnaires asked for additional responses from women in the area of work. They were asked to consider their lives as falling into one of four possible patterns: (a) "I have been primarily a homemaker;" (b) "I have pur-

---

8. Sears, "Sources of Life Satisfactions of the Terman Gifted Men."

sued a career during most of my adult life;" (c) "I have pursued a career except during the period when I was raising a family;" (d) "I have done considerable work for needed income, but would not call it a career." (Unlike the U.S. Census, this study defined homemaking, as well as income-producing jobs, as work.) The measure of work pattern satisfaction was dichotomous.[9] Satisfaction was coded as high if responses to the two columns were identical, whatever pattern it was. Any sort of disagreement between responses in the two columns was considered to imply a moderate or low degree of satisfaction with work. By these criteria, 69 percent of the total sample (N = 429) expressed high satisfaction with their work pattern.

Work pattern satisfaction by demographic variables. Our somewhat naive theory predicted that women who were married, with children, having had income-producing work, and living on a higher than average income, would report higher satisfaction than those in the reverse groups. This could be thought to be the "full life," with rewards from various facets of a woman's potential. Most of these predictions proved false. A satisfying style of work (as viewed at age early sixties) apparently does not need to be that full! Table 1 gives percentages of high satisfaction for the group divided several ways.

There are significant differences in the numbers of women reporting high satisfaction in favor of the Head of Household group, the Income Workers, and those without children. There were no significant differences related to income (not shown in table 1). Median total family income in 1971 for the whole sample of women was $19,000, with a mean of $24,000.

Possibly our naive stereotype of what life-style would prove most satisfying for these women who were born around 1910[10] neglected the fact that they were responding as they felt in 1972. Whereas 41 percent of the women indicated "primarily a homemaker" as their work pattern in the "as it was" column, only 29 percent "would now choose" that life-style. Thirty percent placed

9. Sears and Barbee, "Career and Life Satisfaction among Terman's Gifted Women."

10. Both men and women were born, on the average, about 1910. The standard deviation for age was a little less than four years.

TABLE 1

PERCENTAGES OF VARIOUS SUBSAMPLES
SHOWING HIGH SATISFACTION WITH WORK PATTERN

SUBSAMPLE	N	PERCENT HIGH SATSFACTION
Head of Household (single, divorced, widowed for all of period 1960–72)...................	82	80
Income worker*........................	65	92
With children.........................	21	76
No children..........................	44	93
Homemaker*...........................	17	41
With children.........................	13	46
No children..........................	4	25
Non-Head of Household (married, living with husband for all or part of period 1960–72).....	347	67
Income worker*........................	119	74
With children.........................	86	71
No children..........................	33	82
Homemaker*...........................	228	64
With children.........................	202	61
No children..........................	26	81

* Income worker is defined as one having had steady income-producing work for four of six half-decade periods, 1941-1972. Homemaker is defined as one having had steady income-producing work for less than four of six of these periods.

themselves in the "career" category; 37 percent would now choose this option. The comparable figures for "career except when raising a family" are 12 percent and 29 percent; for the "income only" category, they are 18 percent and 5 percent. Many of these women thus would now choose a career, or a career except when raising a family, rather than the homemaker or work-for-income-only work patterns.

The proportion of women in the U.S. "work force" (which, according to definition, does not include homemaking as "work") has been steadily rising, and possibly some of the homemaker women felt they had missed an interesting and challenging part of life. As shown in table 1, 43 percent of the women were coded as income workers according to the criterion of being employed for four out of six five-year periods. The current (1972) status, however, shows 65 percent as either employed or recently retired from employment (48 percent working, 17 percent retired).

Early predictors of work pattern satisfaction. In the case of women, these predictors included the status of the occupation engaged in. Those women in professional jobs, the arts, and managerial jobs reported higher satisfaction than those in clerical, sales, or homemaking occupations. Those high on work-pattern satisfaction rated not only their occupational success as high but also their success in family life and cultural activity. Other aspects of life they found satisfying were work, income, and children, even though the childless women had higher work-pattern satisfaction. Self-rating on ambition for excellence in work, made in 1960, was also predictive.

Family Life: Marriage, Divorce, Children

EARLIER PREDICTORS OF MARITAL STATUS

Men. Intact marriages, as compared to those broken by divorce, were significantly predicted in the men by self-ratings of the subjects' affectionate relations with and attachment to parents, especially the mother. The ratings were made in 1950. Terman's "Marital Happiness Test" predicted unbroken marriage to 1972, although the scores on this instrument were obtained in 1940.[11] An older age at marriage and a favorable research staff rating on subject's mental health were also predictive of stable marriage.

Women. A different analysis was made for the women. The following groups were compared: (a) women currently (1972) married (not necessarily a first marriage), (b) women currently divorced, and (c) women who had been always single. The married women felt their own parents' marriage had been happier than was the case with the other two groups. Their level of education was considerably lower than that of either of the other groups, perhaps partly because marriage and/or children interrupted education or because the women were willing to have it interrupted. Their husbands were well educated and often held professional or managerial jobs. Family income was high.

FAMILY LIFE SATISFACTION: MEN

This variable was measured in the same way as occupational satisfaction. Of the six areas, family experience was reported retrospectively to have been the one most important for securing satisfaction; success in it proved, on the average, to have been the greatest also.

11. Terman and Oden, *The Gifted Child Grows Up*, p. 239.

A path analysis for prediction of 1972 family life satisfaction disclosed positive weights for the "Marital Happiness Test," and a favorable attitude by the subject toward his own parents, especially the father, in this case. A high amount of income work by the wife seems to have had a negative effect on the husband's family life satisfaction. Whether this was a cause or an effect relationship is indeterminable from the present analysis.

ECONOMIC PREDICTORS OF INTACT MARRIAGES

Several economists have made fruitful use of the Terman longitudinal data. Michael, for example, used the women of the group for prediction of potential divorce.[12]

Women. Using regression and logit analysis based on theoretical deductions about stability of marriage, Michael found the following variables predicting stability: wife's older age at marriage, husband's longer education, wife's shorter education, the fact that at least one of the two spouses was Catholic, and the fact that the two spouses expressed the same religious affiliation.

Men and Women. Another study used both the Terman sample and a nationwide survey of approximately 30,000 households, which had been conducted by the U.S. Bureau of the Census in 1967 (the Survey of Economic Opportunity).[13] Personality developmentalists and educators can translate these economic terms into those more familiar. These economists find that "each person maximizes his or her expected utility as he decides to marry or remain married."[14] "The expected gain from marriage also depends systematically on the level of different characteristics. For example, an increase in the intelligence or attractiveness of men or women or the earnings of men tends to raise the gain, whereas an increase in the earnings of women tends to lower the gain."[15] "The probability and speed of remarriage are positively related to the expected gain

12. Robert T. Michael, "Factors Affecting Divorce: A Study of the Terman Sample," Working Paper No. 147 (Stanford, Calif.: National Bureau of Economic Research, 1976).

13. Gary S. Becker, Elisabeth M. Landes, and Robert T. Michael, "Economics of Marital Instability," Working paper No. 153 (Stanford, Calif.: National Bureau of Economic Research, 1976).

14. Ibid., p. 57.

15. Ibid., p. 58.

from remarriage, which depends on earnings, age, number of children from the previous marriage, and other characteristics."[16]

These authors found that 27 percent of the Terman women had been divorced from their first husbands by 1972—a little higher rate than the U.S. Census shows for the generality. Among the men, we found 21 percent of the men with a history of divorce or separation.

With regard to income of husband and wife, these economists theorized and found that income of men reduces the probability of dissolution of first marriages. The income of wives, however, raises the probability of dissolution of marriage, and reduces the propensity of women to remarry. These results are quite in line with other data reported earlier.[17]

Tomes is using the Terman data set to provide an empirical test of an expanded model incorporating variables of child "quality" (childhood IQ, excluding variation in IQ due to income, education, and home training by the parents) and "quantity" (number of children in the family).[18]

Schooling Investments in Gifted Children: Home and School

Of particular interest to educators are the payoffs for special education for the gifted. Another economist has approached this question less romantically than some educators by asking: "How much money do they make later if they have had early home instruction or acceleration in school?"[19]

HOME INVESTMENTS

Leibowitz examined the Terman data on both boys and girls to gauge the effects of: (a) "home investments" (parent instruc-

16. Ibid.

17. Sears and Barbee, "Career and Life Satisfaction among Terman's Gifted Women"; Sears, "Sources of Life Satisfaction of the Terman Gifted Men."

18. Nigel Tomes, "A Model of Child Quality, Endowments and Quantity: Empirical Results from the Terman Data" (Paper presented at the Workshop in Applications of Economics, Department of Economics, University of Chicago, October, 1976.)

19. Arleen Leibowitz, "Home Investments in Children," *Journal of Political Economy* 82 (1974): S111-S131.

tion of the young child) on "preschool stocks of human capital" (IQ); (b) early stocks of human capital and later home investments on amount of schooling; (c) home investments on later adult earnings; and (d) early measure of ability (IQ) on later earnings.

Her results should be considered in the light of the limited range of the sample on IQ, socioeconomic status, and education/occupation of the parents of the gifted. Census data on studies using less restricted samples are quoted to buttress her findings on the Terman sample.

Leibowitz found that "home investments" do increase measured stocks of childhood human capital, for boys and for older girls. "A mother's education [assumption that mothers spent more time than fathers in instruction of young children] was significantly related to IQ, while the father's was not, thus indicating that home investments rather than wholly genetic factors underlie the relationship."[20]

The measure of preschool time inputs on instruction, however, did not predict later level of education achieved by ages twenty-nine and thirty-nine by men and women in the sample. Nor did family income. Most of the Terman group made it to college regardless of family income and 44 percent had more than sixteen years of schooling. Subjects' education did depend on parents' education and family size. Boys' education also depended on IQ, indicating perhaps greater opportunity for bright boys to get higher education than for bright girls.[21] Leibowitz also found that:

Men's earnings at ages twenty-nine, thirty-nine, and forty-nine were strongly related to schooling and experience variables. The addition of home investment and IQ variables did not significantly decrease the coefficients on schooling and experience, although family income was positively and significantly related to earnings in the early years of the life cycle.[22]

SCHOOLING INVESTMENT

In another paper, Leibowitz looked at acceleration in school and college, with estimates of the direct costs of men's undergraduate

20. Ibid., p. 129.

21. One female Terman subject reported: "When it came time to go to college, it was deep depression for the family. Of course, my brother went to college, but not I."

22. Leibowitz, "Home Investments in Children," p. S129.

schooling.[23] On the question of the relation between years of schooling and lifetime earning patterns, Leibowitz found that the Terman men had greater "intensity" of earlier schooling (acceleration in school; possibly more intensive personal investment in their learning) than a U.S. Census sample comparable in age. "This may allow high ability students to enter the labor force earlier than their peers of average ability."[24] The gifted group's earnings were higher at all ages than the normative census figures for similar ages (from 10 percent to 280 percent), but they rose at a less rapid rate; the greatest differential was in the earlier years.

With regard to special interventions for gifted children, there is evidence on only two: (a) home instruction, and (b) school acceleration, which was a procedure much more used when these subjects were young than it is today. Parental instruction was coded in two ways, both based on parents' estimates in 1922 of how much direct instruction they provided for their child: (a) parents conducted "an appreciable amount of instruction along particular lines," and (b) parents spent a "considerable number of hours, but chiefly reading, telling stories, and writing." For these, the first Leibowitz study shows that the quality of time inputs by parents was associated with higher IQ and special instruction had more of an impact than generalized time inputs. However, mother's education (but not father's) had a much larger effect on IQ. These effects were stronger in first-born as contrasted to later-born children.[25]

With regard to acceleration in school, 67 percent of the group were accelerated in elementary school, and 74 percent of the boys and 84 percent of the girls as they approached or were in high school. This is called by Leibowitz "greater intensity of schooling" and "permits the high ability students to enter the labor force earlier than their peers of average ability. The consequent increase in discounted value of lifetime earnings may be a major route of collecting the returns to high ability."[26]

23. Arleen Leibowitz, "Years and Intensity of Schooling Investment," *American Economic Review* 66 (1976): 321-34.

24. Ibid., p. 334.

25. Leibowitz, "Home Investments in Children," p. S119.

26. Leibowitz, "Years and Intensity of Schooling Investment," p. 334.

It should be noted that generalization from facts on this sample is very much curtailed by (a) the range of IQs to the upper 1 percent of the population, and (b) the analyses in terms of correlation, which gives no information as to causation. Thus we can not conclude that either home instruction or acceleration will improve IQ or increase adult earnings in gifted children, and much less apply these findings to another sample less advantaged in initial IQ or education of parents.

Prediction of Possible Suicide

Shneidman has analyzed life history data, especially affective material, in thirty Terman males for evidence of prodromal clues to suicide.[27] With the cooperation of the Terman staff, he was presented with files from which had been deleted data on whether a man was or was not living. Five of these men had committed suicide, ten matched men had died natural deaths from cancer or heart disease, and fifteen were still living. The files as presented showed the subjects to be about age fifty. Using his concepts of signals of perturbation and lethality in the life history, Shneidman ranked the thirty cases for probability of suicide. The five actual suicides he ranked 1, 2, 4, 5, and 6. The predictive signals were found as early as age thirty. It was clear that suicidal men had carried the seeds of their self-destruction for many years and that somewhere along the line they had failed to find compensating support from their outer world.

Anthropometric Measurements

A study of the cranial measurements of 600 members of the gifted group is currently under way. These were obtained in the 1920s.[28] Measures for the gifted children will be compared to ones obtained from a normative sample in that same decade. Intragroup comparisons will be made as well, correlating the cranial measures with other variables available on the sample.

27. Edwin S. Shneidman, "Perturbation and Lethality as Precursors of Suicide in a Gifted Group," *Life-threatening Behavior* 1 (1971): 24-25.

28. A. S. Dekaban, personal communication.

Comparison of Subjects with Extremely High IQs

Feldman is currently examining records of twenty-six Terman subjects who scored IQ 180 or above,[29] comparing them with equally high IQ subjects reported by Hollingworth.[30] A comparison sample of twenty-six individuals, gifted but with IQs below 180, has been drawn randomly from the Terman files for qualitative analysis of intellectual processes.

Perspectives for the Future[31]

Few of the thousands of variables measured in the gifted group show the homogeneity of the original IQ scores. Some, like education, income, and other demographic measures, do have skewed distributions with means much higher than comparable data from unselected groups, but wide within-group variability is a prime characteristic of the sample. This fact guides strongly toward intragroup analyses in search of both antecedents and consequences of life history events and experiences. The recent studies summarized here have been oriented largely toward causal analyses of satisfaction outcomes as viewed from the 1960s, occupational choices about retirement, marital experience, and economic outcomes. In the data as they stand today, there are many other aspects of experience that can be examined by similar analytical methods. Self-concepts, health status, second generation parent-child adjustments, and persistence of intellectual liveliness are a few.

The group is moving toward later maturity, however, and it would be wrong to allow prepossession with causal themes among the variables measured during the past, and more vigorous, part of life to interfere with continued data collection. From a gerontological view, the group is a unique asset for the study of the aging process in a significantly productive part of the population. Continued follow-up, probably at five-year intervals, is planned in order that new age-relevant outcome variables can be measured while the

29. David Feldman, personal communication.

30. Leta S. Hollingworth, *Children above 180 IQ, Stanford-Binet* (Yonkers-on-Hudson, N.Y.: World Book Co., 1942).

31. This section of the chapter was written by Robert R. Sears.

life events they represent are occurring. Guidance from specialists in aging will be welcomed as an aid to selecting the most appropriate variables.

Intragroup analysis has been emphasized partly because the variability permits it, partly because the data are so suitable for longitudinal analysis, but partly, too, because there have been so few data on the generality available for normative comparison. In recent years, however, several agencies have begun massive data collection programs on random samples of the U.S. population. The Social Security Administration has pressing need for exactly the kinds of data our present study has obtained, but the data are needed on the whole population, not just our specialized sample. Their data, and those of others, can now serve for comparison with the Terman data in a way not possible even a dozen years ago. It is expected that our further follow-ups will be planned with such comparisons in mind—that data parallel to the data of other agencies will be especially sought.

How long will the research continue? Into the foreseeable future, in any event, for "on actuarial grounds, there is considerable likelihood that the last of Terman's Gifted Children will not have yielded his last report to the files before the year 2010!"[32] And of course, on the same grounds, it is most likely that the last one will be *her* report, not *his*!

32. Robert R. Sears, "Introduction," in *The Gifted Group at Mid-life.*

Educational Policies, Programs, and Practices for the Gifted and Talented

A. HARRY PASSOW

Earlier yearbooks of the National Society for the Study of Education have discussed programs for the gifted from organizational and/or curricular vantage points. The Committee for the Twenty-third Yearbook observed that it was "certainly a fact that there is much administrative timidity before the problem of organizing and conditioning practice to meet the newly conceived needs of superior children" (p. 49). Having studied the problems of organization, the Committee concluded:

It is quite evident that the most difficult aspects of the gifted child problem do not lie in the field of formal organization of the school. Grade skipping, segregation, grouping within a class, sectioning according to ability within a grade are simple enough to manage. There is increasing agreement on the desirability of enriching the experience, rather than speeding the rate of the capable children through the all-too-meager offerings of the school years. The biggest question and the most difficult of solution is undoubtedly recognized as this: "How shall their superior powers be challenged, and how shall curriculum and schoolroom procedure be modified to meet more fully the rightful demands of superior endowments?" (pp. 63-64).

In the Fifty-seventh Yearbook, published in 1958, I reviewed various approaches to providing for gifted students. Administrative adaptations, including enrichment in the regular classroom, special groupings, and various kinds of acceleration, were discussed in terms of their potential for helping gifted children attain desired goals. After noting that particular modifications seemed to be of value for specific kinds of achievement, I concluded that "no single administrative plan has provided a 'package formula' for all schools to use with equal effectiveness for the variety of talents among its students" (p. 201). Various programs and provisions were reviewed in that yearbook with descriptions of specific school plans.

In the following chapters of this volume, educational policies, programs, and practices for the gifted and talented are reviewed. Lynn H. Fox provides an overview of programs, pointing out that while state and national legislation often speaks of "qualitatively differentiated programs for the gifted," the nature of that qualitative differentiation lacks precise definition. Fox suggests that programs can differ in their goals, in the manipulation of the instructional components, and in the "delivery systems" used. Eleven kinds of delivery systems are discussed by Fox and then compared with respect to the changes required in instructional components (that is, rate of learning, content, mode of instruction, and homogeneous grouping), staffing and facilities needed (that is, additional staff, staff training, and facilities or equipment required), and the ease of evaluation. Fox concludes that a variety of program options must be designed and implemented since no single program concept can effectively meet the varied needs of the gifted and talented.

A number of prototypes of various kinds of programs for different age levels, in different settings, and under the auspices of diverse institutions are presented. These descriptions are intended to illustrate the variety of program options developed to serve the needs of gifted and talented children and youth. The examples are illustrative and are not intended to be comprehensive in terms of cataloging all of the program options available.

The Calasanctius School in Buffalo, New York, is an independent school for intellectually talented and gifted children in grades five through twelve. Stephen Gerencser describes the organization and instructional program of the school, including the development of a unified program built on the psychological and sociological needs of the gifted population. The curriculum was planned to prepare students for exacting college-level study, with attention to the integrative value of the various elements. The unique program includes historical studies, foreign language study, Advanced Placement courses, colloquia, seminars, and field study. In the seminar program, an independent research/study program under the guidance of a proctor, a serious research paper or creative art work is required. A "Phenomenon-of-Man Program" introduces students to the richness of the history of ideas. Many of the programmatic features of the Calasanctius School are seen as transferable to other settings.

The Child Development Research Group at the University of
Washington has been engaged in a longitudinal study of intellectually advanced young children and in the provision of a preschool program for some of the children as well as a counseling
and diagnostic service for their families. Young children (through
age five) who demonstrate unusual intellectual ability are identified
and the development of each child's pattern of abilities is carefully
monitored. The effects of the preschool program on the development of intellectually advanced children are also studied. Halbert
B. Robinson, Wendy C. Roedell, and Nancy E. Jackson describe
the characteristics of intellectually advanced preschoolers and the
methods used to identify them. Early intervention is seen as serving two purposes—providing a supportive educational environment for the children and providing aid in guidance and planning
for their parents. Longitudinal study makes possible collection of
data that could shed light on issues involved in the development of
gifted persons.

Sandra Kaplan discusses the language arts and social studies
curriculums for gifted children in the elementary school. The language arts curriculum for gifted students requires a definition of
the purpose and scope of language arts as a subject area, the setting
of expectations and perimeters matched to the special characteristics
of the gifted, and adaptation of a theoretical structure that supports the content, processes, and products or outcomes. The social
studies curriculum includes skills, facts, concepts, and generalizations dealing with the study of human beings, including the study
of man's relationship to his environment, institutions created by
man, and human interactions and transactions. Kaplan explores
curricular and instructional adaptations in these areas for the gifted
and talented.

The Study of Mathematically Precocious Youth (SMPY) at
Johns Hopkins University has been engaged in a systematic attempt to identify students who reason extremely well mathematically and to facilitate their development through special educational
provisions. Julian C. Stanley reports on the experience of the

SMPY. Stanley argues for accelerating the pace of mathematics instruction for the young gifted students of junior high school age. In his view, the special fast-mathematics classes, often taught by college instructors, have proved to be "spectacularly successful" for most of the mathematically precocious youth. He suggests a variety of ways of providing for acceleration, ranging from simple grade skipping to bypassing the baccalaureate degree and going on to graduate study after two years of undergraduate study. Convinced of the value of acceleration in mathematics, Stanley suggests similar studies to test the principles and practices of SMPY in other areas such as verbal reasoning and general vocabulary development.

Issues concerning secondary school programs for the gifted are explored by Daniel P. Keating. These include social changes that have affected programs, the perennial argument about acceleration and/or enrichment, global differences versus differences in specific abilities, and attitudes toward gifted students. Keating describes types of secondary-school programs, ranging from special schools and special classes to accelerated programs. He suggests that schools should create a variety of appropriate opportunities and provide for counseling so that experiences can be integrated into a rational program for individual students.

One of the oldest, continuous public school programs for gifted students is Cleveland's Major Work Classes, which have been operated in the Cleveland schools since 1921. E. Jean Thom describes the Major Work Classes in terms of the philosophy, the selection procedures, the instructional program, and the staffing. Thom notes that the Major Work Classes program has not only provided for thousands of gifted students but has been a valuable resource for evaluative and descriptive studies of the education of gifted children.

A summer residential school for exceptionally talented youth, the Governor's School of North Carolina, is described by Virgil S. Ward. The Governor's School has served as a prototype for similar schools that have been established in other states. In Ward's view, the school has provided an opportunity to understand "differential education for the gifted," relating theory to practice and, in turn, developing theory from practice. Time blocks focus on aptitude development, general intellectual development, and personal development. Ward's design for differential education for the gifted includes the following dimensions—(a) experiential and behavioral potentiality, (b) developmental objectives, (c) curricular substance, (d) curricular process, and (e) goals and outcomes.

A review of some of the conditions in higher education over the past two decades and of programs for talented students in colleges and universities is presented by Milton J. Gold. Gold discusses selection procedures, acceleration programs, honors programs, curricular adaptations, modes of instruction, and counseling provisions for able college students. He illustrates such programs with descriptions of three examples of current programs, two of which have considerable structure, while the third has a great deal of flexibility. In Gold's view, colleges and universities during the past decade have moved the focus from superior students to those in need of remedial attention. He suggests that such institutions now clarify their missions and create areas of excellence that will meet the needs of the academically gifted and talented.

June Cox urges concerned parents and educators to look to the larger community beyond the schools for underused resources for educating the gifted and the talented. She points to the variety of community resources, including individuals, that can enrich the educational experiences of gifted and talented. Several exemplary programs are described by Cox, some of which, like the Dallas Theater Center and the Gifted Students Institute for Research and Development, are local in character while others, such as the Executive High School Internships and the Junior Great Books Reading and Discussion Program, are national in nature.

"Career Education" is a rather recent movement on the American scene but the concern for career development is of long standing. Bruce G. Milne discusses career education for the gifted and talented, pointing out that their special interests, abilities, and career aspirations can only be met through individualized and differentiated programs and services beyond those usually offered in regular instructional and counseling programs. Milne suggests that the gifted and talented should be provided with opportunities for work and play that will enable them to discover satisfaction and dissatisfaction for themselves. He cautions that not all gifts and talents can be readily translated into careers and that giftedness may have its release in avocational as well as in vocational outlets. Milne proposes that career education must make provision for the gifted and talented to live effectively in the world of leisure as well as in the world of the intellect—to enrich their lives as well as to enable them to make a living and a contribution to society through the world of work.

Parents have important roles to play in the education of the gifted and talented, ranging from careful nurture of their children in the home to participation in organizational activities advocating improved programs for the gifted and talented. Carol N. Nathan examines the precedents for parent involvement, describing the "success within limits" of California Parents for the Gifted. She discusses some of the unique functions of organizations of parents of gifted children, including advocacy for appropriate national, state, and local legislation and funding as well as the provision of out-of-school enrichment programs and study groups for parents. Education of parents of gifted children is often neglected and Nathan suggests aid to parents so that they will better understand their roles as parents of gifted children. What parents must do for themselves and what they can do for their children are areas of concern that Nathan explores in the belief that parent involvement is absolutely essential if giftedness and talent are to be developed and realized.

The significance of teachers and mentors in the development of the gifted and the talented is pretty much taken for granted. Marvin J. Gold points out that whatever divergence exists concerning other aspects of education of the gifted and talented, gifted students need some degree of expert help in realizing their superior potentials. He reviews the literature on the qualities that teachers of the gifted should have, as well as characteristics of the successful teacher. Preservice and in-service preparation of teachers for the gifted are summarized and the controversy concerning certification of teachers is reviewed. Gold observes that there is much more opinion than fact available concerning the teacher of the gifted and talented children, with the result that confusion exists with respect to requisite characteristics, specific preparation, and programs of continuing education, as well as with respect to procedures for certification.

General issues and problems related to evaluating programs for the gifted and talented are discussed by Joseph Renzulli and Linda H. Smith. They identify some basic concepts in program evaluation, two dealing with evaluation design and three with types of evaluative data. They then examine some special problems in evaluating programs for the gifted and talented, including those of "higher-level" and highly individualized objectives, of testing and measurement, and of providing resources for evaluation. They describe the Key Features Evaluation System, a general design for evaluation that they have found to be particularly effective in evaluating programs for the gifted and talented. In their view, evaluation must be an essential and ongoing part of the planning of such programs.

Finally, William W. Brickman reviews educational provisions for the gifted and talented, focusing mostly on Great Britain, the Federal Republic of Germany, and USSR. Prior yearbooks of the Society have not included discussions of programs for the gifted in other nations. Brickman points out the problems encountered in such surveys and notes an increase in the development of programs for the gifted and talented in several nations, as well as the formation of international groups (for example, the World Conference on Gifted Children) for the purposes of sharing research and experience as well as increasing advocacy for the gifted and talented. In his survey of provisions in Great Britain and Russia, Brickman notes that there is considerable emphasis on intellectual and academic giftedness. Both countries, however, also provide for the development of talents in other areas such as ballet, drama, and the fine arts. Selection procedures as well as programs in these countries are discussed. Programs in other nations around the world are touched on briefly. Brickman concludes his discussion with some reflections concerning the development of talent within certain kinds of societal contexts and philosophical frameworks.

CHAPTER VI

Programs for the Gifted and Talented: An Overview

LYNN H. FOX

The term "qualitatively differentiated programs for the gifted" has recently been used in state and national legislation. Alas, the term has not been precisely defined. Most educators would agree, however, that the intellectually gifted child is one for whom the typical in-grade learning experiences are inappropriate by virtue of the child's ability to learn at a faster pace, to master high levels of content at an earlier age, and to handle abstract concepts with greater insight. For example, students who score at the 99th percentile on achievement tests in grades five and seven are more likely to master Piagetian formal operations tasks than students at the 50th percentile.[1] For the purpose of this chapter, the term "programs for the gifted" will be used loosely to encompass a wide variety of means of providing learning experiences for children of well above average general intellectual and/or specific academic aptitude. In some cases the discussion is also relevant to specific nonacademic abilities that are provided for within the curriculum of many schools, by such offerings as art, music, and athletics.

Programs can differ in their goals, in the instructional components they manipulate, and in the means of delivery they employ. Programs are not restricted to any specific administrative unit. Thus, there can be programs at the national, state, local, school, or classroom level.

All programs at any level should be designed to include certain key processes or elements. There is no absolute logical ordering

I wish to thank Linda Brody, Maryellen Cunnion, Dianne Tobin, and Ilse Harrop (the staff of the Intellectually Gifted Child Study Group) for their comments and help in the preparation of this chapter.

1. Daniel P. Keating, "Discovering Quantitative Precocity," in *Intellectual Talent: Research and Development*, ed. Daniel P. Keating (Baltimore: Johns Hopkins University Press, 1976), pp. 90-99.

for the development of these elements. Many of the decisions in program development must be made in conjunction with one another.

Every program must have an operational definition of giftedness that includes procedures for identification of the target population. Whether a program utilizes a multitalent or global intellectual approach, specific steps to screen students must be outlined. The identification of the target population leads to the determination of the educational needs of that group. Needs assessment includes many considerations, such as geographic and administrative considerations, characteristics of the population, and scope of the program.

Once the population has been defined and student needs assessed, a variety of strategies to meet those needs must be generated. This also involves the formulation of goals for the students and for the administrative unit. The wide range of individual differences in needs of students should be kept in mind so that a program consists of a list of goals and multiple strategies for meeting them.

Once the population and multiple strategies are defined, a plan of action can be outlined.[2] This may include a time table for implementing various components of the program. Such a plan should include consideration of the need for hiring new personnel, retaining existing personnel, and matching students to alternative strategies by means of counseling programs for students, teachers, and parents. Suggestions for teacher training and selection are detailed in a later chapter of this volume.

Once a program is initiated, it must be continually evaluated and monitored. Evaluation should include an analysis of the cost-effectiveness of the various program strategies, as well as measures of the social or human values of the program. Models and guidelines for evaluation are discussed in a later chapter.

The goal of any program for the gifted should be to provide meaningful learning experiences in the most efficient and effective way in order to maximize learning and individual development and to minimize boredom, confusion, and frustration. Thus, given a

2. Irving S. Sato, Martin Birnbaum, and Jane E. LoCicero, *Developing a Written Plan for the Education of Gifted and Talented Students* (Ventura, Calif.: Office of the Ventura County Superintendent of Schools, 1974).

group of gifted individuals, we should assess what they know, determine what they can do and like to do, and specify what knowledge and skills they lack and in what manner to best provide this learning. Not all educators in the field of the gifted agree on how best to accomplish this. Gallagher has noted that instruction has four major components: content, rate, mode, and environment.[3] Programs vary to the degree that they manipulate each of the four instructional components.

Instructional Components

THE CONTROVERSY OVER CONTENT VERSUS RATE

Gallagher argues that the provision of appropriate content is the major focus for attack. Stanley, Keating, and Fox, on the other hand, argue that rate and, to some extent, mode of instruction are the key components.[4] Although this sounds like the continuing enrichment versus acceleration controversy, the differences are largely a result of differential focus in content areas.[5] By and large, the acceleration of learning in science and mathematics leads to higher levels of abstraction, more creative thinking, and more difficult content. In social studies and language arts the hierarchy of the curriculum is less clear.

If "enrichment" is defined as the provision for learning experiences that develop higher processes of thinking and creativity in a subject area, and if "acceleration" is defined as the adjustment of learning time to meet the individual capabilities of the students, the two terms are complementary rather than conflicting. If one assumes that the goal of educational programs for the gifted is to

3. James J. Gallagher, "Needed: A New Partnership for the Gifted," in *Gifted Children: Looking to Their Future*, ed. Joy Gibson and Prue Chennells (London: Latimer New Dimensions, 1976), pp. 57-72.

4. *Mathematical Talent: Discovery, Description, and Development*, ed. Julian C. Stanley, Daniel P. Keating, and Lynn H. Fox (Baltimore: Johns Hopkins University Press, 1974).

5. A. Harry Passow, "Enrichment of Education for the Gifted," in *Education for the Gifted*, Fifty-seventh Yearbook of the National Society for the Study of Education, Part II, ed. Nelson B. Henry (Chicago: University of Chicago Press, 1958), pp. 193-221. The arguments pro and con acceleration, grouping, and enrichment, together with research findings, are summarized here.

meet their learning needs, *both* enrichment and acceleration are necessary. Thus, the gifted learner can proceed at a faster pace, to a higher level of content, and to more abstract and evaluative thinking than his age peers.

At the risk of overgeneralizing, we can conclude that the controversy over enrichment versus acceleration is partly a function of the specific curriculum for a given content area. (One caution is indicated regardless of the subject: the level at which a course is taught may be determined more by the abilities and characteristics of the students and the instructors than by any written course guide.) Another dimension of the acceleration versus enrichment argument involves the administrative level for instruction. If a gifted student is taught concepts of computer science, algebra, logic, a foreign language, and so forth, as a supplement to in-grade work provided at the elementary, middle school or junior high school level without any high school or college credit, it is likely to be called enrichment. If the same student studied the same content in a course at the high school or college level for credit, it would be called acceleration. Acceleration typically leads to either early graduation from high school or entrance to college with advanced standing or earned credit, whereas enrichment implies the student is exposed to the higher level material without having to break away from age peers, and without earning credit. In the latter case, students at a later point in their education may be required to repeat content already mastered.

Numerous studies have reported that acceleration is not harmful and can benefit students in many ways.[6] There is less evidence to demonstrate the benefits of enrichment without acceleration. The acceleration strategy may have been more carefully researched because the goals are more immediately measurable.

THE MODE OF INSTRUCTION

Perhaps the most useful instructional mode or strategy for fostering acceleration of learning rate is diagnostic-prescriptive teaching. In this mode, the skills, knowledge, and learning needs of each

6. Sidney P. Marland, Jr., *Education of the Gifted and Talented*, Report to the Congress of the United States by the U.S. Commissioner of Education (Washington, D.C.: U.S. Government Printing Office, 1972), pp. 51-59.

individual are assessed by a variety of standardized and nonstandardized measures. A sequential program of learning is then developed for each student. The actual process by which the student is taught the necessary skills and facts could include tutoring, programmed instruction, learning centers, or other variations.

Although self-paced study, especially by means of programmed instruction, is useful for some students in some subject areas, it should be used with caution and never as the total program for the gifted child. The gifted child needs opportunities for interaction with peers and knowledgeable teachers. Such structured programs can be helpful for mastering routine skills, but they provide little or no opportunity for the development of skills necessary for creative problem solving, thinking, and expression.

Gifted students can benefit from opportunities for self-initiated learning. Self-directed research projects may, however, be nonproductive if they are not carefully planned and monitored by the teacher. Students need instruction in library research skills and the use of the scientific method. Renzulli has noted that too often self-directed activities deteriorate into game playing rather than productive learning.[7] Most experts would agree that attempts to stimulate more creative and productive thinking should be incorporated into content areas rather than taught as a separate unit. A publication by Feldhusen and Treffinger catalogues some commercial materials that could be integrated into different content areas.[8] Additional ideas for developing curriculum and instructional strategies to foster greater creative and critical thinking skills are found in materials by Kaplan and by Gallagher.[9]

Fast-paced instruction, somewhat like that of a typical college class, has been highly effective with small or large groups of stu-

7. Joseph S. Renzulli, "The Enrichment Triad Model: A Guide for Developing Defensible Programs for the Gifted and Talented," *Gifted Child Quarterly* 20 (Fall, 1976): 303-26.

8. John F. Feldhusen and Donald J. Treffinger, *Teaching Creative Thinking and Problem Solving* (Dubuque, Iowa: Kendall/Hunt, 1977).

9. Sandra N. Kaplan, *Providing Programs for the Gifted and Talented: A Handbook* (Ventura, Calif.: Office of the Ventura County Superintendent of Schools, 1974), pp. 197-207; James J. Gallagher, *Teaching the Gifted Child* (Boston: Allyn and Bacon, 1975).

dents gifted in mathematics.[10] This approach has also been modified and used for science instruction.[11] It could conceivably be adapted to other subject areas. The college seminar model can be used for courses in the humanities.

THE LEARNING ENVIRONMENT

Although the design and condition of the physical plant may not be an important factor for educating the gifted, the provision of appropriate equipment and materials is important. Some programs may involve the transporting of students for varying periods of time to locations that offer essential facilities such as computer terminals, science or language laboratories, video taping equipment, and so forth. For older students, the manipulation of the learning environment might be viewed as the provision for internship experiences in governmental offices, scientific and medical laboratories, industrial and business complexes, theater groups, art studios, and other community agencies.

Peers and teachers are also a part of the learning environment. Homogeneous grouping of students on the basis of aptitude and interest and the provision of well-trained teachers can foster learning if the curriculum and rate of learning are adjusted to meet the needs of the group. Grouping without corresponding changes in instructional content and rate, however, is not very potent if the students are given only more work of the same grade level.

Perhaps the most crucial aspect of the learning environment is the development of an atmosphere of mutual trust and respect among individuals and a commitment to self-improvement. Although it may be impossible to teach a child directly to love learning for its own sake, some environments can clearly either stifle or enhance the student's natural interest.

10. Lynn H. Fox, "A Mathematics Program for Fostering Precocious Achievement," in *Mathematical Talent: Discovery, Description, and Development*, ed. Stanley, Keating, and Fox, pp. 101-125; William C. George and Susanne A. Denham, "Curriculum Experimentation for the Mathematically Talented," in *Intellectual Talent: Research and Development*, ed. Keating, pp. 103-131.

11. Sanford J. Cohn, "Developing a Program in the Physical Sciences for the Intellectually Gifted and Talented," in *Second Annual Report to the Spencer Foundation*, ed. Lynn H. Fox (Baltimore: Intellectually Gifted Child Study Group, Johns Hopkins University, 1976), Appendix C-1.

Once the goals have been operationalized to the degree that the issue of acceleration has been understood and resolved, alternative program strategies can be designed. If the program is to be both accelerative and enriched, the rate of learning, the content, and the mode of learning must be adjusted. If a program is to be purely accelerative, only the rate of learning need be manipulated. Changing the rate of learning may or may not influence the choice of instructional mode. Skipping grades does not necessitate changes in instructional modes, while acceleration accomplished by programmed instruction or tutor does require such changes. If the program goal is restricted to enrichment, the content must be changed. This may also include changes in instructional mode. Enrichment could be provided in a traditional didactic classroom mode or by using more unconventional means, such as self-directed independent projects, learning centers, field trips, or mentors. Accelerative or enriched programs can involve the manipulation of instructional style to focus on more learner-initiated and learner-directed activities and to put greater emphasis upon higher-order thought processes and creative, productive thinking tasks.

Since gifted students differ from each other in a variety of ways, alternative programs need to be developed. For students gifted in science and mathematics, program options should include acceleration. For gifted students interested in creative writing and the humanities, options other than acceleration might be more appropriate.

The delivery of the program can take many different forms. Acceleration of learning, for example, could be accomplished by such means as permitting early admission to kindergarten or first grade, or by having telescoped programs in which three years of course work are covered in two years. Some examples of delivery approaches at system, school, and classroom levels are described in the following section.

Delivery Systems

SPECIAL SCHOOLS

In theory, special schools for the gifted would seem to be the most efficient and effective way to provide for gifted students. Content, instructional modes and pace, and learning environments could be designed and continually adjusted to meet the needs of the students. Such a school could conceivably be run more like a college than a traditional elementary or secondary school and, thus, provide a wide variety of courses and flexible scheduling. The instructional staff could be selected on the basis of knowledge of subject matter and ability to relate to creative and brilliant students. Problems relating to social adjustment, across-age-grouping, and scheduling should be lessened; for example, college-level courses could be taught at the school. The Calasanctius School in Buffalo, to be described in a later chapter, is an example of the special school concept. Perhaps the greatest advantage of such schools is their ability to concentrate resources and programming efforts within one building to serve a large number of students.

There are, however, some real barriers to the creation of special schools. Such schools may be too costly and impractical, except in large metropolitan areas where the pool of gifted students is large and transportation can be readily provided. Another objection to special schools is that students will become too isolated from the rest of the student population and an artificial sense of elitism will develop. Given the financial and political realities of today, it is probably more practical to provide for students of all ability levels by focusing on more flexibility in existing school programs than to advocate special schools for the gifted. Two compromises or variations of the total school concept are possible: the satellite school and the school-within-a-school. Neither program will totally eliminate transportation problems, but both appear promising and practical. Indeed, these concepts have been practiced successfully in large cities such as Baltimore and New York.

The satellite school concept is practical for high schools. In such a program, one school may become designated as the school for the sciences and/or engineering, while another becomes a center for creative and performing arts, and so forth. Thus, opportunities for specialization and individualization can be provided within one or more content areas for multiple levels of ability.

At the elementary or secondary level, the school-within-a-school concept can be used. The gifted portion of the school population would then receive instruction from special teachers in specific subjects, while mixing within the total school for social events and nonacademic subjects.

LEARNING CENTERS OR LABORATORIES

The learning center approach is similar to the school-within-a-school concept but requires separate treatment. One school building, or a portion of a school building, can be designated as a special center for the gifted on a system-wide or within-school basis. Students would attend special programs at the centers on a part-time basis. Centers could be used for accelerated or nonaccelerated classes and seminars, or as resource rooms and work areas for independent study projects or tutoring. In the latter case, a full-time teacher might be needed to supervise the center. If the class or seminar approach is used, teachers from within or outside the school or system could be scheduled to conduct the classes on a daily, weekly, or other basis.

The learning center approach can also be used with a single classroom setting. A part of the room can be set aside for students to pursue their own projects, or activities designed by the teacher, at certain times of the day or week. Of course, the use of learning centers need not be limited to the gifted. This technique, however, does allow for the provision of more advanced assignments and instructional materials for the gifted learner, which usually places a burden on the teacher to develop and monitor the activities to ensure their appropriateness and continuity. Classroom learning centers can, unfortunately, become centers for busy work or play rather than centers to stimulate creative and productive thinking and learning.

EARLY ADMISSION TO SCHOOL

Early admission to kindergarten or first grade for gifted learners has never been a widespread practice. Yet, research has shown that such a practice has no negative effects for students.[12] Although this practice primarily affects the rate of learning rather than content or learning environments, it does provide a better match between the child's learning needs and the content and level of abstraction in the learning situation. Many gifted children are clearly ready for structured learning experiences as early as age four. Whether or not

12. Marland, *Education of the Gifted and Talented.*

a child can adequately adjust to school a year or two early depends
not only on cognitive factors, but on physical and social factors as
well.

The major barriers to early entrance are the lack of provisions
for identifying students who are ready for school on the basis of
social and cognitive measures instead of birth date and legal or
school board regulations. The development of preschool programs
for gifted students should promote early admissions, as well as
provide transition and preparation experiences for the gifted child.
This is particularly crucial for the economically or socially disadvantaged students who suffer from impoverished learning environments at home. Efforts to identify gifted children at an early
age and provide for their educational needs are discussed in a following chapter.

EARLY ADMISSION TO COLLEGE OR
ADMISSION WITH ADVANCED STANDING

There is a growing body of research indicating that large numbers of gifted students are ready for college level experiences at
ages fourteen, fifteen, sixteen, and, in rare instances, at even
younger ages.[13] Few students can jump from grade six, seven, or
eight into full-time college, although it has been done. Most gifted
students need programs at the elementary and secondary levels that
provide for a more gradual transition from secondary school to
college and that enable growth along cognitive and affective dimensions.

There are numerous ways to telescope the time spent in the
elementary and secondary school years and thereby provide for
gradual, rather than radical, acceleration to college at an early age.
If students do not wish to enter college one or more years early,
they can still telescope time by entering college with advanced
standing. The bridging mechanisms include grade or subject skipping, fast-paced and enriched classes, credit by examination, college
courses-in-escrow, and telescoped junior and senior high school

13. Cecilia H. Solano and William C. George, "College Courses and Educational Facilitation of the Gifted," *Gifted Child Quarterly* 20 (Fall, 1976):
274-85.

programs. These program mechanisms are discussed in the following section. It should be noted that, contrary to popular belief, a high school diploma is not required by all colleges for admittance; indeed, many colleges willingly accept younger students on the basis of test scores or other evidence.

GRADE SKIPPING

Although evidence from research shows that skipping one or two years of school is not harmful for gifted students, the practice is employed less today than fifty years ago.[14] For the extremely gifted student, some grade skipping is desirable if not mandatory. Few gifted children need six years to master the basics of reading, writing, and arithmetic as taught in the typical elementary school. Yet, objections to grade skipping are strong. Why? Many educators and parents fear social maladjustment will ensue from moving ahead to be with an older peer group, and also they fear that some important learning will be missed. Although the research indicates that these fears are not justified, this information has not been widely disseminated or understood.

Actually, there are alternatives to grade skipping that may accomplish the same degree of acceleration, but in better ways. Grade skipping primarily affects the rate of learning. Alternative practices, such as homogeneously grouped accelerated and enriched classes, and telescoped programs are probably preferable to grade skipping. When grade skipping is used, it is best done at natural transition points. Thus, it is better to skip the grades between elementary and junior high school or between junior and senior high school than within schools. This lessens the pressure of making new friends and may be particularly crucial for females.[15] Total grade skipping is probably also more practical in the elementary years than in high school. One could, indeed, miss total content areas like biology or chemistry in the latter case. Skipping the sixth grade, however, is

14. Ibid.

15. Lynn H. Fox, "Sex Differences: Implications for Program Planning for the Academically Gifted," in *The Gifted and the Creative: Fifty Year Perspective*, ed. Julian C. Stanley, William C. George, and Cecilia H. Solano (Baltimore: Johns Hopkins University Press, 1977), pp. 113-38.

likely to be little problem for the student who already tests at the twelfth-grade level in reading and mathematics.

TELESCOPED PROGRAMS

One way to provide the advantages of grade skipping without omitting content is to cover the basic content of three years of work in two, or four years of work in three. There are basically two ways to telescope.

The first method, typically used at the junior high school level, provides for gifted classes homogeneously grouped for purposes of acceleration. In such a program, three years of work are covered in two. This allows for systematic coverage of content areas while simultaneously providing enrichment with greater depth and breadth of coverage and special opportunities. Time out for independent and creative learning experiences, such as self-directed study and mentor programs, could also be provided. There would also be fewer social pressures than in grade skipping. The only obvious disadvantage of such a program lies in the need to accelerate all content areas at the same time. Like grade skipping, this telescoping requires the student to be equally or at least relatively gifted in all subject areas. Given a large pool of gifted students in geographic proximity, this plan could work well at the junior high level. This method could be used very effectively at the elementary level for any number of students by employing flexible, across-age groupings and, possibly, the use of itinerant resource teachers.

The second method, more often used at the high school than junior high or elementary school level, allows the student to complete the high school graduation requirements in three years rather than in four by eliminating or reducing electives, earning credit by examination, skipping grade levels in some subjects but not others, taking college or summer courses outside of school, and combinations of all of these. This method is very easy to implement with no extra costs. It does require, however, advanced planning, and good counseling programs at grades eight, nine, and/or ten are needed to ensure that the student plans a balanced program of experiences and meets the requirements. Such telescoping at the high school level could accommodate individual differences in ability profiles quite easily.

SUBJECT MATTER ACCELERATION

Subject matter acceleration by means of course skipping has advantages over the skipping of a total grade, but is not equally feasible in all subject areas. A student who already knows the fundamentals of algebra before completing the sixth or seventh grade does not need Algebra I, but could take Algebra II or Plane Geometry. Whether a student can skip a grade-level subject in mathematics, science, or a foreign language can be easily assessed with tests. Language arts and social studies present a more difficult problem. In some schools, the differences between ninth- and tenth-grade English may be very small and may simply be the difference between reading *Julius Caesar* and *Romeo and Juliet.* In other schools, the curriculum may be more developmental. Appropriate use of diagnostic testing and teaching could, however, help solve such problems.

Another variation of subject matter acceleration is the use of individualized instruction by tutors and/or programmed materials at the elementary level. This method allows gifted students to move rapidly through mathematics or reading materials at a rate appropriate for them, but far faster than that of their classmates, without being removed from the regular classroom, except perhaps for short periods of time. Unfortunately, the regular classroom teacher may not have ready access to good self-pacing materials or to the aid of tutors. In such a case, the teacher may be hard pressed to provide the time for such acceleration. Also, teachers, particularly at the elementary level, may not necessarily possess the requisite knowledge of subject matter to provide the accelerated experiences in some subjects, particularly in mathematics and science. When the number of gifted students in a given class, school, or system is small, the subject acceleration at the elementary level could be facilitated by an itinerant specialist or resource person. Subject matter acceleration would also include the concept of students taking college courses while still enrolled in their secondary school programs. College courses could even be taken by correspondence if necessary.

A major objection to subject matter acceleration often raised by school administrators is that such a practice will lead a student to exhaust the curriculum offerings in one or more subjects before the student is ready to graduate from the school. Although this could be a real problem, it is certainly not a valid reason for holding gifted students back from developing their full potential. For example, if only one student in an elementary school is in need of instruction in algebra, or biology, or advanced music, it is possible to provide for that child without creating a special class within the school. The child could take the course at a nearby junior high school or study the material with a tutor or itinerant resource teacher once or twice a week.

ACCELERATED AND ENRICHED CLASSES

Perhaps the most efficient way to deliver appropriate learning experiences to gifted students, particularly at the secondary level, appears to be by means of special classes for students grouped homogeneously on the basis of interest and aptitude in a specific subject area, and taught the content at a rate and in a style most appropriate for them. The Study of Mathematically Precocious Youth and the Intellectually Gifted Child Study Group have repeatedly found this approach to be successful for mathematically gifted students at the upper elementary and junior high school levels.[16] Although research on this technique has been primarily focused on mathematics classes, the model should work equally well in other subject areas, particularly science, foreign languages, music, and art.

The goal of the accelerated class is to provide students with the opportunity to move quickly through basic subject material and advance to the higher levels of abstraction and creative problem-solving under the guidance of a master teacher. Classes can be conducted within or outside of the regular school schedule. Classes can be school-based or draw from a larger school system pool. Teachers can be itinerant specialists or part of the regular school staff.

This concept is really a refinement of a program for the gifted that has a long history of success—the Advanced Placement Pro-

16. Stanley, Keating, and Fox, *Mathematical Talent: Discovery, Description, and Development*; Keating, *Intellectual Talent: Research and Development*; *Second Annual Report to the Spencer Foundation*, ed. Fox.

gram (APP).[17] Until recently, however, APP courses were limited to juniors and seniors in high school. In the APP, students have the opportunity to learn a subject at an advanced level for high school credit with the possibility of simultaneously earning college credit by later examination.

This concept embodies the advantages of a special school without the creation of special administrative or physical structures. Content, instructional modes, learning rates, and environments can all be adjusted to meet the needs of the gifted learner. Students need not be gifted or interested in all areas to participate in a particular accelerated program. Students can be accelerated in a subject area without being promoted to a higher grade or taking courses with older students. Opportunities for contact with mentors and independent study projects can be incorporated into the learning experience. This program approach fits well into the concept of condensed time learning programs.

The success of such a program appears to be dependent upon three factors. First, students must be carefully selected for the program on the basis of their abilities and interests. Second, they must be well motivated to work. Third, the teacher must be an expert in the subject matter area, as well as a gifted teacher. Gifted students benefit greatly from the interaction with both gifted teachers and gifted peers.

One way to deliver intensive learning experiences that are radically different from the typical classroom procedure is by means of residential summer camps. Several states have tried such approaches, often called "Governor's Schools," particularly in the area of the performing and visual arts.[18] Although these programs are expensive, they do have merit. They can provide students, especially those from disadvantaged backgrounds or rural communities, with some unique opportunities for contact with peers and mentors who have similar interests. For example, professional artists, writers, or musicians could be brought to the summer centers to teach a small number of very talented students from all over the state.

17. Information on the Advanced Placement Program is available from the Educational Testing Service, Princeton, N.J.

18. Examples include the Georgia Governor's School, the North Carolina Governor's School, and the Maryland Center for the Performing Arts.

These programs are often popular because they have high visibility. Unfortunately, they can typically only reach a small number of students for a brief period of time. It is an empirical question as to whether the investment in such programs has the same cost-effectiveness as programs with less visibility and intensity that reach larger numbers of students in different ways.

NONACCELERATIVE ENRICHED CLASSES

The concept of enrichment is not well defined or understood. Homogeneous grouping of gifted students for the purpose of enrichment may have value. If enrichment becomes only the playing of games or busy work, however, it is probably of little value to the gifted student. Although many people advocate some free time or periods of incubation for the gifted, there is little evidence that gifted students can, without direction or training, profit from such experiences. Free time can, indeed, become empty and lost time.

On the other hand, there are valuable learning experiences that cannot be categorized as purely accelerative. Career education, for example, is not accelerative, but presumably enriches a child's experience. Courses in creative writing, logic, law, archeology, statistics, journalism, astronomy, psychology, environmental studies, and so forth, have value but are often not incorporated into the basic curriculum. Gifted students who have mastered the more basic curriculum and skills areas could profit from exposure to such courses. Not all students, however, will be interested in all of the extra course topics. Self-selection should be considered.

The problem of scheduling can be greater for nonaccelerative enriched classes than for accelerated ones. The accelerated classes are, typically, substituted for regular classes in the curriculum. Since the enriched classes do not overlap with basic subjects, it is difficult to schedule them within the regular school day. In order to attend such a class, a student must be pulled out of some other class one or more days a week. The student is often held responsible for making up the "missed" assignments. This sometimes causes conflicts for students. The success of enriched programs is dependent upon good communication and cooperation among the special class teachers and those in the regular classes.

INDIVIDUALIZED STUDY

The concept of individualized study has multiple interpretations. Perhaps the most common, but least creative, is self-paced independent study by means of programmed text materials. Such an approach may work well for learning elementary skills such as arithmetic computation, or basic vocabulary skills in English, or foreign languages. It is, however, not the best method for teaching creative or higher-level thinking and reasoning skills. Even subjects as logical and sequenced as algebra are probably learned better through interaction with a tutor or master teacher. Unless students are unusually highly motivated, they are likely to lose interest in the materials and progress through them at a slow rate.

Correspondence courses at the high school or college level are another form of individualized study. Problems of clarification and the time lapse between working problems and reaction from the reader or grader may lead to boredom and frustration. Although this method may work for the well-motivated learner, it is less desirable than other alternatives, such as a tutor-mentor.

Self-directed independent study projects have great value for some students, at least in theory. Such projects allow students to explore in depth topics not typically covered in the regular curriculum, and/or to gain hands-on experience in a laboratory. Without some basic training and skills in research or close guidance and supervision, some students' projects will degenerate into exercises in busy work or play. For projects to be meaningful, they should challenge but not overwhelm and should build on basic skills and knowledge the student possesses. Even in the elementary grades students can be taught and guided by teachers to develop a systematic approach to such projects.[19] Projects should begin at a simple level and become more complex and self-directed as the students acquire the skills needed to pursue their projects.

One way to make projects more productive for the student is to involve the student with a tutor/mentor or resource person in the design and conduct of the project. Setting specific goals and deadlines also helps ensure logical progression towards a measurable

19. E. Paul Torrance, "Changing Reactions of Preadolescent Girls to Tasks Requiring Creative Scientific Thinking," *Journal of Genetic Psychology* 102 (1963): 217-23.

and meaningful outcome. This does not mean that "failure" can not sometimes be a valuable learning experience, but failure due to poor planning and unrealistic goals should generally be avoided.

Perhaps the most intriguing interpretation of individualized education is the diagnostic prescriptive teaching strategy. This approach is widely advocated for students with learning disabilities, but seldom discussed as an appropriate way to accelerate and enrich the program of a gifted student. The diagnostic approach can be used to teach basic skills in mathematics, reading, or vocabulary and grammar in any language. For example, mathematically gifted students in grades five, six, and seven sometimes know a great many concepts from the Algebra I curriculum without having formally studied the subject in school. A standardized test can be used to determine which concepts have or have not been mastered. The concepts not yet known can often be quickly taught by a tutor or resource specialist, and the student can skip the regular Algebra I course and move directly into an Algebra II class.

TUTORS, MENTORS, AND INTERNSHIP PROGRAMS

There is a subtle difference between the tutor and the mentor. The tutor presumably teaches some body of content in a systematic way in a one-on-one relationship. Tutors need not be strictly remediators but can be used effectively to challenge, pace, and motivate the young learner. Tutors, unfortunately, can be expensive. Special tutors for the highly precocious child may be, however, preferable to radical acceleration. The success of such a program depends largely upon the personal effectiveness and knowledge of the tutor. An older gifted child may or may not be a good tutor and role-model for a younger gifted child. Informal evaluations of such programs suggest that they have merit but need careful monitoring by a knowledgeable educator.

The mentor, unlike the tutor, may have no organized agenda for instruction. A gifted child merely meets with an adult expert in a field of mutual interest for general sharing of ideas and reading. The mentor program appears promising, but has not been systematically evaluated on a large scale. Potential pitfalls include the possibility that the expert is not able to relate effectively to a young child or adolescent in a meaningful way. The mentor system may be applicable in the areas of the fine arts and the performing arts, as well as the sciences.

At the secondary level, a semiformal internship program may be the best way of providing for the development of a mentor relationship. The concept of learning by doing is still valid for education. This concept should probably be incorporated directly into the domain of enrichment or career education. The opportunity to "apprentice" with a professional in any field is clearly a potent experience. The student who works in a congressional office, a business firm, a scientific laboratory, a school, a hospital, and so forth, can observe firsthand the dynamics of the field and the characteristics of those employed in such fields. This type of program, however, should never be considered the sole domain of the gifted.

WITHIN-CLASS INDIVIDUALIZATION (MAINSTREAMING)

Present research suggests that administrative practices such as grade skipping or the provision of accelerated classes offer more direct service to the gifted learner than "mainstreaming" in heterogeneous classes. Unfortunately, at present many teachers are expected to provide for the gifted student without the aid of tutors or other facilities.

The classroom teacher who is faced with a class of thirty or more students of varying ability often finds it difficult to provide appropriate learning experiences for the gifted students in the class. Several practices already discussed, such as learning centers, diagnostic teaching techniques, and independent projects, can be used to individualize instruction for all the students.

Unfortunately, many teachers, especially at the elementary school level, lack expertise in a variety of subjects, particularly mathematics and science. Thus, it is difficult for them to provide the appropriate instruction for the most gifted students in their classes. Also, teachers may find they spend two or more hours to develop a learning center activity that occupies the gifted child for less than half an hour; this can be frustrating for both teacher and child.

Itinerant resource teachers, tutors, and mentors should be used to develop and teach the appropriate curriculum. Ungraded classes, flexible grouping, and team teaching are all likely to promote greater individualization of instruction. Not all teachers, however, enjoy the challenge of working with the gifted student. Knowledge of subject matter and interest in the gifted child should be the main criteria for determining which teachers or teams work with the gifted student.

A few materials or texts are available that describe ways of enriching the curriculum for the gifted learner.[20] A catalogue of materials for developing creative and productive thinking has also been published recently.[21] A few programs in mathematics and science have been designed for the gifted learner.[22] Generally, teachers must rely on their own resources and those in the community.

In-service training for teachers should probably include instruction in the creation of learning centers, diagnostic-prescriptive teaching techniques, and content areas.

Additional Considerations in Program Design

Ideally, it would be helpful to provide all of the possible alternatives. Two major concerns in the planning of programs for the gifted, cost and staff requirements, are likely to restrict offerings. Also, administrative and geographic limitations must be considered. Table 1 is provided as a summary of factors involved in different strategies for delivery of programs. The specific cost-effectiveness of a given program is dependent upon many considerations.

Special schools and system-wide learning centers are likely to involve special costs, particularly transportation costs. Administrative practices such as providing for early admission to first grade, grade skipping, and early graduation, fast-paced and enriched

20. Kaplan, *Providing Programs for the Gifted and Talented: A Handbook*; Gallagher, *Teaching the Gifted Child*.

21. Feldhusen and Treffinger, *Teaching Creative Thinking and Problem Solving*.

22. Although not specifically developed for use with the gifted, appropriate materials for use with the gifted include the *Comprehensive School Mathematics Program* developed by Cemrel, Inc., 3120 Fifty-ninth Street, St. Louis, Missouri 63139, and the *Unified Science and Mathematics for Elementary Schools*, Educational Development Center, 55 Chapel Street, Newton, Massachusetts 02160.

TABLE I

REQUIRED CHANGES IN INSTRUCTIONAL COMPONENTS, PROBABLE COST-EFFECTIVENESS, AND EVALUATION FACTORS ASSOCIATED WITH EACH OF ELEVEN PROGRAM DELIVERY SYSTEMS

Delivery Systems	Required Changes in Instructional Components				Staff and Housing Requirements			Easily Evaluated
	Rate of Learning	Content	Mode of Instruction	Homogeneous Grouping	Additional Staff	Staff Training	Facilities or Equipment	
Special schools or learning centers	possibly	possibly	possibly	yes	yes	yes	yes	possibly
Early admission to school	yes	no	no	no	no	no	no	yes
Grade skipping	yes	no	no	no	no	no	no	yes
Subject matter acceleration	yes	no	no	no	no	no	no	yes
Accelerated and enriched classes	yes	possibly	possibly	yes	possibly	possibly	possibly	yes
Telescoped programs	yes	possibly	possibly	yes	possibly	possibly	possibly	yes
Enriched classes	no	yes	possibly	yes	possibly	possibly	possibly	no
Independent study	possibly	possibly	yes	no	possibly	possibly	no	yes
Tutors	possibly	possibly	yes	no	yes	possibly	no	yes
Mentors or internships	no	possibly	yes	no	possibly	no	no	no
Mainstreaming	possibly	possibly	possibly	no	no	yes	no	possibly

classes, and telescoped programs may actually save money in the long run. Tutor and mentor programs may be costly or, in some communities, may be available at no cost.

Some program strategies will require training of existing personnel rather than hiring of additional teachers. It may be more effective to designate a handful of teachers as itinerant resource teachers or teachers of special classes than to try to provide inservice programs for all teachers in the system. A few hours a week spent with a tutor in an accelerated class may have a greater impact on student learning than the regular classroom teacher's use of individualized learning centers.

Measurable outcomes are clearer for some programs than others. For example, the benefits of accelerative strategies can be assessed by the number of students who complete high school early and are successful in college, as well as by standardized tests. The impact of internships or mentors must be evaluated in more informal and subjective ways.

Gallagher reports that educators say that the reason for the paucity of programs for the gifted is the lack of funds.[23] Yet, a quick look at table 1 shows that many program strategies would not be very costly. Real barriers to programs are more likely to be misinformation and apathy. Few teachers receive information about the special needs of the gifted learner at any stage of their training. Unfortunately, parents are rarely as forceful advocates for their children as they might be.

Conclusion

Gifted students vary greatly in abilities, interests, knowledge of specific content, and attitudes toward learning while still meeting some general criteria for giftedness. Such individual differences should not be ignored. There is no single program concept that can effectively meet the needs of all gifted students. A variety of program options should be designed and implemented. The appropriate matching of students to program goals and strategies will require more testing and counseling than is typically practiced. Student self-selection should also be considered. The provision of greater flexibility and individualized programs may or may not

23. Gallagher, *Teaching the Gifted Child.*

involve additional dollar costs. Accelerative strategies might actually save money. The cost-effectiveness of programs can not be measured solely by dollar amounts for additional testing, counseling, staff, and so forth. There are also affective or human values to be considered that can not be measured in dollars. We must face the fact that perhaps as many as a fifth of our nation's children are bored and frustrated in classrooms where their gifts, talents, and needs are ignored. The child from the educationally and/or economically deprived background may be the most overlooked. If children can be viewed as our nation's greatest natural resource, we should not ask if we can afford special programs for the gifted student, but rather if we can afford not to provide them.

CHAPTER VII

The Calasanctius Experience

STEPHEN GERENCSER

The Calasanctius School is located in Buffalo, New York, close to the city's museums and libraries. Founded in 1957 as an independent school, it is chartered and registered by the Regents of the University of the State of New York and accredited by the Middle States Association of Colleges and Secondary Schools.

My experience as a teacher for many years in different countries, and most especially my experience as a clinical psychologist, led to the idea of the Calasanctius School as an experiment in the education of gifted and talented children. After many consultations with educators, psychologists, and members of the academic and business community, the decision was made to formulate a special program for intellectually talented and gifted children from grade five to college level. The suggestion was for a separate school with a comprehensive program, where the only criteria for acceptance were ability and interest. It was envisioned that the curriculum would not be a copy of any other design. Nor would it employ the so-called enrichment or acceleration methods, but rather it would have a unified program built around the psychological and sociological needs of gifted children.

The school carries the name of a very innovative educator, Joseph Calasanctius (1556-1648), and aims at continuing his dauntless spirit. In baroque Rome, but in the spirit of enlightenment, he pioneered in opening schools without discrimination. His idea of free and compulsory education without regard to class structure, his friendship with Galileo to whom he provided mathematicians even after Galileo's trial, and his contact with other leading dissenters of his age brought him in collision with the extremely conservative and class-conscious circles of Rome.

Organization

BEGINNING OF THE SCHOOL

A fundamental question was faced at the outset: Was there a need in the Buffalo area for the kind of school envisioned? Buffalo is a heavily industrialized, blue-collar city with strong ethnic concentrations. The Buffalo Diocese, the largest school system in the area, provided a list of students who had obtained scores of 130 or above on the *Kuhlman-Anderson Intelligence Test* and who had proved to be "good students" in the third to fifth grades. The parents of these children were asked if they would be interested in a program for gifted students. About twenty-two people attended the first meeting and were enthusiastic. The curriculum plan and admission procedures were explained to them. Individual evaluations would be carried out for each candidate, using the *Wechsler Intelligence Scale for Children* (WISC) and other supplementary tests. Sixteen boys were accepted. At that time the school was planned for boys only, but after its third year it became coeducational. With this small group, plus $2,000 donated by two local businessmen and the enthusiastic collaboration of a good number of people, Calasanctius School opened its doors on September 8, 1957 in a small private home donated for its use for one year. The enthusiasm was remarkable, extending to the students, parents, the Buffalo business community, and various religious groups.

DEVELOPING A CURRICULUM

It was not enough to recruit students; it was imperative to develop and implement a well-organized and comprehensive curriculum. The basic curriculum of the school was planned for a six-year sequence, commencing usually after the fourth or fifth grade, in preparation for exacting college-level study. Features of various curricula were incorporated: the English grammar school, the central European gymnasium, the French lycée, the eastern (American) private schools, and aspects of American comprehensive high schools. In integrating these various approaches, specific features were added that had grown out of research in developmental and differential psychology. In 1972, the program was extended downward to include five-year-olds.

At Calasanctius, all students were exposed to a great variety of learning experiences in clearly circumscribed fields early in their schooling. In the first three years of the school, all courses were required with the only choices being in foreign languages and some areas of creative arts.

There was a good deal of serious resistance to the idea of ten to fifteen subjects weekly, following the college method of scheduling, instead of the usual four to five subjects uniformly scheduled each day. Considering that one of the characteristics of giftedness is an insatiable intellectual curiosity, channeling the interest of children in only a few directions is a questionable method. If students are not exposed to varied learning experiences from early childhood, they are restricted to limited resources. Their imaginations and lives become very one-sided. Calasanctius was intended to enlarge the intellectual and artistic horizons of the gifted.

The students responded to the challenge. They preferred the variety of offerings, and indeed a very full school day, rather than the boredom and uniformity of the daily schedule and the futility of the typical study hall, of which there is none at Calasanctius.

If students were bombarded with many different experiences, is there room for creativity? To be creative, one first needs a great variety of experiences stored in his mind. Human creativity is, essentially, finding new combinations and connections. The Calasanctius curriculum tries to open as many "windows" in the mind as is possible, and to enhance the richness of imagination. Similarly, spontaneity comes when children are immersed in many areas and when through self-assessment they find ways to channel their general interests in more specific areas. This usually occurs at about age thirteen to fourteen, when their interests become more career-oriented and when they "fall in love" with certain areas of academic or artistic endeavor.

CALASANCTIUS PROGRAMS

Some of the Calasanctius programs are unique, not only as individual programs in themselves, but from the viewpoint of their integrating value as well.

The Historical (not "social") Studies Program exposes students, beginning about age ten, to a six- to seven-year sequence in the history of civilization. Because there was no appropriate secondary school text that exposed the students to the richness of the human heritage, a college textbook is used that gives a balanced approach to the great civilizations of past and present (Asia, Europe, Africa, the Americas) in a vertical way. This is not an area-study course, but a sequential and coordinated six- to seven-year program in history. American history is integrated into the course; it is not removed from the continuity of history. In the present age, when history is considered irrelevant in many programs, the historical dimension of our culture is emphasized.

The Language Program is unique, with instruction in a foreign language beginning at the age of five or six. The modern languages offered include German, French, Russian, Spanish, or Japanese. A second language (Latin, Italian, Chinese) may also be taken. In addition, other languages are available for credit through the National Association of Self-Instructional Language Program. The objectives of the language program are twofold: (a) to introduce the student, through a direct method, into conversational language patterns, and (b) to prepare him to reach some understanding of the particular culture and literature. Students are expected to attain the Advanced Placement standard in at least one language by the time of graduation. Most of them do. Calasanctius takes seriously the significance of language learning.

Although the following features may not be unique to Calasanctius, in their combination they constitute a unique approach to learning. All the Advanced Placement courses are offered and three are required for graduation with a Calasanctius diploma. The Science Program is built vertically and culminates in Advanced Placement courses. The English Program concludes with two years of History of Literature and Criticism, taught only at college level. Art History and Music are taught at all grade levels, and Studio Art in the lower and middle schools (ages five to thirteen). They are integrated into the regular curriculum and are not merely electives; they culminate in Advanced Placement courses. Mathematics is considered an integrating subject between humanities and sciences.

The Physical Education program is integrated into the regular program. The role of carry-over sports and gymnastics is emphasized with less stress on team sports. School assemblies are replaced by Colloquia, that is, weekly round-table discussions of books and issues, in small groups in the upper school, and in the form of Academia in the middle and lower schools where the students have a chance to express themselves and are confronted in group situations.

Some of these programs exist in other schools as well. However, perhaps the strongest integrating aspects of the program are presently found only in Calasanctius. These include: the Seminar Program, which is intended to integrate the personal academic or artistic interest of the student with his career orientation and future professional plan; the Field Study Trip Program, which integrates book experience with actual live experiences; and the Phenomenon-of-Man Program, which integrates, on a more conceptual level, the fragmented knowledge gained from various courses into a deeper understanding.

The Seminar Program is an independent research/study program, under the guidance of a proctor. Students are expected to do serious research in the field of their choice, under the guidance of a professional in that particular field who is interested in sharing his knowledge or talent. For each of three consecutive years, students are expected to present a serious paper based upon research (laboratory work and other sources) or creative art work. The presentation is made in front of a committee of experts. The student is expected to stand up for his findings in a serious, sometimes traumatic, but in all cases a maturing confrontation. Former students almost unanimously consider the seminar program their best experience in the school, even after their graduation from college. They report that the program assisted them in finding their career orientation, and in facing demanding programs and challenges.

The following titles give some idea of the scope of the Seminar Program:

"The Design and Construction of a Solid State Doppler Radar with Digital Readout."
"Ecclesia Rex and Sacerdotium, A Study of Carolingian Political Thought in the Reign of Louis the Pious as Presented at the 6th Synod of Paris, A.D. 829."
"The Canadian Dilemma."
"The Construction of a Jotto Playing Program."

"Separation and Aggression Anxiety in Children's Responses to Story Completions Following Arousal by Death Oriented Questioning."

"The Effects of Amytal on the Electron and Energy Transfer Systems in the Mitochondria in the Liver of Rats."

"Critical Interpretation of the Flute Concerto in D-Major (K. 314), by Wolfgang Mozart."

"Exaggeration of Opinion: The Nineties."

Between 1960-1976, of the 380 humanities seminar papers presented, 309 were accepted; 33 of the 45 mathematics papers were accepted; and 176 of the 207 science papers were approved. Seminar papers in the science fields are the result of laboratory research and are usually twenty to eighty pages in length. Seminar papers in the humanities fields range between fifty and two hundred pages. In studio art and music, the presentation is in the selected art field.

From the very first year, the student participates in the Field Study Trip Program, with study trips lasting two to three weeks and somewhat less for the youngest children. The trips take place during the school year. The objectives of the program are to coordinate and integrate school learning experiences with real life situations; to assist growing children to open their minds to the variety of natural beauties of the land as well as to the exceptional achievement of American scholarship, art, and industry; to foster among them the spirit of community through the rigors of camping and outdoor experiences; and, through contact with students of other areas of the country, to nurture an understanding of the diversity of the American experience. For language students, extended trips are available to Germany, France, Russia, and Quebec.

Still another unique feature of the Calasanctius curriculum is the Phenomenon-of-Man Program, a cluster of courses taken in the fourth, fifth, and sixth levels of study (comparable to the sophomore to senior years). The purpose of the courses, which are taken for one, two, three, or four semesters, is to introduce the students to the richness of the history of ideas.

Phenomenon-of-Man Courses include: History of Philosophy —Indian and Chinese, Greek and Medieval, Modern and Contemporary; History of Music; History of Art; Comparative Religion; Philosophy of Religion; Ethics; Anthropology; Sociology; Aspects of World Literature; Basic Concepts of Science; Basic Concepts of Economics; Experimental Psychology; Developmental Psychology;

and Introduction to Personality. The student gains a new and integrated insight into the meaning of "being cultured," perhaps in the sense of the "Renaissance man." These courses are part of the regular curriculum and are intended to be not so much chores as intellectual adventures.

At the end of their stay in Calasanctius, the students participate in a comprehensive colloquium on their understanding of the complexity and adventure of the ideas underlying human culture. It is clear that this program is demanding, but capable students with proper motivation are able to cope and respond to the challenge.

Finally, in evaluating our students we assess actual knowledge in an area, not time spent in a course.

The school has always tried to develop and test experimental programs. Some examples include: the enrichment program for ages four through eight, on Saturdays during the spring and fall, and daily in July; the three-year high school sequence for students admitted after the eighth grade; the admission of "special" students who indicate talents in fields such as music, art, and so forth; the enrollment of post-graduate students. Today, these are integral parts of the curriculum; some other ideas that were tested were abandoned.

EXPANDING THE PROGRAM

The program was extended to include younger children, ages five through nine, in 1972. An enrichment program for talented four- through eight-year-olds was already in operation and a number of applicants had been evaluated. About half of the four- and five-year-olds were already reading, some even on the third, fourth, and fifth grade levels. Parents were concerned that if these children attended regular school their high level of reading skill and intellectual curiosity could become more a liability than an asset.

In developing this section of the school, three psychologically well-founded theories were combined: (a) the Piagetian developmental sequences were followed in many respects, (b) the Jungian archtypical approach was used with regard to content, and (c) the riches of the children's eidetic imagery were to be respected. To this was added foreign language teaching, among others the rather unique experiment of teaching Japanese.

In further expansion, a Talent Search Program and Galileo Study Center have been organized, aimed at the very talented men and women who dropped out of high school or were turned off in college.

STUDENTS

What kinds of students are able and willing to take this demanding program? In the Buffalo area every year there are about 200 from each age who can meet the IQ qualification of 130. The Wechsler Scales have proved to be an excellent tool for insight into mental functioning. To determine visual creativity and some aspects of perceptual ability, the *Wartegg Picture Completion Test* and a modified draw-a-person test are administered. To this is added a standardized short reading test plus a discussion of topics related to a given text. For those who are able (usually by age seven), a written story of about 200 words entitled "My Ideal" is requested. Immediately after the testing, the results are discussed with the parents and they are informed whether the child is capable of facing the challenge of the program. If the child is of the age to benefit, he is included in the discussion. In borderline cases the parents are informed why it would be better for the child to attend a different school. In a few instances, children are accepted on a trial basis, for example, when the child shows a high level of motivation. In some of these cases, the motivational forces are so strong that the difficulties that might have arisen due to the lower measured mental functioning are overcome. Proper placement is especially important in such cases. Each year, four to five emotionally disturbed but highly talented children are admitted. In looking back to their school histories and later lives, about half not only adjusted well, but blossomed in the not rigid but still patterned environment.

When a student is accepted in the school, he is asked: Why do you want to come to Calasanctius? If he himself is not interested, he is not accepted. Each year the student is asked: Do you want to return? If not, a meeting is arranged with the child and his parents to determine what is best for him. There could be many reasons for a child who was previously enthusiastic about the program to change his mind: peer pressures, a too demanding program, problems faced during physical maturation.

Students are usually retested on the Stanford Binet when they are thirteen to fourteen years of age and again before graduation on the *Wechsler Adult Intelligence Scale* (WAIS) or on the WISC-revised. A student's progress is evaluated against standard norms (various national and state tests), as well as against Calasanctius's own requirements.

FACULTY

The teaching staff is international and represents various religious, philosophical, and ethnic traditions. Due to the fact that the program is extremely complicated and a great number of courses are offered (1957-58, 42; 1967-68, 135; 1975-76, 204), the faculty is assisted by members of the academic community. The Buffalo academic community assists our program, mostly as proctors in the seminar program. Their contribution, very specifically the contribution of the scientific community, is of high value and gives inspiration to the students.

In selecting the faculty, no special certificates are demanded in the education of the gifted, but it is considered very beneficial for a teacher to have a good differential psychology course in his background. A course of this nature offers insight into the problems of giftedness. What a person needs most to teach the gifted are intelligence, excellent imagination, richness of personality, and continuous learning and deepening experiences in his field and related areas. The faculty is not forced to follow one particular method of teaching. Each group or student needs a somewhat different approach; there are many ways to open windows for children's minds. To keep the faculty up-to-date, workshops are conducted every year and individuals are encouraged to visit other schools.

On the whole, the rapport between teachers and students in Calasanctius is very relaxed and friendly. The faculty actively participates with the students, especially on field trips, when they act as supervisors and bus drivers. This creates a lively community of students and teachers.

PHYSICAL ENVIRONMENT

The original philosophy was to create a home-library-laboratory atmosphere in an appropriate location. The campus presently consists of seven buildings, six of which are converted private mansions, while the seventh is a new building containing additional class-rooms, the dining hall, library (18,000 books and 80 journals), and gymnasium. There are no signs to indicate that this complex is a school. The grounds are flowery in the spring, with plants from the school's own greenhouse. In the internal spaces the beauty of human art is emphasized. Various classrooms are decorated with repro-ductions of ancient, modern, and original art. The library is be-coming a collection place for exhibition of Buffalo-based artists and for the best work of the students. In the philosophy of the school, the beauty of the environment, which includes the dining hall (not a cafeteria), is a great educational force in developing the student's sensitivity toward the appreciation of the beautiful.

FINANCES

Practically no tax funds are presently available for the educa-tion of the gifted in independent schools. Thus, the school relies on three resources: tuition and fees, donations, and contributed ser-vices. In 1957-58, the tuition was $660; in 1976-77, tuition ranged from $2000 to $2250. This causes serious problems since the student body is not rich. Most come from middle- and lower-middle in-come families, and some are even on welfare. On the other hand, many interested people and local foundations have become involved in the school. Donations to the development fund have been in excess of $500,000. To this are added the donations received through a variety of fund raising activities.

Outcomes

The Calasanctius experience—was it worthwhile? It was and is an exciting, worthwhile experience. To meet with and teach so many bright young people, to see their lives unfolding, their prob-lems, their growth, even to see some going a rather confused way in life, yet in all cases, building at least somewhat on the experience gained through the program—this is the greatest reward. Through the school, the public has become more aware of the gifted and talented child. In that sense, Calasanctius was truly a pioneer school in western New York.

In 1976, in honor of the Twentieth Anniversary, "Calasanctius Day" was proclaimed in Buffalo and Erie County to honor the school as one of the few in the United States solely devoted to teaching the gifted child and a school that has contributed greatly to the educational and cultural life of Buffalo and western New York.

Ongoing psychological research has been conducted regarding such topics as changes in IQ, the correlations between talent, leadership, and responsibility, the emotional problems of gifted children, and so forth. Alumni will participate in a planned publication titled, "Talent-Elite-Leadership-Responsibility."

The school was the breeding ground for the western New York and central Canada-based Foundation for the Education of the Academically Talented, which, in cooperation with the school and other educational agencies, sponsored workshops regarding the educational problems of the gifted and talented.

One of the most important achievements of the school was that a good number of children from middle- and lower-income families and from disadvantaged ethnic groups grew out from their environmental restrictions, were motivated to select the best colleges, and eventually found a place where they could be productive for the whole society. Of the Calasanctius graduates, 90 percent work outside the Buffalo area, in the national or international community.

The school has demonstrated very clearly that a pluralistic (multiethnic, religious, cultural) community is possible and works well. Yet, the real recognition afforded the school and its founder is in the contribution our students make to society. It is in this sense that the Calasanctius experience contributed to the "aristocracy of merit and talent" and to the "democracy of opportunity" as seen by Thomas Jefferson and the great founding fathers of the American republic.

The impression should not be gained that the Calasanctius program is so unique that it would be irrelevant in other schools for gifted or average students, although to copy the school exactly would be practically impossible. Any institution is unique, if the psychological and sociological backgrounds of its founders and collaborators are considered. There are, however, many features of the school that can be used very well for gifted students in other schools, and there are many others that can be utilized in general education.

CHAPTER VIII

Early Identification and Intervention

HALBERT B. ROBINSON, WENDY C. ROEDELL, AND
NANCY E. JACKSON

The information and ideas presented in this chapter have been generated in the context of the Seattle Project—a longitudinal study of intellectually advanced children undertaken by the Child Development Research Group at the University of Washington. Service activities connected with the study include a preschool program for some of the project children and a counseling and diagnostic service which provides families of intellectually advanced children with assessment and information on school placement.

The strategy followed in the longitudinal study is to identify very young children through age five who demonstrate extraordinary intellectual superiority and to monitor the development of each child's individual pattern of abilities. In brief, children are selected whose development as measured by standard indices of overall intelligence, spatial reasoning, reading skill, mathematics skill, and/or memory has proceeded at twice the average rate. The study also includes children whose documented abilities are less advanced, but whose behaviors indicate they might be "at risk" for the development of extraordinary intellectual abilities.

The effects of early educational intervention on the development of intellectually advanced children are monitored in a preschool program accommodating thirty-five children. The preschool program attempts to provide an optimal match between educational programming and each child's level of competence in various subject areas, and to nurture each child's intellectual, social, emotional, and physical growth in a supportive atmosphere.

The Importance of Early Identification

Some might argue that there is no practical reason to expend time and effort in identifying children who demonstrate advanced intellectual abilities at an early age. The continuing study of Terman and his colleagues (see chapter 5 in this volume) is often cited as evidence that bright children have few significant problems in growing up. This monumental longitudinal study has suggested that superior intelligence, defined during childhood by performance on a standard intelligence test, is associated with a high degree of academic and professional success, and with a degree of personal and social adjustment which is equal to or better than that of the population at large. A number of smaller scale studies[1] have tended to confirm Terman's findings with, as Getzels and Dillon have noted, "a regularity bordering on redundancy."[2]

There are some questions, however, about the applicability of Terman's findings to the full range of children who might reasonably be defined as gifted.[3] There is, also, a considerable body of evidence indicating that intellectually advanced children do not develop equally well under all circumstances. This may be particularly true for those who are extraordinarily gifted. In a case study report of children with IQs above 180, Hollingworth has provided convincing evidence that not all extraordinarily bright children do well in life.[4] Other case studies report similar findings.[5]

1. Walter Barbe, "A Study of Family Background of the Gifted," *Journal of Educational Psychology* 47 (1956): 302-9; Hunter M. Breland, "Birth Order, Family Configuration and Verbal Achievement," *Child Development* 45 (1974): 1011-19; Norma J. Groth, "Mothers of Gifted," *Gifted Child Quarterly* 19 (1975): 217-22; Elizabeth M. Hitchfield, *In Search of Promise* (London: Longman, 1973); Donald Kincaid, "A Study of Highly Gifted Elementary Pupils," *Gifted Child Quarterly* 13 (1969): 264-67; Paul M. Sheldon, "The Families of Highly Gifted Children," *Marriage and Family Living* 16 (1954): 59-60, 67.

2. Jacob W. Getzels and J. T. Dillon, "The Nature of Giftedness and the Education of the Gifted Child," in *Second Handbook of Research on Teaching*, ed. Robert M. W. Travers (Chicago: Rand McNally, 1973), p. 694.

3. Herbert F. Hughes and Harold D. Converse, "Characteristics of the Gifted: A Case for a Sequel to Terman's Study," *Exceptional Children* 29 (1962): 179-83.

4. Leta S. Hollingworth, *Children above 180 IQ Stanford-Binet: Origin and Development* (Yonkers-on-Hudson, N.Y.: World Book Co., 1942).

5. Harold McCurdy, "The Childhood Pattern of Genius," *Journal of the Elisha Mitchell Scientific Society* 73 (1957): 448-62.

Hollingworth noted that the earlier very superior children are identified, the more favorable is their development.

Early identification and special educational programming have been implicated in the successful careers of remarkably gifted people such as John Locke and Francis Bacon, whose lives have been studied retrospectively by Cox, McCurdy, and others.[6] Almost all of these persons were recognized by their families as exceptional, were carefully nurtured within the family, and were given a high degree of adult attention. Many of them were educated entirely within the family setting, at least until entrance into a university. Pressey notes that children who became extraordinary geniuses as adults tended to have been identified very early and "had excellent early opportunities . . . to develop. . . . [They] had the opportunity frequently and continuingly to practice and extend their special ability. . . . [They] had the stimulation of many . . . increasingly strong success experiences—and [their] world acclaimed these successes."[7]

It is reasonable to hypothesize, then, that early identification of children with exceptional abilities is important. How, though, can we assure that such children are actually identified and helped? Several studies have reported that kindergarten teachers are woefully inaccurate in recognizing those children whose intellectual talents can be confirmed with intelligence tests.[8] This inaccuracy is particularly disturbing since there is further evidence to suggest that truly superior children who are perceived by their teachers to have only average intelligence decline in intelligence and achievement test performance relative to equally superior children whose abilities are recognized by their teachers.[9] Children who are iden-

6. Catherine M. Cox, *Genetic Studies of Genius*, vol. 2, *The Early Mental Traits of Three Hundred Geniuses* (Stanford, Calif.: Stanford University Press, 1926); McCurdy, "The Childhood Pattern of Genius."

7. Sidney L. Pressey, "Concerning the Nature and Nurture of Genius," *Scientific Monthly* 81 (1955): 124.

8. Jon C. Jacobs, "Effectiveness of Teacher and Parent Identification of Gifted Children as a Function of School Level," *Psychology in the Schools* 8 (1971): 140-42; Judith S. Ryan, "Early Identification of Intellectually Superior Black Children" (Doct. diss., Univerity of Michigan, 1975).

9. Ann Sutherland and Marcel L. Goldschmid, "Negative Teacher Expectation and Change in Children with Superior Intellectual Potential," *Child Development* 45 (1974): 852-56.

tified as gifted and placed in special programs tend to achieve better. In one study, gifted first-grade students who had been placed in special programs were compared with equally gifted pupils who remained in regular classes. The children in special programs gained an average of two academic years during a single nine-month period, while the gifted children in regular classes gained only the usual one year.[10] Similarly, bright children who have been allowed to enter first grade early learn more during their first year of school than equally bright children who have remained in kindergarten.[11] Superior abilities that are not nurtured will not develop, and the resulting waste is inestimable.

The reasons for identifying intellectually advanced children at an early age are, therefore, eminently practical. Early identification creates the opportunity for early intervention. The parent who is aware of a child's special abilities can plan intelligently for appropriate, challenging educational experiences. The educator who has direct information about a child's advanced abilities can develop programs geared to the child's actual level of competence rather than to a level calibrated on the basis of chronological age alone. Since intellectually advanced children have skills beyond those usual for their age, their educational needs are different—in some instances, radically different—from the needs of their same-age peers. The earlier these needs are identified, the sooner educational programs can be tailored to fit them.

Characteristics of Intellectually Advanced Children

Most of the studies which provide data about gifted children have relied for their operational definition of superior intelligence on a single test score weighted in favor of verbal and abstract reasoning abilities.[12] This approach to the assessment of intelligence

10. Ruth A. Martinson, *Educational Programs for Gifted Pupils* (Sacramento, Calif.: California State Department of Education, 1961), cited in Sidney P. Marland, Jr., *Education of the Gifted and Talented*, Report to the Congress of the United States by the U.S. Commissioner of Education (Washington, D.C.: U.S. Government Printing Office, 1972), p. 105.

11. School Board of Broward County, Florida, "A Study of Early Entry into First Grade, 1973-74" (Fort Lauderdale, Fla.: School Board of Broward County, 1974). ERIC ED 122 929.

12. Getzels and Dillon, "The Nature of Giftedness and the Education of the Gifted Child."

still has both theoretical and practical worth. There are limits, however, to the usefulness of a single test score in estimating a child's intellectual abilities.

Certainly, any screening system that identifies children for educational programming will be more successful if it measures intellectual abilities germane to the program than if it taps irrelevant abilities. It makes little sense to identify a group of children with high scores on a test of vocabulary in order to provide them with a special program in science and mathematics. In addition, differential patterns of mental abilities and skills may reflect individual differences in children's problem-solving styles, which may in turn have direct relevance for curriculum planning and teaching strategies.

Many educators have emphasized that gifted children form a heterogeneous population. Individual case studies also dramatize this point.[13] Even when a population of gifted children is defined by an IQ cutoff score, a variety of abilities may be represented. It has long been established that children of varying ages and/or intellectual levels can achieve the same score on a general intelligence test with very different profiles of specific abilities.[14] It is also probable that different children may solve the same problems, and therefore receive identical credit, by utilizing quite different cognitive strategies.[15]

The matter of organization of cognitive abilities in young children is of considerable current interest and controversy. A popular view is that "growth during the developmental period proceeds

13. Barbara B. Hauck and Maurice F. Freehill, *The Gifted: Case Studies* (Dubuque, Iowa: William C. Brown, 1972).

14. Thomas M. Achenbach, "Comparison of Stanford-Binet Performance of Nonretarded and Retarded Persons Matched for MA and Sex," *American Journal of Mental Deficiency* 74 (1970): 488-94; Quinn McNemar, *The Revision of the Stanford-Binet Scale* (Boston: Houghton Mifflin, 1942); Clare W. Thompson and Ann Magaret, "Differential Test Responses of Normals and Mental Defectives," *Journal of Abnormal and Social Psychology* 42 (1947): 284-93; David Wechsler, *The Measurement and Appraisal of Adult Intelligence*, 4th ed. (Baltimore: William and Wilkins, 1958).

15. Barbel Inhelder, *The Diagnosis of Reasoning in the Mentally Retarded*, 2d ed., trans. Will B. Stephens (New York: Chandler, 1968); Robert B. McCall, Pamela S. Hogarty, and Nancy Hurlburt, "Transitions in Sensorimotor Development and the Prediction of Childhood IQ," *American Psychologist* 27 (1972): 728-48.

from a relatively unitary system to one with independent parts,"[16] that is, that progressive differentiation occurs during prenatal, infant, and early childhood growth. Several investigators, however, have been able to uncover separable cognitive dimensions in the test performance of very young children.[17] The distinctiveness of these components and their precise relationship to the factors appearing later in life are unclear. It is possible that such factors may be more easily distinguished in young children who are extremely advanced in particular areas of cognitive functioning. If intellectually advanced children are precocious not only in overall rate of development but also in the differentiation of their abilities, the planning of educational programs may have to be adapted to consider variations in talents and learning styles appearing at very early ages.

The heterogeneity among intellectually advanced children is even more evident, of course, when one considers nonintellectual attributes. While some studies have reported that the average levels of personal and social adjustment, physical health, and the like are slightly higher for gifted children than for the population as a whole, the mean differences favoring the gifted group tend to be small and sometimes disappear when the comparison group is appropriately matched for variables such as social class.[18] Much more

16. William R. Thompson and Joan Grusec, "Studies of Early Experience," in *Carmichael's Manual of Child Psychology*, vol. 1, ed. Paul H. Mussen (New York: Wiley, 1970), pp. 565-654.

17. John G. Hurst, "A Factor Analysis of the Merrill-Palmer with Reference to Theory and Test Construction," *Educational and Psychological Measurement* 20 (1960): 219-532; McCall, Hogarty, and Hurlburt, "Transitions in Sensorimotor Development and the Prediction of Childhood IQ"; C. Edward Meyers et al., *Primary Abilities at Mental Age Six, Monographs of the Society for Research in Child Development*, vol. 27, no. 1, (1962); C. Edward Meyers et al., *Four Ability-Factor Hypotheses at Three Preliterate Levels in Normal and Retarded Children, Monographs of the Society for Research in Child Development*, vol. 29, no. 5 (1964); Sister Rose Amata McCartin and C. Edward Meyers, "An Exploration of Six Semantic Factors at First Grade," *Multivariate Behavioral Research* 1 (1966): 74-94; Leland H. Stott and Rachel S. Ball, *Infant and Preschool Mental Tests: Review and Evaluation, Monographs of the Society for Research in Child Development*, vol. 30, no. 3 (1965).

18. K. Lovell and J. B. Shields, "Some Aspects of a Study of the Gifted Child," *British Journal of Educational Psychology* 37 (1967): 201-8; Melita Oden, "The Fulfillment of Promise: Forty-year Follow-up of the Terman Gifted Group," *Genetic Psychology Monographs* 77 (1968): 3-93; Lewis M.

striking than the mean differences is the variability within any gifted group. In fact, intellectually advanced children are about as heterogeneous as any other population on measures other than those directly related to the instruments used to identify them. Statements such as "gifted children are typically larger, healthier, and more socially mature than other children their age" are more misleading than they are helpful.

The heterogeneity of this population in both intellectual and nonintellectual domains has been consistently evident among the children involved in the Seattle project. Young children have been identified who are able to perform extraordinary intellectual feats but who do not necessarily score in the highest ranges on tests of general intelligence. A substantial group of children have been located, for example, who at the age of two or three years were reading at the second-grade level or above. The IQs of these children have ranged from scores in the 120s to above the scale limits as measured by the *Stanford-Binet Intelligence Scale*. One child at the age of three enjoyed drawing detailed and accurate maps of his surroundings, and could copy geometric block designs and trace paths through pencil mazes as quickly and precisely as the average eight-year-old, yet his Stanford-Binet IQ at the time of these accomplishments was a modest 132.

Teachers' impressions of the social abilities of the intellectually advanced children in the preschool of the Seattle project have been collected via the *California Preschool Social Competency* rating scale. In social ability, as in specific intellectual abilities, heterogeneity is the rule. Teacher ratings for intellectually advanced children attending the preschool program have yielded percentile ranks ranging from the 21st percentile to the 98th percentile.

This evidence calls into serious question a prevailing conception of giftedness that might be labeled the "myth of the gifted child."

Terman et al., *Genetic Studies of Genius*, vol. 1, *Mental and Physical Traits of a Thousand Gifted Children* (Stanford, Calif.: Stanford University Press, 1925); Lewis M. Terman and Melita Oden, *Genetic Studies of Genius*, vol. 4, *The Gifted Child Grows Up: Twenty-five Years' Follow-up of a Superior Group* (Stanford, Calif.: Stanford University Press, 1947); idem., *Genetic Studies of Genius*, vol. 5, *The Gifted Group at Mid-life: Thirty-five Years' Follow-up of the Superior Child* (Stanford, Calif.: Stanford University Press, 1959).

According to this viewpoint, certain individuals possess a general superiority in intellectual potential. This superiority is most reliably indicated by a high IQ. Many theorists, research people, and practitioners have argued that it can also be inferred on the basis of behaviors such as superior leadership, creative talent, and so forth. These diverse talents, while valued in themselves, have also become accepted indices of the "syndrome" entity of giftedness.[19]

There is, however, no such thing as a "typical gifted child." Rather, there are many individual children who demonstrate a variety of surprising skills in both intellective and nonintellective domains. Many two- and three-year-old children can do things one would not normally expect—they can read, they are proficient at arithmetic, they can speak several languages, they can use maps, and so forth. Typically, however, children do not do all of these amazing things equally well, and they differ from one another in personality and style of functioning.

Methods of Identification

There are several points to consider when designing a system for the identification of children of preschool age with advanced intellectual abilities. First, the identification system must include opportunities for children who have extremely advanced abilities to display those skills. Bright children may perform like average children unless they are presented with sufficiently challenging material. Thus, many of the "readiness" tests used to identify children who are not adequately prepared for the typical kindergarten or first-grade program are wholly inadequate for identifying preschool children with advanced abilities. These tests simply do not provide any opportunity for intellectually advanced children to show the extent of what they can do.

Second, an identification system must allow for the inconsistency that often characterizes the performance of young children. If a testing session includes a broad range of tasks, it is more likely that some of the items will both capture the child's interest and elicit the best performance of which the child is capable. A useful

19. Pennsylvania Department of Public Instruction, *Mentally Gifted Children and Youth: A Guide for Parents* (Harrisburg, Pa.: Bureau of Special and Compensatory Education, Pennsylvania Department of Public Instruction, 1973).

maxim is to look for evidence of what the child *can* do, and not be discouraged by what the child cannot, or will not, do.

Finally, experience in the Seattle project has provided ample evidence that even the most comprehensive battery of tests, administered by the most skillful of testers, may not provide a good estimate of a young child's capabilities. For this reason, any identification system should include a detailed parents' report of a child's abilities in addition to the sample of behavior that is collected in a test session.

IDENTIFICATION BY TEST PERFORMANCE

The test battery used to select children for the preschool program in the Seattle project samples a broad spectrum of intellectual and academic skills. Each component of the test battery presents a separate opportunity for children to display the best, most advanced performance of which they are capable. If a child does perform exceptionally well on a test, there can be little doubt about the child's advanced ability. If, however, the child does not score at an advanced level, we do not assume that lack of ability is the problem. Young children's test scores are often depressed by the child's nervousness at being closeted in a strange room with an unfamiliar examiner. Many two- and three-year-olds are more interested in playing their own games with the test materials or conversing with the tester than in solving the particular problems presented by the tests. In evaluating a testing session, one should look for the areas of the child's best performance. Data from the Seattle project suggest that these scores may provide the best information about the child's capabilities. Our identification system does not, then, require that children score consistently at high levels on all test items.

As of 1978, the test battery included the short-form (starred items only) *Stanford-Binet Intelligence Scale*; the Block Design, Mazes, and Arithmetic Subtests of the *Wechsler Preschool and Primary Scale of Intelligence* (WPPSI); the Numerical Memory subtest from the *McCarthy Scales of Children's Abilities*; and a brief, informal test of reading. This battery gives estimates of the child's general reasoning ability, spatial-perceptual reasoning ability, arithmetic skill, short-term memory, and reading skill. When a child performs unusually well on the Block Design, Mazes, and/ or Arithmetic subtests of the WPPSI, the tester continues into the parallel subtests from the more advanced *Wechsler Intelligence Scale for Children—Revised* (WISC-R). Such flexibility can be very important, for preschool and kindergarten-aged children can score at norms for fifteen- or sixteen-year-olds on the Block Design and Mazes subtests.

This test battery is far from perfect, but it does test the limits of a child's abilities in a broad range of intellectual and academic areas within a single testing session that usually lasts less than one hour. To date, the battery has worked somewhat more effectively with children who are four years old or older than with younger children.

Whenever there is an opportunity for more extensive testing of young children's academic skills, the *Peabody Individual Achievement Test* (PIAT) is administered. This test is easy to give to very young, bright children; many of the children with whom we work score at advanced levels on all areas. Virtually all of our three-year-olds have had reading and mathematics skills at the kindergarten level by the time they have completed a year in the preschool program; reading scores at the fourth-, fifth-, or sixth-grade level have not been uncommon.

Our test battery has been developed to identify children with a diverse array of advanced intellectual and academic skills. An identification program should be tailored to the program it serves. A different test battery might well be more appropriate for a different type of program.

IDENTIFICATION BY PARENT INFORMATION

A single test session provides a limited sample of a child's behavior, which may or may not include some indication of the child's best possible performance. Parents, on the other hand, have an opportunity to observe their child's behavior under a wide variety of conditions. The use of parents' reports as a major source of information is an obvious practical alternative for any project involving intellectually advanced children of preschool-age. Moreover, there is evidence from previous research that parents are reasonably accurate in estimating their children's intellectual abilities—sometimes better, in fact, than kindergarten teachers assigned the same task.[20] Parents' reports can be even more useful if parents are asked to provide examples of their child's actual behaviors rather than to estimate their child's ability level.

The strategy adopted by the Seattle project has been to use questionnaire and interview formats to obtain information from parents about specific child behaviors chosen from psychometric and theoretical research literature. Theoretical domains of intellectual ability have been translated into particular behaviors that a child might naturally perform at home and that might be easily observed by parents. Parents' responses to questions about their child's current interests and accomplishments have provided a moderately good prediction of how well the child will perform during a testing session. On the other hand, parents' responses to retrospective questions about the age at which their child first began talking or achieved other developmental milestones do not predict test performance and appear to be unrelated to any other measure of the child's current abilities.

While parents' objective responses to specific questions about a child's behavior have provided useful information, equally good prediction of test performance has been obtained from global evaluations of the qualitative information provided by parents. Our questionnaires are designed to encourage parents to provide lengthy anecdotal descriptions of their child's behavior. Parents' comments often provide a vivid picture of a child's behavior which could never be gleaned from a series of yes-no responses. The following are just a few examples of the detailed remarks which parents have provided us:

Does your child easily put together puzzles of over twenty pieces in which the pieces are all part of the same picture?
"Yes (at twenty months). At about age two and a half she had mastered a Springbok forty-eight-piece puzzle, The Three Bears, working entirely by the shape of the pieces, not by the picture. When she was given a Calico Cat puzzle cut with the same stamp, she quickly recognized that the shapes were the same, and put it together." (girl, aged four years, two months at time of report)

20. Jacobs, "Effectiveness of Teacher and Parent Identification of Gifted Children as a Function of School Level"; Ryan, "Early Identification of Intellectually Superior Black Children."

Does your child use the word "because" or "cause" even though the child may confuse the meaning of the word?
"Yes. She has been doing this since age three years. For instance, she recently said, 'It is fall, a season of the year, because it is getting ready for winter, because it snows in the winter, because it gets so cold and I wear my heavy coat, because I need to keep warm because I might catch cold. . . .' She frequently talks in paragraphs with all the thoughts connected by 'because.' " (girl, aged three years, five months at time of report)

Does your child recognize and name two-digit numbers?
"Yes, he only starts losing track when numbers get into the ten thousands." (boy, aged five years, two months at time of report)

The information that parents provide in response to a questionnaire can be rated by trained judges to yield an overall estimate of the degree of the child's intellectual precocity. In successive years, independent raters were able to reach substantial agreement in judging the data obtained from parents.

We have been encouraged by several years' evidence that evaluations of children based on information from parents consistently show a positive relationship with the child's performance on tests. Our long-term goal, however, is to use parent information, together with test performance, as a predictor of the child's long-range intellectual development. Parent information is based on more extensive samples of a child's behavior than is information from standardized test sessions. For this reason, parent information may ultimately prove to be a better estimate of a very young child's intellectual competence than a test score based on a possibly suboptimal, and certainly limited, behavior sample. Preliminary findings from our longitudinal follow-up are consistent with this hypothesis. Several of the children who have demonstrated extraordinary test performance at age four earned average test scores at age two. Evaluations of the parent reports obtained when these children were two years of age did, however, predict their later extraordinary test performance.

Goals of Early Intervention

Early intervention programs for intellectually advanced preschool children can serve two general purposes: they can provide guidance and planning aid to parents, and they can provide a supportive educational environment for children.

The counseling and diagnostic service associated with the Seattle project has provided a forum for parents of intellectually advanced children to discuss concerns associated with their children's abilities. A degree of ambivalence is evident in the comments of these parents. They tend to be proud of their child's accomplishments, but are worried about meeting their child's special educational needs, and are frequently uncomfortable about public displays of their child's precocity. A three-year-old who reads the menu in a restaurant can, for example, become the focus of unwanted public attention for the family. Family acquaintances frequently comment that parents must have "pushed" the child into advanced accomplishments. Parents may begin to feel guilty about their child's advanced abilities. Some parents go so far as to attempt to decelerate their child's learning rate by resorting to such measures as hiding advanced schoolbooks. Almost all are concerned that advanced academic abilities will cause difficulty when the child enters public school.

An early intervention program can often confirm for parents that their own estimates of their child's unusual abilities are quite accurate. Parents can be put in contact with families with similar children, and can be assured that intellectual precocity is not the parents' "fault," but is, in fact, a natural occurrence for a good number of children. Early documentation of a child's abilities can also aid parents in planning for their child's education, and may help educators attune school programs to the need for individually tailored programs. Individualization of programs becomes more feasible when information is available that gives a full picture of a child's abilities and interests.

Parents frequently mention that they cannot find enough challenges to keep their intellectually advanced preschoolers occupied at home. A carefully planned educational program can provide supportive nurturance for children's rapidly developing intellectual abilities. Traditionally, preschools have had the general goal of helping children get "ready" for elementary school. Intellectually advanced preschoolers, however, frequently have acquired an impressive array of traditional academic skills before they enter a preschool program. In terms of their intellectual prowess, they have been "ready" for school for a long time.

Most descriptions of educational programs for gifted children assume that these children are somehow "qualitatively different" from other children. In actuality, the behaviors described as qualitatively different are usually behaviors similar to those of children who are older than the child in question. There is currently little, if any, good evidence to support the notion that the thinking of intellectually gifted young children is qualitatively different from the thinking of children who are older than they are. The differences that have been demonstrated seem to be differences in *rate* of intellectual development rather than in *type* of development.

The differences in rate of growth *within* individual children do produce characteristics which are, to say the least, unusual. A three-year-old child who can read at the sixth-grade level but cannot draw a square or a diamond is not an ordinary child; neither is a two-year-old who is not toilet-trained but is learning to multiply and divide. Nonetheless, basic strategies of education do apply to these children.

One of the most widely stated educational truths, agreed upon by educators and psychologists alike, is that the key to successful learning experiences lies in providing an optimal match between the child's skill level and the material presented.[21] The material should be sufficiently difficult to provide a challenge, but not so difficult that the child cannot relate it to previous learning. Providing such an optimal match for intellectually precocious young children requires a good deal of individual planning because of the unevenness of skills development within individual children. Care must be taken to challenge each child's particular intellectual strengths, while allowing opportunity for the development of less advanced skills. The heterogeneity inherent in any group of intellectually advanced students makes individual planning essential.

To the extent that a child's skill levels are widely disparate, existing program strategies must be modified to provide an appro-

---

21. J. McVicker Hunt, *Intelligence and Experience* (New York: Ronald Press, 1961); Nancy E. Jackson, Halbert B. Robinson, and Philip S. Dale, *Cognitive Development in Young Children* (Monterey, Calif.: Brooks/Cole, 1977).

priate match. A three-year-old child who reads at the fifth-grade level, has the attention span of a five-year-old, and has average small motor skills cannot be treated like a small fifth grader. Neither can the child be treated like an ordinary preschooler. Nonetheless, materials designed to enhance the reading skills of fifth graders can be successfully adapted to meet the attention span and motor skill requirements of such a child and at the same time challenge the child's area of intellectual strength. Too frequently, educational programs are designed to teach at the child's weakest level of ability, rather than being adapted to match all levels appropriately. A child who reads but cannot write will be taught to write, and the reading ignored. Just as a successful identification system focuses on each child's areas of best performance, so too a successful educational program encourages each child's strengths at the same time that it provides help for weaker areas.

In the preschool associated with the Seattle project, allowance has been made for unevenness of skill levels within as well as among children. Advanced material usually presented to older children has been adapted for preschool children whose attention span and reading and writing abilities may not equal their grasp of conceptual material. Intellectual content of such materials may remain at an advanced level, but often the activities are changed to include things to touch and manipulate and to provide alternatives to written responses.

Activities are also planned to provide experiences in group discussion and group decision making. Discussion with peers provides a unique forum for testing ideas, a forum that cannot be duplicated in the usual home environment.

In addition to challenging children's intellectual strengths, the program emphasizes the development of large and small motor skills. This area is particularly important for children whose advanced intellectual abilities frequently outstrip their physical development. Three-year-olds who read at the fourth-grade level but cannot hold a pencil cannot take full advantage of many experiences appropriate to their reading level. The preschool therefore provides many opportunities for children to develop small muscle skills and eye-hand coordination.

The program also contains a strong emphasis on the development of social skills. In many cases, the children's intellectual skills have progressed far beyond their level of social maturity, creating what might be called an "intellectual-social gap." People often become angry at children when their social skills fall short of the expectations generated by their general intellectual maturity. This unevenness in skill level can be particularly difficult for young children who must cope either with being more advanced in intellectual ability than many of their same-age peers, or with being the youngest in a group of older children who are their intellectual peers. Such children need a large repertoire of social skills, a strong self-image, and a realistic appraisal of what their particular intellectual advancement means and does not mean.

The most important characteristic of the Seattle project is individual planning related to the particular strengths and weaknesses evident in each child's pattern of abilities. The educator's task is not, as with compensatory programs, to bring children up to a minimum level of performance. Rather, the task is to provide a match of learning experience with competence level in each subject area, and to facilitate the child's progress at his or her own rate. With such a program of systematic nurturance, it may well be possible to transform early precocity in intellectual achievements into adult intellectual excellence.[22]

Directions for Future Research

It seems obvious that the identification and nurturance of exceptional talents should be of the highest priority for our society. Yet, public support for such programs has occurred in sporadic bursts of limited financial, scientific, and philosophical commitment.

Little is known about the long-term implications of various types of intellectual precocity. Would it be possible to identify at an early age those children who might, with proper educational opportunities, become the leading scientists, mathematicians, artists,

22. Wendy C. Roedell and Halbert B. Robinson, *Programming for Intellectually Advanced Preschool Children: A Program Development Guide*, Technical report of the Child Development Research Group (Seattle, Wash.: Child Development Research Group, University of Washington, 1977). ERIC ED 151 094.

poets, and social leaders of the future? Retrospective evidence indicates that most individuals who demonstrated intellectual superiority in adulthood were also precocious in some intellective domain in early childhood. Prospective evidence, however, is not available. Many eminent "gifted" adults taught themselves to read at the early age of two or three. We do not know, though, whether all children who learn to read early have the capacity for remarkable intellectual performance in adulthood. Only careful longitudinal research can answer such questions.

Even less information is available concerning the issue of actual differences in thinking and problem-solving strategies between intellectually advanced children and children with average abilities. At present, we have no evidence that would require us to reject a description of the bright child as being mentally equal to the average older child. Yet for good reasons, the doctrine that the thought processes of gifted children are "qualitatively different" persists. Research focused on a process analysis of the thinking strategies of children with differing intellectual talents is needed to clarify this issue. Such information would be of considerable theoretical as well as practical importance.

CHAPTER IX

Language Arts and Social Studies Curriculum in the Elementary School

SANDRA N. KAPLAN

Although a good deal of information concerning the language arts and social studies curriculum for the gifted is well articulated and readily available in the literature, there is a gap between this information and its application in classroom practice. Several factors contribute to this situation. A recognition of the need to accommodate the gifted often surpasses the educator's understanding of the alternatives that qualify as suitable curricular activities for these students. In addition, the pressure on educators to do something for the gifted causes them to be susceptible and responsive to superficial rather than developmental learning experiences.

Some activities labeled as "superficial" might be justified as relevant to the gifted, but such activities are usually addenda to the content, structure, and/or organization of the total curriculum. They are fragmented learning experiences that can be associated with gimmickry and are used to fill the need for a differentiated curriculum for the gifted. In contrast, developmental activities are those that are integrated into the structure of the content area and are continuously reinforced within the curriculum. These activities are referenced to the characteristics of the gifted and are related to a system or pattern of curriculum development that correlates with preselected goals for educating the gifted. Attention to these factors ultimately determines the construction and/or selection of developmental activities for the language arts and social studies curriculum.

Language Arts

A language arts curriculum for gifted students requires defining the purpose and scope of the language arts as a subject area, estab-

155

lishing perimeters and expectations appropriately matched to the characteristics of the gifted, and adapting a philosophical or theoretical structure that supports the content, processes, and products or outcomes to be derived from the above decisions.

Moffett uses communication concepts to define the language arts as a set of receptive (reading and writing) and expressive or productive (speaking and listening) experiences. Within this framework, receptive and expressive or productive experiences are interrelated and the language arts curriculum becomes the "place where all forms and contents can be learned in relation to each other: the functional and actual side by side, comprehension and composition as reverses of each other, spoken and written speech interplaying and language competing with and complementing other media."[1] Although this definition and description of language arts is applicable to all types of learners, Ward's proposition, "that the nature of language, its structures and functions, its integral relationship to thought and behavior should be part of the education of the intellectually superior child and youth,"[2] relates Moffett's concept of the language arts to the gifted. Selecting experiences that provide this type of language arts curriculum is one of the crucial challenges confronting educators responsible for the gifted.

The language arts curriculum should include specific content related to literature and composition, and skills related to usage and comprehension. The common or unifying element for each activity should be the understanding of the meaning and uses of language so that it is perceived, as Ward describes it, "as an art and science of communication." Three experiential processes can be used within a single curricular structure to achieve a comprehensive curriculum. "Exposure" is defined as an introduction to what is to be learned and can be exemplified by the various communication modes in literary, structural, and behavioral forms. "Analysis" is exemplified by such activities as dissecting characterization through verbal and nonverbal clues in a drama and determining the impli-

1. James Moffett and Betty Jane Wagner, *Student Centered Language Arts and Reading* (Boston: Houghton Mifflin, 1976), p. 16.

2. Virgil S. Ward, *Educating the Gifted: An Axiomatic Approach* (Columbus, Ohio: Charles E. Merrill, 1961), p. 165.

cations of words in a selected passage. "Expression" is the "doing" part of the language arts learning experience. It is the presentation of messages and information by new and personalized techniques. Therefore, a unit on "Epistemology of Words" would include opportunities for receiving knowledge about words (exposure), opportunities for determining the purpose and impact of words on senders and receivers (analysis), and provisions for applying acquired understandings in the culmination of a different type of communication (expression).

Neither the introduction of content beyond the regular curriculum nor the extension of the curriculum beyond the prescribed age-grade curriculum will automatically designate these modifications as appropriate for the gifted. The relevance of curricular experiences for the gifted is contingent upon more than newness, uniqueness, or difficulty. Within a unit on "Science Fiction," for example, the activity that requires the gifted student to rewrite a selected science fiction story for the pre- and post-Sputnik era is quite different from the activity that requires the gifted student to read a more difficult selection from this literary form. The first activity differentiates the content (exposure), skills (analysis), and product (expression) in relationship to the purpose and scope of language arts as a subject area, while simultaneously attending to generally accepted goals or aims of gifted educations, such as developing and applying generalizations and practicing divergent thinking. Too often an adjustment in the content area is considered as the sole criterion for making the curriculum area appropriate for the gifted. To develop a language arts curriculum effectively, both the elements that specify the content area for the gifted and the underlying goals of gifted education must be considered in concert.

Content and skills to be learned and goals to be achieved as a result of experiences in the language arts constitute only one set of factors to be included in the development of the curriculum. A philosophical structure that serves to formalize the content, skills, and goals into a structured whole is needed. Goodlad has proposed that an "organizing center" can become the "catch-hold point" for advancing content and for mental operations within that content. The concept of the organizing center could be used effectively in developing a comprehensive language arts program for the gifted. According to Goodlad, an organizing center has the following characteristics: it contributes to the simultaneous attainment of several objectives; it encompasses ability floors and ceilings of the groups; it builds on what has gone before and prepares for what is to come; it permits inclusion of several ideas and points for differing student interest; and it has capacity for intellectual, social, geographic, and chronological movement.[3]

The utilization of major themes, for example, as a basis of an organizing center allows for delineation of receptive and expressive language arts activities within a single framework. Themes should be broad enough to include past, present, and future concepts and generalizations that are related to a cluster of content and skill areas and a set of goals for the gifted. Examples of such themes might be titled: "Style: A Mirror of Thoughts," "Yeas and Boos Expressed in Biographical Sketches." Another consideration in selecting receptive and expressive experiences within a curricular theme is the introduction of new materials, such as brochures and pamphlets, and the outgrowth of new products, such as abstracts and proposals, that expose gifted students to a variety of sources of input and output.

The use of organizing centers is one way to insure that language arts experiences are treated as an integral part of all learning experiences rather than as a separate subject. When language arts skills and content are treated as an isolated rather than an integrated subject, the gifted are placed at a disadvantage. Problems of integration and transfer are manifested when a gifted student demonstrates superior ability to use a skill such as locating a main idea in an advanced reading assignment, but is unable to use exactly the same skill in another context for a different purpose, such as determining the main idea of a debate. Questions concerning the student's giftedness and the appropriateness of the language arts curriculum for the gifted sometimes stem directly from the need to integrate and transfer language arts learnings within the subject area and to other subject areas. Thus, the content and skills of lan-

3. John I. Goodlad, "The Teacher Selects, Plans, Organizes" in *Learning and the Teacher*, Yearbook of the Association for Supervision and Curriculum Development (Washington, D.C.: National Education Association, 1959), pp. 55-58.

guage arts should be introduced and practiced as they relate to other subject areas for different purposes and varied times. Gold describes activities in the language arts as fundamentally important to gifted students because "they represent both a means to achieve in other areas and an area for accomplishment in themselves."[4] (See table 1).

TABLE 1.

EXAMPLES OF INTEGRATING WRITING WITH VARIOUS CONTENT AREAS

Types of Writing	Mathematics	Social Studies	Science	Art
Responsive writing	Speech about a class-determined mathematical problem	Letters requesting information	Editorial about a specific need or problem	Poetry evoked from something observed
Descriptive writing	Dictionary of terms	Lyrics for song about a historic event	News article about a discovery	Advertisement for an "opening"
Technical writing	Directions to perform an operation	Interview with an individual	Labels for a display	Recipe for a process
Reflective writing	Diary of a number: "The Life of a Million"	Memoirs of a famous individual	Journal article about a scientific discovery	Monologue of an artist about his or her works

Organizing centers can also be employed in the development of a language arts curriculum for the gifted in order to prevent emphasizing language arts activities in one direction to the neglect and/or exclusion of other directions. In addition, the use of organizing centers can prevent the curriculum from becoming a series of disjointed experiences or activities. For example, one feature that has traditionally differentiated the language arts curriculum for the gifted has been creative writing. An overemphasis on creative writing constricts the potential development of creativity in other areas of the language arts program. It also restricts the definition of language arts and thus excludes the other areas that comprise this subject area. Many factors have contributed to the adop-

4. Milton J. Gold, *Education of the Intellectually Gifted* (Columbus, Ohio: Charles E. Merrill, 1965), p. 236.

tion of creative writing as the sole identifier of the language arts program for the gifted. Among these are the continuous references in the literature to creativity both as a correlate of giftedness and as a requirement for academic success. The plethora of instructional materials to promote creative writing makes it easier for the teacher to include it as part of the language arts curriculum. Written products are often more valued because they are easier to schedule and validate. Creativity should be developed, however, as a process to be generalized to all areas encompassed within the language arts curriculum. Creative thinking processes, such as hypothesizing, substituting, combining, and redesigning, can elicit creativity in all forms of reading, listening, speaking, and writing (see table 2).

TABLE 2.

EXAMPLES OF APPLYING CREATIVITY TO LANGUAGE ARTS AREAS

LANGUAGE ARTS AREAS	LANGUAGE ARTS CONCEPTS OR SKILLS	CREATIVE PROCESS	ACTIVITY RELATED TO ANY CONTENT AREA
Writing	Developing or extending vocabulary	Substitute	After writing a story substitute new words to: –say the same thing in a different way –emphasize a different idea within the context –change the message
Reading	Determining main idea	Symbolize	After reading a passage, develop a formula, equation of recipe to exemplify the main idea
Speaking	Using precise language to communicate a message	Reorganize	After writing a speech, reorganize it to make it appropriate for delivery to different audiences, such as the Geriatric Society, College Professors, and Teens Club
Listening	Discriminating the purpose of a communication	Minimize and maximize	After listening to a report, write or tell the effect of the communication if an idea was minimized rather than maximized, and conversely the effect of maximizing an idea that was minimized.

While a curriculum stressing creativity is often regarded as *the* language arts curriculum for the gifted, little attention is paid to reading as an element of that curriculum. With a large vocabulary, advanced reading ability, and interests that are multiple and varied, the gifted student is usually expected to proceed in reading without a need for activities that further strengthen the creative skills of reading. Restructuring the language arts program around the reading of various literary forms and requiring the practice of various advanced skills do not suffice as *the* language arts curriculum for the gifted any more than does creative writing. Witty discusses creative reading as "the highest and most neglected aspect of reading," and quotes Torrance's description of creative reading as the ability "to understand the reasons behind discrepant accounts and to reach sound conclusions about what is true."[5] The integration of reading with writing and the inclusion of activities that generalize such thinking processes as are involved in creativity combine to identify a language arts curriculum for the gifted.

Creative thinking skills are not the only thinking processes that the language arts curriculum should introduce, reinforce, or extend. Because language is the medium for thought and because the acquisition of thinking skills is a major area of emphasis for the gifted, the language arts curriculum should stress the attainment of thinking skills as tools for learning and as reciprocal and inseparable units. Sprinkling problem solving or some higher-level thinking process, such as divergent thinking, into the existing language arts curriculum is not a sufficient method of differentiating the curriculum for the gifted. Frequently, higher-level thinking processes are added to the curriculum without coordinating those processes with concepts or generalizations that adequately activate them or make them meaningful experiences for the learner. The selection and coupling of thinking processes with the content should be based on theoretical constructs that lead to the development of thinking as a usable skill and not simply as a game strategy, as often occurs in programs for the gifted. For instance, redesigning

5. Paul A. Witty, "Rationale for Fostering Creative Reading in the Gifted and the Talented," in *Creative Reading for Gifted Learners: A Design for Excellence*, ed. Michael Labuda (Newark, Del., International Reading Association, 1974), pp. 15, 21.

the story of Cinderella into a biography can be a credible activity for the gifted under the following conditions: (a) if the skill of redesigning is taught as one element of creative thinking; (b) if the student understands the value and validity of the skill being practiced; (c) if the purpose for which the skill is applied has relevance for the content; and (d) if the student is able to transfer the skill to other academic and personal experiences.

The very characteristics that distinguish the gifted from other learners and should determine the scope and sequence of the language arts often act as deterrents to the type of experiences with which gifted learners are presented and the degree of progress they achieve within this curriculum area. Language arts experiences and expectations for the gifted, however, are sometimes related to characteristics of giftedness as if those characteristics were absolute, constant, and possessed only by gifted persons. Consequently, curriculum experiences and expectations of performance are tailored to a stereotypical description of giftedness rather than to an analysis of the entry skills, abilities, and interests of the individual gifted student. For example, the trait of a "keen power of observation" should not be automatically equated with a gifted child's inherent ability for descriptive speech or writing. Or, the characteristic of a "liking for structure and order" should not be automatically equated with the gifted child's inherent ability to produce precise and grammatically correct written or verbal products.

Lack of understanding of the specific behaviors that exemplify the general characteristics of the gifted, and a misunderstanding of the difference between a propensity for and the actual manifestation of an ability in a given area of the curriculum, have led to some problems in structuring and implementing a language arts curriculum for the gifted. The characteristics used to identify the gifted students for whom the language arts curriculum is to be used must also serve as a benchmark for decisions made regarding the content, processes, and products that will be included within the curriculum design. If, for example, the referent for identifying giftedness has been "fluency in speaking," then activities that extend or reinforce this characteristic must be considered. The construction of a curriculum based on the educator's preconceived idea of the gifted should give way to the construction of a curriculum that centers on the collection of specific behaviors actually possessed by the gifted population to be served by this curriculum.

Social Studies

The social studies curriculum includes the skills, facts, concepts, and generalizations in the following subject areas dealing with the study of human beings: institutions created by man, interactions between people, and man's relationship to his environment.[6] Because the social studies are comprised of a variety of content areas, they reinforce the interrelationships of information and allow for the practicing of multiple and diverse methods of learning and thinking. For this reason, it is a curricular area appropriate to extend and/or enhance the unique differences that characterize the gifted as a group of learners and to accommodate the unique differences among individual gifted learners. Thus the problem of creating a social studies curriculum is twofold: differentiating the curriculum for the general characteristics of the gifted and adapting the curriculum for individual manifestations of these characteristics.

A major problem arises from the belief that differentiating the curriculum for the gifted group at large automatically differentiates it for each gifted student within this group. One solution to this problem is to perceive each characteristic on a developmental continuum. Although the learner's general placement in relationship to the characteristic may be determined, it is also necessary to analyze the student's specific status with regard to the characteristic. A gifted child may be able to use the skill of determining cause-and-effect relationships generally but may not know how to apply this skill in a specific content area within the social studies curriculum. The integration of social science disciplines into broadly defined themes, such as "Man's Need for Survival," is more appropriate for the gifted than is a social studies curriculum designed around discrete or separate subjects. This interdisciplinary approach to social studies enables curriculum developers to incorporate activities into the curriculum that accommodate both general and individualistic expressions of the characteristics that signify giftedness.

6. California State Department of Education, *Curriculum Guide for Teaching Gifted Children Social Sciences in Grades One through Three* (Sacramento, Calif.: California State Department of Education, 1970), p. 1.

Ways of adapting or modifying the social studies curriculum for the gifted often include the following: replacing the regular social studies curriculum with a "new" curricular subject or unit, applying higher-level thinking processes to the regular or prescribed curriculum, or changing the instructional mode for the teaching and learning of either the regular or the "new" social studies content. While each of these could qualify as a method of differentiating the social studies curriculum for the gifted, each represents only a partial solution.

A "new" curricular subject or area can result in gaps in the learning of basic skills, concepts, and generalizations as well as in isolated experiences that negate the application and transfer of acquired learnings. Such action presupposes that the regular curriculum is not necessary or has not been previously learned, when in fact aspects of the regular curriculum could be vital to the student's ability to master the "new" curriculum. Simply applying-higher-level thinking processes to the regular or to the "new" curriculum often dilutes the content by using it as a vehicle rather than as an integral part of the learning experience. Merely changing the instructional mode for the teaching and learning of the curriculum often places a disproportionate emphasis on how and when learning takes place rather than emphasizing what learning occurs.

The building of a social studies curriculum for the gifted necessitates a blend of the following: replacing what is not needed for the gifted with what is needed; recognizing that, as Gold states, "social studies deals with open-ended problems and issues that . . . [provide] genuine opportunities for improving the quality of children's thinking";[7] and realizing that learning how to learn is a primary skill in the social studies curriculum.

The incorporation of the three traditionally recognized dimensions of enrichment (horizontal, vertical, supplementary) into a *single structure* centered on a given content area or body of knowledge is one approach to the development of a social studies curriculum for the gifted.[8] Within this framework, the three dimen-

7. Gold, *Education of the Intellectually Gifted*, p. 242.

8. William K. Durr, "Dimensions of Enrichment," in *Readings in the Language Arts* (New York: Macmillan, 1964), pp. 441-54.

sions of enrichment are not considered as separate entities to be individually employed with content. Each dimension represents a facet of a total social studies curriculum. These dimensions determine and reinforce the general principles to be considered in curriculum design for the gifted. The nature of the learning experiences within the social studies curriculum are selected and/or structured with reference to and in support of the following criteria:

1. The horizontal dimension includes activities that provide further practice of learned skills, concepts, and generalizations. The focus is on application of acquired knowledge. The dichotomy between accumulation of knowledge and utility of knowledge as an either/or controversy is resolved by presenting opportunities that extend learnings into a variety of personal and socially relevant situations. The gifted child studying the effects of news releases from various media sources on friends and family members after studying a unit on "Man's Need to Communicate" is an example of this dimension within a particular social studies curriculum.

2. The vertical dimension includes activities that afford the gifted student with opportunities for learning beyond those considered to be basic or the core of the curricular experience. As a result of understanding the fundamentals that constitute the core of the content, emphasis is placed on presenting the gifted learner with opportunities to *transfer* specific and general learnings. A gifted child who is assessing the effects of linguistic style within the black culture after participating in the unit on "Man's Need to Communicate" is an example of vertical enrichment as an aspect of the total social studies curriculum.

3. The supplementary dimension is defined as the set of learning experiences that allows the child entry into areas usually omitted from the regular curriculum. This dimension caters to the gifted child's need to stylize learning to individual needs and interests. The purpose underlying this set of curricular activities is to encourage the integration of previous learnings with new learnings and to provide opportunities for tangential learning. The gifted child who is interested in electronics and consequently pursues research on this subject after or while studying "Man's Need to

Communicate" is acquiring supplementary experience within a particular content area. The independent study topic can be a self-selected choice made from a collection of related subtopics or from topics of interest that are extensions of the major theme. This promotes the "learning-to-learn" goal of gifted education, taps student interest for in-depth knowledge, and provides opportunities for firsthand investigations.

Many educators believe that independent study may be an important vehicle within the curriculum to make it appropriate for gifted learners. Renzulli proposes that "students become actual investigators of a real problem or topic by using appropriate methods of inquiry."[9] Ward states that the "abler learner should be encouraged to use knowledge of research techniques to ascertain information for himself."[10] Independent study affords the student with opportunities to pursue what is particularly relevant within a framework that is already relevant for gifted students generally.

The analysis of the operations of an independent study shown in table 3 illustrates how this instructional mode can facilitate the introduction and development of the basic goals delineated for gifted students.

Independent study fails for the gifted when it is perceived as a process independent of teaching. Taba notes that "the task of curriculum is to develop an appropriate balance between discovery learning and receptive learning and to articulate the content organization accordingly."[11] When the concept of independent study as an instructional mode is confused with the concept of independence, independent study is also likely to fail. Gifted learners need to know when, how, and under what conditions individual and group learning and sharing of experiences are available and effective for them. Likewise, teachers must recognize that independent study requires the attainment of prerequisite skills that eventually enable the learner to operate in a self-sufficient and self-directed way. Most importantly, independent study neces-

9. Joseph S. Renzulli, *The Enrichment Triad Model: A Guide for Developing Defensible Programs for the Gifted and Talented* (Wethersfield, Conn.: Creative Learning Press, 1977).

10. Ward, *Educating the Gifted: An Axiomatic Approach*, p. 158.

11. Hilda Taba, "Learning by Discovery: Psychological and Educational Rationale" (Paper given at a symposium of the American Educational Research Association, Atlantic City, N.J., 1962), p. 10.

TABLE 3

OPERATIONS AND GOALS IN INDEPENDENT STUDY

OPERATIONS	GOALS
Searching: The development of techniques and the introduction to materials that develop learning-to-learn skills. Example: Students using journal articles, and interviews to gleen important information.	Access to an array of persons, ideas, materials, experiences and environments and the ability to evaluate the validity of information.
Assimilating: The process of "digesting" acquired information. Example: Students hypothesize solutions and make inferences.	Experiences at various levels of conceptualization including memory, translation, interpretation, application, analyses, synthesis, and evaluation.
Reporting: The expression of learned information or skills in some formalized outcome. Example: Students present information from a comparative study in a research paper.	Applying acquired information to the real-life world.

SOURCE: California State Department of Education, *Principles, Objectives, and Curricula for Programs in the Education of Mentally Gifted Minors* (Sacramento, Calif.: California State Department of Education, 1971), pp. 55-59.

sitates the relinquishing of some time and skills from the basic curriculum so that students can direct their studies with reference to the needs of self as well as to imposed needs. Independent study is thus a way to retain what is important to be learned in the social studies curriculum for all gifted students and to replace general activities with individualized experiences.

Summary

Within the language arts curriculum for gifted students, the purpose and scope of the subject area must be defined in relationship to the appropriate expectations regarding the gifted. A philosophical structure should be adopted that supports and directs the content, processes, and products to be included in the curriculum. The use of an "organizing center" is one way to insure that each language arts experience is treated as an integral part of all language arts experiences rather than as a separate activity.

Because of its scope and diversity, the social studies is a curricular area appropriate to extend and enhance the general differences of the gifted learners as well as to accommodate their unique individual differences. One approach to the development of a curriculum in the social studies for the gifted is to incorporate the horizontal, vertical, and supplementary concepts of enrichment into a single structure. Independent study, as a supplementary experience, becomes a viable instructional mode to foster the acquisition of the content and processes and the development of products appropriate to the gifted.

CHAPTER X

The Study and Facilitation of Talent for Mathematics

JULIAN C. STANLEY

Introduction

GENERAL VERSUS SPECIAL ABILITY

In their preoccupation with the IQ as the principal criterion for defining intellectual giftedness, those who study or help the gifted have not given much attention to special mental abilities. For them the approach of Galton, Binet, Terman, and Wechsler has triumphed over that of Spearman and Thurstone.[1] The assessment of global IQ that Terman established so firmly on the basis of the work of Binet and Simon (1904-11) is one of the greatest contributions of psychology to education, but like all single indices it has sharp limitations.[2] The deliberate averaging of various abilities produces a generally useful score but does not highlight special abilities. The *Stanford-Binet Intelligence Scale* is indifferent, for example, to whether one excels on memory and is less strong on mathematical reasoning, or vice versa. Either can compensate for the other. A high IQ, even 140 or more, does not guarantee any particular special ability.

This creates a problem in those parts of the United States where giftedness is defined by the state departments of education as a minimum overall IQ such as 130 or 132. Because intellectually gifted students are identified in this way, there is a strong tendency to

1. Florence L. Goodenough, *Mental Testing: Its History, Principles, and Applications* (New York: Rinehart, 1949).

2. For a translation of these early articles from the French, see Alfred Binet and Th. Simon, *The Development of Intelligence in Children (The Binet-Simon Scale)*, trans. Elizabeth S. Kite (Baltimore: Williams and Wilkins, 1916). For theoretical contributions that began in 1904, see Charles E. Spearman, *The Abilities of Man* (New York: Macmillan, 1927).

group them for instruction in most subjects according to IQ instead of determining their actual readiness for each subject separately. The outcome is usually inefficiency and frustration for both student and teacher. If David, whose IQ is 140, does not do as well in mathematics as Bill, who is his age and whose IQ on the same test is also 140, it is likely to be said that David is poorly motivated, inattentive, or lazy. Actually, there is no reason to suppose that the two are anywhere near equal in mathematical reasoning ability. Grouping on that special ability first, with some consideration also being given to IQ as a measure of learning rate, will produce much more homogeneous classes than could possibly be produced using IQ as the primary grouping variable.[3]

Underlying the above discussion is a basic difference in philosophy between two approaches to identifying intellectual talent. If youths are required to *average* high by earning a high IQ, some with excellent special abilities will be missed. If they are chosen entirely via a test of special ability such as mathematical reasoning, nonverbal reasoning, mechanical comprehension, or spatial relationships, some will not have a high IQ (although if the criterion score is quite high, few are likely to have a low IQ). An obvious solution is to administer several tests of various special abilities, such as the *Differential Aptitude Test Battery*, that cover a variety of abilities and that reveal much about the youth's intellectual functioning. This approach has limitations when the examinee does not read well. For such persons, an individually administered test of intelligence such as the Stanford-Binet or one of the Wechsler series will usually give more valid information about general ability than will group tests, which are often somewhat speeded and demand

3. Lynn H. Fox, "A Mathematics Program for Fostering Precocious Achievement," in *Mathematical Talent: Discovery, Description, and Development,* ed. Julian C. Stanley, Daniel P. Keating, and Lynn H. Fox (Baltimore: Johns Hopkins University Press, 1974), pp. 101-25; William C. George and Susanne A. Denham, "Curriculum Experimentation for the Mathematically Talented," in *Intellectual Talent: Research and Development,* ed. Daniel P. Keating (Baltimore: Johns Hopkins University Press, 1976), pp. 103-31; Julian C. Stanley, "Special Fast-Mathematics Classes Taught by College Professors to Fourth- through Twelfth-Graders," in *Intellectual Talent: Research and Development,* ed. Keating, pp. 132-59; idem, "Rationale of the Study of Mathematically Precocious Youth (SMPY) During Its First Five Years of Promoting Educational Acceleration," in *The Gifted and the Creative: Fifty-year Perspective,* ed. Julian C. Stanley, William C. George, and Cecilia H. Solano (Baltimore: Johns Hopkins University Press, 1977), pp. 75-112.

reading skills. This multiaptitude, group-test approach can be supplemented by other tests such as the *Raven Progressive Matrices* that can be administered somewhat individually without a time limit.

A related approach is to test mainly for a particular special ability, such as knowledge of general vocabulary, and *then* test the high scorers on it further to see what they are like in other cognitive and affective aspects. One will inevitably lose any persons, however bright, who do not score well in the special area. The less the special-ability scores load factorially on general intelligence, the greater the loss of high-IQ individuals will be. For spelling, clerical speed and accuracy, certain types of spatial abilities, and many other abilities the loss might be considerable. If one's chief aim is to locate persons highly talented in a particular way, however, failure to identify those with a high IQ who are not especially talented in the desired field will not be important.

MATHEMATICAL REASONING ABILITY

One of the most valuable types of intellectual talent for both society and the individual is mathematical reasoning ability. It undergirds much of current achievement in technology, science, and social science. Usually this ability is poorly assessed by in-school mathematics tests, because often they consist of a mixture of computation, learned concepts, and reasoning. Also, it is difficult to measure mathematical reasoning ability until the young student has acquired enough knowledge of elementary general mathematics with which to reason. The basic content of the test items must be fairly well known so that reasoning can be the chief trait measured.[4]

The SMPY Annual Mathematics Talent Search

With these considerations in mind, the Study of Mathematically Precocious Youth (SMPY) at Johns Hopkins University began in 1971 a large-scale, systematic attempt to identify at some optimum

---

4. Richard R. Skemp, *The Psychology of Learning Mathematics* (Baltimore: Penguin Books, 1971); V. A. Krutetskii, *The Psychology of Mathematical Abilities in School Children*, trans. Joan Teller (Chicago: University of Chicago Press, 1976); William B. Michael, "Cognitive and Affective Components of Creativity in Mathematics and the Physical Sciences," in *The Gifted and the Creative: Fifty-year Perspective*, ed. Stanley, George, and Solano, pp. 141-72.

age students who reason extremely well mathematically as determined by their scoring high on a test of mathematical reasoning
ability quite difficult for youths their age. Various studies of the
problem were made in order to choose the appropriate age level,
test, and testing conditions. These studies led in March, 1972 to the
first SMPY Annual Mathematics Talent Search among seventh,
eighth, and under-age ninth graders in the Baltimore vicinity. A
total of 396 students, most of whom had already scored in the top
5 percent of national norms on an in-grade mathematics test from
an achievement-test battery, volunteered to take two tests designed
primarily for above-average eleventh and twelfth graders. These
were the College Board's *Scholastic Aptitude Test*, mathematical
part (SAT-M), and its *Mathematics Achievement Test*, Level 1.[5]

The staff of SMPY, consisting then of Lynn H. Fox, Daniel P.
Keating, and the writer, was surprised and pleased at how high a
number of the contestants scored on these two difficult tests. It
was found that 49 percent of the boys and 30 percent of the girls
already exceeded the average college-bound male twelfth grader's
SAT-M score of 497. The top score earned on SAT-M was 790,
only ten points below the highest possible score for this test.[6] The

5. *Mathematical Talent: Discovery, Description, and Development*, ed.
Stanley, Keating, and Fox, especially pp. 23-46. For results from the second,
third, and fourth talent searches, see *Intellectual Talent: Research and Devel-
opment*, ed. Keating, especially pp. 23-31 and 55-89; William C. George and
Sanford J. Cohn, "The 1976 Talent Search Results Are In!" *Intellectually
Talented Youth Bulletin* 3 (15 February 1977), pp. 1-2; and Sanford J. Cohn,
"Cognitive Characteristics of the Top-scoring Third of 1976 Talent Search
Contestants," *Intellectually Talented Youth Bulletin* 3 (15 July 1977), pp. 3-6.

6. The reported score scale runs from 200 through 800, but the chance-
score level is represented by a score of about 260 to 280, and 800 does not
necessarily represent a perfect score. For comparison, the entering class at
Johns Hopkins University in the fall of 1977 was composed of persons who
as eleventh or twelfth graders had averaged 667 on SAT-M, with a standard
deviation of about 80 points. The young man who scored 790 in March of
1972 while still thirteen years old became a senior at Johns Hopkins in September of 1977 at age nineteen years five months, two years ahead of schedule,
majoring in engineering science. (Had he wished, he could have received the
baccalaureate in May of 1977.) The top science scorer from the March 1972
contest, who was then a twelve-year-old seventh grader, received his B.A.
from Johns Hopkins in May of 1977, four years ahead of schedule at age
seventeen years nine months. His major field is electrical engineering, with
emphasis on computer science. Graduated with both general and departmental
honors, he was elected to membership in Phi Beta Kappa and won a three-
year National Science Foundation graduate fellowship with which to work
toward a Ph.D. in computer science at Cornell University, where he went in
the fall of 1977.

Mathematics I scores added little to the information provided by the SAT-M scores. Because the latter are less affected by differences among the mathematics curricula of schools in the grades kindergarten through seven, we settled on SAT-M for future use. In light of our cumulative findings about the remarkable predictive validity of SAT-M, this was probably a fortunate decision.

Table 1 shows data concerning SAT-M scores in each of the four SMPY mathematics talent searches (1972-1976). The first three

TABLE 1

MEAN SCORES AND STANDARD DEVIATIONS BY SEX ON SAT-M
FOR THE FOUR TALENT SEARCHES HELD BY SMPY (1972-1976)

STATISTICS	1972*		1973*		1974*		1976**	
	GIRLS	BOYS	GIRLS	BOYS	GIRLS	BOYS	GIRLS	BOYS
Number	173	223	416	537	591	928	366	507
Mean scores	442	501	461	518	479	513	422	459
Standard deviation	84	110	82	94	77	90	65	88

* Seventh and eighth graders, and a few students in higher grades who were no older than age-in-grade eighth graders.
** Seventh graders, and a few seventh-grade-age students in higher grades.

groups were roughly comparable in age, being composed mostly of seventh and eighth graders, whereas the fourth group consisted only of seventh graders and a few underage students in higher grades. There have been some fluctuations from year to year, such as in the highest SAT-M scores obtained (790, two 800s, 760, and two 780s during the respective four years), but considering the variety of recruiting methods used and the increasing geographical area covered each succeeding year, that variation is not great. It is clear that a large reservoir of virtually untapped mathematical reasoning ability exists all around the region, although it is much greater in some places than in others. For further statistics from the 1976 search, see figures 1 and 2.

Besides administering SAT-M each of the four years, the SMPY staff varied from year to year the other aptitude and achievement tests used in the competition. In 1972, there was also a general science talent search; it involved taking college-level Forms 1A and 1B of the *Sequential Tests of Educational Progress* (STEP-II). A total of 192 students entered it, 138 of whom were also in the

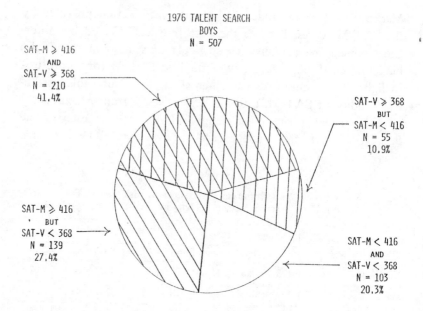

FIG. 1. Males in the 1976 Talent Search who as seventh graders (or under-age eighth graders) scored as well as or better than the average random sample of eleventh- and twelfth-grade males on SAT-M, and as well as or better than the average random sample of eleventh- and twelfth-grade students in general on SAT-V.
Source: William C. George and Sanford J. Cohn, "The 1976 Talent Search Results Are In!" *Intellectually Talented Youth Bulletin* 3 (15 February 1977).

mathematics competition. In 1973, all 953 contestants took both parts of the SAT, mathematical and verbal. In 1974, the 1519 contestants took only SAT-M. Besides these ability tests, self-report inventories of interests and values were used during some of the years.

The model for the SMPY talent searches is the same as the subtitle of its book on *Mathematical Talent: Discovery* (finding the talented), *Description* (testing the highest scorers a great deal more), and *Development* (facilitating their education, especially in mathematics and related subjects). After the mathematically talented youth is identified and studied, it is feasible for someone to devise a smorgasbord of educationally accelerative options from which the student may choose *ad lib*. This flexible counseling ap-

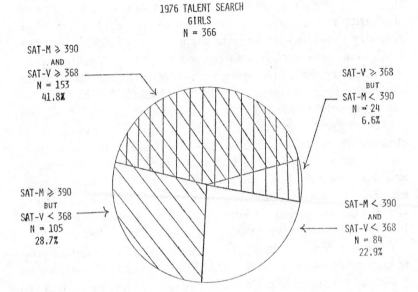

1976 TALENT SEARCH
GIRLS
N = 366

SAT-M ⩾ 390
AND
SAT-V ⩾ 368
N = 153
41.8%

SAT-V ⩾ 368
BUT
SAT-M < 390
N = 24
6.6%

SAT-M ⩾ 390
BUT
SAT-V < 368
N = 105
28.7%

SAT-M < 390
AND
SAT-V < 368
N = 84
22.9%

Fig. 2. Females in the 1976 Talent Search who as seventh graders (or under-age eighth graders) scored as well as or better than the average random sample of eleventh- and twelfth-grade females on SAT-M, and as well as or better than the average random sample of eleventh- and twelfth-grade students in general on SAT-V.
Source: George and Cohn, "The 1976 Talent Search Results Are In!"

proach, adapted to the abilities, interests, motivations, and individual circumstances of each youth, does not constitute *a* program in the same sense that the usual procedures for helping gifted children do. Some highly talented students choose little or nothing from the bountiful possibilities, whereas others gorge themselves almost to the point of having to be restrained. No two tend to do exactly the same things at the same time.

Special Educational Provisions for the Mathematically Talented

What are the educational opportunities that constitute the smorgasbord? The chief theme is getting along faster and better with mathematics from Algebra I straight through the second year of college mathematics (usually Calculus III, linear algebra, and differential equations). An able youth may take the first year of high school algebra a year earlier than usual, or complete two years of algebra in one, or study both second-year algebra and plane geometry the same year, or learn the first year of algebra independently and move rapidly into the second year of algebra and/or into geometry, or if able enough do even more than that. For example, one brilliant eleven-year-old earned credit for the freshman year of calculus at Johns Hopkins by means of a grade of "4" (on a five-point scale) on the Advanced Placement Program Level BC examination in mathematics. At Brooklyn College, another eleven-year-old simply skipped the first year of college calculus entirely and was among the best students in Calculus III. These are extreme examples, of course, but indicative of how incredibly slow-paced 180 fifty-minute periods of introductory high school algebra would have been for these students had not SMPY intervened.

The boredom and frustration of even the average-scoring contestants when incarcerated in a year-long introductory algebra class is difficult to appreciate. Often, highly able youths themselves are not aware of the extent of the slowdown, because it has been their lot from kindergarten onward. Actually, because of the more abstract nature of algebra and the abler-than-average students who enroll for it in the eighth or ninth grade the already bored student may experience a "lift" in spirits when entering beginning algebra. Only by being given opportunities to move ahead at a more appropriate rate and on a better level of rigor can the student realize how much time was being wasted and how much more enjoyment can be gained from studying mathematics.

That is why various SMPY special fast-mathematics classes, usually taught by a college professor, have been so spectacularly successful for a considerable percentage of the students who entered them. Being paced by their intellectual peers rather than merely by their agemates and being moved ahead quickly by an excellent teacher make a world of difference in the students' progress and their sense of accomplishment. Often they take off like rockets intellectually when allowed to do so. Several brief case studies reported later in this chapter will illustrate this point.

GRADE SKIPPING

There are also other options available. One is skipping whole grades in school, especially the grade at the end of the middle school or the junior high school, so that the student can enter earlier a senior high school, where the intellectual fare is usually more varied and appropriate for able youths.

EARLY PART-TIME COLLEGE STUDY

Another opportunity is the taking of college classes for credit on a part-time basis before becoming a full-time college student. An occasional student may be able to do this at age nine or ten. For example, the boy who earned credit for college calculus by examination at age eleven also had been an extremely successful college student in courses on "Introduction to Computer Science" and "Mini-computers" while still ten years old. Other highly able students need to wait until they are twelve to fourteen years old before taking a college course. Still others who are somewhat less able should wait until they are fifteen to seventeen years old, but not necessarily until they have completed high school. Nothing seems to boost a student's level of aspiration more than earning an "A" in a college course with regular college students. The SMPY participants' favorite such course is "Introduction to Computer Science." Other courses often taken are in college algebra and trigonometry, descriptive astronomy, and the calculus, but the range of courses taken by an appreciable number of the students is quite great.

Since 1972, SMPY has seen hundreds of youths take college courses for credit before becoming full-time college students. The cumulative gradepoint average of the group is about 3.6, well above the requirement for being placed on the Dean's List at Johns Hopkins.[7]

CREDIT BY EXAMINATIONS

Another way for the gifted student to move ahead is via college-credit examinations, particularly those of the Advanced Placement Program (APP) and College Level Examination Program (CLEP). Many high schools do not facilitate or encourage this until the twelfth grade, if at all. The staff of SMPY has been alerting highly

---

7. Cecilia H. Solano and William C. George, "College Courses and Educational Facilitation of the Gifted," *Gifted Child Quarterly* 20 (Fall, 1976): 274-85.

able youths to this method of cutting both educational time and cost. It makes little sense for a student who, at age twelve or thirteen, reasons extremely well mathematically—better than the typical male college-bound twelfth grader—to enter college later without having already gained credit for the first year of calculus as well as for several other subjects such as physics, chemistry, biology, and whatever else the student finds feasible. In a time of rapidly rising college costs, this type of acceleration can make an important difference in the institution a students' parents can afford. It can mean five to seven semesters of undergraduate study rather than eight.

The SMPY contestant who, as a twelve-year-old seventh grader in a public school, scored 800 on SAT-M in January 1973, managed to earn credit for two semesters of college calculus at age thirteen and two semesters each of biology, chemistry, and physics at age fifteen by making the highest possible grade ("5") on all four APP examinations. While age fourteen, the student earned an "A" from a major university by correspondence study in a third-semester college calculus course. As a twelfth grader he earned other college credits by examination. In the fall of 1977, he entered the Massachusetts Institute of Technology a year early with sophomore standing.

EARLY COLLEGE ENTRANCE

Quite a few of the participants in SMPY programs come to college early by simply leaving high school before completing the last grade(s) or by doubling up in their subjects and thereby being graduated early. During the 1976-77 school year, there were at Johns Hopkins alone twenty-six such students whom SMPY had sponsored for admission, and even more elsewhere whom it had helped to become "radical accelerants." Five of those twenty-six were graduated during the 1976-77 academic year three to five and one-half years ahead of schedule, three of them while still seventeen years old, one at eighteen, and one at nineteen. All had done well and had enjoyed the intellectual and social stimulation of college as compared with the inappropriate pace and level of the earlier grades. Two were elected to membership in Phi Beta Kappa and one barely missed this honor. Three were graduated with both general and departmental honors. Three won three-year National Science Foundation graduate fellowships.[8]

Again, it must be noted that these are exceptionally able youths, perhaps one in 200 or more of their age group in scientific ability. There are, however, many like them across the country who can hardly get permission to move even one year ahead of the age-in-grade lockstep. The efforts of SMPY in this respect are virtually in their infancy because the students in even the earliest of its talent searches were, at most, accelerated ninth graders during the school year 1971-72. Nearly all of them were only seventh or eighth graders then and one would expect them to have been in the twelfth grade or freshman year in college during the 1976-77 academic year. When the five early college graduates mentioned above were first identified (in the fall of 1971 or the spring of 1972) only one of them had skipped even one school grade. None had yet done anything else that accelerated their progress through the grades.

COLLEGE GRADUATION IN LESS THAN FOUR YEARS

There are several ways to go through college in less than four years. Perhaps the most straightforward is by entering with sophomore standing attained by some combination of college courses taken while still in high school and credits by examination.[9] Another is by taking heavier-than-required course loads and/or attending summer school. With the comparatively recent advent of inter-sessions—periods between terms—it has become possible in many colleges to get extra credits during those periods via courses or work experiences. A third method, feasible at Johns Hopkins and at only a few other institutions, is taking a master's degree concurrently with the last year or two of the baccalaureate. SMPY's

8. *Time*, "Smorgasbord for an IQ of 150," 6 June 1977, p. 64; David Nevin, "Young Prodigies Take Off under Special Program," *Smithsonian* 8, no. 7 (October, 1977): 76-82, 160.

9. The main national programs by means of which high school students may earn college credit by examination are the Advanced Placement Program (APP) and the College Level Examination Program (CLEP), both sponsored by the College Entrance Examination Board and administered by the Educational Testing Service. Also, of course, it is possible, although often not easy or convenient, to get college credit for a subject by taking an examination in the relevant department of the college or university one attends or plans to attend.

first radical accelerant did this, entering Johns Hopkins in the fall of 1969 as a regular freshman at age thirteen after completing the eighth grade of a public school. Four years later, he had received the B.A. degree, with a major in the area of quantitative studies, at age seventeen years seven months. Three months later, he completed the thesis required for the M.S. in Engineering with a major in computer science. (Had he done it during the senior year the two degrees could have been awarded in May.)[10]

Some students simply shun the baccalaureate and go directly into graduate work after two years or so of undergraduate study. Most major universities will permit this for an occasional meteoric student, albeit perhaps reluctantly. Of course, many colleges and the undergraduate divisions of many universities are so rigidly addicted to the "Class of _____" concept that a student wishing to progress more rapidly must be extraordinarily planful and persistent. The ablest and best-motivated intellectually precocious youths can usually find ways, however, especially by being careful which collegiate institution they choose. The facts about how the accelerative policies of a school actually operate, as contrasted with what their promotional literature says, should be obtained *in writing* before enrolling.

Few students who at an early age score startlingly well on SAT-M will major in "pure" mathematics at a highly selective college. Most of them will go instead into fields that are undergirded by mathematics or even into those, such as the practice of medicine, where great mathematical ability is not essential or even very helpful. Often this is appropriate, because the need for persons holding a Ph.D. degree in mathematical science is being rather fully met by fewer than 1,000 such degrees annually, except, of course, that there will probably never be enough of the ablest, most creative mathematicians. As in most specialties, room exists at the very top. Also, a bachelor's or master's degree in pure mathematics can be an excellent background for graduate work in a number of fields.

10. Julian C. Stanley, "Use of Tests to Discover Talent," in *Intellectual Talent: Research and Development*, ed. Keating, p. 9.

Illustrations of How the Smorgasbord Works

To see how the smorgasbord of educationally accelerative opportunities is used by its most ravenous partakers, consider the progress of two similar boys *A* and *B*, from the fall of 1971 through June, 1978.

A was born December 4, 1959. In October 1971, when the SMPY staff first met this remarkable youth, he was an eleven-year-old sixth grader in a public school. In June 1972, he entered the first SMPY fast-mathematics class. By August 1973, after about sixty two-hour periods of rapidly paced instruction, he had completed two years of high school algebra, college algebra, plane geometry, trigonometry, and analytic geometry. Before then, he had skipped the seventh grade and earned a grade of "A" in a regular college course in computer science at Johns Hopkins, a course taken on released time from the eighth grade. After one year in the middle grade of a junior high school, he skipped the ninth and tenth grades and entered the eleventh grade of a large, excellent senior high school. There he took Advanced Placement calculus and studied physics on his own, besides taking a normal schedule of college preparatory eleventh-grade courses. In addition, he enrolled at night and during the summer in several college courses. This left him time to win a varsity letter in wrestling, be the mathematics and science expert on the school's TV academic-games team, tutor a brilliant young friend in mathematics, and play an excellent game of golf. In spare moments he directed the successful campaign of his fourteen-year-old sophomore friend for the presidency of the student council.

After just this one year in junior high and one in senior high, *A* entered Johns Hopkins at age fourteen as a sophomore, with fourteen credits by APP examinations (calculus and physics) and twenty credits from the college courses he had already taken. In January 1977, he completed all requirements for the B.A. degree in quantitative studies at age seventeen years one month, perhaps the youngest student ever graduated from Johns Hopkins. Although a full-time college student only five semesters, he had taken advanced work in a number of different fields, including political science, economics, astronomy, and management.

To sum up: *A* skipped grades seven, nine, ten, and twelve. He utilized the SMPY fast-mathematics class, the APP examination opportunity, and college courses taken part-time. He completed college in five-eighths of the usual time. In the fall of 1977 *A* began studying toward the M.B.A. and the Ph.D. in economics at the University of Chicago, specializing in finance.

By contrast, *B* (born July 10, 1959) simply skipped grades two, eleven, and twelve. He took a college course each semester and summer term from the second semester of the eighth grade at age twelve onward, entered Johns Hopkins after the tenth grade with thirty-nine college credits, and in six semesters finished his B.A. in electrical engineering with emphasis on computers. During the two summers while in college he did high-level research in major industries. His B.A. was received at age seventeen years and ten months. In the fall of 1977, aided by a three-year National Science Foundation graduate fellowship, he went to the Massachusetts Institute of Technology to work toward a Ph.D. in electrical engineering, stressing computer science.

B was not in any special mathematics classes, but he enrolled instead in regular college courses after completing only the first year of high-school algebra. Also, he did not attempt any of the APP examinations, but had completed two years of college chemistry (earning four grades of "A") before enrolling at Johns Hopkins. He skipped the second grade and spent three years in junior high school, compared with *A*'s one, but got considerable released time from those studies in order to pursue college courses.

Both of these young men are highly promising, although for different fields. Both are intellectually brilliant and powerfully motivated, of course, but they are by no means unique, even in the experience of SMPY.[11] What they did, or variations on it, can be accomplished by a considerable number of mathematically highly apt youths anywhere who also have excellent overall intellectual ability and are eager to move ahead.

Conclusion

Specialists in the education of mathematically talented youths do not have the resources with which to develop mathematics

11. Ibid., pp. 19-21.

courses and curricula. Instead, they must help such students use the best available courses in wisely accelerative ways. Special mathematics curricula such as SMSG (School Mathematics Study Group) and CEMREL (Central Midwestern Regional Educational Laboratory, Inc.) are designed for above-average students, so at their *regular* pace they do not meet the needs of the mathematically most precocious youths well. Private schools are not in themselves a solution, either, though increased pace and stimulating competition within a selective school—whether private or public—can be helpful.

Except for table 1, no attention has been given in this chapter to sex differences in mathematical aptitude and achievement. This subject is discussed by Callahan in chapter 26 of this volume. Utilizing the mathematical potentialities of women better is an important topic that deserves far more research and development than it has yet received.

One can sum up by reaffirming that great mathematical reasoning ability at an early age is a resource of inestimable value to individuals and society, but only to the extent that its expression is facilitated through the various subject-matter fields for which it is relevant. The highly precocious mathematical reasoner does not need anything like the Procrustean fit of five or six school years of 180 periods each in which to progress from first-year high school algebra through the high school calculus. In fact, such a student is likely to be hurt severely in mathematics by being forced to do so. That persistent finding by SMPY is not contradicted by any other studies of which we are aware.

Candidates for substantial acceleration in mathematics and related subjects must be found, studied, and helped to move ahead fast and well. Doing this requires far more ingenuity, determination, and persistence than money. The procedures that SMPY recommends actually tend to save a school certain costs of instruction. A little special effort on behalf of the mathematically talented can easily yield large outcomes. Precocious students, their parents, and educators genuinely concerned with the students' educational and personal welfare can spark local efforts to provide the smorgasbord of educationally accelerative opportunities from which each such youth needs freedom to choose over the years of school and college.

As noted earlier, SMPY is not a curriculum development project. It was obvious from the beginning that for SMPY to become concerned with the development of special materials for the top one in 200 or so young mathematical reasoners would go far beyond available resources of personnel and money. We fully appreciate the importance of the various unified mathematics curricula that hard-working, insightful mathematics educators have devised and tried out. Nothing in the philosophy or practice of SMPY prevents helping youths who reason extremely well mathematically to move through a special curriculum faster than most of the other students in it do. Even in a mathematics program designed for the upper third or fourth of the age group, the mathematically brilliant students are almost certain to move too slowly for their abilities unless appropriate provisions are made. Perhaps in the standard algebra—geometry—trigonometry—analytic geometry—calculus sequence it is somewhat easier to determine what the exceptional student does not know, but the method of diagnostic testing followed by prescriptive teaching is just as applicable to "modern mathematics" as it is to the older version.

To what extent are the recommendations for educational acceleration contained in this chapter applicable to school areas other than mathematics and related subjects such as physics, chemistry, and computer science? While those subjects depend far less on life experiences than do more verbal areas such as social studies and the language arts, still there are strong reasons for believing that youths who score extremely high on SAT-Verbal have managed to acquire many of those experiences and therefore (if well motivated to do so) are ready to forge ahead faster than the usual age-in-grade lockstep. As the extensive review by Daurio[12] shows, the research literature contains many substantial studies showing that educational acceleration is widely successful, both academically and personally, with virtually no substantial study showing harmful effects. Despite this, the beliefs of educators and their educational practices tend to

12. Stephen P. Daurio, "Educational Enrichment versus Acceleration: A Review of the Literature," in *Acceleration and Enrichment: Strategies for Educating the Gifted*, ed. William C. George, Sanford J. Cohn, and Julian C. Stanley (Baltimore: Study of Mathematically Precocious Youth, Johns Hopkins University, 1979).

be strongly antiacceleration. Large, longitudinal studies are badly needed to try some of the principles and practices of SMPY systematically in the areas of verbal reasoning and general vocabulary tested by SAT-V.

CHAPTER XI

Secondary-School Programs

DANIEL P. KEATING

Issues Concerning Programs for the Gifted and Talented

SOCIAL CHANGES AFFECTING PROGRAMS

Since the last yearbook of the National Society for the Study of Education in which secondary-school programs for the gifted and the talented were discussed,[1] several significant changes in the larger society have required rethinking of some of the programs described there. Most striking perhaps is a strong egalitarian mood, which led to the dismantling of many special schools for highly able students throughout the country. Some of these have, of course, survived (for example, the Bronx High School of Science), and recently there have been some indications that renewed efforts in this direction can be anticipated. By and large, however, plans to facilitate effectively the education of the highly able student at the secondary level are currently required to operate within comprehensive, nonselective high schools. Some private schools remain an exception to this trend, and this issue will be discussed in more detail later.

Another constraint placed on such programs is the scarcity of resources available for their implementation. A significant historical source of this problem has been the heavy funding of research and development efforts in the areas of mental retardation, learning disabilities, and compensatory education during the 1960s. Although one may simultaneously advocate such efforts and regret their

1. Lloyd S. Michael, "Secondary-School Programs," in *Education for the Gifted*, Fifty-seventh Yearbook of the National Society for the Study of Education, Part II, ed. Nelson B. Henry (Chicago: University of Chicago Press, 1958), pp. 263-315.

dampening impact on research and development for the gifted, there are difficulties inherent in such a position. It is possible to argue that funds for special learning programs are not necessarily best appropriated as a block to be subdivided among the several categories. Such a block approach places programs for gifted and talented in the unenviable and probably untenable position of seeking funding primarily at the expense of reduced funding for programs dealing with mental retardation and learning disability.[2] Few advocates of programs for the gifted, no matter how staunch, find that a pleasing or promising position. A better approach might place programs for the gifted in a separate category altogether, to compete equally with all other demands for educational resources, and not just against programs for cognitively impaired children. Anastasi has observed that it may well be today's gifted children who, if their education is adequately facilitated, will make tomorrow's important breakthroughs in helping the least able.[3]

The long-run opportunities for increased resources are unclear. The short-run implication of this dearth of funding is that practical programs for gifted and talented in secondary schools require considerable financing ingenuity. Many excellent opportunities can be made available with rather modest expenditure.[4]

ACCELERATION AND/OR ENRICHMENT

A perennial controversy that goes to the heart of the question of what to do for gifted and talented young people is whether the programs should be principally accelerative or enriching in nature. It is important to understand the roots of the controversy, because there are serious implications both for the implementation and justification of successful programs.[5]

2. Carl E. Bereiter, "SMPY in Social Perspective," in *Intellectual Talent: Research and Development*, ed. Daniel Keating (Baltimore: Johns Hopkins University Press, 1976), pp. 308-15.

3. Anne Anastasi, "Commentary on the Precocity Project," in *Mathematical Talent: Discovery, Description, and Development*, ed. Julian Stanley, Daniel Keating, and Lynn Fox (Baltimore: Johns Hopkins University Press, 1974), pp. 87-100.

4. "General Discussion," in *Intellectual Talent: Research and Development*, ed. Keating, pp. 316-342.

5. Julian C. Stanley, "Concern for Intellectually Talented Youths: How It Originated and Fluctuated," *Journal of Clinical Child Psychology* 5 (1976): 38-42.

Advocates of acceleration point out that one major characteristic of gifted and talented youth, perhaps the key characteristic, is that their rate of dealing with new information is much faster than average. Evidence for this comes from both evaluation of gifted students' learning in classroom situations as well as from experimental psychology.[6] For exceptionally gifted students, the time needed to deal with new information may be anywhere from 50 to 75 percent less than for students of average ability. Given these facts, the argument goes, the most sensible and defensible facilitation of gifted students is to move them through the curriculum content of secondary school at as rapid a pace as is appropriate to their ability. The principal goal of special programs is to accomplish this purpose with as little disruption as possible, and a variety of ways in which this might be done are described below.

The arguments in favor of enrichment rather than acceleration are both positive and negative. On the negative side, it is argued that accelerative programs may be disruptive to the overall educational goals of the school, both for the individual gifted student as well as for other students. On the positive side are arguments of practicality (such programs are often easier to implement) and of greater educational benefit (the broadening rather than the hastening of the process of education).

These arguments seem mostly to concern poorly designed accelerative or enriching educational plans.[7] Thoughtless acceleration can be harmful, and unplanned enrichment can turn out to be mostly busywork. Good educational acceleration is always enriching, however, and solid enrichment programs always advance the student's learning of new and relevant material and are consequently accelerating. The major distinction between the two concepts is thus reduced to the level of administrative convenience, with respect to what the program will be called and how it will be

6. William C. George and Susanne A. Denham, "Curriculum Experimentation for the Mathematically Talented," in *Intellectual Talent: Research and Development*, ed. Keating, pp. 103-131. Also, Daniel P. Keating and Bruce L. Bobbitt, "Individual and Developmental Differences in Cognitive Processing Components of Mental Ability," *Child Development* 49 (1978): 155-67.

7. Daniel P. Keating, "Acceleration vs. Enrichment: Competing or Complementary Approaches?" (Paper presented at the annual meeting of the American Educational Research Association, New York, 1977).

handled in terms of classroom assignment and the allocation of the student's time.

It seems more appropriate to concentrate instead on what is being made available to the student. If challenging, novel, and educationally relevant material is being provided in such a way that the student can continue to capitalize on these educational experiences, then the program is a sound one, irrespective of the label attached to it. To the extent that this is not accomplished, calling some other adjustment to the student's school time "acceleration" or "enrichment" does not increase the appropriateness of those experiences.

DIFFERENCES IN AREAS OF ABILITY

Another major shift in educational thinking in the last few decades has been a growing questioning of the concept of global ability for purposes of planning for gifted students. The global ability (as measured by most intelligence tests) is a useful initial index of general ability, but its utility for informed decisions about facilitation of good education for gifted students is quite limited in two important respects. First, it obscures significant underlying differences in specific academic aptitudes within groups of individuals at the same score levels. Second, it may focus attention so exclusively on academic skills that we ignore other socially important areas of human endeavor where it is, or may prove to be, necessary to make special efforts to foster talent and achievement.

The recognition of the different areas of academic ability is especially important for program planning during the secondary school years, as those years appear to be a time of significant differentiation in the factor structure of ability.[8] Whereas most ability variance seems well accounted for by a single general factor during the primary grades, much of the variance in ability during the adolescent years and subsequently is better accounted for by a number of major group factors such as verbal ability, mathematical ability, logical reasoning, spatial visualization, and so on.

8. John L. Horn, "Human Abilities: A Review of Research and Theory in the Early 1970s," in *Annual Review of Psychology*, vol. 27, ed. Mark R. Rosenzweig and Lyman W. Porter (Palo Alto, Calif.: Annual Reviews, 1976), pp. 437-85.

Programs designed on the assumption of a single factor of academic ability are likely to result in wide distributions of specific abilities in each class. If an IQ or composite score is used, for example, the range of mathematical aptitude among students thus selected is likely to remain quite large.

There may be important differences in the programs adopted for facilitating the learning of gifted students, depending upon the nature of the subject matter itself. Two dimensions are important, one relating to the nature of subject matter and the other relating to methods of facilitating the learning of gifted students. The first dimension has been characterized as open versus closed systems of knowledge, closed systems being those subjects in which a more linear, step-by-step learning progression is possible, without the addition of outside "life" experience.[9] The second dimension is that of horizontal expansion of learning versus vertical progression. Horizontal programs may be more appropriate for open systems whereas vertical programs are perhaps best for closed systems.

An example serves to illustrate the distinction. A teacher discovers that a particular student is quite able in mathematics, and is capable of doing assigned work in much less time than is used by the rest of the class. As a "reward" for such excellent performance, the student is assigned twice as many of the same problems to work on. This is not only an abuse of the enrichment concept, substituting busywork for truly enriching experiences, but is also a failure to recognize the nature of much of learning in mathematics. Once a student has fully grasped the principle underlying a particular concept (for example, simultaneous equations), continued routine drilling, especially for the highly able student, is both a waste of time and potentially counterproductive if it leads to a decreased interest in the subject matter. The student with high quantitative ability will need fewer, not more, sample problems to grasp the principle underlying concepts. Progression vertically into more difficult material, for which the current learning is the groundwork, is needed to meet the earlier stated criterion of challenging, novel, and educationally relevant work.

9. Daniel P. Keating, "The Study of Mathematically Precocious Youth," in *Mathematical Talent: Discovery, Description, and Development*, ed. Stanley, Keating, and Fox, pp. 23-46.

The study of literature, on the other hand, provides an example of the other end of the two dimensions. As Bereiter has noted, "*To Kill a Mocking Bird* and *Julius Caesar* are worth reading, even by children who have already read them or comparable works. . . ."[10] Similarly, reading several of Shakespeare's plays rather than one is quite different from solving fifty simultaneous equations rather than thirty. In literature and other areas there exists no obvious linear progression of learning, and expanding the scope of material horizontally makes good educational sense if it is done well.

A second limitation of reliance on a single global academic composite is more problematic. Neisser, among others, has noted the propensity of educators and psychologists to assume, on the basis of modest or nonexistent evidence, that assessments of academic intelligence will generalize to other areas of human ability (for example, social intelligence).[11] The concern of schools has always been thought to extend beyond strictly academic domains,[12] and recently there has been a renewed interest in direct facilitation in such areas as moral development, interpersonal relations, and others.[13] The U.S. Office of Education definition includes six areas of talent, only two of which are traditionally academic domains.

Unfortunately, interest and concern regarding these "nonacademic" areas of ability have significantly preceded the development of the educational and psychological measurement and technology needed to support selection and facilitation efforts. The scientific status of such constructs as social or leadership ability is questionable at best.[14] The importance of these areas should be recognized and research efforts encouraged in order to lead to a better understanding of such domains. There are those who believe that it may

10. Bereiter, "SMPY in Social Perspective," p. 383.

11. Ulric Neisser, "General, Academic, and Artificial Intelligence," in *The Nature of Intelligence*, ed. Lauren B. Resnick (Hillsdale, N.J.: Lawrence Erlbaum, 1976), pp. 135-44.

12. A. Harry Passow, "The Comprehensive High School and Gifted Youth," *Teachers College Record* 58 (1956): 144-52.

13. James Rest, "Developmental Psychology as a Guide to Value Education: A Review of 'Kohlbergian' Programs," *Review of Educational Research* 44 (1974): 241-59.

14. Daniel P. Keating, "A Search for Social Intelligence," *Journal of Educational Psychology* 70 (1978): 218-23.

be premature to make a major investment in projects to identify high-ability students in these domains and to facilitate their development, lacking a firmer base of knowledge about them. This is especially true since we have not yet approached a satisfactory level of programming for students with high academic ability.

ATTITUDES TOWARD GIFTED STUDENTS

An additional constraining factor in planning programs for gifted and talented students is the fact that they must be workable in the "real world," in this case the world of the secondary school. Otherwise, excellent programs can founder because of misunderstanding or resistance. Such feelings may be more likely when there is already a tendency to view gifted students negatively.

Research suggests that the initial reactions of both teachers and other students are likely to be somewhat negative.[15] This may be especially true for gifted female students.[16] The picture is not unrelentingly bleak, however. Teachers' attitudes grow more positive with exposure to identified gifted students, especially if the teachers are actively involved with these students. Also, there are major school-by-school variations in the extent to which gifted students are perceived negatively. In those schools where negative feelings run high, it may prove quite difficult to establish solid programs in which the gifted students will be willing to participate. If attitudinal shifts within the school can be brought about, however, there can be considerable support for a wide range of programs.

Types of Programs

SPECIAL SCHOOLS

Perhaps the most straightforward way of dealing with the myriad of problems besetting effective programming at the second-

---

15. Abraham J. Tannenbaum, *Adolescent Attitudes toward Academic Brilliance* (New York: Teachers College, Columbia University, 1962). Also, Richard J. Haier and Cecilia H. Solano, "Educators' Stereotypes of Mathematically Gifted Boys," in *Intellectual Talent: Research and Development*, ed. Keating, pp. 215-22.

16. Lynn H. Fox, "Sex Differences in Mathematical Precocity: Bridging the Gap," in *Intellectual Talent: Research and Development*, ed. Keating, pp. 183-214.

ary level for gifted and talented students is to create a school especially for them. In this way, adequately stimulating courses can be
devised and taught without concern for the remainder of the students who are unable to keep up with such a rapid pace. Also, since
teachers as well as students can be recruited specifically for such
schools, many of the negative attitudinal problems are absent or
minimal.

For a variety of social and economic reasons already noted,
such schools are less in vogue today than they once were. Support
for them has declined for reasons other than the adequacy of their
programs. In the public sector particularly, administrators and
school boards have perceived less popular support for such complete separation of these gifted students from the general population. Major difficulties exist in launching new efforts along these
lines, but some excellent public schools for high-ability students
remain.

Some private schools claim to serve this population especially
well. Many excellent private institutions do enroll a significant
number of gifted students and provide challenging educational opportunities for them. Some of these schools, however, may not be
as useful as possible to the exceptionally gifted student. Often the
assertion is that "all our students are gifted"; hence, nothing special
need be done even for the students who are exceptional in their
ability, even within a high-level group. As research indicates and
another chapter in this volume explores, the needs of the exceptionally gifted student may be as different from the general group of
gifted students as the latter's needs are from the general population
of students.[17]

Even within special schools, whether public or private, one needs
to take account of the different patterns of ability (in terms of
group factors) if appropriate planning is to be done. The first major
division is usually along the lines of mathematics and science versus
literature, languages, and humanities. In fact, separate schools have
been established on occasion to reflect this division. Beyond the
strictly academic areas, schools for the performing arts have had
a long and distinguished history.

17. Keating, "The Study of Mathematically Precocious Youth," pp. 36-44.

SPECIAL CLASSES

The option of establishing special classes is normally both more flexible and more practical than special schools. Classes can be set up on a continuing or short-term basis, in any subject area, with the intention of either enriching or accelerating the student (or, in the terminology suggested above, expanding horizontally or progressing vertically). A major advantage of such classes is that they reduce the variance among the students, usually both in ability and interest, and the instruction or discussion can be carried out with a lesser risk of losing some students or leaving others unchallenged.

The level of selection for such classes can vary enormously. Within a given school, honors classes that involve relatively little selection can be organized to give interested and able students an opportunity to cover the normal course material in a given subject at a somewhat deeper level, but with little or no attempt to include substantial amounts of extra coursework. On the other hand, it is also possible to select a small group of students who excel in a given subject from a number of schools with the express purpose of accelerating their coverage of that subject.

This type of accelerated course, with a rigorous selection procedure and a fast pace, has been shown to be effective in a variety of settings, especially in mathematics at the junior high school level. Such courses seem to be highly appropriate for settings where there is a large enough target population to justify a rigorous selection procedure.

Fast-mathematics classes. The reported success of accelerated special classes in mathematics at the junior- and senior-high level merits fuller consideration. Such classes run by the Study of Mathematically Precocious Youth (SMPY) at Johns Hopkins University have been described in detail elsewhere.[18] These successes appear to be generalizable to other settings, as reflected in the Minnesota Talented Youth Mathematics Project (MTYMP).[19]

18. George and Denham, "Curriculum Experimentation for the Mathematically Talented"; Fox, "Sex Differences in Mathematical Precocity: Bridging the Gap."

19. Peggy A. House, "Minnesota Talented Youth Mathematics Project: Evaluation Report, 1976-77" (St. Paul, Minn.: Minnesota State Department of Education, 1977).

The first crucial element in such a class is selection of the students. They need to be as homogeneous as possible in terms of ability (but not necessarily in age), and highly motivated. Both the SMPY and MTYMP classes have been after-school or Saturday experiences, and poorly motivated students are less likely to continue in them long enough to derive the benefits. Even if they were held during regular school hours, the content is more challenging, and less motivated students may not respond well in that situation.

In the MTYMP, selection for mathematics ability took place through a talent search among teacher-nominated or test-score qualifying seventh-, eighth-, and ninth-graders. In the Twin Cities metropolitan area, 527 students (278 boys, 249 girls) took the *School and College Ability Test* (SCAT) normed for grades nine through twelve. It is important to note that the test used would be far too difficult for the average seventh to ninth grader, but the difficulty level was appropriate for selecting within a high-ability group.[20] Of these students, forty-eight were selected to participate in two special classes beginning with Algebra I (which none of the students had yet taken) and finishing with Algebra II after approximately thirty-five two-hour meetings.

The second important element is excellent teaching, which appears to be abundant among teachers who are especially interested in working with such students. For the MTYMP classes, there were many applications from teachers for this extra class, despite very modest financial reward. The major commitment the teacher of such a class should have is to moving the group at an appropriately rapid pace, since the advantage of the student selection is otherwise lost. There must also be motivation for the students to work through materials between meetings, since the meetings are few in number.

As in other similar classes, the students in the MTYMP classes met mastery criteria for mathematics knowledge far higher than would ever be required in a regular class, and did it in about half the time. These results were similar to those reported for SMPY classes. This successful replication of a special fast-paced mathe-

20. Daniel P. Keating, "Testing Those in the Top Percentiles," *Exceptional Children* 41 (1975): 435-36.

matics class demonstrates the utility and generalizability of such an approach.

Other considerations. As noted above, acceleration through subject matter in a linear fashion is not the only possible use of special classes. In literature and humanities, special classes can and have been used to provide the opportunity for much deeper exploration of issues not normally covered in regular classes. The "Great Books" have been used as a supplementary curriculum for gifted students at the secondary level and even earlier, and can provide the basis for a truly enriched education.[21]

Because of these significant advantages of flexibility, range of applicability across subject areas and levels of selectivity, and practicality, special classes remain one of the most widely used alternatives for the facilitation of gifted students at the secondary level.

There are some potential problems associated with their use, however. They can be simply diversionary. For example, establishing an extra art appreciation class for students who are advancing rapidly in mathematics and need something to do with their time, rather than working out a suitable mathematics program for these students, seems highly inappropriate. Also, such classes may mislead counselors into thinking that appropriate measures have been taken for all the students in the class, when in fact some of them are exceptionally able and require different arrangements. In a large school, for example, a single honors section may leave some students in that section still unchallenged. Finally, they may prove to be major disappointments for students if the progress they have made in such classes is not followed up with additional opportunities. Such a "hurry up and wait" syndrome can be particularly damaging to students who make major commitments in time and effort to the programs. If such pitfalls are avoided, however, special classes can be among the most useful alternatives in program planning.

DIRECT EDUCATIONAL ACCELERATION

There are a variety of ways to facilitate the learning of gifted students through direct acceleration of their education. This would primarily entail earning credit for various courses prior to

21. Bereiter, "SMPY in Social Perspective," p. 313.

the time when they would regularly be taken. In many ways these alternatives are the easiest administratively, because they typically require little of the school beyond the willingness to make the necessary administrative adjustments. Both academic and nonacademic factors need to be considered in recommending individual students for these methods of acceleration, but at the same time nonacademic concerns, such as social and emotional development, should not prohibit their use. The preponderance of systematic evidence indicates convincingly that such adjustments, when thoughtfully employed, are highly beneficial educationally and neutral or mildly beneficial in other developmental domains.[22] The description of such programs by Fox (see chapter 6 in this volume) demonstrates the range of alternatives that can be considered. Such variations as grade skipping, early college entrance, subject matter acceleration, early college courses, and advanced placement courses merit serious consideration.

COORDINATING PROGRAMS

For individuals familiar with the history of gifted education, a strong sense of *déjà vu* must accompany a reading of this discussion of educational alternatives for highly able students. There are no truly novel items in the list above, and each of them has been used at some times in some places. Many programs exist for only a short time, however, and there is often little continuity for a given student. One of the major needs for coherent, sensible programming for gifted students in secondary schools is to provide a mechanism for coordination.

A vitally important part of this mechanism will almost certainly have to be intensive, continuing counseling for gifted students. It is perhaps most appropriate to think of the specific programs as items in a cafeteria, and the task of the student and the counselor is to select a balanced set appropriate to the needs of each student. Fox has constructed a matrix to examine the pros and cons of each type of contemplated facilitation.[23] This matrix notion can be used

22. Stanley, "Concern for Intellectually Talented Youths: How It Originated," p. 41.

23. Lynn H. Fox, "Identification and Program Planning: Models and Methods," in *Intellectual Talent: Research and Development*, ed. Keating, pp. 32-54.

to sort out some of the confusion about the best course of action for a particular student.

In summary, then, there are two related goals necessary for the improvement of education for gifted students at the secondary level. First, there must be a concerted effort to create a variety of appropriate opportunities, whether these involve new instructional offerings, wider use of existing opportunities, administrative rearrangement, or some combination of these. Second, equal effort should be devoted to creating a counseling system whereby these opportunities can be brought together in an integrated, rational program for individual students.

Chapter XII

A Systemwide Program

E. JEAN THOM

Shortly after World War I, the Education Committee of the Cleveland Women's City Club became convinced that able children in the Cleveland Public Schools were not being sufficiently challenged and that, as a result, the nation was being deprived of some of its most valuable assets. At the same time, Florence Hungerford, a general supervisor in the Cleveland school system, established the first class for gifted children in grades four, five, and six at the Denison Elementary School. On learning of these efforts, the Women's City Club joined forces with the school system and the Major Work Program was born. Major Work classes have operated in the Cleveland schools since 1921. While classes for the gifted in many other cities floundered, the classes in Cleveland survived because of the broad base of community support and because of adherence to goals that have been set. The classes have always been housed in regular schools and the children in Major Work classes and their teachers have always been an integral part of these schools. As Superintendent of Schools Paul Briggs observed on the occasion of the fiftieth anniversary of the Major Work classes, "They have never been allowed to become an elite society."

Between 1921 and 1927, fourteen elementary and two junior high schools were designated as centers for gifted children. Dorothy Norris took charge of a new class for gifted children at Miles school in 1924 and later became, in turn, Supervisor and Directing Supervisor of the Major Work Department, serving until 1965. Her continuous, active, and dedicated leadership during these years provided the impetus and strength of purpose needed for the program to thrive during times when interest in the education of gifted children waned in other areas of the country.

As the Cleveland plan for gifted children developed, an experimental Major Work class was started at Oliver Hazard Perry School in 1942 for children who seemed unchallenged by regular school work, yet were not quite able to reach the requirements for admission to a regular Major Work class. Several similar classes were subsequently started, and by the 1944-45 school year were referred to as "Enrichment classes." The addition of these classes played an important role in maintaining the program for gifted children in Cleveland. Enrichment classes have served, and still serve, as a bridge between the regular classes and the Major Work classes in the school system. They provide added flexibility for the program by offering alternative placement for brighter children who for a variety of reasons are not ready for the challenge of a Major Work class but who are not being fully challenged in the regular class setting.

In October 1977, total enrollment in the program was 5,723. Of this number, 629 were enrolled in elementary Major Work classes in seven centers; 2,033 were enrolled in elementary Enrichment classes in twenty-seven centers; 766 were enrolled in junior high school Major Work and Honors classes in five centers; 824 were enrolled in senior high school Honors classes in four centers; and 1,471 were enrolled in Honors classes in other schools. Thus, the Major Work Program has grown through the years into an articulated program serving academically and intellectually gifted children from the primary grades through the high-school years.

The Major Work—Enrichment—Honors—Advanced Placement Program is an integral part of the Cleveland school system, a system that is committed to an educational program that recognizes the unique value, needs, and talents of the individual student. The program is designed to challenge gifted students through a multidimensional approach to teaching that involves special curricula, enrichment, and the acceleration of course content. The ultimate goal of the program is to develop in the student a desire for excellence and a sense of individual responsibility to the school community and to a changing society.[1]

1. Cleveland Public Schools, *Manual for Junior and Senior High School Major Work—Honors—Advanced Placement Program* (Cleveland: Cleveland Public Schools, 1970), p. 4.

Major Work children have outstanding intellectual and/or academic ability. They have a myriad of talents in all possible combinations. No group is more diversified. Their most distinguishing characteristics, however, include their perceptive and inquiring minds, their extraordinary insight and intellectual curiosity, and their critical attitude toward fact and argument. They have extensive vocabularies, learn rapidly, have a long span of concentration, and deal readily with abstractions and generalizations. They prefer to work independently. They are divergent thinkers who show signs of creativity. They show initiative and assume responsibility. They have an advanced sense of humor, have a tremendous quantity of psychic energy, and seek sincere and honest approval.[2] They have a strong sense of ethics and values.

Determination of Eligibility for Special Classes

The following criteria have been established for the assessment of every candidate in order to determine eligibility for the classes in the various components of the Cleveland program for gifted children:

For candidates for Enrichment classes, grades three through six: a stanine rank of seven or eight on an individual or group intelligence test; an average or above-average school record, or unusual ability in reading or mathematics based on standardized tests; emotional stability; recommendation of the principal and teacher; parental approval; and approval of the Division of Major Work Classes.

For candidates for Major Work classes, grades two through eight: a stanine rank of eight or nine on an individual intelligence test administered by a school psychologist; an above-average school record; evidence of substantial achievement in reading and mathematics; emotional stability; recommendation of the principal and teacher; parental approval; approval of the Division of Psychological Services; and approval of the Division of Major Work Classes.

For candidates for Special Major Work classes: the same as for the candidate for Major Work classes and, in addition, superior

2. Cleveland Public Schools, *The Right to Be Accepted, Respected, Educated: Programs Serving the Exceptional Child* (Cleveland: Cleveland Public Schools, 1975), p. 36.

achievement, good work habits, and maturity in relationships with others.

For candidates for Honors classes: criteria vary depending on the subject area but generally include a "Probable Learning Rate" score of 115 or above or a stanine rank of seven or above on a group intelligence test, standardized test performance indicated by a stanine rank of seven, eight, or nine; an "A" or "B" average in scholastic achievement in the particular subject area (a "C" average is acceptable only for Major Work students); recommendations of teachers, counselors, principals and/or department chairpersons.

Referrals are made by parents, teachers, counselors, principals, and psychologists.[3] The Division of Major Work Classes enlists the services of guidance counselors, teachers, psychologists, social workers, administrators, and supervisors to determine the best procedures to follow in serving the needs of particular children.

Placement Procedures

Forms have been developed for use in recommending candidates for placement in the various classes. These forms are revised as procedures are modified from time to time.

The procedures for placing candidates new to Major Work and Enrichment classes are as follows:

1. The principal of the contributing school uses a "Teacher's Appraisal Form" to identify candidates, initiates a "Recommendation and Placement Form" for possible candidates, and recommends students for testing by the school psychologist.

2. The psychologist from the Division of Psychological Services tests the child and makes a recommendation, returns the "Recommendation and Placement Form" to the principal of the contributing school, and sends notation of the recommendation to the Division of Major Work Classes.

3. The principal of the contributing school then makes contact with the parents, completes the school's section of the "Recommendation and Placement Form," and forwards the form to the Division of Major Work Classes.

4. The Division of Major Work Classes informs the contrib-

3. Ibid., pp. 36-38.

uting school when an opening occurs for placement of the child and sends the "Recommendation and Placement Form" to the Center School. (Placement in Major Work or Enrichment classes generally takes place at the beginning of the school year except when it is to the advantage of the child to enter later.)

5. The principal of the contributing school then issues a transfer to the Major Work or Enrichment class center. The principal of the Major Work or Enrichment Center holds a preentry conference with parents and child to explain standards of the program, completes the Center School's section of the "Recommendation and Placement Form," and forwards it to the Division of Major Work Classes. The principal keeps the Division informed at all times of openings at a particular grade level and the availability of additional rooms for use by the Division.

6. The Division of Major Work Classes keeps an up-to-date record of openings at the centers, of children eligible for placement in the classes, of children who have qualified but whose parents have refused permission, and of children who have been removed from the classes.[4]

The procedures for placing candidates for the Honors classes are as follows:

1. The Division of Major Work Classes sends "Recommendations for Senior High Honors Placement" forms to all junior high schools. Teachers and department chairpersons of the contributing schools provide the guidance counselor in the contributing school with names of students being recommended.

2. Guidance counselors complete a "Recommendation for Senior High Honors Placement" form for each student meeting the criteria for Honors classes in particular subjects and submits these forms to the principal of the contributing school, who signs the forms and forwards them to the Division of Major Work Classes.

3. The Division of Major Work Classes sends copies of recommendation forms that are approved and those that are not approved to the principal of the contributing school. Copies of the approved forms are also sent to the principal of the Senior High School Honors Center.

4. Cleveland Public Schools, *New Dimensions in the Major Work Program* (Cleveland: Cleveland Public Schools, 1967), pp. 5-6.

4. The guidance counselor of the contributing school contacts the student and parents regarding approval for placement in an Honors class.

5. The principal of the contributing school then issues a transfer to a Senior High Honors Center.

The Instructional Program

Close cooperation between subject area divisions and the Division of Major Work Classes has made possible the development of curriculum guides for use by teachers of gifted students. Materials and instructional strategies are customized to fit the learning styles of gifted children. The Major Work Program places much emphasis on group discussion, group planning and evaluation, independent research, independent study, self-discipline, and the development of the higher-level thinking processes. In all classes emphasis is placed upon high levels of development in both the affective and the cognitive domains.

The content in mathematics is accelerated beginning at the third-grade level and leading into twelfth-grade courses in calculus and analytic geometry. The study of social studies progresses to the study of Advanced Placement American History or Advanced Placement European History at the eleventh- or twelfth-grade level. In science, the laboratory approach is begun at the elementary-school level. Currently, both Advanced Placement Biology and Advanced Placement Chemistry are offered at the twelfth-grade level. Among the activities in which gifted students in science have shown interest are the Earthwatch Scholarships. Several students have been granted funds enabling them to participate in scientific field expeditions.

Released time has been granted individual students whose needs could not be met within the Major Work or Honors classrooms. For example, one tenth-grade student spent time in the Division of Research of the Cleveland Metropolitan General Hospital conducting research on white blood cells, while a ninth-grade student spent time at the Cleveland Metroparks Zoo working with one of the veterinarians there.

The Major Work Program is probably best known for its elementary language arts program. Among the components of the program are the literature club, outlining, and daily talks.[5] In the secondary school the English language arts program culminates with the study of Advanced Placement English in the twelfth grade. Study of one or more foreign languages is an integral part of the program. At the elementary-school level the main emphasis is on speaking and understanding the language. At the upper-elementary level some reading and writing are introduced. In secondary school all four skills are developed.

Beginning with the 1975-76 school year, pupils in fifth- and sixth-grade Major Work and Enrichment classes were offered the opportunity to participate in the French Snow Class program under the auspices of Campus International Ltd. This program affords American children the experience of living with French children in the French Alps for a month. They pursue their regular academic subjects in the classroom in the morning and learn to ski in the afternoon. The Cleveland school system considers the Snow Class program an extension of the elementary foreign language program and an excellent intercultural experience for young people.

A further development of plans with Campus International Ltd. involved the visit of French children to the United States in May, 1977. The first stop on their American itinerary was in Cleveland where they attended school with children in two Major Work Centers and were housed with families in areas served by those two Centers. This program was continued in 1978.

The Staff

The headquarters staff of the Division of Major Work Classes is composed of a director, a supervisor, and a secretary. Personnel from the Division of Psychological Services, the Division of Research and Development, the Division of Guidance, and the Divisions of English and Language Arts, Mathematics, Science, Social Studies, Foreign Languages, and Fine Arts all play important roles in providing appropriate educational experiences for the academically and intellectually gifted young people.

In the schools, teachers, department chairpersons, counselors,

5. Detailed explanations of these components can be found in Cleveland Public Schools, *Jump into a Treasury of Ideas* (Cleveland: Cleveland Public Schools, 1969).

and principals are all important to the smooth functioning of the program. The role of the teacher in the classroom is critical to the success of a program. In cooperation with the Division of Major Work Classes, the Case Western Reserve University recently developed and implemented a three-year staff development effort in affective and humanistic education. This in-service program, known as Project Impact, was funded under Title III of the Elementary and Secondary Education Act.[6]

Basic to the Cleveland program for gifted children is the philosophy that each child and each teacher should be helped to become the very best person possible. Keeping in mind the interests and needs of these children, it is believed that teachers should have a strong self-concept and an ego that is not threatened by students who may know more about a subject than the teacher. They should like, have empathy for, and understand gifted students, should be able to challenge them without threatening, and should understand the use of motivational strategies that will "turn them on." Teachers should be good listeners and allow time for students to think. They should take into account the learning styles of students and be able to develop a broad spectrum of effective teaching strategies. It is also important that teachers should have demonstrated superior scholarship in the subject to be taught and should also be committed to continuous personal and professional growth. A classroom learning climate should be developed that encourages students to take intellectual risks and allows them to probe, to wonder, to guess, to try, to inquire, to deal in fantasy, to play with questions and discrepancies, to toy with possibilities, and to test ideas.[7]

Assistance is available to teachers in the programs of the Division of Major Work Classes from supervisory personnel in the division and in the school system. Teachers in the Major Work Division are willing and eager to exchange ideas and help one another. They also welcome educators from other school systems who are seeking assistance in working with gifted young people.

All-day or half-day workshops are held periodically to keep teachers abreast of the latest developments in curriculum. In recent

6. *Project Impact: A Humanistic Approach to Instruction* (Cleveland: Department of Education, Case Western Reserve University, 1976).

7. Cleveland Public Schools, *The Right to Be Accepted, Respected, Educated*, p. 39.

years, these workshops have dealt with such topics as Language Arts, Mathematics, Science for the Gifted, Strategies for Teaching the Gifted, Developing Creative Thinking, the Cognitive Domain, the Affective Domain, Drama, and Creativity. In addition, an orientation meeting is held each August for teachers new to elementary Major Work and Enrichment classes. A meeting of all elementary Major Work and Enrichment teachers is held each September. Teachers also play vital roles in the development of curriculum guides and the selection of books for use by the Division of Major Work Classes.

In each junior high school Major Work-Honors Center and each senior high school Honors Center one or more counselors are designated as Major Work and/or Honors Counselors. In the senior high centers the college counselor is generally the designee. The Major Work-Honors counselor is responsible for all aspects of the guidance program with respect to Major Work and Honors students. The responsibilities of the counselor include the following: (a) working with principals, teachers, and other counselors and visiting contributing schools to improve articulation between elementary, junior, and senior high school Major Work and Honors programs; (b) planning a special orientation program early in the seventh grade and tenth grade for Major Work and Honors students and their parents; (c) conducting an orientation program in the eighth grade for students (and their parents) who qualify for one or more ninth-grade Honors classes; (d) acting as a liaison between department chairpersons, principals, subject matter supervisors, and the Division of Major Work Classes; (e) promoting understanding of the Major Work-Honors programs through P.T.A. meetings, faculty meetings, and other school and community functions; and (f) providing special information on competitive scholarship activities.[8]

Conclusion

For more than half a century, the Division of Major Work Classes has served gifted children in Cleveland. Continuity of the program can be attributed to many factors, including support from parents, from the community as a whole, from the Women's City

8. *Manual for Junior and Senior High School Major Work—Honors—Advanced Placement Program*, p. 18.

Club, from the Board of Education, from administrative, supervisory, and teaching personnel, and from graduates of the program. Changes made as the result of studies of the program have also contributed to its continuity.

The Major Work Program has served as a valuable resource for evaluative and descriptive studies of the education of gifted children. Over the years the program has been described in detail by Goddard, by Hall, and by Sumption.[9] The program has been studied in connection with research carried on for doctoral dissertations.[10] In his follow-up study of graduates of the Major Work Program, Barbe noted that "almost without exception [the graduates] praised the Major Work Program as having given them the intellectual challenge to ask, 'Why?' and to know the real value of education."[11]

On the occasion of the fiftieth anniversary of the Major Work Program, a sixth-grade student made the following comment:

The Major Work literature program has been a rare and precious experience to me. It was there in the reading circle that I learned the importance of what I, as an individual, think and feel. I truly believe that I am a Child of the Universe; no less than the trees and the stars, I have a right to be here, as I am, with all of the little points that distinguish me from everyone else. It was in the circle that I learned to respect the opinions of others. The ideas that I carried with me to the discussion were expanded by the thoughts and opinions of others. This does not happen when I read alone.[12]

9. Henry Herbert Goddard, *School Training of Gifted Children* (Yonkers-on-Hudson, N.Y.: World Book Co., 1928); Theodore Hall, *Gifted Children: The Cleveland Story* (Cleveland: World Publishing Co., 1956); Merle R. Sumption, *Three Hundred Gifted Children* (Yonkers-on-Hudson, N.Y.: World Book Co., 1941).

10. Walter Barbe, "A Follow-up Study of Graduates of Special Classes for Gifted Children" (Ph.D. diss., Northwestern University, 1953); Charles N. Jordan, "An Analysis of the Abilities and Achievement of High IQ Pupils in Cleveland's Major Work and Enrichment Classes, Grades 4B-6A" (Ph.D. diss., Western Reserve University, 1961); Edward C. Frierson, "A Study of Selected Characteristics of Gifted Children from Upper and Lower Socioeconomic Backgrounds" (Ph.D. diss., Kent State University, 1964).

11. Cleveland Public Schools, *Thirty Years After: A Digest of Dr. Walter Barbe's Dissertation "A Follow-up Study of Graduates of Special Classes for Gifted Children,"* (Cleveland: Cleveland Public Schools, 1960), pp. 9-10.

12. Donna Weathers, "Memoirs of the Reading Circle" (Speech delivered at a dinner commemorating the fiftieth anniversary of the Major Work Program, Cleveland, April 13, 1972).

CHAPTER XIII

The Governor's School of North Carolina

VIRGIL S. WARD

The Formative Years of the Governor's School—1963-65

The Governor's School of North Carolina is a summer residential school for exceptionally talented secondary-school youth. The school originated in 1963 as one of several innovative educational developments stemming from the office of the then Governor Terry Sanford. As Special Assistant to the Governor, novelist John Ehle, a devotee of the arts in his native state, developed and proposed the idea of the Governor's School.

The project was supported in the beginning mainly by the Carnegie Corporation of New York and additionally by business and foundation interests within the state. The school is now an established feature of public education in North Carolina, operating under a special Board of Governors and administered through the North Carolina Department of Public Instruction.

Some 400 senior high-school students, selected by competition in academic areas, and by auditions in the fine and performing arts, are brought each summer to the school site at Salem College in the Old Salem community of Winston-Salem for a seven-week period. There they pursue a program of study supplementing but not supplanting their studies in their home communities, in a curricular pattern geared as closely as possible to their respective aptitudes and interests. Tuition is free. There are no grades in the usual sense. The faculties for the various areas are meticulously selected for competence and distinction within the respective curricular fields, and they come from secondary schools and colleges in North Carolina and in other states.

The Governor's School is a prototype in differential education for the gifted, the first such institution among several that were to follow with similar concepts of purpose and program. Initially, it provided occasion for some exciting and adventurous thought on the part of its progenitors. And while a succession of able faculties and administrative personnel have made notable contributions in the operation of the program and in the substance of curricular activities over the intervening years, the character of the school has remained remarkably true to the original concepts as to the organization of the program and the structure of the curriculum.

In describing the general plan and rationale worked out in the formative years of the school I shall illustrate how the theoretical foundations have established curricular areas and boundaries designed to achieve specific objectives.[1] I shall try to show that efforts to relate theory to practice can contribute to a developing body of theory of differential education for the gifted.

From Theory into Practice: Foundations of the Program

The task of conceptualizing the Governor's School took place between January and May of the first project year and under such pressure of time that implicit understandings and impulses could exist only in a generalized way in the initial concepts of both program and curriculum. There were two principal foundations in psychological and epistemological thought on which the institution was established.

First, a concept about the nature of the human mind and its

---

1. Virgil S. Ward, "The Governor's School of North Carolina: The Formative Years: 1963-65. Collected Papers of the Project Director." This unpublished compilation of papers was prepared in connection with a newly commissioned "Study of the Institution: 1977" for presentation to the present Board of Governors and the State Department of Public Instruction.

Two conference papers in this collection are of principal relevance in the present explanatory essay, both developed during the formative period: (a) "A Case Study in Curricular Designing for Gifted Secondary School Students," Forty-second annual conference of the Council for Exceptional Children, Chicago, 1964, in which the details of the planning sessions and preparations for the first summer session are provided; and (b) "Differential Education for the Gifted: Theory and Application," Forty-third annual conference of the Council for Exceptional Children, Portland, Oregon, 1965. In this second paper, the curricular structure, which by then appeared to be standing the implementation process reasonably well, was put into general form so that it might serve as a model transferable in essence to other situations, without the necessity of specific duplication. A chart taken from that paper is shown in fig. 1. The design as originally set forth was subsequently edited and expanded (1968) for use in other connections.

inner organization provided a basis for understanding the aptitudes or talents manifest among exceptional youth of secondary-school age. The concepts that guided planning were not the currently popular psychological concepts of mental organization that emphasize a large number of finely distinguished elements, but rather the historically important "two-factor" theory of mind.[2] In this view, both general intelligence (a g factor) and a small number of specific aptitudes (s factors) are functionally related. This theoretical concept provides for a parallel relationship in the specially constructed curriculum between both the general and pervasive perceptivity of gifted youth and their peak excellence in one or more capacities of mind and personality, such as that for mathematics, dance, or music.

The parallel between the hypothesized mental organization, inclusive of both general and specific capacity, and the three areas or divisions within the curricular whole can be readily observed. The principal emphasis in a three-hour daily time block is on Area I, the objective of which is aptitude development. The student body is divided into subgroups for studies in this phase of the curriculum, according to identified peaks of capability and interest. Experiences leading to the objective of general intellectual development (Area II) include studies and activities relating to the formal and the substantive aspects of general learning capability. Studies in Area III alternate with those in Area II in the daily schedule. These activities are targeted toward development in the affective and purposive domains. Thus, the pattern is as follows:

Area I: Aptitude development. In this major curricular phase, a block of time each day is devoted to the pursuit of studies related to the student's first choice among eight curricular divisions:

2. Historic origins of concepts as to the nature and organization of mind are of special interest in that contemporary publications tend understandably to emphasize the currently prevailing views. The reference to the "two-factor" theory is based upon a selection in *Studies in Individual Differences: The Search for Intelligence,* ed. James J. Jenkins and Donald G. Paterson (New York: Appleton-Century-Crofts, 1961), in which several excerpts from Charles Spearman, *The Abilities of Man* (London: Macmillan and Co., 1927) are reprinted. Spearman's paper marks a turning point from the earlier unifactor theories of intelligence toward the predominant multifactor concepts of today. Other readings in a similar vein are conveniently set forth in the Jenkins and Paterson volume.

humanities, mathematics, social science, natural science, dance, drama, music (instrumental and choral), and painting.

Area II: General intellectual development. In this aspect of the curricular plan, the students meet for three days a week in a shorter time block for the pursuit of studies and activities intended to involve general intellectual operations and/or an emphasis upon general forms of knowledge, ideas, or issues.

Area III: Personal development. In this phase of the curriculum, the affective and purposive aspects of the student's potential are brought to the fore, the intent being to anticipate typical gratifications, problems, and frustrations that tend to occur in the life careers of creative and idealistic persons, and to facilitate those kinds of personal and social adjustment that are commensurate with productivity and leadership.

A second background resource in the conceptualization of the Governor's School was more immediate. A body of psychological and epistemological principles, cast in axiomatic form and comprised of twelve propositions and twenty-nine corollaries, had been developed in research in 1952 and had been recently published.[3] These descriptive and prescriptive generalizations were available during the first summer session of the school for the orientation of staff members as they worked within the curricular plan given above. The following is an example of a single subset of those principles:

That the educative experience of the intellectually superior should be consciously designed as generative of further development, extensively and intensively, along similar and related avenues.

1. That in the education of the gifted child and youth the scope of the content should extend into the general nature of all the chief branches of knowledge.
2. That the curriculum for the gifted should but introduce and initially explore the concepts extending over broad expanses of knowledge.
3. That the content of the curriculum should be organized in a manner which reduces to generic areas the concepts undertaken for instruction.

3. Virgil S. Ward, *Educating the Gifted: An Axiomatic Approach* (Columbus, Ohio: Charles E. Merrill, 1961). This volume is based on Virgil S. Ward, "Principles of Education for Intellectually Superior Individuals" (Doct. diss., University of North Carolina at Chapel Hill, 1952).

4. That the theoretical bases should always be given for the facts, opinions, and principles presented to the gifted individual.

From Reality to Generality: The Analysis of a Design for Differential Education for the Gifted

By the third year of the project, with all principal aspects of the projected curriculum proving generally feasible, it seemed possible to set forth a general plan or design that would be transferable in essence to other settings. The sense of the matter is that if requisite theoretic foundations have been successfully incorporated, then further advances can be more certainly achieved. When the principal substance holds, variations in practice contribute to the further testing of the theory.

Figure 1 provides a model of the curricular plan. Only a few reference points in the matrix and a few interpretive comments can be provided here. These are intended to suggest the fuller range of linkages derived from the external resource theories that lead into both the actual curriculum and the generalized design.

The order of the curricular divisions described earlier (Areas I, II, and III) differs from the order in which the cells in column 1 of the chart are presented. The curricular outline was designed for ready communicability of the emphases intended in the ground plan of the Governor's School. The entries in the cells of column 1 from top to bottom represent an increasing magnitude in the deviance of the gifted from the average in experiential and behavioral potentiality. The magnitudes range from the affective and purposive aspects of personality (which are the least deviant and provide the psychological bases of curricular Area III), through the two cells b and c (representing the general intellectual capacities that comprise the psychological bases of curricular Area II), and finally to the peak degrees of aptitude (the psychological bases for curricular Area I, which comprises the first priority in the curricular plan of the school).

The entries in column 2 are simply transformations from the respective psychological potentialities (that is, experiential and behavioral) into the form of parallel developmental objectives to which the various aspects of the educational task relate. All the cells within this column add up to the summary designation at the

(1) Experiential and Behavioral Potentiality	(2) Developmental Objectives	Curricular Design; Developmental Experience		(5) Goals, Outcomes: Actualized Experiential and Behavioral Potentiality
		(3) Substance: Knowledge of and about Arts and Sciences; Values: Behavioral Skills	(4) Process: Learning and Instruction	
a) Ordinary emotional response potentiality plus possible extremes in temperament, sensitivity	Personal development	Value information: valuational and affective situational experience and activity	Cognitive and situational experience and guidance involving motive and emotion	Mature, healthy personality; actualized self with constructive and gratifying involvement of productive or creative disposition
b) Superior intellective potentiality, moderate to extreme	Conceptual development	All knowledge and derivative activity arranged in an epistemological taxonomy	Lifetime learning and behavioral development: Mainly personal exploration according to interest or need; instruction and social interaction only where these significantly facilitate individual learning and performance	Understanding and skill of every nature and in whatever degree required by the actualized self for satisfying experience
c) (Superior intellective potentiality, moderate to extreme)	Intellectual development	Any knowledge or activity involving these complex mental processes subject to structural or functional modification through experience	Functional exercise, supervision and evaluation involving available intellective potentiality	Optimally developed potentiality for general intellective operations: reflective, critical, creative
d) Extreme superiority in localized experiential and behavioral potentiality	Aptitude development	Relevant technical knowledge or activity in full subtlety and complexity; systematic knowledge of one or more particular fields	Sustained, exacting experience, supervised and evaluated in light of most sophisticated developmental theory and technology	Extraordinary understanding and skill, localized; actualized talent
All significant, identifiable human potentialities sufficiently extreme to warrant special treatment	Integrative development of all significant exceptional potentialities	Every significant kind of knowledge and human activity utilized as required by and for the individual in life-long personal growth and contributory social interaction		Optimally developed, continually becoming person, free and responsible universalized human mind and character, educated for social and cultural interaction

Fig. 1. Differential Education for the Gifted: A Chart of the Theoretical Rationale.

SOURCE: Virgil S. Ward, "Differential Education for the Gifted; Theory and Application" (Paper given at the forty-third annual conference of the Council for Exceptional Children, Portland, Oreg., 1965).

bottom of the column: "integrative development of all significant exceptional potentialities." These respective cells, of course, lead laterally in the chart toward related activities in columns 3 and 4 and in turn to the anticipated outcomes in column 5.

The collective entries in columns 3 and 4, following across the respective rows b and c, are intended to differentiate the nature of developmental experience that takes its point of departure in the total aptitudes of the person and leads toward the anticipated social roles identified elsewhere as those involving the reconstruction of human culture as distinct from the simpler devices of participation in and maintenance thereof.[4]

Area II of the Governor's School curriculum takes into account the emphasis intended in the design upon both general understanding and the uses of general intelligence. There is a division noted in the chart between sections 2b and 3b ("conceptual development," involving knowledge in general) and sections 2c and 3c ("intellectual development," involving any knowledge promising to result in structural or functional improvements in general intelligence). In fact, the ongoing activities in this curricular area, while employing exciting and worthy epistemological and psychological processes, have not as yet come firmly to respect the division.

Finally, the grandly summative juncture at the extreme right of the bottom row represents the fully developed (actualized) person, whose gifts of extraordinary mind and personality have benefitted in this ideal sense from appropriately evocative experience in every main psychological domain and epistemological realm, across the youthful years and into what should be a continuously productive adulthood. Needless to say, while history records the names of some who appear to qualify as encompassing genii, few among the living can aspire to such stature within their own life span.

The purpose of the chart is to provide a theoretical rationale to guide curriculum planners in the design of differentiated educational experiences for the gifted. As such, it is intended to relate the special characteristics of the gifted and talented to appropriate developmental objectives, to developmental experiences through a curriculum design, and to outcomes resulting in actualized behavior.

4. Virgil S. Ward et al., *The Gifted Student: A Manual for Program Improvement* (Atlanta: Southern Regional Education Board, 1962), pp. 31, 64.

Theoretic Authenticity and Institutional Generativity

It is hoped that the applications of theory in the Governor's School program and curricular design comprise a kind of "theoretic authenticity" for that institution. If so, what further inquiries and suggestions would seem to be useful?

The Governor's School has been established as a continuing feature of public instruction in the state of North Carolina. More than 6,000 students have apparently been elevated to previously unexperienced heights of educational insight and aspiration through participation in the program. The durability and appeal of the Governor's School and its impact on the students suggest that the idea and design have theoretic authenticity.

If it is the underlying soundness of the theory of differential education for the gifted that accounts for the continuation of the school, could the institutional philosophy and curricular design be adapted to the regular academic program of a local school? For instance, could it function in a year-round plan for a school-within-school program? Is the rationale sufficiently clear and strong to support a K-12 district plan for differential education for the gifted, with primary and intermediate levels appropriately designed for developmental readiness and student interest? In sum, is the Governor's School pattern generalizable directly to other endeavors with similar intent and purpose such that it is generative in that sense? Experience with the Governor's School of North Carolina clearly suggests that it is.

If the movement from theory into practice is possible, what about the reverse—practice into theory? Can activity authenticated through a grounding in principle provide a base for inquiry for more sophisticated empirical research than might otherwise occur? Could it contribute to the opportunity for students at advanced stages to move into more penetrating concentration upon issues? Could the Governor's School itself, with its history, be expected to show some transcending inquiry and observations on its own? Obviously, this is possible.

Finally, it is clear that further energy and resources should be invested in studying the strategies for inquiry and action. More than a half century has elapsed since the progenitors of differential education for the gifted, Terman and Hollingworth, began their insightful and imaginative inquiries. During this period a knowledge base has emerged that has become attenuated, discontinuous within itself, disparate in emphasis and redirection, and divided by massive sociocultural upheavals in both school and community. We must now employ imagination and reason to harness the more dependable of yesterday's understandings and to set them forth in various theoretical statements so that further empirical inquiry can then indeed lead to significant upward transformations in our understanding of this inordinately consequential human problem of nurturing the potential of the gifted and the talented. The Governor's School suggests that this is possible.

CHAPTER XIV

College Programs

MILTON J. GOLD

In the score of years since publication in 1958 of the fifty-seventh yearbook of the National Society for the Study of Education on education of the gifted, higher education witnessed a surge of interest in academic excellence followed by a student protest movement with a powerful egalitarian drive. The same period saw an enormous outpouring of government and private funds in the interest of first-rate scholarship, followed by a shrinking of financial support that threatened the continued existence, let alone the quality, of major public and independent colleges and universities. Through this all, interest in superior students reached its apogee in the early 1960s, fell to a nadir in the early 1970s, and shows signs of revival at the end of the decade. Fortunately, many programs that began in the 1950s and 1960s laid down viable roots nad persevered.

By 1958, programs supported by major foundations had already borne their first fruit in the development or expansion of plans leading to acceleration, individualization, and enrichment in higher education. Soviet success in launching Sputnik in 1957 stimulated public as well as foundation concern with the quality of education that America was offering its most promising students. This concern was reflected in massive assistance from the federal government and from some state and local units to students in the form of scholarships, to universities for institutional improvement, but most particularly to scholars, teachers, and researchers through grants from health, science, education, and manpower agencies.

Funds given in the interest of academic excellence helped move many institutions in the direction of the research university that had served as the exemplar for graduate universities since Daniel

Colt Gilman had first introduced the German model to Johns Hopkins in 1875. For twenty years following World War II, major universities proceeded along this path, recruiting researchers, developing research facilities, and promoting development of young scholars committed to research ideals. Unfortunately, teaching in undergraduate programs earned but a low priority. A researcher for the Carnegie Commission on Higher Education is quoted as saying, "The faculty is not hostile to teaching, just not enthusiastic." [1]

At the same time, some segments of the academic community and some foundations sought to establish programs that would identify superior college students early and provide them with instruction and counseling that could counteract apathy or alienation. The rapid expansion of honors programs (to be discussed later in this chapter) and advanced placement provide evidence of these efforts. These efforts, however, proved inadequate in the face of the student protest movement that is generally dated from the free speech movement in Berkeley in 1964 and which peaked in the aftermath of demonstrations at Kent State University that resulted in the death of four students in 1970. The disruptions of this period were obviously related to circumstances outside the university as well as those within it—the war in Viet Nam, the civil rights movement, and political motivation on the part of a few groups with social-revolutionary objectives. Within the university, large numbers of students and some faculty protested depersonalization, remoteness from the problems of the contemporary world, irrelevant criteria of scholarship, and a servile relationship to the military-industrial complex. The cry for "relevance," for contemporaneity, for access to higher education for the poor and the minorities, and for egalitarian rather than elitist values and operation led in many cases to inflation of grades, to progressive elimination of foreign language requirements, to a steady dilution of distribution requirements, and to curricular changes that almost systematically reduced emphasis on reading and writing.[2] Many superior students capable of greater challenge were unfortunately

1. John S. Brubacher and Willis Rudy, *Higher Education in Transition* (New York: Harper and Row, 1976), p. 284.

2. Charles Frankel, "Reflections on a Worn-Out Model," *Daedalus* 103 (Fall 1974): 25.

leaders in pressing these demands and the victims as a result of a less demanding curriculum.

Even more unfortunate were many bright young people who opted out of the "academic grind" and what they perceived as a materialistic culture in order to join the "counterculture." Frequently from upper middle-class backgrounds and professional families, large numbers of intellectually endowed youth dropped out from, or never entered, college in the late 1960s and early 1970s, pursuing an aimless life because they rejected the achievement-oriented values of their parents and middle-class society.

The civil rights drive and the "War on Poverty" of the 1960s moved the theme of excellence off center-stage and focussed attention instead on equal access of deprived groups to higher education. "Open admissions" programs led to entry of large numbers of poorly prepared students. Many colleges had to devote their major energy not to the talented but to those desperately in need of remediation. Unfortunately, financial strictures at the same time prevented colleges from pursuing simultaneously two essential purposes—equal access and the pursuit of academic excellence.

Foundation and government support also shifted. A letter from the Ford Foundation in 1976 noted that "few, if any, Foundation-supported activities during the past ten years were designed explicitly for 'gifted' or 'superior' college students." [3] At the same time, the Secretary of the Carnegie Corporation regretted "that Carnegie Corporation has not been active in support of programs for the intellectually gifted during the past ten years," but noted that "our emphasis in the past decade has been more on students who formerly would not have had access to higher education." [4] In the preceding decade, Ford and Carnegie had been among the main sponsors of programs for superior students.

Against this setting, programs for talented students in colleges and universities become all the more urgent. A return to achievement values is discernible in the economically distressed years of

3. Letter from Fred E. Crossland, Program Officer, Division of Education and Research, Ford Foundation, September 23, 1976.

4. Letter from Sara L. Engelhardt, Secretary, Carnegie Corporation of New York, October 7, 1976.

the mid-1970s, more concern with "making it" in college and graduate school, and anxiety over employment thereafter. These attitudes have been leading to greater application, but to a concomitant "vocationalism," which places career specialization above the values of a broad and liberal education.

Special Programs for the Able

In mounting special programs for students of high ability, many institutions have declared their concern with maintaining the interest of superior students in academic achievement, in offering a challenge to them, and in developing their potential. Seeking to recruit the very best students, they have also sought to set the tone for the college as a whole, and in doing so, to attract and to retain highly able faculty members.

In order to update information on college programs,[5] inquiries were addressed to 176 institutions, including the major colleges in each state and those that reported special programs for the gifted in the 1973 edition of *American Colleges and Universities*.[6] Of these, 115 responded. The responses should be regarded as representing practices that are worthy of note but not necessarily typical of colleges and universities in general.

SELECTION

Pressures to increase access to higher education have reduced the tendency in many colleges to provide for the gifted by limiting admission to superior applicants. A few private colleges responded to the questionnaire, however, indicating that continuing selectivity made special programs unnecessary in their institutions.

In most colleges, selection for special programs takes place at or after admission. Rank in high-school class, grade-point averages, scores on nationally administered tests such as the *Scholastic Aptitude Test* (SAT) and the *American College Testing Program*

5. For summary of developments in the decade preeeding 1964, see Milton J. Gold, *Education of the Intellectually Gifted* (Columbus, Ohio: Charles E. Merrill, 1965).

6. *American Colleges and Universities*, 11th ed., ed. W. Todd Furness (Washington, D.C.: American Council on Education, 1973).

(ACT), locally developed examinations, and interviews with applicants are among mechanisms mentioned by practically every institution seeking to give greater assistance to superior students. A small handful of colleges, however, expressed concern with the injustices of mass testing, the effects of early negative experiences upon achievement records, and the handicaps of impoverished culture. Schudson noted that students of high socioeconomic status stand a better chance on the widely used SAT and ACT. While access to college has become increasingly important to provide the credentials needed for upward mobility, higher education has grown more stratified as a result of overuse of standardized testing.[7] Accordingly, some colleges give greater value to informal assessment devices (for example, self-selection, interviewing by college faculty and student peers) in selecting students for special educational experiences. An argument to support self-selection is implied by Suczek, who evaluated self-selectees at the University of California (Berkeley) as being relatively more flexible, tolerant, and realistic in their thinking, less bound by authority, and possessing broader intellectual and aesthetic interests.[8]

ACCELERATION

Lehman's classic studies on age and achievement provide a major justification for accelerating progress of superior students through formal education so that they can get on with their life's work.[9] Seeking a relationship between age and the period of one's greatest contribution to scholarship, research, industry, literature, and the arts, Lehman found that man's greatest achievements in all fields occur at early ages, some before age thirty and only a few after age forty-five. For the most able individuals, the major contribution of college may be to give them the tools that an education provides and to get them involved in their career at an early age. The work

7. Michael Schudson, "Organizing the Meritocracy: A History of the College Entrance Examination Board," *Harvard Education Review* 42 (February 1972): 34-69.

8. Robert F. Suczek, "Self-Selection and Special Educational Programs," *Journal of Higher Education* 41 (November 1970): 607-17.

9. Harvey C. Lehman, *Age and Achievement* (Princeton, N.J.: Princeton University Press, 1953).

of Terman[10] and Pressey[11] reporting the superior achievement of accelerated children gave research support for the Early Admission to College Program and the Advanced Placement Program, which the Fund for the Advancement of Education initiated in 1951 and 1952 respectively. The early admission venture built upon ten years of experience at the University of Chicago in admitting selected students after completion of their junior and occasionally their sophomore year in high school.[12] Both programs proved successful. In 1976, about one college in five admitted some students before graduation from high school, generally making arrangements for students to secure their high school diplomas after completing their freshman year in college.[13]

The most commonly used device for acceleration is the Advanced Placement (AP) Examination. Advanced Placement courses started in high schools in 1952, offering college-level work following specially developed syllabi in a number of subjects, and qualifying students to take examinations administered by the Educational Testing Service. In 1976, over 75,000 students in 3,939 schools took almost 99,000 examinations, and success on these tests was accepted by 1,580 colleges. Studies indicate that AP candidates "are solidly successful in their academic work in college." They do very well when placed in advanced courses; as many as 87 percent of them often take advanced work in the subject of their AP examination; they "generally get higher grades in sequent courses than do other students"; they appear to "have an edge over non-AP students, even those from the secondary schools, . . . and they are more likely to take advanced work in the field." Generally, AP students do not

10. Lewis M. Terman and Melita H. Oden, *The Gifted Child Grows Up: Twenty-five Years' Follow-up of a Superior Group* (Stanford, Calif.: Stanford University Press, 1947).

11. Sidney L. Pressey, *Educational Acceleration: Appraisals and Basic Problems, Bureau of Educational Research Monographs,* No. 31 (Columbus, Ohio: Bureau of Educational Research, Ohio State University, 1949).

12. Fund for the Advancement of Education, *They Went to College Early* (New York: The Fund, 1957); also Anthony T. G. Pallett, "Early Freshman Entrance at the University of Chicago," *School and Society* 100 (January 1972): 8, 28.

13. Baird W. Whitlock, "Simon's Rock: The Early College," *Community and Junior College Journal* 44 (February 1974): 18-20.

use credit they receive to shorten their term in college but use the
exemption in order to take extra credits and do more advanced
work instead. They also attribute increased enthusiasm for learning
to their involvement in AP.[14]

Students earning specified grades in AP examinations receive
differing kinds of recognition in the colleges they enter. Some
colleges give sophomore standing to students who have achieved
required grades (generally grades of "4" or "5"—occasionally "3,"
"4," or "5"—on a scale from 1 to 5) in three or four examinations.
Some colleges give credit toward graduation as for comparable
courses taken in college. Some colleges give no credit but waive
parallel requirements.

After admission to college, various devices are offered to accelerate progress. A few colleges have systematic programs to permit
graduation in three years. A larger number make available the
option of taking a heavy load in order to accumulate the usual
number of credits at an earlier date. "Dual degree" programs are
much in evidence—completion of an academic and a professional
degree (both at the bachelor's level) in four years, or a B.A.-M.A.
combination where the student qualifies for the first graduate degree in reduced time. Finally, there is increasing use of credit by
examination.

In 1966, with support from the Carnegie Corporation and the
College Entrance Examination Board, the Educational Testing Service developed the *College Level Examinations of Proficiency*
(CLEP). CLEP tests were designed to evaluate the educational
achievement of persons, primarily adults, "no matter where you
learned it."[15] Tests are offered in five general areas and in forty-one
subjects. Some 1800 institutions grant CLEP credit, exempting students from basic requirements, allowing distribution credit, or
granting elective credits.[16] The tests have been used unexpectedly

14. Letter from Carl H. Haag, Director, College Board Placement Test
Programs, Educational Testing Service, October 4, 1976.

15. Jack N. Arbolino, "No Matter Where You Learned It: The 10-year
Promise of the College Level Examination Program," *College Board Review*,
no. 99 (Spring 1976): 13-20.

16. Jerilee Grandy and Walter M. Shea, *The CLEP General Examinations
in American Colleges and Universities* (New York: College Entrance Examination Board, 1976).

by students of traditional college age as well as those "who, for whatever reason, missed their first chance when they were young." They reached a high point of almost 100,000 candidates in 1974-75, with half the candidates taking the general examinations only. The number of older candidates has been increasing, with the 1976 figures showing 42 percent eighteen years of age under, 21 percent nineteen to twenty-one years, 18 percent twenty-two to twenty-nine, and 19 percent thirty years or over. It should be apparent, then, that two out of five of these candidates seek advanced placement via CLEP at admission; almost three out of five are older applicants for admission or are seeking credit by examination during their course in college.[17]

In 1971, the Carnegie Commission on Higher Education proposed shortening the baccalaureate program to three years by moving the freshman college year to the high school.[18] Despite the Carnegie proposal and the options for advanced placement and early admissions, relatively few students avail themselves of opportunities for acceleration, few colleges have restructured their programs, and only one college in five recruits candidates for early admission extensively at the eleventh-grade level.[19]

HONORS PROGRAMS

The past twenty years have seen phenomenal development of honors programs. Award of degrees "with honors" (*cum laude, magna cum laude, summa cum laude*) is an ancient institution, but was at one time based simply on a grade-point average or grade-point average plus thesis. In 1921, Frank Aydelotte introduced to Swarthmore College the "pass-honors" program initiated in Oxford in 1904, basically an upper-division program calling for independent study in the student's major department with faculty guidance and culminating in a senior thesis. A number of smaller, private

17. Ibid.

18. Carnegie Commission on Higher Education, *Less Time, More Options: Education beyond the High School* (New York: McGraw-Hill Book Co., 1971).

19. A new exception is the University of Delaware, which initiated a Freshman Honors Program in 1976, recruiting eleventh graders and establishing a separate campus with special curriculum for outstanding applicants.

colleges took up the program, but major expansion awaited the post-World War II period. The three-year honors program estab-lished at Columbia College in 1909 is generally recognized as the first "general honors" program that characterizes most current honors efforts.

In 1957, Joseph W. Cohen, who had initiated a general honors program at the University of Colorado a decade earlier, succeeded in obtaining a grant from the Carnegie Corporation to establish the Inter-University Committee on the Superior Student.[20] Between 1957 and 1965, the Committee promoted the development of a large number of general honors programs in large and small institu-tions. These programs were an important departure because they placed emphasis on the entering student who needed recognition and encouragement and were as concerned with the student's gen-eral education as a departmental faculty is with specialized study. Cohen identified sixteen major features of a "full honors program," including the following six:

1. Early selection and identification of superior students and initiating them into special programs immediately upon admission to college or subsequent identification;
2. Formulating a continuous, cumulative program through all four years, including work in the student's major department;
3. Employing a varied, flexible program that sets aside restrictive re-quirements and features instruction in small groups, active rather than passive learning procedures, counseling by teaching personnel, inde-pendent study, and terminal projects or examinations to evaluate results;
4. Providing for acceleration both at admission and during college en-rollment;
5. Involving students in contributing roles where possible as assistants to stimulating faculty members, teaching apprentices, peer counselors for younger honors students, and members of a committee of honors students to serve as liaison with the honors council;
6. Selecting faculty who identify fully with the program and who are qualified to give the best intellectual leadership.[21]

A recent survey of colleges and universities shows the impressive

20. With subsequent support from other foundations, corporations, the U.S. Office of Education, and the National Science Foundation.

21. Condensed from *The Superior Student in American Higher Educa-tion*, ed. Joseph W. Cohen (New York: McGraw-Hill Book Co., 1966), pp. 46-69.

effect of the Inter-University Committee and its successor, the National Collegiate Honors Council.[22] "Honors program" is no longer limited to a grade-point distinction. As a minimum, it includes departmental honors, generally consisting of special work within the student's major department. Major emphasis is usually given to "general honors" work in the first two years as well. Interdisciplinary studies form part of the lower-division honors student's program, generally in a small seminar restricted to honors students. In most cases, these seminars take the place of other courses in the college's basic prescription; sometimes they are additional requirements. Honors courses have also been designed for nonmajors in various departments so that the more able student can get more than a cursory look at fields of knowledge outside his own specialty.

The next step in building a "full honors program" is to establish an honors school or college either for the lower division or for all four years. A director of honors is given responsibility for program planning and student advising and usually works with a Council on Honors representative of the undergraduate faculty, more often in arts and sciences than in professional schools. Students normally take some of their work outside the honors program and are not confined to the honors college alone. In a few cases, there are even separate residences for honors students, although such separation is a controversial matter. Special privileges are often attached to membership in the program—access such as a graduate student has to the library, special study lounges, waiver of prerequisites where appropriate, and admission to special seminars and programs. In some colleges, the Honors Program has been labelled as a special "Scholars' Program." In others, a "Scholars' Program" designates a pattern even more selective that the Honors Program with which it runs side by side. The Scholars' Program offers still more freedom, opportunity, and special features to students, at times with stipends and research funds attached.

Honors programs do not go unchallenged. The strong egalitarian drive in American life causes some college faculties to reject implicit elitism and particularly removing the "yeast" of high ability students from the "dough" of the general population in

22. See C. Grey Austin, "Honors Learning in the Seventies," *Educational Record* 56 (Summer 1975): 160-69.

lower-division classes. Similarly, many students do not respond to invitations to enroll in honors programs, sometimes because they opt for more egalitarian modes, sometimes because of fear of competition with an elite, and sometimes because the culture often commends taking the easier road.

CURRICULAR ADAPTATIONS

Recognizing that the standard curriculum may not be the appropriate curriculum for the very best students, institutions have made a variety of changes. In the lower division, these changes include a special "core curriculum" for honors students, frequently featuring interdisciplinary studies, special research methods, and seminar-colloquium classes. Some institutions offer only one special course in each semester of the first year or two; others simply offer special sections of required courses. A number of institutions free the student of all requirements other than the total number of credits to be earned, leaving the design of an individual program to the student and his advisors. In some colleges, the special honors courses take the place of normal requirements; in others, they are added to the usual basic prescription. Advanced placement and "placing out" via examinations are generally used to exempt the well-prepared student from introductory courses and some prerequisites.

In the upper division, and at times in the lower division as well, "reading for departmental honors" may include variations of independent study. These are found in tutorial programs, special research projects and theses, and programs of individually designed reading. A few colleges maintain an interdisciplinary focus even at the upper-division level requiring of (or offering to) honors students one or more courses each term around a theme requiring an interdisciplinary approach. Writing and defending an honors thesis or project are required in some colleges, and course credit for one or more semesters is allowed to develop the thesis.

Particularly at the lower-division level, but in some cases extending through all four years, the influence of the honors and general education movements may be seen. There is concern with the total educational program and not with departmental achievement alone; there is a growing trend toward freedom from requirements and toward individual planning under informed guidance; interdisciplinary studies command special interest.

MODES OF INSTRUCTION

Engaging the individual in greater control of his own education is a major aspect of instructional adaptation for the superior student. In many instances, the colloquium is called the "heart" of the honors program. Independent study and the tutorial are frequently cited. The superior student may work more quickly and with greater interest in self-paced programs like the Keller Personalized System of Instruction[23] and programmed patterns as used in computer-assisted instruction.

Farther removed from the conventional classroom-library-laboratory setting are various off-campus experiences accepted for academic credit. Some colleges have succeeded in setting up internships in industry, the arts, government, public and private agencies, and in special urban and rural environments. Such internships provide supervised learning experiences while offering the student actual work experience in his chosen field or one related to it. Extended to a full-time activity, the internships become the "work-study" programs pioneered early in this century by the University of Cincinnati as professional preparation, and since 1921 by Antioch College as general education as well. At a less intensive level, field-work opportunities have been explored by a growing number of institutions in various areas. Proponents of off-campus programs assert that "students in them mature more rapidly, develop a sense of purpose, exhibit greater self-discipline and see their classroom studies within a broader context." [24] Farther afield, a number of universities have developed centers for study abroad in Europe, Asia, Latin America, and Africa.

Interdisciplinary team teaching is also used to offer a greater challenge to the more able student.[25] Interplay between scholars

23. For description of the Keller Program, see Paul N. Protopapas, "The Keller Plan," *Science Teacher* 41 (May 1974): 44-46.

24. Ohmer Milton, "Curriculum Reform," *Current Issues in Higher Education* 25 (1970): 223.

25. For example, see Thomas F. Gallant, "Interdisciplinary Boom in Higher Education," *Liberal Education* 58 (October 1972): 347-58.

in these programs sets a model of intellectual activity for students who can appreciate the academic subtleties and differences in the approach of varying disciplines to a particular issue or problem.

COUNSELING

Because the superior student presents special concerns in higher education, individualization depends upon personal counseling. The structure of an Honors Program normally provides for a director who assumes responsibility for the special academic advising needed by the unusual student. In larger programs, he may have a staff that includes counselors competent to deal with personal problems as well as with academic advising. In general, there is agreement that academic advising should be done by teaching faculty rather than professional counselors with a different orientation.[26] A few colleges recognize the potential value to honors students in serving as counselors themselves to younger students and provide such an opportunity to upper-division honors students.

Particularly in the lower division, students need information and direction in the strange new world of academe—information as to college and career options, advising that prevents premature specialization, counseling into the most suitable major, and help in design of a total program where able students are freed from normal college requirements.

Colleges report a variety of provisions for guidance. Some indicate no special arrangements for counseling the most able. Most tie counseling of gifted students to the honors program—in the first two years (prior to selection of a major) to counseling in the honors office and beyond that, through specially designated advisors in departmental offices.

Some Illustrative Programs

Descriptions of a few operating programs will illustrate the generalized features already noted. For this purpose, three honors programs have been selected: two with considerable structure and one with a great amount of flexibility.

26. Austin, "Honors Learning in the Seventies."

UNIVERSITY OF NORTH CAROLINA-CHAPEL HILL

The program at the University of North Carolina includes a
Freshman Honors Program, a Sophomore Honors Program, and
Departmental Honors designed for seniors within their major department. Approximately 125 freshmen are invited to join the program by the Faculty Council on Honors, based upon the student's
high school record, rank in high school class, and performance on
the *Scholastic Aptitude Test*. The descriptive brochure reports:

> The student may enroll in special honors courses and advanced sections
> which have been set up and reserved especially for him. . . . Students in
> the Freshman Honors Program have the additional benefit of a special
> academic adviser in the General College. The adviser is available to
> these students to assist them in planning their curricula and to advise
> them on post-graduate plans. . . . The Academic Residence Area, an
> informal and coeducational housing unit . . . is available for honors stu-
> dents. A completely furnished honors reading room is available for
> honors students in the Undergraduate Library.[27]

Most students are exempt from the freshman English composition
courses and are encouraged instead to take special sections of a
literature course. Honors or advanced sections are offered in history, foreign languages, mathematics, natural sciences, philosophy,
political science, and economics.

The 125 students who have done best in the freshman year are
invited to join the Sophomore Honors Program. The advanced and
honors sections of General College courses are available to them.
In addition, they are encouraged to enroll in at least one of the
sophomore honors seminars, three or four of which are offered
each semester.

Special programs of independent study are also available. Students who have acquired knowledge of the contents of a course
through independent study or experience may receive credit hours
(though no grade) by passing a special examination for the course.
Directed reading courses, conducted as individual tutorials on topics
agreed upon by the student and a faculty member, carry full grade
and course credit. "Double registration" enables a student to obtain
wider and more comprehensive study than is normally offered in

27. University of North Carolina, *Honors: UNC-CH* (Chapel Hill, N.C.:
University of North Carolina, 1976).

a given course by registering, not only for the course, but also for a three-hour "H" (or Honors) section of it. This amounts to independent work done in the same subject under the supervision of the course instructor. Independent honors study is encouraged during the summer, with credit offered for superior performance on a term paper and on an examination for the course.

The "UNC Year" at Seville or Montpelier offers foreign study through an exchange program with the University of Toronto and through the Intercollegiate Center for Classical Studies in Rome.

During the senior year students may undertake a project leading to graduation "with honors" or "with highest honors." Each department has designated one of its faculty as the honors adviser who works with the student to determine the nature of his project. Departments also set course and grade requirements for granting honors degrees.

WASHINGTON STATE UNIVERSITY

A second program with a high degree of structure is that at Washington State University where over 600 students are enrolled in the Honors Program. Students are pursuing work in all departments but also take special Honors courses required of all those enrolled in the program. The descriptive brochure reports:

Honors courses often correspond to the usual undergraduate courses but with important differences. The Honors Program is not an accelerated program. Rather, it attempts to provide a richer, more challenging experience in general education than might otherwise be available to students. Most Honors classes are small, and students can establish a close intellectual relationship with their instructors. Honors students are expected to do more than the usual out-of-class reading and to spend less time on routine class assignments. They are encouraged to write more, to talk more, and to think more. They have the opportunity to develop their own individual talents and to become creative participants in their own education. . . .

In lieu of the General University Requirements, Honors students are expected to complete all Honors Program requirements. In all instances, the best interest of the individual student is the determining factor in planning the course of study. . . . Each student is assigned an advisor under the university's Curriculum Advisory Program. All Honors students have access to additional counsel on Honors-related questions from the Academic Advisor for the Program. . . . In addition, students are encouraged to confer with the staff of the Honors Center and associates of the faculty Honors Council who are in fields of particular interest to them. Students may also take advantage of the Honors Students Advisory Committee. This group consists of approximately twenty Honors students who assist other Honors students with curricular and related problems.[28]

All honors students are required to take special honors courses in English, mathematics, social science, and, if they do not plan to take additional advanced courses in physical and biological sciences, honors courses in those sciences. In addition to departmentally offered honors courses, the following interdisciplinary courses (called University Honors) are offered: Development of Western Civilization, Development of Eastern Civilizations, Domain of the Arts, a senior thesis or project, and seminars involving study in depth of selected topics.

Independent study is a necessary and important part of the Honors Program, with all students required to complete a minimum of three credits in this way. Independent study may be accomplished through the Summer Reading Program, through Special Problems enrollment (either departmental or interdisciplinary), through an approved program of reading without credit, or through other individual arrangements with prior approval. Exchange and foreign study programs are also available, with special arrangements at the University College of South Wales and with Denmark. An Honors Center is made available to students in the Program. The Center includes a reading room and lounge, an honors library, a listening room, a seminar room, and the Honors Program Office.

MICHIGAN STATE UNIVERSITY

A program with a lower degree of structure is offered at Michigan State University. The descriptive brochure states that the purpose of the program is to create "rigorous and challenging academic opportunities for undergraduate students of high ability."

Flexible program planning is the distinguishing feature of Honors College membership. The student, *under the supervision and with the approval of his academic advisor*, may redefine all the requirements for

28. Washington State University, *Honors Program* (Pullman, Wash.: Washington State University, n.d.).

graduation with the exception of the total number of credit hours. . . .
It is the responsibility of the Honors College advisor to "provide a situation which makes certain that students of high ability constantly are
challenged by the most advanced work for which each is ready."[29]

It is the corollary responsibility of the student to take advantage of
enriched opportunities. The goal is greater mastery of "subject
matter both within and without his field of specialization," and
development of a graduate who is "more alive to intellectual concerns, more skilled in analysis, more comprehensive in judgment,
and more cognizant of the responsibility of talent."

Students are admitted as freshmen by invitation only, based on
high school records and national test scores. Others may be admitted after completing forty quarter hours of study. Applicants
are asked to describe the honors elements of the program they
intend to pursue upon admission. This statement follows consultation with, and approval by, the Honors advisor in the student's
major field. Honors students are expected to average at least one
course per quarter of clear Honors calibre (for example, Honors
courses, Honors sections, Honors options, Honors independent
study and research projects, or graduate courses).

Most academic departments permit honors students to construct
totally individualized programs, but a few departments do have
fully articulated honors programs. Students enrolled in departmental honors program are reminded that they are also expected
to pursue "an enriched course of study leading to greater breadth
in areas outside their major."

This opportunity to develop a truly individualized program of study is
the primary privilege conferred by Honors College membership. It is
expected that with the help of their advisors, students will choose as
elements in those programs the most relevant, exacting, and enriched
experiences offered by the University. It is not likely that the elements
of any two programs will be precisely the same; it is expected, however,
that they will share basic characteristics of *flexibility, breadth, and
depth.*[30]

Students file a proposed program each year for the three ensuing

29. Michigan State University, *Honors College Student Handbook* (Lansing, Mich.: Michigan State University, n.d.).

30. Ibid., *The Honors College* (Lansing, Mich.: Michigan State University,
n.d.).

quarters. The planning form asks students to list courses in which they are exercising the "H-option," that is, regular courses in which they are arranging with the instructor to follow an alternative syllabus, or to engage in special group or individual projects. They are also asked to list and describe other honors-type study: "substantial alternatives for the required general education courses," "substantial alternatives for major area requirements," and independent study plans. Students also respond to a question on the relevance of their proposed program to career objectives.

An Honors College building houses staff offices, lounge, and study space for honors students, rooms for honors seminars, and a small browsing library. Students are granted the same library privileges as graduate students, permission to check out periodicals not normally circulated among undergraduates, and complete access to graduate stacks.

Conclusion

In summary, the events of the past decade that have moved the spotlight from superior students to those needing remedial attention are the same events that should be evoking new emphasis on the special needs of the most able undergraduates. To the extent that program quality may be diluted overall in responding to needs dictated by wider access to higher education, there is increased need to stimulate and maintain the involvement and academic commitment of superior students.

One recommendation is increasing diversity among postsecondary institutions and concentrating superior students in universities with a high level of research and scholarship.[31] A more realistic solution than invention of new institutions is clearer definition by each institution of its own mission. If that mission includes education of the most able, a coherent program needs to be developed. Precedents for such programs exist within the experience of many institutions whose example has filled the preceding pages. These include identification of academic talent and designing experiences for students that permit a maximum of independence and challenge,

31. Martin Mayerson, "After a Decade of Levellers in Higher Education: Reinforcing Quality while Maintaining Mass Education," *Daedalus* 103 (Winter 1975): 304-321.

association with top-flight minds among the faculty and their fellow students, exposure to the best that has been thought and said and to the world of current research as well, assistance in getting started as an independent citizen in any walk of life, and counseling along the way to uncover challenging opportunities and to avoid personal and academic pitfalls.

CHAPTER XV

Community-based Programs

JUNE COX

Introduction

Although there is a resurgence of programs for the gifted and talented in progress all over the country, concerned educators and parents would do well to look to the larger community beyond the schools for a wealth of underutilized resources.

A school may have no programs for the gifted and talented. The location may be a ghetto, a small rural community, or an affluent suburb. But community-based programs for the gifted and talented abound, if only they can be brought to the attention of parents and educators. The directors of the facilities themselves may not be sensitive to the special needs of the gifted nor recognize the potential in their domains to fulfill those needs. Parent groups and others who are active on behalf of the gifted would be well advised to add to their lists of resources all a community has to offer, whether or not those resources are in formally announced programs for the gifted and talented or are in programs no one has thought to fit to the needs of such students.

These community resources include the libraries, the museums, the galleries, the theaters, the studios, shops, offices, hospitals, radio and television stations, to name a few. If asked if they have a special program for the gifted and talented, the executives of these establishments would generally respond negatively. Many of them are unaware of the unique learning opportunities their facilities could provide for the most able youth of the community.

Whatever the resources of the school itself, it would do well to push back the four walls that confine the experiences for the gifted and talented and reach out into the larger community.

Since few schools can afford the resources required for spe-

cialized education in the creative and performing arts, a good case
can be made that such education should be provided by community resources such as art institutes, museums, theaters, and
similar facilities. Likewise, specialized scientific equipment may be
minimal in the schools; few can afford a cyclotron or an electron
miscroscope, for instance, but these instruments exist in some communities, and once the need for their use by gifted youth is made
known, experience has shown that civic-minded personnel are
generous in making them available.

Associations for the gifted and talented could sponsor workshops to assist the staffs of community agencies to achieve more
awareness of the needs of gifted children and youth. Such a project
would also help bring to the attention of museums, theaters, and
libraries the many aspects of their facilities that could easily be
geared to meet the needs of the gifted, needs that cannot be easily
met in our public schools under present conditions.

The history of community-based programs for the gifted is
sketchy at best. For the most part, programs have emerged here and
there and flourished briefly before fading into oblivion. This lack
of continuity is perhaps one of the greatest weaknessess of the
community concept. Generally, the programs are offered on a
volunteer basis, which is not sustained when other pressures emerge.
A school-community liaison might solve part of this problem.
Other problems inherent in community programs that require
school cooperation include scheduling difficulties, funding, transportation, and the insurance coverage needed to take students out
of their buildings into the community. One of the most difficult
problems in any community-based program, school-related or not,
is that of evaluation. How does one know that such programs are,
in fact, effective? Since most deal with "widening of interests," the
effects can only be measured on a long-term basis.

Training staffs to deal specifically with the needs of the gifted
and talented is still another problem shared by many sponsors of
programs. Since few programs are regarded by sponsors solely as
resources for the gifted, special training for staff members to develop sensitivity to students who are highly endowed intellectually
or artistically is not even perceived as a necessity.

Exemplary Programs

Despite the many problems attending such efforts, a number of exemplary programs do exist. Some of the illustrations presented here were especially designed for and offered exclusively to the gifted and talented. Others, while not restricted to the gifted, are particularly appropriate to their needs.

THE DALLAS THEATER CENTER

The Dallas Theater Center, a remarkable Frank Lloyd Wright structure in Dallas, Texas, presents an equally remarkable program for students. In addition to its regular productions, the theater offers a comprehensive program for students four through eighteen years of age. Although enrollment is not restricted to gifted and talented students, by its very nature the Center attracts such students and holds their interest as they continue year after year in the comprehensive and progressive program. Students may begin at the Center at age four and continue through high school without repetition.

Reflecting the philosophy of the Center's gifted director, Paul Baker, the goal is not to develop young professional actors, but rather to lead the young students to honest self-appraisal, self-expression, and a deep sense of their inner strength.

Sessions are held during the summer as well as after school and on Saturdays during the academic year. Most of the faculty members are working toward or have received their degrees in the graduate programs of the Center. This arrangement provides professionally trained teachers at minimal costs, and keeps the student fees at a modest level.

THE LYCEUM OF THE MONTEREY PENINSULA

The Lyceum of the Monterey Peninsula is located in Carmel, California. Founded in 1960 and taking its name from the school established by Aristotle, the Lyceum brings together talented students and adults in special seminars, conferences, and workshops. A nonprofit organization, the Lyceum charges modest fees for registration and materials, but no tuition. Its work is supported by philanthropic minded individuals and groups.

Although the Lyceum works closely with the public and private schools in the entire peninsula, serving students from kindergarten through the twelfth grade, it is a separate entity and is not directly affiliated with the schools or with any group. The stated objective of the organization is "to supplement and extend but not duplicate school offerings."

Leadership is provided by talented adults with expertise in various fields of endeavor. In addition to sessions held at the Lyceum itself, others are scheduled throughout the peninsula, depending on the area of study. For example, one flyer announces lifesaving sessions at the Coast Guard Station; introduction to medicine at the U. S. Army Health Clinic; animal care at an animal hospital; an introduction to aviation at a local airport; cartooning at a local public library; horse care at a riding center; painting in an art gallery; and a study of Japan at the Monterey Institute of Foreign Studies. The list goes on, but these activities indicate the great diversity of the Lyceum program, one which could be replicated throughout the country with immeasurable benefit to countless numbers of gifted and talented students.

THE GIFTED STUDENTS INSTITUTE FOR RESEARCH AND DEVELOPMENT

Based in Arlington, Texas, The Gifted Students Institute for Research and Development is a nonprofit educational organization that sponsors sessions throughout the country each summer. To qualify, students must rank in the upper 5 percent of the student population, as verified by leadership abilities, IQ, achievement test scores, or evidence of special talent. Generally, they are recommended by their school guidance counselors.

Currently, programs are scheduled at the University of Michigan, at Texas Christian University, and at the University of Guadalajara. In addition to these sessions that are open to students all over the country, one scheduled at the Dallas Theater Center is for commuting students only. One session at the University of Michigan focuses on career orientation. Another on that campus focuses on creativity and problem solving. Both are open to students entering the seventh, eighth, or ninth grades.

Texas Christian University also hosts two sessions, divided according to grade levels. One is open to students entering the sixth, seventh, and eighth grades. The other is for senior high school students. Both emphasize the importance of the humanities in all career planning.

At the University of Guadalajara, students live with university approved Mexican families for the five-week session. Teams of teachers and students are encouraged to apply. High school students earn up to six semester hours of college credit in Spanish. Teachers and graduating seniors may earn up to nine semester hours of credit. They may enroll in a variety of courses, including Latin American Culture and Problems, Methods of Teaching Spanish, as well as courses in the Spanish language.

The session at the Dallas Theater Center, emphasizing creativity and imagination, encourages students to expand their conceptions of themselves and their capacities as human beings. All activities are designed to help students discover their own extraordinary inner potential. The techniques and experiences presented in the course are new—new, that is, to contemporary western education. They draw, however, on ancient Eastern philosophy in presenting simple and natural methods for developing one's creativity.

This course represents community involvement in a significant manner. The resources of the Dallas Theater Center are combined with those of the Gifted Students Institute for Research and Development to present an unusual program for talented students in the area. Because excellent resources are too limited and special programs much too costly, combined efforts are essential. Individual projects can be jealously guarded only at an unconscionable cost to the students served. The Gifted Students Institute sessions are supported by student fees, foundation grants, and private contributions. Scholarship assistance is available for some sessions.

THE EXECUTIVE HIGH SCHOOL INTERNSHIPS OF AMERICA

The Executive High School Internships of America, headquartered in New York, assists school districts throughout the country to develop and implement programs for high ability junior and senior high school students. Selection criteria include initiative, perseverance, creativity, leadership, maturity, and sensitivity. Participating schools grant qualified students a one-term leave from all classes. During the term, students receive academic credit in regular subject areas while they work with key decision makers in their communities. Each student serves as a special assistant to leading executives in government, business, media, the arts, law, social services, health, and civic affairs. Weekly seminars reinforce management and decision-making skills. Students receive no salary, but their work experience sometimes leads to summer or permanent employment. More often, students use the knowledge gained to help them select a college where they can acquire the required skills and credentials for their chosen career.

The value to the student in this type of program is obvious. The student learns about a particular area of interest from a top level executive already working in the field. Many sponsors who accept this challenge open every door possible for their young assistants, including them in conferences and board meetings. The value of the program to the school district itself may be less obvious, but it is no less real. Through their participation, local Chambers of Commerce and other community leaders intensify their interest in the local schools and increase their support to the district.

High School Executive Internships receive support from foundations and from the National Institute of Education. Participating schools pay a fee, for which they receive guidance and materials. It is possible, of course, for local districts to design their own community-based career education programs, and indeed many have done so.

THE JUNIOR GREAT BOOKS READING AND DISCUSSION PROGRAM

The Junior Great Books Reading and Discussion Programs, sponsored by the Great Books Foundation, a national nonprofit organization based in Chicago, attracts intelligent volunteers in every area of the United States. Its income is from the sale of sets of paperback books, fees for training and educational consultation, and philanthropic contributions. The Foundation trains annually approximately 5,000 discussion leaders in their own communities. Teachers, librarians, and other school personnel participate in the training courses and frequently co-lead student groups with the volunteers.

Sometimes the discussions are held in schools, either during or after the regular school day. Often groups meet in libraries, churches, and community centers. Students meet once a week or every other week to discuss a story that everyone has read. With their leader or co-leaders, they gather around a circle for discussions that last thirty to ninety minutes, depending on the grade level. Using questions that reflect their own doubt and interest, the leaders help the group explore and resolve problems about the author's meaning or intention.

Readings for the Junior Great Books series are published only in paperback editions. To be included, a story must be fun to read and sufficiently rich in ideas to produce extended discussion. Formerly comprised entirely of the classics, the collections now include outstanding selections of modern works as well. Only persons who have successfully completed a Great Books Leader Training Course, and schools and libraries that have the services of certified leaders, may purchase the series in quantity.

This policy for the purchase of books reflects the Foundation's belief that trained discussion leaders plus thoughtful reading of carefully selected materials will enable students to attain worthwhile goals. Students at every level, from second grade through senior high school, develop the habit of reading critically, interpreting what they read, and supporting their interpretations with ideas and facts from the readings.

Although the Foundation makes no claim that the program is suitable only for gifted students, many communities have found the discussion technique and the readings themselves particularly appropriate for gifted students. Students who benefit most from this particular program appear to be those who rank high in general intelligence and who read well above grade level. Thus qualified, not only will they learn to read critically and interpretively, they will also develop listening skills. They will develop respect for their own and other's opinions and they will learn to express themselves with confidence and poise. Additionally, students will enter college, if that be their choice, with a remarkable background in reading. Best of all, perhaps they will have developed a lifelong habit of thoughtful reading.

FORT WORTH MUSEUM OF SCIENCE AND HISTORY

The Fort Worth Museum of Science and History offers a remarkable variety of courses for students of all ages, beginning with three-year-olds. Modest fees enable applicants to explore exotic subjects such as dinosaurs, snakes, and the art of lapidary. Other course offerings—astronomy, painting, and photography, to name a few—are more traditional but provide equally exciting learning experiences for the participants.

In addition to the courses above, which are open to all on the basis of interest, the Museum offers year-round experimental art programs for gifted and talented students. The purpose of the program is to offer art instruction above and beyond the level of work in the public schools. The program has now been in existence more than ten years, and its "graduates" have excelled in high school and college. Many of the students have received scholarships. An impressive number have exhibited in the Fort Worth-Dallas area, and several of the students whose teenage years were enhanced by the program now are on the staff of the Museum, sharing their talents and time with a new generation.

EARTHWATCH

Although its offices are located in Belmont, Massachusetts, the activities of an organization known as Earthwatch extend far afield. At Earthwatch the community encompasses the entire world.

Earthwatch is actually two organizations in one. It serves as a clearinghouse, bringing together people and research projects needing people. Earthwatch reviews and approves proposals from professional scholars for expeditions. Not only does the organization fund approved projects, it also provides fellowships for teachers and scholarships for students to staff the projects. A partial listing of projects in 1977 included a study of the feeding and ranging habits of monkeys in Peru, an investigation of the birds and plants in the Out Islands of the Bahamas, a Mayan excavation, an investigation of ancient engineers of Peru, a biological survey of the tropical rain forest in northwestern Ecuador, a study of fossils in the Andes, and a study of tropical birds in Trinidad.

Scholarships are available on a nationwide competitive basis to students aged sixteen to twenty-one who wish to participate in such projects. Competition is keen, but dedicated young scholars are well advised to consider this project a possible option in their educational development.

Fellowships for teachers consist of partial subsidies. Applicants must demonstrate a professional interest in field research and evidence that their experience will enrich their classroom teaching. These activities are neither field trips nor simulated explorations. Students and teachers are expected to do actual scientific work and make a real contribution to the project.

Conclusion

The programs presented here, some simple and others complex, have significant common elements. All involve community resources; all require a cooperative attitude; and all seek to expand and extend rather than replace the regular school program. Schools that cooperate with these or similar programs will enrich the lives of gifted and talented students and those students will find new friends and support in the community. There can be no justification for an isolation stance that says in effect, "Education is our business. Let the museums, the libraries, the scientists, and the doctor tend to their own domain." Education is everyone's business, a lifetime experience, and the gifted and talented can gain much and return much to the society that provides a rich diversity of educational experiences.

CHAPTER XVI

Career Education

BRUCE G. MILNE

Career education for the gifted and the talented carries with it the overwhelming concern for all educational activity for these students. Their unique interests, abilities, needs, and occupational or career aspirations must be met through individualized and differentiated programs and services beyond those provided by the instructional program in regular classrooms. Any school system must be willing to make a commitment to provide for differentiation in its program for these exceptional pupils if they are to fulfill their potential for themselves and for society.

While the limitations placed upon most local schools in the form of trained personnel, resources, time, and leadership must be recognized, there are some critical elements involved in providing adequate career education for the gifted and the talented student. These are set forth here as working assumptions that can be used to guide the development of programs to meet needs of individual pupils.

1. There are probably more than a few individuals who possess outstanding abilities or high potential in one or more of the generally recognized areas of giftedness or talent: general intellectual ability, specific academic aptitude, creative or productive thinking, leadership, visual and performing arts, and psychomotor or psychosocial ability.

2. Early identification of the gifted and the talented is not only desirable, but is advantageous and essential for programming, instruction, counseling, and for providing appropriate experiences that will enhance their potential contributions to self and society.

3. Programs, services, and experiences, including career education, must be modified in varying degrees to meet the unique needs,

diverse interests, advanced accomplishments, and career aspirations of the gifted and the talented students.

4. Career exploration should not be limited to the careers about which the gifted student already knows. It is the responsibility of the school, home, and community to expose this student to a wide range of other career alternatives through programs that provide opportunities for developing awareness, for orientation, for exploration, and for preparation.

5. Gifted and talented students have basic needs and wants like all other persons. Occupational choice or selection is part of the total pursuit of life satisfaction that may or may not relate directly to their perceived gifts or talents.

Identification of the Gifted

An abundance of information is available on identification processes and procedures. It is not the purpose to dwell here on identification, nor to set forth the gifted as a "circle of elites" into which only those with easily recognized gifts and talents can enter. A better mental posture to take is that of searching for gifts and talents in all students. No students should be ruled out as potentially outstanding performers in the world of work in which they can find a life-satisfying career. The following are advanced as hypotheses closely related to concerns about identification:

1. The higher the level of giftedness or talent, the greater the suspension of decision making about career goals, although some gifted and talented youth do make a very early commitment to a career area.

2. The higher the level of giftedness or talent the greater is the probability of reliance upon internal/intrinsic rewards and the rejection of external/extrinsic rewards.

3. Gifted and talented persons establish their own internal standards for utilization of their gifts and talents. Those standards dictate the exacting amounts of physical, mental, and emotional stress they will tolerate from external forces.

4. Gifted and talented individuals learn to avoid external coercion early in life, whether from parent, peer, teacher, or the adult society. They develop an internal conscience that builds a strong barrier between external pressures and the pursuit of personal goals.

5. Gifted and talented persons seek emotional, mental, and physical competency and confidence at a level commensurate with what they perceive as personal interests, aspirations, needs, and life satisfaction.

As we look to the year 2000 and beyond, identification of the gifted and differentiated programming for them in career education becomes imperative. Without making value judgments about the relative worth of any individual compared with another, we must realize that gifted and talented persons do not accept careers —they create them. They synthesize and transfer known processes into new dimensions. Through them, other persons will find careers in yet unknown and undeveloped fields.

Early identification of the gifted and subsequent identification of potentially satisfying careers allow the school, home, and community the opportunity to provide programs that include experiences leading to awareness, orientation, exploration, and preparation. An educational program that provides vocational, technical, and occupational experiences paralleling academic preparation can eliminate much of the indecisiveness in searching for a career.

Assisting the Gifted in the Selection of a Career

The ability to define and predict occupational or career choices is limited to the extent that students can interpret their own interests, needs, and work aspirations. There are several inventories and reliable instruments that can aid in assessing the individual's interests, aptitudes, personality type, and competencies. Wise use of such information can be of great value in working with the gifted child or youth.

The highly gifted or talented individual is probably aware of a wide range of career choices early in life and has greater difficulty in making selections when the number of alternatives is expanded. Thus, when we increase the gifted student's awareness and orientation activities we logically complicate the ultimate selection process. The problem is compounded in that the conceptual theories and methodological practices in career education deal with the scope of various careers on the basis of existing evidence. The gifted and talented individual tends to reach beyond these limitations.

How then can we aid in the process of selecting a career? Presumably, the answer lies somewhere between what we know from the data that are generated from existing careers and what we can learn about the individual gifted and talented student.

Whether the processes leading to greater awareness of careers and further exploration of them are provided through regular classroom activities or occur as a result of differentiated programming is less important than providing breadth of the activities. As indicated in the hypotheses, there is a tendency on the part of the gifted to pursue in depth that which appeals to an interest or perceived need. The regular classroom teacher or coordinator of programs for the gifted should not frustrate the student nor thwart an effort to select a career, but should continue to challenge the gifted student to explore a smorgasbord of clusters of career opportunities. In that further exploration, it is likely that the student will see additional outlets, dimensions, and potential linkages for their interests and aspirations.

One method of approaching the problem of selecting a career might well be that of using a narrowing process through the elimination of alternatives. For example, an effort could be made to find out which of the fifteen career-education clusters the student is *not* interested in. Once limited, awareness, orientation, exploration, and preparation can be directed toward potentials rather than toward all careers.

The *Dictionary of Occupational Titles* published by the U.S. Department of Labor offers some assistance in the narrowing process through its classification system. For example, with assistance the pupil can determine whether he likes to work with data (facts and figures), people, or things. A careful search through the occupational categories allows the student to see these in different combinations of importance and difficulty.

A second coding having predictive value is that of classifying materials by personality characteristics. Holland's codes are used in indexes to relate occupations to personality types.[1] His six basic categories (realistic, investigative, artistic, social, enterprising, and conventional) give additional support to the narrowing process.

Depending somewhat upon the age and abilities of the gifted

---

1. John L. Holland, *Making Vocational Choices: A Theory of Careers* (Englewood Cliffs, N.J.: Prentice-Hall, 1973).

student, some further information for decision making can be gained early from such tests as the *Kuder Preference Record* and the *Strong Vocational Interest Blank*. Such interest inventories give support to the student's own self-perception regarding data, people, and things.[2]

The merits of particular types of tests are not discussed here. There appears to be value, however, in gaining insight into the character and personality of the gifted. Projective tests using words or pictures to elicit free and unstructured responses should be considered. Such instruments allow for greater divergency of response than is the case with nonprojective, convergent tests. Free association, figure drawing, and open-ended responses are good indicators of creative abilities as well as of personality.

A note of caution should be advanced. All gifts and talents can not be readily translated into careers. On the other hand, some gifts and talents can enhance many different and varied careers. To assume that there is a market or dollar value on a gift or talent places an unrealistic, pragmatic, or utilization value on giftedness.

Giftedness may have its release in an avocational as well as in a vocational outlet. Life satisfaction, being largely a process of fulfilling one's potential, comes from choosing alternatives that bring satisfaction in themselves. It is the right of the individual to choose what has meaning in life. The responsibility of educators is to protect the gifted insofar as possible from exploitation and misuse of those gifts and talents.

Programming Career Education for the Gifted

The role of the school in the career development of any student is to provide an adequate information base upon which occupational decision making can occur. Gifted students, although having the same basic needs as all students, operate at a higher rate of efficiency and move more rapidly toward specialization. Provisions for rewarding experiences must be made at times commensurate with their interests and abilities and not necessarily in the sequence set forth for all students in the regular program.

2. Oscar K. Buros, *Eighth Mental Measurements Yearbook* (Highland Park, N.J.: Gryphon Press, 1978); idem, *The National Guidance Handbook: A Guide to Vocational Education Programs* (Chicago: Science Research Associates, 1975).

A variety of activities, both purposeful (work) and random (play), can be provided in the regular program as well as in special classes. Whether these are activities leading toward awareness, orientation, or exploration, they must be tailored to yield potentially satisfying experiences at the students' level. In this light, work is seen as purposeful mental, physical, and emotional activity that deliberately points beyond the present by creating products or values that can be used in the future. Random activity or play is without purpose and may be a spasmodic or indiscriminate response to a chance mood, interest, or passing fancy. Although play can have future benefits of value, it is enjoyed simply for its own sake and gives direct and immediate gratification.

In programming for the gifted, the best axiom to follow is to provide work or play activities that give the gifted the predisposition to discover satisfaction (or dissatisfaction) in the experience for themselves. On this thesis, life satisfaction is total and complete at any point in the growth and development process—the future is always here for the gifted.

Types of work that utilize the gifted student's creative and productive ability, leadership ability, management skills, and psychomotor abilities can be found in a wide variety of clusters or occupations. Commerce, business, communications, transportations, industry, and agriculture have a high demand for persons with specific skills. The students possessing such skills can look to any of those clusters and freely translate their talents into careers.

Career education is also part of the process of becoming. Through the gaining of efficiency and specialization in work activities, the decision-making process in reality is continuous. The student is always seeking satisfaction at a higher level.

To illustrate graphically the need for continuous growth and development in the gifted student's search for a career, the Educational-Occupational Interactive Model shown in figure 1 has been developed.

An educational-occupational interactive model is essential to provide an adequate program for the gifted in career education. Work/play activities, training/retraining, and the updating of educational/occupational experiences all build competencies. Through the gaining of efficiency and specialization there is a continuous upward mobility.

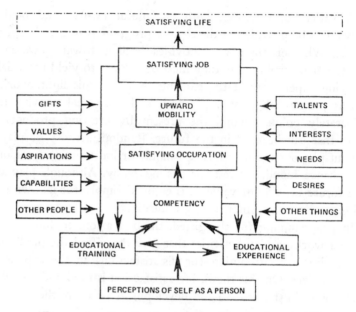

Fig. 1. An educational-occupational interaction model.

SOURCE: Bruce G. Milne et al., *Vocational Education: A Challenging Alternative for the Gifted and Talented Student* (Vermillion, S.D.: Educational Research and Service Center, 1976), p. 12.

Throughout the process of growth and development as indicated in the model, provisions must be made for individuals to reexamine their self-perceptions, gifts, talents, values, needs, and so forth. In total, the interactive model orchestrates the blending of education and occupational experiences with the unique characteristics of the gifted and the talented individual.

The Gifted Individual as a Whole Person

The concept of a well-rounded life still exists as an ideal. Career education should not only give the gifted and the talented student a predisposition toward making a meaningful contribution to the world of work, but it should also make provisions for living in the world of leisure and in the world of the intellect.

The world of leisure here refers to that portion of one's day or life in which there is little concern for making a living. That world may have been alien or very limited in the lives of our forefathers, but it is becoming more and more pronounced in our lives today.

Such terms as hobbies, avocations, recreational outlets, and life-time sports draw from our feelings and emotions rather than from our needs for productivity.

The world of the intellect in a parallel sense draws upon the desires and needs within people to know and to understand more. It is difficult to translate this quest for knowledge without getting involved in a semantic battle. It can be loosely defined as the search for wisdom and involves the process we call thinking.

Gifted and talented persons are often characterized as individuals who dedicate disproportionate amounts of time to one or more activities. These persons often have difficulty in separating those things they do in their vocations, intellectual pursuits, and leisure time. The responsibility for maintaining a well-rounded life-style must be theirs. At the same time, however, parents, educators, and adults should provide guidance and assistance in avocational as well as in vocational preparation.

Current concerns for mental health, excess leisure time, early burn-out, early retirement, and production pressures all dictate the need for a harmonious balance among mental, physical, and emotional drains. A holistic approach to career development for the gifted is essential. Gifted students, in all probability, will develop an intense commitment to the task of fulfilling their potential. In projecting their careers we must also help them to seek complementary harmony and balance in their leisure and intellectual development, for it is within the total self that satisfaction in life is achieved.

Summary

Career education for the gifted and the talented can be summarized by refuting the myth that whatever applies to the gifted also holds true for the regular student. There are significant differences in meeting the needs of those with high degrees of giftedness and talent. These include, but are not limited to, the following:

1. The interests, abilities, needs, and occupational or career aspirations arise at a much earlier age than in the regular student.

2. Gifted students need individualization and differentiation in career awareness, orientation, exploration, and preparation at a

time commensurate with the growth and development of that giftedness.

3. The gifted are aware of a broad range of career alternatives earlier in life; as further awareness of careers occurs, there is an increased difficulty in making decisions about occupations and careers.

4. Gifted students tend to think beyond the known scope of career information and project themselves into nonexistent but highly potential careers.

5. Career selection, leading toward career satisfaction, takes into account the unique characteristics of the gifted individual, including personal, emotional, physical, and psychological traits.

6. Purposeful activity (work) and random activity (play) are essential enrichment experiences in the narrowing of alternatives for a satisfying career.

7. The student's gifts and talents may or may not directly relate to a career, but some gifts and talents can be translated into a wide range of careers.

8. Satisfactory career development for the gifted takes into account a harmonious balance among the physical, emotional, and intellectual drains on energy in one's total life, not merely in one's productive world of work.

9. Life satisfaction is total and complete at any point in the process of growth and development if there is an emerging realization of the potential contributions of the student's gifts and talents.

10. Career education, for the gifted, is part of the total process of becoming and should be continuous in all stages of growth and development.

CHAPTER XVII

Parental Involvement

CAROL N. NATHAN

Introduction

Parents looking for ways to improve educational opportunities for gifted children have a variety of options. They range from careful nurture in the home to participation in organizational activity supporting education for the gifted, and from the local district out to the national scene. Where and how parents choose to participate is, of course, a matter of personal choice. But regardless of how modest the venture, each parent's contribution raises the visibility of the gifted.

Each step a parent takes outside the home in the direction of involvement moves him a little farther away from the center of his concern—his own child. But, at the same time, the broader the participation the greater the possibility of improving gifted education, and hence the greater the ultimate benefit to each child. In public education, the emphasis necessarily is on the specific group, in this case, the gifted, rather than on the individual child—at least for funding and program development. It is obvious, however, that what supports all gifted students supports each gifted student.

When parents elect to work outside the home, one prerequisite for meaningful involvement is knowledge of what already exists at local, state, or federal levels. Recognizing the limits to what is immediately possible affects what long-range goals can be set. Risking a moon shot at the outset almost guarantees failure. With some understanding of the limits and possibilities open to them, parents can then go on to survey the attitudes held by the professionals with whom they must work. Are teachers and administrators sympathetic, apathetic, or downright hostile? Answering that question makes it possible to develop appropriate persuasive techniques for addressing political realities and beginning the process of change.

PRECEDENTS FOR PARENTAL INVOLVEMENT

In many instances, before educators were willing to admit that there were mentally gifted children requiring a specialized kind of education (and there are still some who do not), parents of such children were aware that the general curriculum offerings in most public schools were inadequate for this particular population of students. As a result, the initial push for recognition of gifted children as a special group was often made by parents. First, individual parents struggled, often vainly, to get schools to serve their bright youngsters. Out of a variety of frustrating experiences and perhaps out of the growing success of parent organizations for the handicapped, parents came to realize that the only hope for achieving recognition for gifted students lay in organizing advocacy groups. Organized pressure proved in many instances to be effective in encouraging various school districts to direct attention toward the creation of programs for the gifted.

Parent organizations began at the local level. Personal concern for their own children brought parents together to work toward getting some commitment to the needs of the gifted from local school boards. While occasionally successful, such efforts were disparate and did little to legitimize the concept of education for the gifted at higher levels of education or to stimulate legislation to fund special programs. What developed out of these isolated efforts was the realization that broad organized pressure on state legislatures and state departments of education was the only means for bringing about any substantive change in existing educational patterns.

In the last decade or so, parent support has become vital to the development and maintenance of programs providing appropriate education for gifted children. Because such programs serve a relatively small number of students, educators of the gifted generally acknowledge the importance of such parent participation. Until very recently, parental involvement has been almost exclusively in the area of education for the mentally gifted. But attention has now broadened to serve those students who exhibit outstanding ability in the areas of creativity, performing arts, and leadership. This expanded population, while still relatively small, has raised issues that have weakened organized parent support and have made organized effort beyond the local school district more difficult to realize. The nature of this problem will be discussed later.

A pioneer group to move beyond the local district was the California Parents for the Gifted. This organization grew from a nucleus of parent groups in southern California, pulling together other active parent groups then in existence throughout the state. Together, representatives from these groups launched an effort to influence the California legislature. After much lobbying and many disappointments, their efforts bore fruit in the passage of the Burgener Bill in 1972. This bill not only recognized the special needs for gifted education, but also established methods for identifying mentally gifted students and provided categorical funding both for the identification process and for programs designed to serve gifted students. This was a landmark accomplishment. Not only was education for the gifted legitimized, but the power of parental involvement was indisputably demonstrated.

After having successfully won its point, however, the organization seemed to wither. Elements of its initial proposal, such as statewide mandating of programs that were not included in the legislation, were abandoned. No new action platform was created to continue the work and no preparation was made to respond to cultural and economic changes over the years. Membership dwindled and, for all practical purposes, California Parents for the Gifted ceased to exist as an outspoken advocate. When issues arise that threaten the existence of programs for gifted children in California, it has been able to muster sufficient support to meet the threat, but the organization has never been able to generate the kind of commitment it enjoyed earlier.

The reasons for the falling-away are not clear, but some speculation is possible. First, as districts responded to the new legislation, parent attention turned to overseeing local program development. There are few parents with time for anything more. Second, those who had worked so long and hard were spent. On the surface, it seemed the initial victory was enough, and the subsequent satisfaction undermined interest in pursuing the remaining goals. Regardless of the failure of California Parents for the Gifted to sustain

itself, the achievement of the organization is dramatic evidence of
the power parents possess when they band together.

Organizations and Their Functions

When parents elect to take their concern for gifted children
and their education beyond the home, the most effective means of
involvement is through organization work.[1] Solitary, subjective
parents are rarely successful in effecting change and frequently
do more harm than good by antagonizing professionals who sometimes retaliate by making school life difficult for the children involved. This is less apt to occur through organized appeal, since
the more objective stance of an organization reduces the onus on
individual children. Also, it is more difficult for professionals to
brush off a well-organized plan as the "pushiness" of neurotic
parents.

UNIQUENESS OF ORGANIZATIONS OF PARENTS OF GIFTED CHILDREN

The group of parents of the gifted whose emphasis is on curriculum and academic excellence differs from the usual concept of
parent participation as developed over many years by the PTA.
The former is established to serve a different function from the
usual kinds of support activities undertaken by other parent associations. Curriculum matters have traditionally been considered
outside the purview of parent participation. With the growth of
the concept of parental involvement in academic problems, parents
are coming to be seen as legitimate advisory bodies within the
schools. For example, such participation is required in compensatory
education programs and in programs of early childhood education
in California. While parents of the gifted groups do not usually
enjoy such a mandated role, they have served as the model for these
later groups, with one important difference: they are autonomous.
Their independence enables them to adhere to a set policy of their
own and frees them from being viewed as a rubber stamp for
administration. This does not mean that a group of parents is automatically an adversary of the schools, but rather that it can better

1. An excellent brief paper by Garnet Posa, "So You Want to Start an
Association," may be obtained from Carol Nathan, 40 Beverly Road, Kensington, Calif. 94707.

protect both the schools and the students by working in cooperative partnership with professional educators.

Some problems that beset education for the gifted and parental involvement in it are unique. No other program serving a group of exceptional children must face the same degree of indifference and negligence. Public opinion and sentiment respond quickly to the needs of children whose incapacities are immediately apparent. But there are no visible differences upon which the gifted may rely to emphasize their exceptionality. Of no other group has it ever been said that "they will make it anyhow." In addition, there is, both within public education as well as outside, a suspicion of the intellect. Do students who have so great an initial advantage need any more benefits? Do they not, in fact, really owe something to others less fortunate?

Aside from the professionals who do not accept these notions, there is no one to defend the needs of gifted children except parents and those few who believe that all children, including the gifted, must be provided with an education appropriate to their abilities. Because teachers and administrators who believe in education for the gifted may well be a minority within their profession, they too need the kind of support provided by a parent group.

When the emphasis of a parent group is not on the individual problems of particular children (where this situation occurs, it is the individual parents who must take the initiative), but on the principle of equality of educational opportunity commensurate with all children's skills and abilities, the group can be a powerfully persuasive force in a community, a state, and the nation. It can effectively define the gifted as a valuable part of the whole of education, and persuade others that this part needs to be served. From such a vantage point, parents can often judge and criticize the consequences of school board and administrative decisions when the staff cannot.

While parent groups are chiefly concerned with the structure and effectiveness of programs for the gifted, many have found it necessary to review and assess the overall academic program of a district. Gifted programs, under the most happy circumstances, are usually limited to a few offerings. Funding generally does not permit a parallel total curriculum for gifted students; the best it can provide is some supplementary support. Therefore, it is important that all areas of the academic curriculum be made to provide growth for all, including gifted students. The reason for the concern of a parent group here is obvious. Less obvious, perhaps, is another reason: that attention to the total academic curriculum implies the understanding that gifted students require more than a special program, that a totally homogeneous experience for gifted students may in fact be undesirable. The world in which the gifted function is not homogeneous, and it is important that they learn to live comfortably and compassionately with those who are not so quick or so perceptive. This kind of learning can only take place in a heterogeneous atmosphere. While gifted children should have the opportunity for a continuous educational experience with their intellectual peers, they should not be totally isolated from the larger world in which they will have to live.

With the growing interest in areas of giftedness beyond the intellectual, attention to all elements of the school curriculum becomes more crucial. Not only is it much more difficult to identify the truly talented in all areas of endeavor, it also would be unrealistic to expect a district to be able to finance a myriad of special programs for a wide variety of gifts. Music programs, art programs, creative writing programs, even physical education programs, usually cannot exclude any student who desires to participate. The outstanding students surface finally through the genuine competition that such programming allows. And the student who is elected president of the student body is elected by all his school mates, not just by his peers. Consequently, it is encumbent on organizations of parents of the gifted to recognize the importance of the total school environment. Their effectiveness is greatly diminished by excessive concentration on a few select classes that are identified as gifted.

Parent groups in different communities must follow different paths to reach their goals, but there are a number of methods that, while differing in emphasis, are similar in intention. There is, of course, one primary aim shared by all organizations, whether on the local or state level: to obtain, insure, and guarantee the continuance of programs specifically aimed at educating gifted students. Where the emphasis to gain that universal end is put depends upon local idiosyncracies, community response, and the attitudes prevalent among state legislators and officials, and in state departments of education.

National organization. Only recently have the unique educational needs of gifted students been acknowledged and addressed by the federal government. With that recognition, meager though it is, some representation for the gifted has been established in the regional offices of the U.S. Office of Education as well as in an Office of Gifted and Talented in Washington. In addition, many states now have at least one person in the state department of education responsible for education for the gifted.

Before these developments, the establishment of a national organization of parents of the gifted was less feasible. Now there are states with rapidly growing statewide organizations that could form the nucleus for a national organization of representatives. Several factors, however, affect such activity. One is the fact that the rapid growth of commitment to gifted education has occurred at a time when education generally faces economic difficulties that make adequate funding for gifted programs hard to come by. Another factor is the reaction to the attacks on volunteerism by some elements of the women's movement, which has made parents hesitant to make the effort. Since most active workers for gifted education are volunteer mothers, the criticism has discouraged many from becoming involved without paid professional status. The formation and active development of national parents' organization can only evolve out of a resolution of the contention between the needs of gifted students in a tightening economy and the pressure of social criticism.

There are, of course, two national organizations concerned with gifted education: the Association for the Gifted and the National Association for Gifted Children. Both are primarily professional groups, and while each has made some effort to enlist parent support, neither has gotten beyond a kind of tokenism. Most of the parents involved are also professionals, and they are generally recognized in their professional rather than their parental role.

Statewide organizations. Statewide organizations generally put their energies to work in obtaining some kind of legislative recognition of the need for specially funded gifted education within the state. The intent is to persuade elected representatives of its importance as part of public education. Their persuasive efforts are more successful when the organization is made up of a membership that represents all local constituencies, since elected officials listen more closely when their own electorate speaks.

State departments of education must wait upon the action of legislatures before they can incorporate education for the gifted into their administrative and education codes and before they can allocate funds to support such education. However, legislation is often drafted and supported by state departments, and a statewide organization can establish liaison with the department to the end that the legislation proposed reflects the concerns of parents as well as the technical requirements of the department.

Such efforts have little result if there is not a statewide plan of action with suitable goals that all local affiliates agree to support. Of course, there will never be unanimous agreement; but there can be consensus. To achieve that consensus requires compromise and then political reality always calls for further compromise.

Local district organizations. Local organizations must be capable of a variety of stances. On the one hand, their commitment to the principle of gifted education must be clearly spelled out. On the other, they need to recognize the climate in which they have to work. Whenever possible, members of the gifted community must participate on school district committees considering budget, curriculum, integration, and so forth, never losing sight of the fact that gifted education is an integral part of a total educational plan. An organization with a clearly defined policy in this matter is the gifted students' best spokesman. Further, the policy should be thought out in such a way that it assumes the good will of the school system and makes itself acceptable on the grounds of its reasonableness. A stance as adversary should be taken only as a last resort.

To win the support of a community and the confidence and trust of professionals, parent groups need to put aside personal feelings and look at what is actually provided within the district. If there is no recognition of the needs of the gifted, then there is the task of educating the public on its importance. If there is already some evidence of concern with the plight of gifted students, an organization has a foundation on which to build. When criticism is needed, it is also necessary to suggest constructive alternatives.

District and site advisory committees. Superintendents and principals usually do want to accommodate the community they serve, but gifted education may be low on their list of priorities. The job of the organization is then to find ways by which to raise the visibility of the gifted.

Advisory committees can be of great benefit to a district staff, since parent representatives can provide accurate reflections of community thinking. The truth of this assertion can be found in the growing desire on the part of school districts to include parents in their planning. Such representatives can often help to prevent a massive and irrational response within the community by discovering and correcting a situation before it becomes intolerable for either the parents or the students.

Professionals often fear parental interference, and equally often parents feel threatened by what seems to be complacence and condescension on the part of professionals. Both of these situations need to be relieved by a cooperative commitment to the matter at hand— in this case, the need for special education for gifted children. Parents on an advisory committee have to remember that they are there only in an advisory capacity, just as staff has to remember that they are there to serve the community.

Newsletters. Information about programs is a necessity for parents to support a gifted program in their district, or to support legislation when it is needed. Communication is a knotty problem from the professional standpoint. Most local organizations do publish an informational paper on a more or less regular basis, usually quarterly.

A newsletter provides three important services to the membership of a group. First, it supplies its members with an ongoing resumé of gifted programs in the schools, what is happening, and what difficulties the program may be suffering. Since the majority of members of any parent organization are relatively inactive, aside from paying dues, a newsletter is tangible evidence of what they are supporting. The second benefit is that it provides the possibility of dialogue between parents and professionals and alerts each to the reactions of the other. Finally, the newsletter can generate involvement of the inactive parents at moments of crisis. When important matters concerning the gifted are to be considered at a district school board meeting, the newsletter provides a vehicle for drawing a large supporting audience to attend the discussions and participate in the decisions to be made.[2]

Some local parent groups go beyond the simple newsletter and provide their membership with reviews of significant books, assessment of relevant programs, and reports on matters that affect the children's education generally. A survey, done by parents, on the districtwide objectives in a music program, a mathematics program, a foreign language program, and so forth, gives other parents an awareness of the continuity, or lack of it, in the existing curriculum.[3] Such reviews, if they are done objectively, assist the district in its planning in various areas of the curriculum, particularly where they tend to produce response from parents.

Study Committees. Parental influence contributes to the uniformity and continuity of a gifted program from classroom to classroom and from grade to grade. Establishing parent study committees at individual school sites provides the organization with up-to-date information on specific needs that parents can fill at their own children's schools. Many parents are willing to be involved where their children are directly concerned, even if they do not see the importance of broader involvement. The school-site committees enable parents to familiarize themselves with what is of immediate interest to them—the education of their gifted children. Beyond that, there is often growth in parents from the school-site sensibility to an awareness of the larger responsibilities of a parent organization. Hence, a constantly developing pool of experienced parents is available to provide the continuity needed for the survival of the parent organization as an effective tool for gifted education.

2. Some newsletters of good quality are published by statewide and local organizations. A few examples follow: Newsletter of the Michigan Association for the Academically Talented, Inc., 29976 Hennepin, Garden City, Michigan 48135; *DIALOGUE: A Journal for Education of the Gifted*, 40 Beverly Road, Kensington, Calif. 94707; Newsletter of the Gifted Children's Association of San Fernando Valley, 17915 Ventura Blvd., #230, Encino, Calif. 91316; *Gifted Gab*, Gifted Children's Association of the Foothills, P.O. Box 4132, Covina, Calif. 91723.

3. For instance, a fact sheet format has been developed by Berkeleyans for Academic Excellence, P.O. Box 492, Berkeley, Calif. 94701.

An out-of-school alternative. Enrichment classes outside the public schools are often one part of the undertakings of a local organization.[4] By providing gifted children with additional experiences in a variety of disciplines, parent groups can enhance their children's education. In areas where gifted education stands little chance of official recognition, this way of serving gifted children is a necessity.

Lyceum classes, however, should never be considered as an excuse for districts or states to do nothing. They should always be clearly seen as a supplement to, not a substitution for, public school responsibility for the education of gifted students. Wherever they live and whatever their ethnic background and economic status, gifted children are entitled to a public education commensurate with learning potential. Lyceum classes have to be paid for, and many parents are not financially able to provide such benefits for their children. Scholarships serve to some extent in these cases; but unhappily there can never be enough of them to take the place of quality programs within the schools.

If the exigencies of present circumstances leave no other way of serving gifted students in a community except through special after-school or Saturday classes, then by all means they should be offered. At the same time, however, parents should consider organization to bring concentrated pressure on whatever public agency can bring about legitimate educational opportunities for all gifted students.

The range of parent-supported programs is limited only by the opportunities available within a community and the energy of parents to pursue them. The intent is to provide gifted children with enriching experiences in subjects in which they excel far beyond what the public schools can offer and to make available a variety of options that challenge their curiosity. Subjects are as varied as the chemistry of cooking, the relation of humans to their environment, the mystery of the ocean, the intricacies of the computer, how to make and use puppets, the understanding of music and art, to name a few.

Classes meet in almost any setting, ranging from a public club-

4. Model enrichment programs are offered by the Gifted Child Society of New Jersey, 59 Glen Gray Rd., Oakland, N.J. 07436 and the Gifted Children's Association of San Fernando Valley (see footnote 2 for address).

house or college campus to an instructor's home workshop or garden. They benefit children in two major ways: (a) they offer gifted children the opportunity to interact intimately with their intellectual peers; and (b) they expand the world of possibilities by focusing on materials outside the limits on learning imposed by the restrictions of a formal classroom.

ASSESSING THE STUMBLING BLOCKS

Establishing an organization with both sufficient numbers and some assurance of continuity can run into several difficulties. Some parents of gifted children are reluctant to identify themselves and expose their children's difference in a public way. Whether their reticence arises out of ambiguous feelings about intellectual pursuits or out of embarrassment in seeking special attention for children already obviously blessed, they are slow to involve themselves. Dorothy A. Sisk, director of the federal Office of Gifted and Talented, recently stated the issue as follows:

One of the problems in stimulating support for education of the gifted is the inherent feeling of parents that it is not quite appropriate to demand programs for their children. If those same parents had children with defects, they would be willing to seek every bit of professional and educational help for their children.[5]

In our egalitarian society, it seems that the idea of demanding special educational opportunities for those already well endowed is sometimes seen as unacceptable. Therefore, rather than actively pursuing suitable provisions for educating the very bright appropriately, parents may settle for token gestures.

While some parents are eager to work at the local level for their own and their friends' children, they are unable to see beyond the narrow limits of such activity to the broad necessity for such aid to all gifted children. As a result, there is only a small pool of parents spread throughout the United States to develop either a network of statewide organizations or a national one. And among this small group, there are profound philosophical differences regarding the scope of such an endeavor. Many parents insist that the only legitimate emphasis· must be on securing support for the

5. Quoted in G. I. Maeroff, "The Unfavored Gifted Few," *New York Times Magazine*, 21 August 1977, p. 31.

mentally gifted exclusively. Their arguments make three points: (a) that legitimate and adequate tools do not exist for identifying any but the mentally gifted; (b) that the movement historically was founded on the needs of the mentally gifted; and (c) that until recognition is won for the mentally gifted, no other area of giftedness should be supported. An equal number contend that only by working within the broader area of gifted and talented now established at the federal level, and generally reflected by state offices, can there be any hope of succeeding. They believe that a more congenial atmosphere exists when it is recognized that all gifted and talented children must be served by our educational institutions.

By and large, active parents tend to be affluent, well educated, articulate, and white. Few parents of gifted minority or culturally different children participate in decision making in organizations. Such an organization is an easy target for accusations of elitism and classism. And there is some justification in the charge, since little attention is given to the problems of gifted students coming from less fortunate backgrounds.

There are no pat solutions for any of the above problems. What is needed, is a change of attitude to reinforce the statement that an organization is nondiscriminatory and a willingness to follow as well as lead. Those changes are personal decisions, but without them parent organizations for gifted education cannot flourish as they should.

Parents and Their Gifted Children

What is often neglected in concentration on gifted education is the need for education of parents of gifted children. An ideal program cannot serve gifted children well without parents who understand what giftedness is, that is, parents who comprehend their responsibility as significant adults in the life of a bright child. Probably the most general area of parental confusion arises out of the notion that potential (which says a child is gifted) and achievement (which can sometimes indicate otherwise) are synonymous. Sometimes the contradiction between the identification score and school grades results in tension between parent and child. The discrepancies can be the fault of the schools, but often they develop out of an unsympathetic, even hostile, home life.

It is not any easier to be the parents of a gifted child than it is to be a gifted child. Expectations insisting that brightness should manifest itself in success, conformity, and perfection are a gifted child's greatest hazard. A gifted child is still a child and should be allowed the prerogative of being like all children—cooperative/negative, happy/sad, smart/stupid. Life becomes a heavy burden for the child whose parents assume that a gifted child is not going to be childish. Brightness is praised when it reflects well on the parents, but that same brightness is rejected when the child's perceptions embarrass them. That is, of course, true for all children, but a gifted child's potential is even more badly damaged by the confusions that arise from what is perceived as parental caprice. When there are too many pressures at home, the gifted child quickly learns that one way to handle the situation, both at home and in school, is to opt for averageness. Nothing is more exasperating to parents whose expectations are unrealistic than the child who knows they are unrealistic and refuses to accommodate to them.

There is a great waste of mental potential among our gifted population. The schools cannot be blamed for all of it; parents are culpable too. For children to achieve to their full potential, they have to believe that they can achieve and that achievement has a value and respect in the most important place of all—the home. The extent to which they do achieve, given proper educational opportunities, reflects how successful parents have been in understanding their role as parents of gifted children.[6]

WHAT PARENTS MUST DO FOR THEMSELVES

That bright, perceptive, achieving, delightful child with whom parents have lived from day one of his life is not changed by being formally identified as gifted. Whatever the means of identification, but particularly by a standardized intelligence test, the child who comes out of the testing room is the same child who

---

6. See Gina Ginsberg, *How to Help Your Gifted Child* (Oakland, N.J.: Gifted Child's Society of New Jersey, 1977); Jeanne L. Delp and Ruth Martinson, *The Gifted and Talented: A Handbook for Parents* (Ventura, Calif.: National/State Leadership Training Institute, 1974); Kay Coffey et al., *Parentspeak on Gifted and Talented Children* (Ventura, Calif.: National/State Leadership Training Institute, 1976).

went in. The parent who emerges from a subsequent conference with the tester can be a very different person—bemused, confused, a little frightened and terribly proud—and carrying a whole new set of expectations. For the child sitting at a table drawing or reading while waiting, this parent is a stranger.

The most common question parents ask, according to psychologists, is "What should I do now?" The inevitable answer, often only partially heard, is "Don't change. What you have been doing is right, because you have a bright child eager to learn and grow. Just go on loving him, respecting his individuality, supporting his achievements, and satisfying his curiosity." One other bit of information that often gets lost is that the test indicates *potential*, nothing else. Part of a parent's job is to assist in the realization of that potential.

Two of the best ways for parents to learn about the unique qualities of gifted children are to talk with other parents who have experienced the joy and anguish of raising their own gifted child and to read some books that describe the characteristics of the gifted and the parenting of them. And keeping the lines of communication open between parents and child is of major importance. Gifted children will tell their parents a great deal about themselves if the parents take the time to listen and to understand. With an extremely verbal child, it is very hard not to stop listening from time to time; there is so much to listen to. It need not happen, however, if parents point out from the very beginning that they can only take in so much, that they can understand and sympathize, but that they cannot always share equally in enthusiasm. Parents need to be left alone sometimes too. Setting up a regular time for talk is the best way to solve the need for constant attention; no one should be eternally available. Set limits; make home values clear; no gifted child has ever been harmed by learning that other people also have needs.

Grant the gifted children genuine respect for their individuality; accept them as they are; trust them to be responsible; respect their decisions even when they are different, unless they fly in the face of rational behavior. Above all, when parents say that all they want is for their child to be happy or successful or contented, they should be sure they know how the child defines happiness, success, contentment. Those definitions may be very different from theirs.

WHAT PARENTS CAN DO FOR THEIR GIFTED CHILD

Satisfying the curiosity of gifted children about the world around them is a rewarding experience for both parents and children.[7] To do this means more than just supplying children with information; it means being open to their perceptions and evaluations and considering seriously what they have to say. A child's IQ may be higher than that of the parents, but they have experience on their side. That counts for a great deal. But experience should not result in either condescension or cynicism. Those are two attitudes to which a gifted child is most vulnerable.

Museums, theater, ballet, art shows, nature walks, sporting events may not be a child's immediate idea of fun, but if parents truly enjoy them and share their pleasure with the child, no activity need be without good effects. On no account should parents ever insist upon the child participating in something they can not stand themselves just because they think it might "enrich" the child. The useful outings are those to which both parents and children can respond positively. What a gifted child discovers in those adventures may be unique; but that is part of the fun.

Sometimes it is important to share the child's delights. The board walk or the amusement park may offer few gratifications to a parent. They need not subject themselves to upsetting experiences but they can be involved by accepting the child's delight with delight. The impish grins and sparkling eyes that greet one at the end of a wild roller coaster ride let parents know that their children have proved themselves braver or more daring than the parents. More than that, the careful description of their sensations shows that they are learning to communicate their experiences.

Books—good fiction and nonfiction—need to be part of the gifted child's world. The wealth of inexpensive but valuable paperbacks makes this economically possible. A personal library card broadens horizons and at the same time teaches responsibility.

One word of warning is needed: parents of gifted youngsters often tend to concentrate activities and gifts in the area of a child's greatest ability. This can be a mistake. The schools will of necessity

7. See Herbert Kanigher, *Everyday Enrichment for Gifted Children at Home and School* (Ventura, Calif.: National/State Leadership Training Institute, 1977).

emphasize that part of a child's gifts. It is up to parents more often than not to help the child become a fully knowing person. The mathematician who hates to read or write is only a half-realized person. Strategy games are great, but so is the *Odyssey*. The reader who shuns physical activity may really need a basketball.

Finally, the gifted child needs some privacy. A place for day-dreaming and secret thoughts is imperative. When the door to the child's room is closed, that child wants to be alone. Knocking and waiting for an invitation to enter is just good manners. Parents have to learn to deal with the uneasiness over what goes on in that solitary time. They can rest assured that it is a lot of growing. But it only happens and then reveals itself when there is trust on both sides of the door.

Conclusion

This chapter does not pretend to be an exhaustive survey of the possibilities for parent support of gifted programs and children. Experiences in many places and under a variety of circumstances have demonstrated the effectiveness of the activities described.

Parental involvement has produced many good things for gifted children where it has been seriously undertaken. While organization work is demanding and exacting, the reward is great. As programs develop and deepen, it is satisfying to know that one had some small hand in that happening. Moreover, learning about giftedness makes for better understanding between parents and children.

CHAPTER XVIII

Teachers and Mentors

MARVIN J. GOLD

In the field of education for the gifted and talented there are differences of opinion as to philosophic goals, programmatic considerations, and future directions. Yet one view remains fairly constant: the gifted student needs some degree of expert help in fulfilling his superior potential. "Some degree" is the all-important modifier, however, for it will take its meaning from the interaction of all the necessary components of any program: philosophy, definition(s), goals, curricular articulation, and so forth. The interaction of these components will lead to decisions as to which personality characteristics will be deemed essential for the teacher of the gifted, what sort of training is necessary, what additional criteria are needed for the selection of teachers, as well as whether or not certification is essential to give the schools and the public assurance of professional competence. Indeed, followed to a logical conclusion, the interaction of components could even give the administrator of programs for the gifted a rationale for avoiding professional teachers and for using community mentors exclusively.

The Role of the Teacher

It is not uncommon for the uninformed person to say, "*Anyone* can teach." Similarly, many professional educators believe that *any* teacher can teach gifted children. The second opinion is as fallacious as the first.

Regardless of philosophy or educational goals, the very nature of the gifted or talented child leads to necessary modifications in the education and the role of teachers for such children. That role might be viewed somewhere on a continuum ranging from a resource person, whose task is determined exclusively by the varying demands put upon him by the gifted children with whom he deals, to a completely authoritarian figure, who acts both as a task-master to get the children to acquire high-level knowledge as well as the ultimate authority on the knowledge itself.

It can certainly be assumed that the specific criteria employed in identifying candidates for any role will give direction and scope to that role. Yet significant differences were found among more than 200 experts on the education of the gifted as to the ranking of criteria to be used in selecting teachers of gifted children.[1] Not unexpectedly, there was a difference as to the first-ranked criterion for selection of teachers of the gifted as compared with the first-ranked criterion for teachers of the talented. According to the weighted scores, respondents believed that teachers of the gifted should first have "proven teaching ability." "Competence in a specified skill (art, music)" was ranked twelfth and "a strong academic background" was ninth. Teachers of the talented, however, were seen as needing "competence in a specified skill," and "proven teaching ability," which were ranked first and second respectively, while "a strong academic background" was ranked eleventh. Table 1 shows other differences in the rankings. The conclusion could be drawn that the advocates perceived the criteria for teachers of the gifted as differing from those of the teachers of the talented. Programmatic implications can be inferred from the data in table 1.

Approaching the issue another way, Spaulding underscores how attention to different types of giftedness would lead to different responsibilities:

The "creative intellectual" or creatively gifted appears most highly motivated and constructively occupied in settings where limits are clearly set but which permit a wide range of choice for self-direction. . . . The "conforming achiever" seems most at ease and most productive when the lines of expectation are closely drawn and the instructions clearly given.[2]

1. *The Advocate Survey: A Survey of Experts in the Education of Gifted Children* (Silver Spring, Md.: Operations Research, 1971), pp. 72-75.

2. Robert L. Spaulding, "What Teacher Attributes Bring Out the Best in Gifted Children? Affective Dimensions of Creative Processes," in *Teaching Gifted Students*, ed. James J. Gallagher (Boston: Allyn and Bacon, 1965), p. 233.

TABLE 1

ADVOCATE SURVEY RANKINGS FOR SELECTION OF TEACHERS
OF THE GIFTED AND TEACHERS OF THE TALENTED

CRITERION	RANKING FOR TEACHERS OF GIFTED	RANKING FOR TEACHERS OF TALENTED
Proven teaching ability	1	2
Flexibility, open minded	2	6
Understanding of special problems in teaching the gifted and talented	3	4
Able to relate to children (sensitive, patient, sense of humor, communications)	4	3
Ego strength, self-confidence, maturity	5	7
Enthusiasm toward teaching and children (high motivation, dedicated)	6	5
High intelligence	7	12
Love of learning, intellectual curiosity	8	9
Strong academic background	9	11
Creativity	10	8
Wide interests	11	13
Competence in specified skill (art, music)	12	1
Other	13	10

Source: Adapted from *The Advocate Survey: A Survey of Experts in the Education of Gifted Children* (Silver Spring, Md.: Operations Research, 1971), pp. 73, 75.

The complexity of the professional's task is further compounded by the several hats he has to wear, regardless of the types of giftedness or how he deals with those types in the classroom: "He is partly teacher, partly a psychologist and counselor, partly an ombudsman, partly a public relations man."[3]

The role and the selection of the teacher of the gifted, then, are dependent on a variety of considerations: the program(s) for the gifted and talented, the biases and background of the authorities employed by a community when initiating or maintaining programs, differences in personalities and learning styles of gifted and talented children themselves, and the exceedingly varied demands placed upon the teacher of the gifted.

The Mentor

Although the concept of the mentor is at least as old as recorded history, it has only recently come to be used more regularly in the education of gifted children. A perusal of the index in a dozen

3. Gerald H. Bidlack, "The Special Teacher/Consultant for Gifted Pupils in the Public School System: Two Approaches," *Gifted Child Quarterly* 18 (1974): 151.

texts on the education of gifted children failed to turn up more than a single mention of the term. In fact, although that single reference is included in the revision of his book, Gallagher did not employ the term in the earlier edition.[4] In preparing his pamphlet on the role of the mentor, Boston noted that "a search of the Library of Congress card catalog under the subject heading 'Mentor' turned up nothing."[5]

Basically, the potential mentor in gifted child education possesses a high degree of competency in some particular endeavor (for example, genetics, Chinese history, French impressionists). An arrangement is made between the school and this individual to work on a one-to-one basis with some gifted or talented student interested in the same field. The contact leads ideally to a mutually satisfactory and fulfilling relationship for the mentor and his charge.

A relatively unique approach to working with gifted and talented children, Project Matchmaker, was initiated in Polk County, Florida.[6] Since only one professional could be employed to work with all the gifted children in this large and basically rural county, it was decided that the professional's time could be best used to build school-community contacts for educating those gifted children rather than to provide services directly. The venture was successful, but as more teachers for the gifted became available less reliance was placed on these community mentors.

The major organized mentor effort to be found in the United States today is the Executive High School Internship Program, which was established a decade ago.[7] The program aids local school systems in developing plans in which high-school students are given released time from their formal studies and are put in contact with

4. James J. Gallagher, *Teaching the Gifted Child*, 2d ed. (Boston: Allyn and Bacon, 1975), pp. 284-85.

5. Bruce O. Boston, *The Sorcerer's Apprentice: A Case Study in the Role of the Mentor* (Reston, Va.: Council for Exceptional Children, 1976), p. 1.

6. *Project Matchmaker: A Program Designed to Match School and Community Resources to the Needs of Students for Talent Development* (Bartow, Fla.: Polk County Board of Public Instruction, 1967).

7. Sharlene P. Hirsch, "Executive High School Internships: A Boon for the Gifted and Talented," *Teaching Exceptional Children* 9 (1976): 22-23.

volunteer community leaders in business, industry, and the professions. Although this plan is not for the exclusive use of gifted or talented children, its value to them is of some magnitude. The period of released time is usually a semester, but may vary according to local conditions. In one school system a student might be released for a day per week during the second semester of the senior year, while a student in another system might be released for an entire six-week period or longer, and still another system might opt for two afternoons per week for the entire year.

In explaining why the mentor approach has not been employed more frequently, Gallagher has observed: "(It) has been infrequently used not because of strong counterarguments but because it is administratively awkward."[8] An advantage of the Executive High School Internship Program, however, is that the plan can easily be modified to suit the administrative convenience of the school.

An analysis of the relationship between the mentor and his charge has been made by Boston, who concluded that (a) mentor programs in gifted child education must be rooted in experiential learning; (b) both mentor and pupil to some degree select each other in the context of a commitment that is being shaped (in the case of the pupil) or is already formed (in the case of the mentor); (c) mentoring programs for the gifted will have to be, by the nature of what we hope will happen in them, open-ended; and (d) both instruction and evaluation will necessarily be competency-based rather than norm-based.[9]

Characteristics of the Successful Teacher

Gallagher has observed that "there is probably more nonsense and less evidence dispensed about the needed characteristics of the teacher of the gifted than almost any other single issue."[10] Unfortunately, this statement is difficult to refute. A search of the literature reveals very little meaningful research on characteristics of the teacher of the gifted.

8. Gallagher, *Teaching the Gifted Child*, p. 285.

9. Boston, *The Sorcerer's Apprentice*, pp. 31-33.

10. Gallagher, *Teaching the Gifted Child*, p. 312.

Toler developed a list of questions posed by his sixth-, seventh-, and eighth-grade gifted students relative to their concerns about what makes a good teacher of the gifted.[11] The list of thirty-five questions included, among other items, queries about knowledge of and ability to handle subject matter, racial and other prejudices, intimidation by students, classroom favorites, discipline, friendliness, fairness, classroom control, and sense of humor. Such questions would not seem to be different from those that might be asked about any teacher, nor do they seem to differentiate between questions relating to general characteristics desired in all teachers and characteristics that are of special importance for teachers of the gifted.

After reviewing eighteen basic works on the subject of education for the gifted and talented, Maker brought together a list of personal characteristics believed to be important for teachers of the gifted.[12] The list included such items as "highly intelligent," "flexible and creative," "self-confident," "a wide variety of interests," "sympathy with problems of gifted and talented children," and "enjoyment in working with gifted and talented children." Maker suggested that the list of traits represents characteristics of all good teachers and thus defeats the specific value of such a list for identification of teachers of the gifted or talented.

It would appear, therefore, that the typical list of characteristics of teachers of the gifted and talented would be useful only if attention were given to the specific nature of each of those characteristics with respect to teachers of the gifted and the talented.

Two studies of teachers of the gifted offer some insights, yet each has limitations. McNary correlated measures of academic achievement and of creativity among fourth-, fifth-, and sixth-grade gifted pupils with the characteristics of their teachers (for example, intelligence, personality, age, sex, training, and marital status).[13] In

11. Donald Toler, unpublished study.

12. C. June Maker, *Training Teachers for the Gifted and Talented: A Comparison of Models* (Reston, Va.: Council for Exceptional Children, 1975), p. 11.

13. Shirley R. McNary, *The Relationships between Certain Teacher Characteristics and Achievement and Creativity of Gifted Students* (Syracuse, N.Y.: Syracuse University, 1967).

general, the personality characteristics of teachers, as measured by the *Sixteen Personality Factor Questionnaire*, were found to be more related to change in the children's scores than were the teachers' intelligence, age, socioeconomic level, marital status, family status (presence of children), years of formal education, years of teaching (excluding years of teaching the gifted), years of teaching the gifted, credit hours in courses concerning the gifted, and present grade-level assignment. The personality characteristics identified as being most associated with the achievement of gifted children included submission (versus dominance), happy-go-lucky (versus serious), lack of rigid internal standards (versus superego strength), and naive (versus sophisticated). The factors related to growth in creativity included emotional stability (versus emotional immaturity), superego strength (versus lack of rigid internal standards), accepting (versus suspecting), and uncontrolled (versus controlled).[14] A significant flaw in this study concerns the measured intelligence of the teachers, for whom the mean verbal IQ was found to be approximately 102 and the mean nonverbal IQ approximately 85. It would seem to be essential to replicate this research with a "brighter" group of teachers.

In Bishop's study, students in the Georgia Governor's Honors Program were asked to identify their "most successful" teachers. These teachers were then compared with a random sample of teachers who had previously taught these students but who were not chosen by them as "most successful," using data obtained from the *Ryan Teacher Characteristics Schedule*, interviews with teachers, teachers' verbal scores on the *Wechsler Adult Intelligence Scale*, teachers' college transcripts, the *Edwards Personal Preference Schedule*, and students' responses on questionnaires. The results indicated that the more successful teachers of this gifted group of high school youth were mature, experienced teachers of high intelligence (mean IQ = 128), had intellectual avocational interests, expressed a need for achievement, opted for teaching because it represented an opportunity for intellectual growth, had more positive attitudes toward their students, were student-centered in their approach to teaching, were well versed in their subject

14. Ibid., pp. 18-19.

as well as being able to stimulate and interest their students in the material, and finally, were in favor of special provisions for the gifted.[15] The limitation of the Bishop study is that the majority of the students involved were white, high achievers, basically conforming, and had been nominated for the honors program by teachers and administrators. The findings, therefore, should not be generalized beyond a comparable group.

Both studies described above are now more than a decade old and nothing similar to them has been conducted in the intervening years. More research and less opinion about the characteristics of teachers of the gifted are clearly needed.

The Preparation of Teachers for the Gifted

As is the case with views on the characteristics of teachers of the gifted, the nature of preservice training for future teachers of the gifted and the talented is as varied as the biases held by the teacher educators. In general, however, divergence in models for preparing these teachers probably represents a healthy situation for the field. As graduates of these programs acquire experience and provide feedback to those responsible for teacher education programs, those programs will continue to be modified and improved.

PRESERVICE TRAINING

Several years ago a committee of the Council for Exceptional Children developed some general criteria for the preparation of teachers of the gifted. The committee believed that teacher trainees needed the following: "(a) high-level competence in at least one academic area; (b) opportunities for independent inquiry and research; (c) the study of some topics in great depth; (d) specialized work . . . planned individually on the basis of need; (e) understanding of the meaning of exceptionality . . . in relation to all children; (f) a commitment to differential education for the gifted; (g) understanding of learning theory, . . . [of] higher conceptualization processes, [of] qualitative differences in levels of think-

15. William E. Bishop, "Successful Teachers of the Gifted," *Exceptional Children* 34 (1968): 317-25.

ing, and [of] the development of cognitive abilities; (h) study of various provisions for the gifted; (i) [understanding of] guidance and counseling needs of the gifted and their parents; (j) [understanding of] curriculum planning for the gifted; (k) observation of and participation with gifted children; (l) and student teaching with gifted pupils."[16] In preparing a review of the literature for the report of the U.S. Commissioner of Education to the Congress, Martinson concluded that "studies of successful teachers of the gifted typically have dealt with their characteristics and behavior more often than with their specific preparation."[17]

Undergraduate programs. There are differences of opinion as to whether preservice training programs for teachers of the gifted should be at the undergraduate or graduate level. At present there are relatively few undergraduate programs. A search of college catalogs and of the professional literature, as well as extensive personal communications, failed to identify more than three such programs. The rationale for one of these, the program at the University of South Alabama, is that a relative lack of time constraints and of need for pedagogical remediation makes the undergraduate level particularly appropriate for the training of professionals to work with gifted and talented students. Since the preprofessional trainees in this program are themselves gifted and talented individuals of high caliber, it has seemed reasonable to assume that the level of conceptual comprehension and of assimilation will be very high and that waivers of other course requirements would permit the inclusion in the program of a significant amount of advanced work. A description of the program points out:

With early identification of preprofessionals—the senior high school year is not too early—the undergraduate program could concentrate for all four years on developing and refining appropriate strategies for working with gifted and talented youngsters. Besides its didactic elements, the freshman year could contain observation and low-level participation; the sophomore year, "teacher-aiding"; the junior year, one-to-one

16. *Professional Standards for Personnel in the Education of Exceptional Children,* an interim report (Washington, D.C.: Council for Exceptional Children, 1965), pp. 89-90.

17. Sidney P. Marland, Jr., *Education of the Gifted and Talented,* Report to the Congress of the United States by the U.S. Commissioner of Education (Washington, D.C.: U.S. Government Printing Office, 1972), p. 107.

and small-group involvement of a diagnostic-prescriptive nature; and the senior year, full responsibility for classroom and resource room management.[18]

Regardless of the training model or level, professionals working with gifted and talented children need didactic and practicum experiences in understanding the gifted and in-depth work in at least one substantive (content) area. They need also to receive their education in a style equivalent to styles appropriate for gifted children themselves (for example, time to think, ability to take risks, freedom to fail) and to gain knowledge about intellectual theories, cognitive and affective heirarchies, curricular models, and their interrelationships.

Since the program at the University of South Alabama is comparatively new, there has been no opportunity to evaluate its effectiveness. Supportive data on such programs will have to be collected and analyzed prior to any movement within the field toward acceptance of an undergraduate training approach as readily as the concept of the graduate program is currently accepted.

Graduate programs. In their survey of almost 1600 institutions of higher learning, Laird and Kowalski concluded that fewer than 10 percent (151) of those institutions had at least a single course dealing specifically with the education of the gifted and talented. It certainly can be assumed that only a fraction of that number would have complete training sequences for teachers of the gifted and talented.[19]

A more recent survey indicates that in the United States there are fewer than thirty institutions that offer programs at the master's level and that only about one-third of that number offer doctoral programs. In fact, 60 percent of the states *do not have a single sequential degree program* at any level for teachers of the gifted and talented.[20]

18. Marvin J. Gold, "Preparation of Teachers for Gifted and Talented (G/T) Youngsters," *Talents and Gifts* 19 (November 1976): 22-23.

19. A. W. Laird and C. J. Kowalski, "Survey of 1,564 Colleges and Universities on Courses Offered in the Education of the Gifted—Teacher Training," *Gifted Child Quarterly* 16 (1972): 95.

20. "Master's and Ph.D. Programs in Gifted Education or with Emphasis in Gifted Education," *N/S-LTI-G/T Bulletin* 3 (August, 1976): insert.

At the University of South Florida, there is a program at the master's level designed for individuals who are experienced and certified teachers and another for those who have completed only a liberal arts bachelor's degree. The programs are based on the following "skills and competencies that have been identified for the teachers of the gifted and talented": (a) skills in utilizing tests and test data, utilizing group dynamics, counseling and guidance, developing lessons in creative thinking, utilizing strategies such as simulation, providing learning opportunities at all levels of cognition, relating the cognitive and affective dimensions, demonstrating lessons for the gifted, conducting action research, and (b) knowledge of the nature and needs of the gifted, of new developments in education, and of current research in gifted education.[21] The program attends to professional specialization, liberal arts, and field work, but the liberal arts element is neither mentioned (nor implied) in the above list, nor is it significantly represented in the sample programs presented.[22] Although this program has already produced a number of practitioners, it has not been evaluated as yet. Practically every other teacher training effort for the gifted and talented is in the same situation.

IN-SERVICE EDUCATION

There are differences of opinion as to whether in-service programs for teachers of the gifted and the talented should be of the standard kind as contrasted with programs of technical assistance. Maker has described in some detail a variety of approaches to in-service training, including summer institutes, demonstration projects, and service centers.[23] Although she includes the Technical Assistance Development System (TADS) under "service centers," that approach will be discussed separately here. Again, evaluations of the effectiveness of these programs are generally not available.

Summer institutes. Institutes can be of any duration from a few days to an entire six- or eight-week period. One effort has been

21. Dorothy Sisk, "Teaching the Gifted and Talented Teacher: A Training Model," *Gifted Child Quarterly* 19 (1975): 84.

22. Ibid., pp. 84-85.

23. Maker, *Training Teachers for the Gifted*, pp. 29-52.

that of the National State Leadership Training Institute on Gifted and Talented (N/S-LTI-G/T). Although not designed for teacher training alone, the LTI model underscores the effectiveness of comparatively brief (two-week) but intensive periods of activity that includes components related to the acquisition of knowledge, demonstration, activities, interaction with peers, decision making, familiarization with processes of change, and so forth.[24] A summer institute, as an in-service model, is neither good nor bad but simply an administrative method for implementing educational change. If the components of the institute are weak, it will be weak; if there is vigor in the content, then the summer institute will have a significant impact as a training effort for teachers of the gifted and talented.

Demonstration projects. The demonstration project probably has failed as often as it has succeeded as a training vehicle. When a demonstration effort represents a vital, viable, fluid function, it has a dynamism that can be quite contagious. If, on the other hand, the project has found "the way" and is trying to share its discovery with the in-service participant, it tends to defeat its own purposes. Most demonstration efforts that are not replicated are so firmly set in institutional concrete that they gain few converts among in-service participants.

Demonstration operations also fail as in-service models when they are out of touch with the real world on issues such as pupil-teacher ratio, expenditures for equipment and materials, and space allocation, to mention only a few. If participants see no way to borrow or adapt from the activity being demonstrated because it is not realistic, they are very likely to leave the demonstration feeling that, since money, space, teaching assistants, and so forth are not available to them, they will just keep on doing what makes most sense under their present circumstances.

Service centers. The concept of the area service center is gaining more and more popularity. The center can gather resources effectively, disseminate training with comparative economy, and perform other activities that individual schools or school systems are not able or liable to do as well. Like the institute and the

24. "Third National Summer LTI in Aspen," *N/S-LTI-G/T Bulletin* 2 (February 27, 1975): pp. 1, 7.

demonstration center, however, the service center remains only as good as its program. It is a vehicle. If it transports goods of worth, then it finds most positive results. On the other hand, if it is weak programmatically, then its in-service education for teachers of the gifted and talented will suffer.

Technical assistance. Gallagher points out that those interested in education for the gifted and talented are being deluded if they think that enough professionally qualified teachers and supervisors can be turned out by using a standard preservice training model. Employing data from the National Center for Educational Statistics, he estimates that approximately 41,000 teachers and over 5,000 supervisors are now needed to serve an estimated 1,023,980 gifted students between the ages five and seventeen in the schools.[25] He argues that it is not possible to expect a sufficiently large pool of such personnel to be trained in a reasonable amount of time. Therefore, instead of a preservice approach he suggests a plan called the Technical Assistance Development System (TADS), which he describes as follows:

A technical assistance unit operates to provide systematic aid to local programs upon their request on problems of local concern. It would be staffed by some educators intimately familiar with gifted education but could also include staff who had expertise in such areas as curriculum development, program evaluation, or the stimulation of creative activities.[26]

Gallagher suggests that the major differences between typical consultative services and technical assistance is that no one individual (consultant) has the complete wherewithal to solve the many particular problems of a local system (client). In addition, the consultant comes with his particular expertise, background, and pool of information and usually gives it *all* to the client "whether he wants it or not."

In initiating a technical assistance plan, a *needs assessment,* a formal *contract of agreement* (for the who, when, what, and how of services to be delivered) and a *talent bank* are key elements.

25. James J. Gallagher, "Technical Assistance: A New Device for Quality Educational Services for the Gifted," *TAG Newsletter* 16 (Summer, 1974): 7-8.

26. Ibid., p. 7.

This plan, beginning with an individualized prescription approach, certainly has much to commend it as a means of upgrading education for the gifted and talented. The problem comes with supporting completely the premise that the preservice agencies cannot make more of an impact than Gallagher thinks is possible.

Other activities. The above four in-service approaches are now popular and can be effective ways of dealing with the preparation of the professional for working with the gifted and the talented. Other methods have been employed, as has been noted elsewhere:

Administrative aid. Supervisors and administrators can bring ideas for increased enrichment of the classroom program and procedures.

Workshops. They provide opportunities for hearing authorities in the field present their viewpoints, for exploring the research available about gifted, and for reading and discussing what is being done in other localities.

Classes and study groups. Near many schools are colleges and universities which as part of their extension or field services will organize classes on the expressed interest and need of a number of teachers.

Teacher institutes. County institutes and state meetings of teacher groups ordinarily offer sessions in which they present speakers, panels, and symposia dealing with topics of interest to their teachers.

Reading. Individual reading and study by a teacher who desires to improve his teaching of the gifted can be very significant.

Informal methods. Informal conversation among teachers, the exchange of ideas as they search for ways of helping a student who presents problems, or one with whom they all have contact, [is helpful, as are] . . . a few days of observing an already successful teacher of the gifted in the classroom.[27]

The mode employed to get background and skills through training is less important than the concepts, materials, biases, and other general information to be presented. The administrative plan should be subordinate to the content.

The Problem of Certification

The first state to develop criteria for certification of teachers of the gifted took the pattern of other certification requirements in that state (for example, two semester hours of Art for the Gifted Child, and so forth). This pattern was soon found to be unwork-

27. Merle R. Sumption and Evelyn M. Luecking, *Education of the Gifted* (New York: Ronald Press, 1960), pp. 245-48.

able because of its specificity and its cafeteria approach to the acquiring of competency.

There has been considerable controversy concerning certification of teachers of the gifted. Opponents fear that mediocrity will be legitimized by merely checking off course offerings. Proponents of certification, while arguing against a cafeteria approach, suggest that either competency-based plans or approval of institutional programs will assure a more reasonable alternative. Proponents also imply that administrative patterns should be developed to allow for the employment of field experts, specialists in a subject, and community experts. But they also hold that certified teachers of the gifted must be available for the effective day-to-day operation of programs. Without certification, it is argued, training programs cannot attract future teachers who are being prepared for a "non-field" (as compared, for example, to elementary education), and schools will not employ those teachers as teachers of the gifted and talented for fear of losing state funds because the teacher is working "out-of-field." The vicious cycle must be broken. One way of doing so would be to acknowledge that there is a field of education that can be identified as "gifted child education."

Just as there are types of certification relating to age levels of children, content taught, and the background of teachers, so there could be similar delineations for teachers of the gifted and the talented. There need not be, nor should there be, a single certificate reading "Teacher of the Gifted."

The concept of certification for teachers of the gifted and talented is not a popular one, at least insofar as state departments of education are concerned. In 1975, the Council for Exceptional Children conducted a survey of all states to learn about state laws and regulations regarding exceptional children.[28] Information concerning the gifted was compiled separately, including information about patterns of certification for teachers of the gifted. From that survey it appeared that only Alabama, Georgia, Kansas, Mississippi, and North Carolina had specific certification plans.

Alabama. There is certification at all degree levels. Required

28. *A Summary of State and Federal Laws and Regulations Regarding the Education of Gifted Children* (Reston, Va.: Council for Exceptional Children, 1975).

work includes a background in the education of exceptional children, the nature and needs of the gifted, the testing of exceptional children, methods of teaching children with high potential, practicum activities, and concentrated work in a single arts and sciences area. Presently individuals in Alabama can obtain certification directly from the State Department of Education by presenting a record of having completed approved courses or they may be certified upon completion of a state-approved program for the preparation of teachers of the gifted. The state is currently moving toward the latter method as the primary and perhaps sole approach to certification. Certification in Alabama is specifically for the teacher of the gifted and is not an "add-on" endorsement to an elementary or secondary credential.

Georgia. The field of education for the gifted is considered supplementary in Georgia. A teacher receives endorsement after taking the three following five-quarter-hour courses: nature and needs of the gifted; methods, materials, and curriculum for the gifted; and educational measurement.

Kansas. Both provisional and permanent certification are available. Provisional certification requires a minimum of two years experience, one in a regular class and one with gifted and talented children. For permanent endorsement, the teacher needs an additional twenty-nine semester hours of work beyond the Bachelor's degree, including twelve hours in course work related to the gifted (including characteristics of the gifted, education of the gifted, and practicum), eight hours in *general* special education, and nine hours in "background" courses (for example, learning theory).

Mississippi. Both a *permit* and a *certificate* approach are used in Mississippi. The permit requires a degree in teacher education and the recommendation of the District Superintendent; the certificate calls for additional course work. Certification assumes that permit requirements have been met and that eighteen semester hours in courses on education for the gifted have been completed. This academic requirement includes courses in psychology and education of the gifted, methods, materials, and resources for the gifted, and guidance for the exceptional child. Certification is possible for an individual with a bachelor's degree or for one with a master's degree in a teaching field.

North Carolina. This is apparently the only state employing both a competency-based approach and a course-work approach to certification. In either case, the State Department of Education requires the teacher to hold a bachelor's degree from an approved teacher education program in which there is an emphasis on gifted child education. When pursuing the credit-hour option, the applicant for certification must complete six semester hours in general education for exceptional children and twelve semester hours in the education of gifted children.

Other states are working on certification plans that have not as yet been adopted.

Concluding Statement

There is still more opinion than fact about the teacher of the gifted and the talented. With lack of certainty as to the nature of the role, it is not difficult to see why confusion exists as to specific required characteristics for teachers. A vague list tends to be safer ground on which to rest than a list of specified and verified traits. All of this, of course, has its bearing on programs of teacher training, their differences, and their limited number. Similarly, the certification issue has probably not been faced squarely because of the current stage of development in the field.

CHAPTER XIX

Issues and Procedures in Evaluating Programs

JOSEPH S. RENZULLI AND LINDA H. SMITH

The purpose of this chapter is threefold. First, a brief overview of some of the major concepts that define the field of program evaluation is presented. The focus of this section is upon general issues and problems related to each concept and the ways in which these issues and problems have special relevance to the task of evaluating programs for the gifted. Second, some of the relatively unique characteristics of programs for the gifted are discussed. These characteristics require that special considerations be taken into account in the process of developing evaluative studies that are designed to assess particular objectives and populations. The third purpose is to present an overview of a model that hopefully will provide some practical guidance in designing evaluative studies.

Basic Concepts in Program Evaluation

As the literature on evaluation grows in size and complexity, a whole new language of evaluation is emerging that describes the concepts which have helped to create this area of specialization. The concepts discussed below reflect some of the basic ideas that have been set forth in the general evaluation models of Stake, Stufflebeam, and Provus.[1] The first two concepts, formative and summative evaluations, may be thought of as evaluation designs. They represent the predetermined plans that guide the ways in which an

1. Robert E. Stake, "Measuring What Learners Learn," in *School Evaluation: The Politics and Process*, ed. Ernest R. House (Berkeley, Calif.: McCutchan Publishing Corp., 1973), chapter 16; Daniel L. Stufflebeam, *Educational Evaluation and Decision Making* (Itasca, Ill.: F. E. Peacock Publishers, 1971); Malcolm M. Provus, *Discrepancy Evaluation* (Berkeley, Calif.: McCutchan Publishing Corp., 1972).

evaluation will be carried out and the role that evaluation will fulfill in the overall operation of a project or program. It should be
emphasized that an evaluation need not be either formative or summative, but rather can be a combination of both designs.

The other three concepts—product, process, and presage evaluations—should be thought of as types of evaluative data, that is, the
kind of information that an evaluator focuses upon in organizing
and conducting an evaluative study. Decisions regarding which
types of data an evaluator will seek are, of course, also based on the
role that evaluation is expected to play; and thus, there is a relationship between formative and summative evaluations on one hand,
and product, process, and presage evaluations on the other.

FORMATIVE EVALUATION

Scriven, the originator of the concept, defines formative evaluation as "simply outcome evaluation at an intermediate stage in the
development of [whatever it is that you are evaluating]."[2] The
role of formative evaluation "is to discover deficiencies and successes in the intermediate versions" of educational programs and
activities.[3] The emphasis is on when the data are gathered (intermediate stages as opposed to end-of-program data) rather than on
the types of data that are being used. The major purpose of formative evaluation is to provide continuous in-process feedback so that
appropriate modifications and revisions can be made in a program
as the program develops and matures. One of the primary advantages of formative evaluation is that the data are gathered in close
proximity to specific components of a program, and thus it has
greater potential for pinpointing the successes and failures of particular activities in a program.

All types of data (product, process, presage) can be used in
formative evaluation but it is important to keep the following
guidelines in mind. First, a systematic feedback mechanism must
be developed so that information reaches decision makers in time

2. Michael Scriven, "The Methodology of Evaluation," in *Perspectives of
Curriculum Evaluation*, ed. Ralph W. Tyler, Robert M. Gagné, and Michael
Scriven, American Educational Research Association Monograph Series on
Evaluation, no. 1 (Chicago: Rand McNally, 1967), p. 51.

3. Ibid.

to institute changes that are deemed necessary. Second, decision makers at each level of decision-making responsibility must make a sincere commitment to change. Third, and perhaps most importantly, information should be collected on identifiable program activities about which something can be done. Formative evaluation data are useless unless they indicate where to make changes and unless the changes are within the realm of possibility.

An evaluator expected to engage in formative curriculum evaluation can benefit from some of the strategies that have grown out of experimental curriculum projects. These projects have generally relied on carefully developed mastery tests bearing direct relationship to specific areas of the curriculum. The strategies recommended are based on a detailed analysis of content areas and process objectives which are classified according to the taxonomies of educational objectives.[4] Instructions are given for drawing up tables of specifications and constructing formative evaluation tests.

Curriculum evaluation based on mastery testing represents only one dimension of total program evaluation. Persons who are engaged in formative evaluation will no doubt want to provide continuous feedback in other areas where corrective action can be taken, such as reactions of parents toward the program, the effectiveness of in-service training, and so forth.

SUMMATIVE EVALUATION

Summative evaluation differs from formative evaluation mainly in the role that it fulfills. Whereas formative evaluation is directed toward program revision and improvement through continuous feedback, summative evaluation is more concerned with overall program effectiveness. Thus, summative information is more likely to be used in making decisions about the adoption or continuation of a program. While the results of this type of evaluation are no doubt of interest to persons who may develop and operate programs, they may be of greater interest to boards of education or funding agencies.

---

4. Benjamin S. Bloom et al., *Taxonomy of Educational Objectives, Handbook I: Cognitive Domain* (New York: Longman, 1956); David R. Krathwohl et al., *Taxonomy of Educational Objectives, Handbook II: Affective Domain* (New York: David McKay, 1964).

Although summative data might be gathered through the course of a program, the summative evaluator usually avoids giving any feedback until the end of the program in order to see how the program works in its natural (unaltered) form. In this respect, summative evaluation resembles the classic approach to experimental research design, that is, holding the independent variable (program) constant in order to discover what changes it produces. The main difference between summative evaluation and experimental research design is that the researcher is usually comparing alternative treatments under highly controlled conditions. These conditions almost always include the random assignment of students to experimental treatment groups and to control groups. Although most evaluators would like to respect as many of the mandates of good research as possible, it is difficult to do so in field evaluations. Programs for the gifted are often characterized by a great deal of variety and individualization, and it would be difficult to do high quality research without very substantial resources. The summative evaluator can, however, use the same instruments as the formative evaluator in documenting the overall effects of a program. But in this case there is a greater need to show growth over relatively long periods of time, and for this reason it may be necessary to gather data at the beginning and end of a program.

In actual practice, the evaluator will most often use a combination of approaches and some of his instruments can serve the dual purpose of providing in process feedback for practitioners and documenting student growth for decision-making bodies. The best guide for determining what types of data will be most useful for practitioners and decision makers is to survey each group at the outset of an evaluation study. The techniques for doing this are discussed in a later section under "Front-End Analysis."

PRODUCT OR "PAY-OFF" EVALUATION

Since educational programs are intended to produce certain changes in the attributes of students, product evaluation can be thought of as the assessment of observable and measurable student outcomes that result from a particular educational endeavor. Assuming that there is some consensus about the desirability of intended outcomes, these outcomes then become the pure "pay-off" of an educational program. The important evaluative data are documented indications of change in student performance, change that would not have taken place had the student not been enrolled in a particular course or taken part in a certain educational activity.

Merely obtaining objective measures or descriptions of student growth does not enable the evaluator to make qualitative judgments about what has been learned (for example, how good is an increase of ten points in the mean score for a particular group?). The problem of establishing abstract criteria for judging educational products is compounded as attention is focused on higher-level processes such as creativity and problem-solving abilities. In the final analysis, some form of human judgment must be brought to bear on objective findings; and thus, one of the major responsibilities of the product evaluator is to determine what types of information are most necessary for facilitating the judgment process.

The most obvious and popular type of product evaluation data has been scores on standardized and teacher-made tests. Scriven has pointed out that "the performance of students on the final tests, as upon the tests at intermediate stages, must be analyzed in order to determine the exact location of shortcomings of comprehension, shortages of essential facts, lack of practice in basic skills, and so forth."[5] In other words, test scores, in and of themselves, tell us nothing about cause and effect relationships and the only way to pinpoint such relationships is through a thorough analysis of test items as they relate to course content.

The development of criterion-referenced measurement shows promise of making more effective use of tests in program evaluation.[6] Whereas traditional norm-referenced tests yield only scores that show an individual's relative standing in comparison to a norm group, criterion-referenced tests are designed to show a student's accomplishments in particular areas in relation to a level of performance that the student will be expected to achieve. As such, criterion-referenced tests can help to determine exactly where remedial instruction may be necessary and/or whether or not a

5. Scriven, "The Methodology of Evaluation," p. 61.

6. Jason Millman, "Criterion-referenced Measurement," in *Evaluation in Education: Current Applications*, ed. W. James Popham (Berkeley, Calif.: McCutchan Publishing Corp., 1974), chapter 6.

student is ready to go on to the next step in a learning hierarchy.

Until the present, criterion-referenced testing has been closely tied to the behavioral objectives movement and because of this there has been a tendency to concentrate mainly on basic skills and limited types of learning activities. Unless these tests truly assess the types of learning that are appropriate for gifted and talented students, their use may have the same limiting effects on programs as the rigid application of norm-referenced tests.

Product information can be gathered from a number of sources other than tests. Ratings of student products (or of performance) by experts is one way in which the quality of creative work can be assessed. For example, in a program for gifted and talented students in Warwick, Rhode Island, a group of professional artists and writers were asked to rate students' work that was completed at various stages throughout the program. If specific student attitudes are listed as objectives of a program, the measurement of such attitudes can also be considered product data. Instruments for the measurement of all types of attitudes have been collected in a variety of sourcebooks.

Another type of product data falls under the classification of "frequency counts." This type of data is typically gathered through the use of logs, checklists, or an analysis of school records. Frequency counts qualify as product data if they reflect the accomplishment of an important program objective. Thus, for example, if one of the stated objectives of a particular program is "To increase by 50 percent the number of science books that students select for independent reading," this objective can be evaluated by some relatively simple record keeping. This is a very different kind of product from the qualitative assessment of student performance.

PROCESS EVALUATION

In view of the many problems that product evaluation presents in assessing for the gifted and talented, there is a clear need to seek additional kinds of data that show promise of determining the effectiveness of particular program activities. Process evaluation is concerned with assessing those aspects of student and teacher behavior considered to be worthwhile in their own right. These behaviors or processes are the teaching strategies and learning activities that are believed to be necessary in order to bring about desired educational products. In other words, process evaluation is concerned with "what goes on" in a learning situation rather than "what comes out of it."

Although there is some disagreement among educators about what constitutes a process, most evaluators agree that assessing the actual dynamics of a learning activity can provide very valuable insights about the strengths and weaknesses of certain educational practices. The assessment of educational processes is almost always used in formative evaluation studies. Process data are usually gathered to give immediate feedback to teachers so that they can be used in summative evaluation reports, but a great deal of caution must be exercised when such data are used for summative purposes. Teachers may be genuinely interested in "taking a look at themselves" so that they can improve their teaching techniques, but may feel threatened if they think that process data will be used by others to make judgments about their teaching ability.

The use of process data for purposes of program evaluation can best be discussed by focusing on two specific approaches to systematic observation techniques and to the analysis of classroom climate. One of the most highly developed and widely used systems for gathering observational data is the Flanders Interaction Analysis System.[7] This system focuses on the distinction between direct and indirect teacher influence in the classroom, the underlying assumption being that the first step in modifying one's teaching behaviors is to understand more fully how the teacher is influencing the learning situation. Implicit in the target behaviors of this system (that is, direct and indirect influence) is Flanders's belief that teachers should develop the capability to make their own behaviors appropriate to the requirements of particular learning situations.

Higher achievement, less dependence, and greater self-direction have usually been found in the classrooms of teachers who were classified as highly indirect. Thus, the Flanders system represents a technique that has relevance to the task of evaluating the processes

7. Edmund J. Amidon and Ned A. Flanders, *The Role of the Teacher in the Classroom: A Manual for Understanding and Improving Teacher Classroom Behavior* (Minneapolis, Minn.: Association for Productive Teaching, 1971).

that are frequently encouraged in gifted education. The system is especially useful in gathering data at lower grade levels because students are not required to complete questionnaires or rating scales.

A second approach to the evaluation of process offers some possibilities for overcoming some of the problems of observers in the classroom. Rather than having one or two observers in the classroom for a very limited period of time, the questionnaire or rating-scale approach is based on observations made by numerous observers who are in the classroom all the time. These observers are, of course, the students themselves.

The *Class Activities Questionnaire* (CAQ) was developed by Steele as part of the instrumentation that was used to evaluate the Illinois Gifted Program. Both cognitive and affective dimensions of the instructional climate are measured through a thirty-item instrument that is completed by both students and teachers. Steele describes the dimensions of the instrument as follows:

1 and 2. Lower Thought Processes and Higher Thought Processes assess the dimensions of cognitive emphasis. This part of the CAQ is based on Bloom's taxonomy. Each higher level of thinking is believed to involve the use of all the lower levels. The difference between lower and higher levels is one of complexity. There can be a range of difficulty of activities at each level of thinking.

3. The Classroom Focus dimension assesses whether focus is on the teacher as information-giver with students having a passive role, or on the students being given an active role with the teacher being the facilitator.

4. The Classroom Climate dimension deals with the affective domain. It assesses factors such as how relaxed and open the class is.

5. The Student Opinions dimension represents mini-interviews with each student on the best things and changes to make in the class.[8]

Student responses are considered to be the "actual" emphasis that is placed on each of the factors and these are summarized. Teachers fill out two copies of the questionnaire. On one copy they record the *intended* or *ideal* amount of emphasis that they would like to place on each factor. The second copy records their *predicted* emphasis. In analyzing their results teachers can deter-

8. Joe M. Steele, *Dimensions of the Class Activities Questionnaire* (Urbana, Ill.: Center for Instructional Research and Curriculum Evaluation, University of Illinois, 1969), p. 3.

mine how successful they were in achieving their ideal behavior and how accurately they estimated the way students viewed the class. Discrepancies can be used as the basis for improving instruction through self-analysis and/or inservice training activities.

The fact that the CAQ is based, in part, on Bloom's *Taxonomy of Educational Objectives* makes it particularly relevant to process evaluation in gifted education. As was indicated above, a system such as the taxonomy helps focus attention on those higher cognitive and affective processes which should be given major emphasis in programs for the gifted and talented.

PRESAGE OR INTRINSIC EVALUATION

Some evaluators would argue that due to deficiencies in instruments that measure products (payoff), especially higher-level cognitive and affective products, it is necessary to look for other sources of evaluative data. Presage or intrinsic evaluation focuses on factors which are assumed to have a significant impact on outcomes or products. Thus, intrinsic factors may be thought of as the purposefully planned activities that are designed to bring about changes in student performance. According to Scriven, persons who advocate this approach in curriculum evaluation are likely to be concerned with certain "qualities of a curriculum such as elegance, modernity, structure, integrity, readiness considerations, and so forth, which can best be judged by looking at the materials directly." [9] Renzulli and Ward have used the presage approach more broadly in the development of the *Diagnostic and Evaluation Scale for Differential Education for the Gifted* (DESDEG) by pointing out several dimensions of a program that can be studied through the assessment of information that has an assumed relationship to the quality of a program.[10]

The major problem with presage or intrinsic evaluation is the logical jump that must be made from intrinsic factors to program outcomes. Indeed, very few contemporary evaluation theorists advocate a wholly presage approach, and yet, this concept is of

9. Scriven, "The Methodology of Evaluation," p. 54.

10. Joseph S. Renzulli and Virgil S. Ward, *Diagnostic and Evaluation Scale for Differential Education for the Gifted* (Storrs, Conn.: Bureau of Educational Research, University of Connecticut, 1969).

value in considering the assessment of programs for the gifted and talented because the outcome objectives of such programs are oftentimes not easily measured by existing instruments.

The presage approach also offers a useful model of evaluating nonproduct dimensions of a program. For example, in the DESDEG model, Renzulli and Ward have developed several forms that help to provide an analytic look at identification systems. The comprehensiveness of screening and placement procedures, the variety of criteria used in identification, and the proportion of students selected at each grade level are revealed through the use of these forms. The forms force a breakdown of the information and thus enable the evaluator to see the identification system more clearly and to ask more meaningful questions. A clearer picture of all aspects of the identification process should help the evaluator come to more accurate judgments.

The presage or intrinsic approach is probably more in keeping with Stake's belief that careful and accurate description is a necessary prerequisite to the judgmental process.[11] Information (data) does not in and of itself render opinions; and in the final analysis, it is people who must make judgments. The presage approach can facilitate the judgmental process by helping to present information in its clearest and most useful format.

Special Problems in Evaluating Programs for the Gifted and Talented

THE PROBLEM OF "HIGHER-LEVEL" OBJECTIVES

Programs for the gifted are often characterized by a commitment to the development of higher powers of mind and advanced levels of awareness, interest, and other affective behaviors. This presents a somewhat unique problem for the evaluator because these objectives cannot be measured as easily and precisely as those objectives that deal mainly with the acquisition of basic skills. As one moves up the scale of learning behaviors, from the simple acquisition of knowledge to the development of higher mental processes, it becomes increasingly difficult to find measuring instru-

---

11. Robert E. Stake, "The Countenance of Educational Evaluation," *Teachers College Record* 68 (1967): 523-40.

ments that meet the scientific and practical requirements necessary for good evaluation studies.

A second dimension of this problem is that gifted programs are frequently characterized by highly individualized objectives for each student. Whereas a reading skills program for average or slow learners may have enough uniformity in its objectives to warrant large-scale standardized testing, a program for gifted students may have many *different* objectives for each student. Standardized tests can, of course, be used effectively in evaluating programs for the gifted if they (a) are valid (appropriate) measures of particular objectives, and (b) if they are used in situations where reasonable levels of reliability can be obtained. But when a teacher devises individualized objectives for each child, the appropriateness of tests based on systemwide or nationwide objectives must be seriously questioned.

In recent years there has been a great deal of concern in education about the specification of objectives in terms of observable and measurable student behaviors. Many evaluators have looked upon the "behavioral objectives model" as a panacea for conducting evaluation studies. The nature of gifted programs, however, and their concern for developing higher thought processes may make this model too cumbersome to be applied practically to programs for the gifted and talented. In fact, when the behavioral objectives approach is used in its most rigid form, it may even force program developers to focus their attention on the trivial rather than important behaviors of superior learners.

The rigid behavioral objectives model is inappropriate for programs for the gifted because it forces one to be primarily concerned with those behaviors that are readily measured. Although many experts in testing believe that complex objectives can be evaluated, Stake has suggested that the total cost of measuring such objectives may be one hundred times that of administering a forty-five minute standardized paper-and-pencil test; and the amount of time, personnel, and facilities necessary for such evaluation may be astronomical. Stake also points out that the errors of testing increase markedly when we move from highly specific areas of performance to items which attempt to measure higher mental processes and unreached human potential.[12]

12. Stake, "Measuring What Learners Learn," pp. 196-99.

MEASUREMENT AND STATISTICAL PROBLEMS

Measurement and formal testing often play a major role in evaluation studies, but certain cautions are necessary when considering the use of standardized tests in evaluating programs for the gifted. By definition, the gifted student initially scores at the upper end of the normal curve, where it is much more difficult to show an increase in percentile score points. The same is true for age and grade scores. Generally, there is a slowing down of gains at the upper levels of most performance tests that were normed on the general population. For this reason, when the evaluator uses standardized tests, he should avoid making comparisons between gifted students and other populations. This can be done by developing separate sets of norms for each distinct population whose growth is being evaluated, provided of course, that the test has a broad enough range to allow students to show maximum growth. If a test does not have enough "top" or "ceiling" in it, highly able students may score at the upper limits, but their true growth cannot be determined because of the low ceiling of the test. Since many standardized tests are designed to provide achievement information for the vast middle ranges of ability, their content and interpretive data may not be valid for children who deviate markedly upward from the mean.

The use of conventional tests with gifted and talented students also presents some problems in the statistical treatment of evaluative data. One such problem relates to the fact that test reliability is a function of group diversity—the more heterogeneous the group, the higher the reliability. When dealing with a relatively homogeneous group of students, caution must be exercised in examining the reported reliabilities of standardized tests. Unfortunately, most test publishers do not report reliabilities for subpopulations within their standardization sample and therefore it is necessary to conduct a local reliability study whenever conventional tests are used with special populations.

Another statistical problem encountered when working with the test scores of superior students is the well-known effect of regression toward the mean. Simply stated, this means that predicted scores tend to "move in" toward the mean of the distribution.

Thus, if a pretest and posttest design is used to evaluate the effects of a program for the gifted, and if the students' scores on the pretest are initially high, it is quite likely their posttest scores will actually decrease somewhat due to the regression effect. It is for this reason the evaluator must exercise great caution when considering the pre/post design and other statistical designs that do not take into account the lack of normality in the distribution of gifted students' test scores.

PRACTICAL PROBLEMS

The evaluation of programs for the gifted, like evaluation in all other areas, requires time, money, and trained personnel. When evaluation is "tacked on" to a program as an afterthought, and when the human and financial resources necessary for carrying out a comprehensive evaluation are not available, the evaluator may very well end up being asked to do the impossible. Even when time and resources are available, the evaluator is frequently called upon to develop a plan of evaluation for programs with poorly defined objectives and a very limited conception about what will constitute a successful program.

What can be done about practical problems in evaluation such as time, money, and personnel? There is agreement on the importance of involving the evaluator from the very beginning of any educational endeavor. Through such involvement, the evaluator can continually bring to the attention of program developers the steps that must be taken and the resources that must be allocated if evaluation is to serve useful purposes. Early and continuous involvement on the part of the evaluator will help to overcome many of the difficulties that arise when evaluation is tacked-on as an afterthought.

Another practical problem relates to the attitude that many educators hold toward evaluation. Teachers and other professional personnel often view evaluation as a means of controlling or checking up on a program and the persons responsible for operating a program. In short, evaluation can be very threatening and might result in some rather harsh actions, especially if the evaluation is mandated by a decision-making body or by an outside funding agency.

The evaluator must walk a very thin line in the process of gaining the acceptance and cooperation of persons over whom he may eventually have to pass judgment. In spite of all of the rhetoric about friendly and cooperative relations between evaluator and staff, the fact remains that the evaluator may sometimes have to recommend actions or changes unpleasant to the persons who sponsor and operate a program. This problem can be minimized by spelling out the responsibilities of the evaluator and the staff at the very beginning of an evaluation study.

The Key Features Evaluation System

The Key Features System is a general evaluation design that has proven to be effective in documenting the value of programs for the gifted and talented. It is an approach that translates many of the theoretical concepts in program evaluation into a practical, usable plan and is flexible enough to account for the relatively unique characteristics of programs for the gifted and talented. As indicated in figure 1, this system consists of four sequential steps or phases. The purpose of these steps and the specific activities or procedures involved in each are described in the narrative that follows.

STEP 1: FRONT-END ANALYSIS

The purpose of Front-End Analysis is to help the evaluator identify "key features" in a project or program. Key features may be thought of as major factors or variables that contribute to the effectiveness of a program. Before instruments can be selected and data gathered it is important to determine which factors influence the operation of the program and contribute most to an understanding of it. It is also important to learn what types of information are of major concern to various "Prime Interest Groups." Prime interest groups consist of people who have a direct or indirect interest in the program being evaluated. These groups will almost always include students, parents, teachers, administrators, and school board members. But, depending on the nature of the program, prime interest groups may also include persons who are involved in the program indirectly.

As noted in figure 1, the evaluator can identify key features by

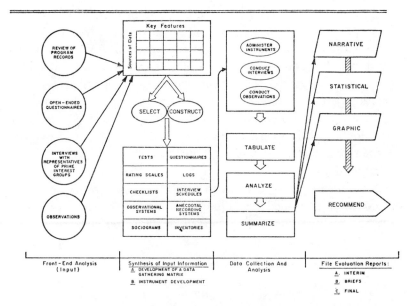

FIG. 1. Overview of the Key Features Evaluation System

Source: Joseph S. Renzulli, *A Guidebook for Evaluating Programs for the Gifted and Talented* (Ventura, Calif.: Office of the Ventura County Superintendent of Schools, 1975), p. 51.

compiling "input" information from four main sources, the first of which is a comprehensive review of all written material relating to the program. These documents should provide the evaluator with an overview of program objectives and a description of the general mode of operation of the program.

As a second source of information, the evaluator can design and administer open-ended questionnaires. These questionnaires should be completed by a representative sample of each prime interest group and should enable the respondents to describe their main concerns about the program. Respondents may simply be asked, for example, to list the major questions that they would like to have answered by the evaluation report.

Knowledge gained from reviewing documents and the questionnaires will enable the evaluator to ask meaningful questions during the third step of Front-End Analysis: interviews with representatives of each prime interest group. Interviews should begin with the director and persons who were involved in the planning phase of the program. These persons will more than likely provide an understanding of the way in which the program was ideally conceived, whereas interviews with teachers and students will probably deal more closely with the way in which the program is actually operating. In all Front-End Analysis interviews, the evaluator should essentially be asking: "How can I help you?" "What information will help to make the program better for you?" "What are the things that are bothering you?"

In the final stage of Front-End Analysis, the evaluator observes the program in operation so as to help clarify and verify some of the concerns identified through previous input procedures. This type of "reality orientation" gives a much better perspective of "the way it is" rather than the ways in which it has been described and discussed.

STEP 2: SYNTHESIS OF INPUT INFORMATION AND INSTRUMENT DEVELOPMENT

At the conclusion of Front-End Analysis the evaluator should be able to list the *major* concerns of each prime interest group. These concerns should be classified and organized according to similarities among the groups and the list which evolves should make up the key features upon which the evaluation will focus. Once identified, these key features should be listed along one dimension of a chart such as the one presented in figure 2. The evaluator must now ask himself two questions: (a) What types of instruments and/or techniques will provide information relevant to each key feature? and (b) From whom can this information be obtained?

The answers to these questions provide the information necessary for completing the other dimension of the chart (Sources of Data) and filling in the actual content, which consists of the instruments that will be used to gather data related to each key feature.

Selecting and constructing appropriate data gathering instruments is perhaps the most difficult aspect of evaluating programs for the gifted and talented. As mentioned in the previous section, standardized tests of cognitive and affective abilities may fail to yield valid information about student growth and it may therefore be necessary to seek out special instruments or to construct instruments that will provide more accurate information about program effectiveness. The list of assessment devices that can be used to supplement or replace standardized evaluation tools is quite lengthy and includes such items as rating scales, checklists, interview schedules, logs, sociograms, and observation techniques. It is important to point out that selection and/or development of these evaluation measures requires a strong background in tests and measurements. The field evaluator without such training should obtain the assistance of a consultant with experience in this area of specialization.

STEP 3: DATA COLLECTION AND ANALYSIS

After the evaluator has identified key features, sources of data, and instruments necessary for obtaining the data, he then begins the third step of the Key Features Evaluation System—data collection and analysis. Data collection requires careful and comprehensive planning so that important information will not be lost due to conflicts with school vacations, special events, or final examinations. Timing is also important in terms of how often information is gathered and how much time is required to obtain the information.

Once data related to each key feature are obtained, they must be broken down into component parts. There are two basic methods of data analysis open to the evaluator: logical analysis and statistical analysis. In logical analysis, information is categorized according to some common characteristic and an attempt is made to discover patterns, trends, or discrepancies that exist within each clearly discernible category. The statistical approach, which incorporates both descriptive and inferential techniques, provides the evaluator with the means by which to summarize large sets of numerical information and to make probability statements regarding the significance of observed differences among groups. Generally speaking, the nature of the data collected will determine which type of analysis is most appropriate for answering specific evaluation questions.

STEP 4: PREPARING EVALUATION REPORTS

Once data are collected and analyzed, the evaluator is ready to prepare a final report. The report should begin with an introductory chapter that contains a description of the program and an

Key Features

		Student Growth	Levels of Thinking and Classroom Conditions	Attitudes Toward Program	Identification Procedures	Etc.
Sources of Data	Students	Pre- and Post-Tests of Creativity, Critical Thinking, etc.	*Class Activities Questionnaire* Interviews	Questionnaires Interviews (Random Sample)		
	Program Teachers	Evaluation of Student Growth Forms (A Structured Anecdotal Report)*	*Class Activities Questionnaire* Logs	Interviews	Time and Effort Reports Follow-up Questionnaire	
	Parents			Questionnaires Interviews (Random Sample)	Follow-up Questionnaire	
	Student Selection Committee (Including Records)				Time and Effort Reports Rating Scale (on Usefulness of Information) Interviews Analysis of Records	
	Non-Program Teachers	Rating Scale		Questionnaires Interviews (Random Sample)	Time and Effort Reports Follow-up Questionnaire	
	Consultants	Student Product Rating Form				
	Building Principals and Coordinators		Questionnaires	Interviews "Problems" Log	Time and Effort Reports "Problems" Log	
	Secretaries				Time and Effort Reports	

FIG. 2. Matrix of Key Features and Sources of Data

Source: Renzulli, *A Guidebook for Evaluating Programs for the Gifted and Talented*, p. 57.

overview of the evaluation design. Each chapter that follows should be organized around one key feature. The methods for data collection and techniques for data analysis should be described, followed by the results as they relate to each activity being evaluated. Statistical information should always be described in narrative form and each chapter should end with a brief summary that highlights the major conclusions derived from the results. The final chapter of the report should contain a general summary of the entire evaluation, highlights of the strengths of the program and areas that are in need of improvement, and recommendations that seem warranted by the findings.

Concluding Remarks

All too often, evaluations have been launched as last-ditch efforts to save programs that are in danger of being eliminated or sharply reduced in the amount of support they receive from sponsoring agencies. Although a hastily conducted evaluation may be better than no evaluation at all, the best weapon in the battle for program support and survival is a carefully planned and comprehensive evaluation that will accurately document all aspects of the services being provided for gifted and talented youngsters. Evaluation should be an essential and ongoing part of total programming and each step of the planning and development phases of a program for the gifted should give careful attention to the ways in which evaluative information can be gathered, organized, and presented to decision-making individuals or groups.

CHAPTER XX

Educational Provisions for the Gifted and Talented in Other Countries

WILLIAM W. BRICKMAN

Ideally, this chapter should have been prepared after a visit to several countries and a close examination of the literature. It has only been possible, however, to analyze what is hopefully a representative sampling of significant literature on the education of the gifted and talented of a few countries—England, Germany, and the USSR. While there is some information on educational provisions for the artistically gifted, most of the writings concentrate on the academically talented.

Previous yearbooks of the National Society for the Study of Education dealing with the education of the gifted did not devote any special attention to developments in other countries. The Twenty-third and Fifty-seventh yearbooks had passing references to Europe in the historical chapters and in the bibliographies.[1] Understandably, the *Year Book of Education* (later called the *World Year Book of Education*) could offer virtually global coverage in its detailed volumes on *Concepts of Excellence in Education* and *The Gifted Child*.[2]

Writers of textbooks and other general works on the gifted

---

1. *The Education of Gifted Children,* Twenty-third Yearbook of the National Society for the Study of Education, Part I, ed. Guy M. Whipple (Bloomington, Ill.: Public School Publishing Co., 1924); *Education of the Gifted,* Fifty-seventh Yearbook of the National Society for the Study of Education, Part II, ed. Robert J. Havighurst (Chicago: University of Chicago Press, 1958).

2. *Concepts of Excellence in Education, Year Book of Education,* 1961, ed. George Z. F. Bereday and Joseph Lauwerys (London: Evans Brothers, 1961); *The Gifted Child, Year Book of Education,* 1962, ed. George Z. F. Bereday and Joseph Lauwerys (London: Evans Brothers, 1962).

generally concentrate on their respective countries, with at most only an incidental reference to any other nation. Among the few exceptions are Hollingworth and Hildreth who in their respective volumes devote several pages to foreign developments.[3] The most unusual treatment is in a composite work that includes chapters on the USSR, on West Germany, and on England within a collection of papers describing educational programs for the gifted.[4]

Among the encouraging signs is the founding of organizations that attend to developments abroad, among them the National Association for Gifted Children, organized in 1965 in England, and the more recent International Foundation for Gifted Children. The former organized the First World Conference on Gifted Children in London in September, 1975. The proceedings of this conference contain a section with brief statements on provisions for gifted children in twenty-four countries.[5]

Underlying the interest in, and provisions for, the education of the gifted and talented in any particular country are several interrelated factors. The historical remembrance of a Leonardo da Vinci in Italy, a Desiderius Erasmus in the Netherlands, and a Mikhail V. Lomonosov in Russia may inspire a national desire for a contemporary counterpart. Such a feeling is a function of national pride, which manifests itself in the form of scholarships, fellowships, competitive contests, public adulation, and in other ways. Also pertinent is the awareness of economic advantage to a nation that can educate persons who are exceptionally efficient in various lines of endeavor. Not to be overlooked, moreover, is the centuries-old intellectual tradition persisting in many European countries, with the result that special note is taken of the academic aptitude of children and young people.

On the other hand, the increasing democratic consciousness in

3. Leta S. Hollingworth, *Gifted Children: Their Nature and Nurture* (New York: Macmillan, 1926), pp. 282-84; Gertrude S. Hildreth, *Introduction to the Gifted* (New York: McGraw-Hill, 1966), pp. 59-62, 123-25. The latter volume treats West Germany, England, France, and the USSR.

4. *Programs for the Gifted: A Case Book in Secondary Education*, ed. Samuel Everett (New York: Harper, 1961), pp. 55-116.

5. *Gifted Children: Looking to Their Future*, ed. Joy Gibson and Prue Chennells (London: Latimer New Dimensions, with the National Association for Gifted Children, 1976).

some countries, for example, Sweden and the United States, has resulted in an anti-elitist ideology that is negatively oriented toward any special provisions for the intellectually gifted. And yet, such an ultra-egalitarian attitude has not been extended to individuals who exhibit talent in art, music, ballet, the theater, the circus, chess, and athletics (especially in the Olympic games).

In analyzing the education of the gifted and talented on an international scale, as on a national scale, it is well to be aware of the components of the study. First, of course, the gifted and talented must be defined. One should then consider the ways of identifying pupils with exceptional abilities. On these foundations it is possible to examine the actual provision for the education of such pupils, as well as the achievements and problems. To fulfill the requirements of such an outline, it would be necessary to have a reasonably representative collection of writings from several countries. This has not proved to be the case, however. If a full analysis in comparative perspective cannot be given, then one is forced to work on what is available and hope for a minimum of misrepresentation and distortion.

Great Britain

A governmental publication confessed in 1975 that in Britain there was "a paucity of investigations dealing with gifted children." [6] A check of the references to the gifted children in the *British Education Index* for 1955-1975 reveals an average of fewer than two articles per annum. A recent British research bibliography listed eighteen titles, all of them in English and most of them of American provenance.[7] Sir Cyril Burt, posthumously controversial, lamented the lack of research studies and discussions on the modification of curricula and instructional methods toward the full realization of "the potentialities of the more gifted individuals." [8]

6. E. Hoyle and J. Wilks, *Gifted Children and Their Education* (London: Department of Education and Science, 1975), p. 3.

7. Ann Start, *The Gifted Child: A Select Annotated Bibliography* (Slough, Bucks: National Foundation for Educational Research in England and Wales, 1972).

8. Sir Cyril Burt, "The Gifted Child," in *Advances in Educational Psychology*, ed. Mia K. Pringle and Ved P. Varma (London: University of London Press, 1974), p. 160.

A possibly plausible explanation, for the past at least, was given by a British educator: "We don't write about the gifted; we educate them. That is what our grammar and public schools exist for." [9]

Regardless of the issue of quantity, the available British literature on the education of the gifted and talented is edifying enough to get a grasp of what is being accomplished. The educational world has long been aware of the academic achievements of the alumni of the British grammar school, particularly of those who completed the Sixth Form. This is a one- to three-year specialized study program just prior to university entrance. Historically, the Sixth Form, which has been closely linked with the British public school, has been reserved for the academically able, as determined by examinations and teachers' judgments. Despite some new tendencies, it seems likely to remain a citadel of the competent in advanced curriculum. [10]

The place of the gifted adolescent in the secondary schools of Britain has been presented in a volume of papers by practicing pedagogues, under the editorship of an American educator. The Manchester Grammar School is open to "all pupils in the area, regardless of socioeconomic status, provided they attain the necessary standard in the competitive entrance examination." [11] A direct-grant school, Manchester has ranked first for a long time in university scholarship awards to secondary-school graduates.

In another type of secondary institution, the Maesydderwen Comprehensive School, Breconshire, near Swansea, in Wales, there is no selection at all. Each pupil receives an education in terms of his own ability and aptitude in a school environment enrolling in-

---

9. Quoted in A. Harry Passow, *Secondary Education for All: The English Approach* (Columbus, Ohio: Ohio State University Press, 1961), p. 6.

10. W. D. Halls, "Sixth Form Studies at Home and Abroad," *Times* (London) *Educational Supplement*, 20 April 1966, p. 1291. On the scope, role, and trends of the Sixth Form, see *The New Sixth Form*, ed. Roger Watkins (London: Ward Lock Educational, 1974); Philip H. Taylor, W. A. Reid, and B. J. Holley, *The English Sixth Form: A Case Study in Curriculum Research* (London: Routledge and Kegan Paul, 1974); Department of Education and Science Library, *Select List of References on Sixth Form Colleges* (London: Department of Education and Science, 1975).

11. Roger Stone, "Manchester Grammar School," in *British Secondary Education: Overview and Appraisal*, ed. Richard E. Gross (London: Oxford University Press, 1965), p. 150.

dividuals of varying capacities. This is accomplished by the procedure known as "setting." The pupils are "segregated" in terms of ability in a particular subject, so that those of high intellectual ability learn at their own pace, while those of average and below-average levels proceed at a rate suitable to them. As members of a single, "mixed community," the pupils of this comprehensive school appear to enjoy both individualization and egalitarian socialization.[12]

English primary education since the mid-1960s has been affected to a large extent by the findings and recommendations in the report of the Central Advisory Council for Education, usually identified as the Plowden report. Welcoming "the trend toward individual learning," the Council recommended a combination of individual and group instruction in the classroom.[13] With regard to the education of the gifted children, the report noted the existence of "an egalitarian suspicion" of giftedness, as well as the difficulties in the identification of the various types of gifted and talented children.[14] Most of the members of the Council insisted that there should not be separate schools for the talented, except in music and ballet. They affirmed that English primary education "at its best is better adapted than any other we have seen" to meet the needs of gifted children without "segregating" them. "We cannot afford to waste their talents."[15] In the closing chapter on talented children, the report recommended long-term studies on their needs and achievements.[16]

Contemporaneous with, and subsequent to, the Plowden report there have appeared various publications dealing with the identification and education of gifted children. One type of literature is in

---

12. Alwyn Thomas, "Maesydderwen Comprehensive School (Breconshire)," in *British Secondary Education*, ed. Gross, pp. 446-66. On setting, see *Grouping in Education: A Report Sponsored by the UNESCO Institute of Hamburg*, ed. Alfred Yates (New York: Wiley, 1966), pp. 63-68.

13. Department of Education and Science, *Children and Their Primary Schools: A Report of the Central Advisory Council for Education (England)*, vol. *1: The Report* (London: Her Majesty's Stationery Office, 1967), p. 474.

14. Ibid., p. 305.

15. Ibid., p. 307.

16. Ibid., p. 308.

the form of guides for parents and teachers.[17] Another is the committee report, such as the Donnison report of 1970, which includes recommendations on the enrichment of courses for the academically able.[18]

Research studies seem to be on the increase, to judge from the evidence of recent years. A summary and interpretation of research was made by Shields.[19] Bridges brought together reports on the positive outcomes of the experiment initiated by the Brentwood College of Education to offer half-day programs for gifted pupils from the area.[20] The problems of highly intelligent pupils were studied by Kellmer Pringle.[21]

Two important studies, possibly inspired by the Plowden report, concentrate on the gifted pupils in primary schools. One study, sponsored by the Schools Council, surveyed over a twelve-month period the provisions by the Local Education Authorities for children aged five to eleven years. This report, based on visits to thirty schools, questionnaires, and interviews, dealt with definition, identification, instruction, and problems of the gifted children. Among the provisions for such children, the report emphasized the Saturday morning classes and the individualization of learning and teaching.[22]

17. Margaret Branch and Aubrey Cash, *Gifted Children: Recognizing and Developing Exceptional Ability* (London: Souvenir Press, 1966); N. R. Tempest, *Teaching Clever Children, 7-11* (London: Routledge and Kegan Paul, 1974); Phyllis M. Pickard, *If You Think Your Child is Gifted* (London: Allen and Unwin, 1976); Sydney Bridges, *Problems of the Gifted Child: IQ-150* (New York: Crane, Russek, 1973). The author of the latter work is a member of the Schools Council Working Party on Gifted Children, England.

18. *Public Schools Commission Second Report, vol. 1: Report on Independent Day Schools and Direct-Grant Grammar Schools* (London: Her Majesty's Stationery Office, 1970).

19. James B. Shields, *The Gifted Child* (Slough, Bucks: National Foundation for Educational Research in England and Wales, 1968).

20. *Gifted Children and the Brentwood Experiment,* ed. Sydney A. Bridges (London: Pitman, 1969).

21. M. L. Kellmer Pringle, *Able Misfits: A Study of Education and Behavior Problems of 103 Very Intelligent Children, IQ 120-200* (London: Longman, 1970).

22. Eric Ogilvie, *Gifted Children in Primary Schools: The Report of Inquiry by Schools Council into the Teaching of Gifted Children of Primary Age, 1970-71* (London: Macmillan, 1973).

What is probably the first national study of gifted children, under the sponsorship of the national Children's Bureau, investigated comparatively and longitudinally 125 boys and 113 girls aged seven to eleven years. Using the survey technique, interviews, tests, and case study procedures, the inquiry involved pupils, parents, and teachers and gave special attention to intelligence, educational achievement, and social and emotional adjustment. The findings indicated that most of the children were "catered for satisfactorily" and that nonsegregation of the gifted was the best policy.[23]

A three-year project inaugurated in 1974 by the Gulbenkian Foundation seeks to analyze the influences exerted by the "total environments" of gifted children "on achievements and personality development."[24] By definition, this study is concerned with the top 2 percent of the pupil population.

Some attention has been paid in the literature to the special schools for children who are talented in music and the dance. The Royal College of Music provides for talented children, but there seem to be few data available. There is more information on Yehudi Menuhin's music school, founded in 1963 in Surrey, which had thirty-six pupils by 1969.[25]

To develop a distinctly British ballet style, in contrast to the prevalent Russian form, Dame Ninette de Valois, a noted dancer, founded in 1931 the Sadler's Wells School, which children could attend after regular school hours. In 1947, the financial situation became favorable enough for the establishment of the Royal Ballet School, which combines "dance training and general education under one roof" in London.[26] The major problems remained those of finance and of the recruitment of boys.

23. Elizabeth M. Hitchfield, *In Search of Promise: A Long-term National Study of Able Children and Their Families* (London: Longman, 1973), pp. 205-206.

24. Joan Freeman, "The Gulbenkian Project on Gifted Children," in *Gifted Children*, ed. Gibson and Chennells, p. 237.

25. Eric Feaby, *Menuhin's House of Music: An Impression of the Yehudi Menuhin School at Stobe d'Albernon, Surrey, England* (London: Icon Books, 1969); *Gifted Children: Recognizing and Developing Educational Ability*, ed. Branch and Cash, pp. 119-23; Antony Brackenbury, "Round the Clock with Gifted Musicians," in *Gifted Children*, ed. Gibson and Chennells, pp. 73-87.

26. Arnold L. Haskell, "The Royal Ballet School: Education for the

The evidence for the increasing concern in Britain for the education of gifted children and adolescents is undeniable. The active leaders and others involved in providing for them are aware of the difficulties and problems, as well as of the values to the nation and to the person. There appears to be a general consensus that the gifted can be adequately cared for in general primary and comprehensive secondary schools and that separate schools for the academically talented are both unnecessary and socially undesirable. One problem that does not seem to have been overcome is pupil attitude regarding giftedness. Thus, an article in the British magazine *Education* for May 26, 1967 noted the comment of teachers of "superintelligent children" in Oxfordshire schools that "unusually gifted children quickly learned to hide their brilliance, if they wanted a smooth passage in school." [27] Most recently, Painter revealed the existence of underachievement among the "covert gifted," pupils unidentified as such by their teachers and peers, in part possibly because of concealment of the fact of their talent.[28] This development helps one recall the observation by Tannenbaum that the "brilliant student" in America is "an exceptionally prominent target for teen-age pressures" and that "there is danger of his deliberately masking his talent in order to relieve these pressures." [29]

Federal Republic of Germany

The awareness in Germany of the special needs of the scholastically superior pupil may be traced to the ideas of Philipp Melanchthon, the leading educator of the Lutheran Reformation. In general, however, because of the developing dual system of education, one track leading to higher education and the other to work

Dancer," in *Concepts of Excellence in Education*, ed. Bereday and Lauwerys, p. 461. See also *Gifted Children: Recognizing and Developing Educational Ability*, ed. Branch and Cash, pp. 114-19.

27. Summarized in the *Times* (London), Educational Supplement, 2 June 1967.

28. Frieda Painter, "Research into Attainment Levels of Gifted British Primary School Children," in *Gifted Children*, ed. Gibson and Chennells, pp. 231-36.

29. Abraham J. Tannenbaum, *Adolescent Attitudes toward Academic Brilliance* (New York: Bureau of Publications, Teachers College, Columbia University, 1962), p. 68.

training, it did not seem necessary to make special provisions for the academically talented. An outstanding exception was the Mannheim School System, which was reorganized during 1895-1923 by Superintendent Anton Sickinger according to a three-level ability plan, with special classes for the scholastically superior pupils in elementary school. This idea, however, was severely criticized by Superintendent Georg Kerschensteiner of Munich as hindering the balanced development of the individual.[30]

Recognizing the principle that academic giftedness could be developed outside the walls of the schools, educators of the Weimar Republic introduced in 1923 the *Begabtenprüfung*, an examination to demonstrate the competency of anyone lacking a formal secondary education to undertake university study. After 1952, this term was replaced by *Prüfung für die Zulassung zum Hochschulstudium ohne Reifezeugnis* (examination for admission to higher education without a secondary school leaving certificate).[31] The idea of an alternate route to higher education, other than the *Gymnasium* (academic secondary school), for those with advanced scholastic aptitude was revived after World War II and in the mid-1950s received the designation of *Zweiter Bildungsweg* (second road to education). This opened educational opportunity to the gifted who for economic or other reasons had to undertake employment and forego academic secondary education.[32]

A noteworthy effort at discovering and developing talented adults in the industrial sector was inaugurated with the founding in 1956 of the *Deutsches Institut für Talentstudien* (German Institute for Talent Studies), with financial aid by government bodies, industry, and the Ford Foundation. This was a significant step in planning provisions for lifelong learning, especially for those whose abilities showed promise for making contributions to industry and society.[33]

---

30. Georg Kerschensteiner, *Theorie der Bildung* (Leipzig: Teubner, 1926), pp. 406-407.

31. Wilhelm Hehlmann, *Wörterbuch der Pädagogik*, 8th ed. (Stuttgart: Kröner, 1967), p. 43; R. Vath, "Begabtenprüfung," in *Lexikon der Pädagogik*, new ed., vol. 1 (Freiburg im Breisgau: Herder, 1970), p. 125.

32. Helmet Belser, *Zweiter Bildungsweg*, 2d ed. (Weinheim/Bergstrasse: Beitz, 1965); Hehlmann, *Wörterbuch der Pädagogik*, p. 586.

33. Reinhold Schairer, "The German Institute of Talent Study in Cologne,"

Perhaps the most substantial step in West Germany toward providing for the gifted on the elementary level was a recommendation in 1959 by the *Deutscher Ausschuss für das Erziehungs und Bildungswesen*, an educational body set up jointly by the Federal Ministry of the Interior and the *Kultusministerkonferenz* (standing conference of *Land* or provincial ministers of education). In its *Rahmenplan zur Umgestaltung und Vereinheitlichung des allgemeinbildenden öffentlichen Schulwesens* (outline or skeleton plan for the restructuring and unification of general secondary education) this group presented a plan for a *Förderstufe*, a two-year program of observation and guidance of pupils aged ten to twelve in grades five and six of the elementary school. In this way, gifted pupils could be identified and guided toward the *Gymnasium* without the traditional selective examination at age ten.[34] The idea of the *Förderstufe* was recognized in 1964 by the *Kultusministerkonferenz* at Hamburg, with leeway to the several states putting it into operation. In recent years, the term *Orientierungsstufe* has replaced *Förderstufe*. In 1972, the *Bund-Länder-Kommission für Bildungsplanung* (federal-state commission for educational planning) recommended that all the states introduce the *Orientierungsstufe* by 1976.[35]

One practice that has been common in West German schools is *Kernunterricht*, or instruction through sets.[36] Similar to the English

---

in *The Gifted Child*, ed. Bereday and Lauwerys, pp. 271-74. More details about the need for talent were given in Reinhold Schairer, *Technische Talente*, 3d ed. (Düsseldorf: Diederichs, 1956) and idem, *Aktivierung der Talente* (Düsseldorf: Diederichs, 1957).

34. *Empfehlungen and Gutachten des Deutschen Ausschusses für das Erziehungs und Bildungswesen, 1953-1965: Gesamtausgabe*, ed. Hans Bohnenkamp, Walter Dirks, and Doris Knab (Stuttgart: Klett, 1966), pp. 81, 83-85; Arthur Hearnden, *Education in the Two Germanies* (Oxford: Blackwell, 1974), pp. 105-106, 254. On the workings of the *Förderstufe*, see Fritz Uppleger Hans Götz, *Die förderstufenähnlichen Schulversuche in Hessen* (Hannover: Schroedel, 1963); Walter Twellmann and Karlheinz Walter, *Begabte Schüler: Der Uebergang zu weiterführenden Schulen, Ein Handbuch für Lehrer* (Düsseldorf: Bagel, 1965); and Wilhelm Seeberger, *Begabung als Problem* (Stuttgart: Klett, 1966).

35. K. E. Maier, "Förderstufe, Orientierungsstufe," in *Wörterbuch der Schulpädagogik* (Freiburg im Breisgau: Herder, 1973), p. 119.

36. Walter Schultze and Christoph Führ, "Federal Republic of Germany," in *Schools in Europe*, vol. 1, part A, ed. Walter Schultze (Weinheim: Beltz, 1968), p. 494.

procedure, it ensures that pupils who are exceptional in a given subject have an opportunity to study that subject in a homogeneous group.

The *Gymnasium* exemplifies the West German way of providing for differences among the academically advanced students. There are special schools concentrating on classical languages, modern languages, mathematics and science, vocations, commerce, social science, technology, music and art, sports, educational science, agriculture, and home economics.[37]

USSR

During the nineteenth century and in the twentieth prior to the October Revolution, the Russian educational system provided a *Gymnasium* education for the academically talented of the upper classes to strengthen "the existing class structure" through preparation of selected persons for the professions. The major exception in Russian gifted education was the ballet, which recruited talent from all social levels. The decade and a half following the revolution, which was marked by the popularity of pedology (child study), saw an emphasis on the identification and promotion of individual aptitude. In 1936, "the pedological perversions" were banned by the Communist Party as anti-Marxist and Soviet education adopted the policy of heterogeneous grouping. Any special provisions for the scholastically superior students were given up.[38]

An ambivalent attitude toward the gifted seems to have characterized the history of Soviet education. On the basis of Pavlovian psychology, Soviet educators insist that talent is not innate and, hence, every child can do well in every field, depending upon the amount of time invested in preparation. On the other hand, since it was not feasible to realize Comenius's ideal of teaching all things to all thoroughly, the practice of separate provisions for the gifted tended to persist. During the debates preceding the school reform

37. Walter Schultze and Christoph Führ, *Das Schulwesen in der Bundesrepublik Deutschland*, 3d ed. (Weinhem: Beltz, 1973), pp. 83-90.

38. George A. Roeper, "Education of the Gifted," in *The Changing Soviet School*, ed. George Z. F. Bereday, William W. Brickman, and Gerald H. Read (Boston: Houghton Mifflin, 1960), pp. 360-361; William W. Brickman, "The Historical Setting after the Revolution," in *The Changing Soviet School*, ed. Bereday, Brickman, and Read, p. 72.

of 1958, N. S. Khrushchev himself advocated "schools for gifted children" in the sciences.[39] Not being or wanting to be a Stalin, Khrushchev did not force his views upon the Central Committee of the Communist Party. There followed a barrage of ideological criticism by politicians, psychologists, and pedagogues asserting that schools for the academically talented would encourage snobbery, egoism, anticollectivism, and other undesirable social outcomes. As a result, this aspect of the reform was tabled for "further study," and it was not included in the new school law of December 25, 1958.[40]

The proponents of special schools and facilities remained undaunted. The concept of *odarennost* (giftedness) and the needs of *odarennye deti* (gifted children) were by no means overlooked. An article in the *Pedagogical Encyclopedia*, published by the prestigious Academy of Pedagogical Sciences, reminds the reader of native creative geniuses of the past—M. V. Lomonosov, I. Y. Repin, A. S. Pushkin, T. H. Shevchenko, M. Gorky, P. I. Tchaikovsky, and N. A. Rimsky-Korsakov—doubtless in support of the idea of special provisions for the artistic-literary gifted.[41] (Lomonosov, of course, was outstanding in a variety of skills, including the scholarly and the scientific). There may not be anything in the nature of an abundance of literature on gifted children, but it cannot be said that the subject does not receive attention.[42]

There are special facilities and schools for the academically talented in the USSR. In 1957-1958, the Moscow State University organized a Mathematics Olympiad for the identification of the mathematically gifted children.[43] In September, 1959, a special class for ninth-grade pupils with aptitude for mathematics was

39. *Pravda*, 21 September 1958, as cited in Nicholas DeWitt, *Education and Professional Employment in the USSR* (Washington, D.C.: U.S. Government Printing Office, 1961), p. 18.

40. Ibid., pp. 18-19.

41. B. F. Baev, "Odarennost," in *Pedagogicheskaya Entsiklopediya*, vol. 3 ed. Ivan A. Kairov et al. (Moscow: Izdatelstvo "Sovetskaya Entsiklopediya," 1966), pp. 186-88.

42. Among the Soviet educational and psychological scholars dealing with giftedness are A. N. Leontiev and B. M. Teplov.

43. Roeper, "Education of the Gifted," p. 373.

organized at School 425 in Moscow under the authorization of the Ministry of Education of the RSFSR.[44] Separate mathematical-scientific schools made their appearance before long. Sponsored by universities and the USSR Academy of Sciences, these were organized with boarding facilities for promising pupils. Of particular note are the schools founded in 1963—the Moscow School of Mathematics and Physics under the auspices of the Moscow State University, and the Novosibirsk School of Mathematics and Physics jointly sponsored by the Novosibirsk State University and the Siberian Department of the USSR Academy of Sciences.[45]

Apparently, the idea of special schools for academically talented has received approval, official and otherwise, in the Soviet Union. That questions of an ideological nature still remain in the world of Communism is evident from a recent comment in a Communist Chinese periodical. The writer criticized the "Soviet revisionists for establishing special schools to teach politics, mathematics, fine art, and music to so-called 'talented students' . . . who consider themselves far superior to the masses" and who will be appointed to "positions at all levels of the power structure to serve the bureaucrat-monopoly capitalist class in the Soviet Union dominated by the revisionists." [46]

The competitive examination for the discovery of specialized scholastic talent has proved to be popular, not only in mathematics but also in other fields. A recent all-Siberian Olympiad in mathematics and physics attracted between 10,000 and 12,000 participants.[47] The literature Olympiad, held in 1967 in Moscow, involved all schools, with 25,000 taking part in the intermediate stage.[48] In

44. Bruce R. Vogeli, *Soviet Secondary Schools for the Mathematically Talented* (Washington, D.C.: National Council of Teachers of Mathematics, 1968), p. 11.

45. Ibid., pp. 49-54.

46. Tai Shan-hung, "New Tsars and New Aristocrats," *Peking Review*, no. 29, 16 July 1976, p. 28.

47. Mikhail Lavrentiev, "A School for Young Mathematicians in Siberia," *Prospects: Quarterly Review of Education* 5, no. 2 (1975): 153-58. The author is vice-president of the USSR Academy of Sciences and chairman of the Siberian Department.

48. "Soviet Olympiad for Literature," *Times* (London), Educational Supplement, 21 July 1967.

addition, there have been contests in the fields of biology, geography, and philology.[49] It is clear that the campaign for the identification of academic aptitude has been going on without abatement since 1934.[50]

The needs of the various types of talented children and adolescents are also provided for outside the school. Inasmuch as curriculum and instruction are generally rather fixed and formal in the schools, the authorities have organized facilities for the development of pupil capacities and interests beyond the walls of the school.

Programs for pupils with various aptitudes and interests, not necessarily for those who are gifted, have been available for some time under the jurisdiction of the Communist Party of the Soviet Union. These are in the form of *kruzhki* (study circles—*kruzhok* in the singular), which cover many types of activities by children and adolescents. For the most part, the circles are located in Pioneer Palaces, Pioneer Houses, and Pioneer Camps. Here the pupils have access to scholastic and recreational facilities and guidance services that are often superior to those offered by the schools. These extracurricular circles help enrich the curriculum and identify the gifted in such academic fields as physics, astronomy, technology, biology, literature, history and others.[51]

As already indicated, the special schools for the artistically talented have been less controversial than those who excel in academic fields. The existence of schools of music, ballet, and art is quite familiar. Less known are those that emphasize chess, the circus, and sports. The first special school for ballet training dates

49. G. V. Berezina and A. I. Foteyeva, "Educational Work and Extracurricular Educational Establishments," in N. P. Kugin et al., *Education in the USSR* (Moscow: Progress Publishers, 1972), p. 75.

50. Detlef Glowka, *Schulreform und Gesellschaft in der Sowjetunion, 1958-1968: Die Differenzierung der allgemeinbildenden Schule als Problem der Sowjetischen Bildungspolitik* (Stuttgart: Klett, 1970), p. 81.

51. On the circles, see Berezina and Foteyeva, "Educational Work and Extracurricular Educational Establishments," pp. 71-79; Roeper, "Education of the Gifted," pp. 371-74; *Narodnoe Obrazovanie v SSSR*, ed. Ivan A. Kairov et al. (Moscow: Izdatelstvo Akademii Pedagogicheskikh Nauk, 1957), pp. 217-35; and A. D. Kalinin, *Narodnoe Obrazovanie v SSSR* (Moscow: Izdatelstvo "Pedagogika," 1972), pp. 61-66.

from the mid-eighteenth century, when the Vaganova School in St. Petersburg began its work. The well-known Ballet School of the Bolshoi Theater originated in 1783 under the aegis of its predecessor, the Petrovsky Theater. After various developments, the school was reorganized in 1926 as a specialized educational institution with a nine-year course of study through adolescence. The current program comprises general education and ballet subjects with the latter constituting 7,501 out of a total of 13,842.5 hours.[52]

Special schools for the musically gifted are relatively new in comparison to those of the dance. The Central Music School, under the guidance of the Moscow Conservatory, dates from the early 1930s. There are also part-time music schools for those with great ability and interest even if they cannot be considered as highly gifted. Still another type is represented by the Leningrad Orphanage for Musically Talented Children.[53] There are also full-time and part-time schools for children and adolescents with unusual talent in the visual arts.[54]

It is clear that the special school for the gifted, whether artistically or academically, has won a place in the Soviet school system. The collective society becomes flexible enough to make some more equal than others.

Other Countries

The international literature on the gifted has been substantially enriched by the *Year Book of Education* for 1961 and for 1962, which have already been cited several times in this chapter. In addition, the proceedings of the first World Conference on Gifted Children (London, 1975), likewise cited, contain concise statements of provisions and plans in twenty-five countries. Thus, the interested reader can find some information about the education of

52. Miriam Morton, *The Arts and the Soviet Child: The Esthetic Education of Children in the USSR* (New York: Free Press, 1972), pp. 365-66, 303-17. See also H. C. Creighton, "The Bolshoi Ballet School," in *Concepts of Excellence in Education*, ed. Bereday and Lauwerys, pp. 467-70.

53. Roeper, "Education of the Gifted," pp. 364-67; Morton, *The Arts and the Soviet Child*, pp. 139-47, 357-63 (courses of study).

54. Morton, *The Arts and the Soviet Child*, pp. 275-84; 364-65 (courses of study). See also Mayo Bryce, *Fine Arts Education in the Soviet Union* (Washington, D.C.: U.S. Government Printing Office, 1963).

gifted children and adolescents in Europe (for example, Belgium, Bulgaria), North America (for example, Canada, Mexico), South America (Brazil), Asia (for example, Pakistan, Syria), Africa (for example, Kenya, Nigeria), and in Australia and New Zealand. This constitutes evidence of the existence of interest and concern in many nations. Even more impressive is the emergence of national bodies dedicated to the education of the talented. Of particular note are the *Association Nationale Française pour les enfants surdoués* (1971), the Association for the Education of Gifted Children in South Africa, and the Department for Gifted Children in the Israeli Ministry of Education and Culture (1972).

In this chapter it is impossible to cover adequately the various countries offering provisions for the gifted. The best that can be done is to refer to a sampling, even if somewhat arbitrary, owing to the lack of sufficient source materials in the original languages.

In western Europe, France has used the system of *l'orientation continue* (progressive guidance), which has enabled the identification of gifted children who would otherwise have been overlooked.[55] The French have retreated from their policy of severe selection for secondary and higher education and have neglected the provision of facilities for the gifted, but recent events indicate a more promising future.[56] Along with other countries, Belgium has faced social and other problems in connection with the academically talented; yet, its history records the founding of *Le fonds des mieux doués* (the fund for the most gifted) in 1921 to provide financial support for the secondary-school study of qualified pupils.[57] Doubtless because of its differentiated school system, the Netherlands has not stressed special classes or schools for gifted pupils. More attention is paid to such children in the Montessori and other nontraditional schools, while the recent literature shows

55. Robert A. Mallet, "Progressive Educational Guidance—France," in *The Gifted Child,* ed. Bereday and Lauwerys, pp. 253-58.

56. Jean-Charles Terrassier, "France," in *Gifted Children,* ed. Gibson and Chennells, p. 303-7.

57. M. Ride Craecker, *Les enfants intellectuellement doués* (Paris: Presses Universitaires de France, 1951). See also Yves Roger, "Problems of Democracy and the Selection of the Gifted in Belgium," in *The Gifted Child,* ed. Bereday and Lauwerys, pp. 246-52.

an increased awareness of their educational needs.[58] Particular interest in the identification and education of the gifted in Italy was manifested after an awareness of the loss of intellectual talent. *Identificazione ed assistenza dei ragazzi dotati*, established in 1961 in Milan, has shifted its focus from the testing of intelligence and creativity to the factor of environment and to the struggle against social discrimination toward the gifted in schools.[59] Of considerable interest is the *Villaggio del Superdotato*, a school for mentally gifted children from economically disadvantaged families, established by Don Calogero La Placa, a priest, near Palermo, Sicily.[60] Evidence of activity for the gifted in Spain seems to be sparse, although some studies are extant.[61] Finally, in Scandinavia, little in the form of special provisions appears to have been made. Except for ballet and music, Denmark has neglected the gifted in favor of the average and below-average children.[62] Swedish educational officials confess that "little that is tangible" has been done for the scholastically talented.[63]

58. Gerard A. van Eldert, "Netherlands," in *Gifted Children*, ed. Gibson and Chennells, pp. 340-43; Th. J. Ijzerman, *Het talentenvraegstuk* (Groningen: Wolters-Noordhoff, 1968); F. vanHeek et al., *Het verborgen talent: Milieu, schoolkeuze en schoolgeschiktheid*, a report on the Nederlandse Talentproject of the Sociologisch Instituut of the University of Leiden (Meppel: Boom, 1968).

59. Egle Becchi, "Italy," in *Gifted Children*, ed. Gibson and Chennells, pp. 327-31. Two studies are cited in this article: O. Andreani and S. Orio, *Le radici psicologiche del talento* (Bologna: Il Mulino, 1972) and O. Andreani, *Classe sociale, intelligenza, personalità* (Bologna: Il Mulino, 1974). Two essays in *The Gifted Child*, ed. Bereday and Lauwerys, are also relevant: H. Boutourline Young, "Detection and Encouragement of the Talented in Italian Schools," pp. 275-80, and A. Benedetti, "Economic Development and Intellectual Resources in Italy," pp. 472-80. See also Luigi Volpicelli, "The Italian School and the Education of the Gifted," in *Concepts of Excellence in Education*, ed. Bereday and Lauwerys, pp. 277-83.

60. Bert Lodge, "A Godfather for the Gifted," *Times* (London), Educational Supplement, 20 August 1976, p. 4.

61. J. Costa Ribas, *España y el cuidado de los bien dotados* (Madrid, 1953), cited in Victor Garcia Hoz, "Methods of Selecting the Gifted: A Spanish Assessment," in *The Gifted Child*, ed. Bereday and Lauwerys, p. 283.

62. Kirsten Morch Vaughan, "Denmark," in *Gifted Children*, ed. Gibson and Chennells, p. 299.

63. Mary Ekdahl and Christina Ekblad, "Sweden," in *Gifted Children*, ed. Gibson and Chennells, p. 363. One wonders to what extent the work of Husén

It is not surprising that countries in eastern Europe, permeated as they are by Communist ideology and dedicated to the Soviet model, include provisions similar to those in the educational systems of the USSR. Thus, Czechoslovakia, Bulgaria, and Poland have *kruzhki*, Pioneer palaces and houses, Pioneer camps, Mathematical Olympiads, and special schools (including ballet.)[64] Many of these features can also be found in Yugoslavia, a non-Soviet oriented Communist country.[65]

Canada and Australia have made use of curriculum enrichment, special classes, and acceleration in providing for the gifted.[66] In New Zealand, there has been a transition from the "pretty rough and ready process" of selection, as Winterbourn put it, to a system of nonstreaming, curricular enrichment, and acceleration.[67]

There is some interest in the gifted in Latin America, although

may have influenced this attitude. See Torsten Husén, "Loss of Talent in Selective School Systems: The Case of Sweden," *Comparative Education Review* 4 (1960): 70-74, and idem, "Detection of Ability and Selection for Educational Purposes in Sweden," in *The Gifted Child*, ed. Bereday and Lauwerys, pp. 295-314.

64. For Poland, see Bogdan Suchodolski, "The Gifted Child: Poland," in *Concepts of Excellence in Education*, ed. Bereday and Lauwerys, pp. 297-307, and Lidia Woloszynowa, "Poland," in *Gifted Children*, ed. Gibson and Chennells, pp. 352-55. For Czechoslovakia, see Oĭga Pačesová, "Czechoslovakia,' in *Gifted Children*, ed. Gibson and Chennells, pp. 295-98. For Bulgaria, see Beatrice King, "The Education of the Gifted Child in Bulgaria," in *Concepts of Excellence in Education*, ed. Bereday and Lauwerys, pp. 241-254. See also "Maths Olympiad for Balkan Countries," *UNESCO Features*, no. 500 (April, 1967): 33.

65. Dragotin Franković, "General Notions on Ability, Talent, and Genius in Yugoslavia," in *Concepts of Excellence in Education*, ed. Bereday and Lauwerys, pp. 128-39.

66. Two essays in *Concepts of Exellence in Education*, ed. Bereday and Lauwerys, deal with Canada. See David Munroe, "The Education of the Gifted Child in an Open Society: Canada," pp. 255-61, and Ian E. Housego, "Current Practices in Handling the Gifted in Alberta, Canada," pp. 489-99. See also Samuel R. Laycock, "Trends in the Education of the Gifted in Canada," in *The Gifted Child*, ed. Bereday and Lauwerys, pp. 226-35, and John P. Maclean, "Canada," in *Gifted Children*, ed. Gibson and Chennells, pp. 292-94. For Australia, see W. C. Radford, "The Gifted Child in Australia," in *Concepts of Excellence in Education*, ed. Bereday and Lauwerys, pp. 227-35.

67. R. Winterbourn, "Identification of the Gifted in a Largely Egalitarian Society (New Zealand)," in *The Gifted Child*, ed. Bereday and Lauwerys, pp. 236-45; Clement G. N. Hill, "New Zealand," in *Gifted Children*, ed. Gibson and Chennells, pp. 343-48.

not much in the way of specific literature has come to light. Brazil provides "special enrichment programmes" and acceleration, while in the late 1960s Mexico established a school for "child geniuses," particularly for pupils from families of the lower classes.[68]

In the Middle East,[69] Egypt established in 1955 a national secondary school for highly gifted boys with an enriched curriculum and a selected staff. Syria has opened schools of art and music for the talented. Turkey founded secondary schools for those exceptionally competent in science, made available special classes for gifted primary pupils, and sent gifted graduates to study languages abroad. Elsewhere in the area, Israeli educators have experimented with multiple setting in the two upper grades of the primary school in Beersheba while parents have organized club activities for exceptionally gifted children and special classes for the highly gifted were introduced into regular primary schools.[70]

Among the Asian countries, India furthers the education of the gifted through accelerated academic programs, experiments with special schools, and national and state talent searches in science,

68. Raquel Braune, "Brazil," in *Gifted Children*, ed. Gibson and Chennells, pp. 288-92; Emil Zubryn, "Fostering Genius," *Times* (London), Educational Supplement, 15 December 1967; Julio Larrea, "The Education of the Gifted and the Promotion of a New World: Latin America," in *The Gifted Child*, ed. Bereday and Lauwerys, pp. 512-27.

69. Nazmi H. Mikhail, "A Secondary School for Highly Gifted Boys at Ain-Shams, Cairo, U.A.R.," in *Concepts of Excellence in Education*, ed. Bereday and Lauwerys, pp. 484-88. For reports on Syria and Turkey see the follow in *Gifted Children*, ed. Gibson and Chennells: Moubina Kouatly, "Syria," pp. 363-65, and Halide Yavuz, "Turkey," pp. 368-73.

70. D. Bitan and Gina R. Ortar, "The Beersheba Experiment in Multiple-Level Setting in Primary Schools," in *Grouping in Education*, ed. Yates, pp. 174-77; "Trying to Solve the High IQ Problem," *Jerusalem Post Weekly*, 3 February 1976, as excerpted in *The Principal* 21 (April, 1976): 8-9; two essays in *Gifted Children*, ed. Gibson and Chennels: Nava Butler, "Israel's First Experiment in Special Classes for Gifted Children within Regular Schools," pp. 169-81, and Dan Bitan, "Israel," pp. 322-27; Moshe Smilansky, "Beit-sefer l'mhonamin B'Yisrael," in *Antziklopediah Hinuchit*, vol. 3, ed. Hayim Y. Ormian (Jerusalem: Ministry of Education and Culture and Bialik Institute, 1967), pp. 246-49; A. Evyater, "Enrichment Therapy," *Educational Research* 15 (February, 1973): 115-22. The latter article describes a mathematics enrichment program for "very gifted children" aged eleven to thirteen at the Technion, Haifa.

sports, and other fields.[71] The Japanese school system, in common with some European systems, has tended to concentrate on the below average and average by raising the national standard as measured by achievement tests, and has "virtually neglected" the needs of the gifted. Yet some progress is evident in the form of experiments in intraclass ability grouping, individualized instruction, special ability classes, and academic clubs and extracurricular activities.[72]

In Africa, the developing countries have been wrestling with the problems of mass education, including linguistic diversity, and hence have not given much attention to the provisions for the academically talented. The assumption appears to be that the selective process for secondary and higher education is, in itself, a guarantee for the gifted. Another important factor is the presence of private, fee-charging schools that offer opportunities for pupils with exceptional abilities.[73]

Reflections

Few, if any, countries are unaware of the needs and values of the academically and creatively talented. Because of history, socio-economic-political status and policy, there are differences in how the various nations provide for the education of such children in the primary and secondary schools. The World Conferences on Gifted Children in 1975 and 1977 revealed a worldwide interest and concern for giftedness and the education of gifted children. It is likely that the international attention given to this educational aspect will spur some countries to greater exertions.

The provision of educational opportunities for the gifted takes

71. K. N. Saxena, "India," in *Gifted Children*, ed. Gibson and Chennells, pp. 311-14. See also Abdul Haq Khan, *Educating the Gifted* (New Delhi: Arya Book Depot, 1967); C. L. Bhatt, *Gifted Children: A Psychological, Sociological, and Educational Study* (Allahabad: United Publishers, 1973).

72. Bunkichi Iwahashi, "Problems of Educating the Gifted in the Primary and Secondary Schools in Japan," in *Concepts of Excellence in Education*, ed. Bereday and Lauwerys, pp. 284-90.

73. For reports on some of the African countries, see the following in *Gifted Children*, ed. Gibson and Chennells: N. O. Anim, "Ghana," pp. 307-10; N. O. Bwibo, "Kenya," pp. 332-33; Christie Ade Adjaui, "Nigeria," pp. 349-51.

on many forms, such as acceleration, setting, individualized instruction, special classes and schools, curricular enrichment within and outside the school, and talent searches through competition. During the past decade, European countries have intensified the withering away of selectivity, homogeneity, and streaming in the interests of social democracy and the elimination of educational and other types of elitism. Proponents of this policy have taken comfort from the conclusions of some leading international educators. Perhaps the most influential of these has been Husén of the University of Stockholm, who sees "the dilemma of meritocracy versus democracy," and who is convinced that "redemptive equality" can only come about "by playing down the rewards, status, and authority connected with superior competence." [74]

Along these lines, it is pertinent to cite some of the research findings in connection with the widespread controversy concerning comprehensive versus selective secondary education. From his international analysis, Schultze, of the *Deutsches Institut für Internationale Pädagogische Forschung*, concluded that comprehensive schools do not necessarily result in lower achievement in mathematics on the part of the very gifted.[75] Similarly, the research studies of the International Association for the Evaluation of Educational Achievement reveal that the test scores of the best students of science are not necessarily affected by the type of school they attend.[76]

These conclusions suggest the desirability of comprehensive education as the "wave of the future" if not indeed of the present. Some educators feel that this policy would tend to submerge the scholastically superior in school and society. Trow views an "austere definition of comprehensive education" as implying coercion, state

74. Torsten Husén, *Talent, Equality, and Meritocracy: Availability and Utilization of Talent* (The Hague: Nijhoff, 1974), p. 243.

75. Walter Schultze, "Die Begabtenförderung in ihrer Abhängigkeit vom Schulaufbau: Eine internationale Umschau," *Paedagogica Europaea*, III (Amsterdam: Agon Elsevier, 1967), pp. 25-45.

76. T. Neville Postlethwaite, "The Surveys of the International Association for the Evaluation of Educational Achievement (IEA)," in *Educational Policy and International Assessment: Implications of the IEA Surveys of Achievement*, ed. Alan C. Purves and Daniel U. Levine (McCutchan Publishing Corp., 1975), p. 23.

control, standardization, and possibly the decline of diversity.[77] Whether or not this fear is justified, it should be possible to have comprehensiveness along with giftedness. This is illustrated by the recent policy statement by the public educational authority of New York State that "the attention given to the gifted and talented should be comprehensively planned, systematic, and focused upon their individual needs." [78]

The dogma that democracy is at the opposite pole from meritocracy based on individual talent, skill, aptitude, ambition, and ability is at least open to serious difference of opinion. It is all too easy to dismiss the ideas of the world's greatest thinkers from ancient times to the present. A democratic society can pursue an egalitarian policy if it provides the fullest possible education for each person without regard to background and status, social, economic, political, religious, racial, sexual, physical, and mental. Under such a policy, all individuals will receive their democratic due, including those who are gifted and talented.

77. Martin Trow, "Commentary II" on Torsten Husén, "Implications of the IEA Findings for the Philosophy of Comprehensive Education," in *Educational Policy and International Assessment,* ed. Purves and Levine, p. 151.

78. Regents of the University of the State of New York, *Educating the Gifted and Talented in New York State* (Albany: New York State Department of Education, 1976), pp. 9-10.

Policies and Practices for Special Populations of the Gifted and the Talented

A. HARRY PASSOW

It has been clear that the gifted and talented populations do not constitute a homogeneous group. There is a tremendous variation within any group of gifted children and a considerable range of differences found among the gifted and talented. Within the general population of the gifted and talented, there are individuals and groups who are unique even with respect to the "generality" of gifted persons. Their uniqueness sets them aside from other gifted individuals in the sense of pointing up their special programming needs. As I noted in a paper prepared for the 1960 White House Conference on Children and Youth, "There are individuals of many gifts, first class in many areas; there are others who shine in a single field. Some persons are just slightly better than the average; others are so unusual as to be rare." Different talents can be identified and nurtured at various developmental stages. Some of these "special populations" are discussed in this section—the child prodigy, the creative child and adult, the artistically talented, the gifted minority person, and the gifted and talented woman.

David Feldman discusses what he calls "the mysterious case of extreme giftedness"—the paucity of studies dealing with the most extreme forms of intellectual giftedness. He points to Terman's use of the term "genius," noting that it was not until thirty years after he had started his studies that Terman realized his gifted subjects could not be labeled as geniuses. The concepts of precocity and prodigiousness are examined in relation to genius. Feldman reports on a study of three individuals who were younger than ten years of age at the time the project began and who were ex-

tremely gifted intellectually. He explores the educational and
psychological aspects of their development, indicating ways in
which early prodigious achievement resembles and differs from
other developmental phenomena. Feldman concludes that the
achievements of child prodigies are not achieved "without intensive, prolonged, *educational* assistance."

The unique needs of the creative child and adult are examined
by E. Paul Torrance. In a rather short time, the concepts of
creativity and of the creatively gifted have gained rather wide
acceptance in the educational community. Torrance argues that
the logic of making the creatively gifted a recognized category of
exceptionality is clear and that supporting evidence is available to
make the case. He proposes that changes in policies and practices
designed to serve the unique needs of creative children and adults
are both necessary and possible. These changes would deal with
the techniques and procedures used to identify creative individuals
and with the environment of the school as it affects the nurturing
of creativity. Torrance proposes that creative individuals be provided with a "refuge" somewhere within the system, that they be
helped to find individuals who would serve as their sponsors or
patrons, and that creative giftedness be acknowledged and rewarded. Policies and practices must be developed to facilitate creative ways of behaving.

A study of talented individuals, from the time they were enrolled in one of America's preeminent art schools to six years after
they were graduated, is reported by Jacob W. Getzels to provide
insights into the nature of art talent and its development. The cognitive, perceptual, personality, and value characteristics of second-
and third-year art students are summarized and those value and
personality determinants of artistic specialization are pinpointed.
Getzels found systematic relationships between the personal-affec-
tive characteristics of art students and their achievement in art
school, relationships that varied by sex and by field of specialization. The social and personal context of becoming a fine artist is
described by Getzels. He proposes for further examination a number of tentative hypotheses about becoming a fine artist. These hypotheses, which center on problem finding and problem solving,
have implications for developing artistic talent.

Culturally different individuals, the disadvantaged, and minority groups have unique needs and problems with respect to developing and using their special gifts and talents. Gwendolyn J. Cooke and Alexinia Baldwin recall W. E. B. DuBois's "Theory of the Talented Tenth," which posited that among blacks, as with other races, "there is a hereditarily controlled elite whose potential would blossom within the proper educational context." DuBois urged identification and nurture of potential talent among blacks in order to provide the intellectual leadership necessary for liberation from poverty and social malaise. Cooke and Baldwin present a matrix to aid in identification of gifted and talented among minority and disadvantaged persons. The Baldwin Identification Matrix uses a variety of techniques for establishing strengths in particular areas. A curriculum/instructional rationale must then be developed to nourish innate abilities so identified and to accommodate stimuli deficits. Cooke and Baldwin urge that unique paradigms be examined to identify and develop talent among the black children and youth.

Ernest M. Bernal, Jr. contends that the education of what he calls "culturally different gifted" children and youth is a relatively new concern among those who have been involved in the education of gifted and talented. Bernal points out that being culturally *different* does not mean being culturally *inferior*, yet the gifted and talented from minority groups have generally fared poorly in terms of being identified and developed. He urges that programs for the culturally different gifted be designed and developed with the psychological, cultural, and linguistic characteristics of such children in mind. Bernal cautions educators against making one of two errors in planning for the culturally different—either adopting a "supercompensatory" approach or seeking simple ethnic integration in the program for gifted children. A valid program should build on the assets of culturally different gifted students while fostering interethnic understanding and broadening the style-of-life options.

It is a fact, Carolyn M. Callahan points out, that the number of men recognized as gifted and talented far exceeds the number of women who have achieved similar levels of success. Callahan reviews the research and literature concerning the intellectual abilities and achievements of males and females and concludes that there is little to account for the overwhelming dominance of males among the identified gifted or to aid in identifying the characteristics that distinguish females who realize their gifted potential from those who do not. Similarly, research on differences in personality, interests, and values are reviewed by Callahan for clues to male-female variations in performance. The possibility of environmental factors impinging upon the success of gifted females is examined and Callahan finds barriers, some subtle and others blatant, that affect achievement. Finally, she explores the appropriateness of models for administrative adaptations in programs for the gifted and talented and notes that they have systematically failed to consider the differential effects of those models on males and females. Callahan discusses the special counseling needs of gifted and talented females.

Finally, Marshall P. Sanborn discusses the counseling and guidance needs of gifted and talented students, drawing upon the twenty-one years of experience of the Research and Guidance Laboratory at the University of Wisconsin. This interdisciplinary program, begun in 1958, uses a research-through-service format. Almost 4,000 young people, together with their parents and teachers, have been involved in identification and guidance programs. Sanborn notes that gifted and talented individuals differ from one another more than they resemble each other. A major purpose of counseling and guidance in schools, he maintains, is to discover the unique patterns of individual characteristics and to help individuals understand how these patterns relate to opportunities available. A related purpose is to help teachers use these characteristics in generating appropriate educational and developmental experiences. Two case studies are presented to compare and contrast the development of two boys identified as gifted. The needs of gifted and talented students for appropriate counseling and guidance are pointed out, but Sanborn suggests guidance personnel must have the assistance of the teaching staff, which has the real control over the student's experience in school. Because gifted and talented children are interested in and concerned about subjects taught in school, it is the curriculum that has the greatest potential as a delivery system for meeting their needs for guidance.

CHAPTER XXI

The Mysterious Case of Extreme Giftedness

DAVID FELDMAN

Introduction

Oddly, perhaps inexplicably, the most extreme forms of intellectual giftedness have been the least studied. If one looks for studies of persons with a very high IQ, there is Hollingworth's 1940 case study of children above 180 IQ and little else.[1] If performance rather than potential is the metric, then there seems to be not a single work in English. In 1930, Baumgarten, a Swiss contemporary of Hollingworth, published a study in which nine child prodigies were subjected to psychological analysis through test and interview.[2] These two works appear to be the sum total of the psychological literature on extreme giftedness, except of course the clinical case studies and biographical or retrospective accounts, such as Cox's estimate of the childhood IQ of prominent individuals living from 1450 to 1850.[3]

One purpose of this chapter is to explain why the most obvious and dramatic manifestations of human intellectual superiority have also been the most neglected. The explanation points to the work of Lewis M. Terman and his colleagues as instrumental in transforming the meaning of extreme giftedness even as they were try-

1. Leta Hollingworth, *Children above 180 IQ* (New York: World Book Co., 1942).

2. Franziska Baumgarten, *Wunderkinder psychologische Untersuchungen* (Leipzig: Johann Ambrosius Barth, 1930).

3. Catherine Cox, *The Early Mental Traits of Three Hundred Geniuses* (Stanford, Calif.: Stanford University Press, 1926). After completing the preparation of this chapter, I learned of an important work on child prodigies that had not previously come to my attention: Géza Révész, *The Psychology of a Musical Prodigy* (Westport, Conn.: Greenwood Press, 1970). This volume was originally published in 1925, in New York by Harcourt, Brace and Co. and in London by Kegan Paul, Trench, Trubner, and Co.

ing to study it. This transformation appears relevant to the virtual nonexistence of extreme giftedness as a field of psychological study. A second purpose is to describe efforts begun recently at Tufts University to learn more about extreme manifestations of intellectual capability.

Interest in extreme forms of giftedness may be seen as part of the more general attempts to rejuvenate the field,[4] but it is important to distinguish between work with the more moderately gifted, who have in the past received much attention, and work with the extremely gifted, who have not. It could well be that the preoccupation of earlier workers with less extreme forms of giftedness (for example, with subjects whose IQs are in the range of from 125 to 165) was itself a contributing factor to the neglect of the extremely gifted. The concept of giftedness established by the early workers in the field seemed to render unnecessary the study of the most exceptional forms of intellectual expression.

TERMAN'S "GENIUS"

Ironically, the one who looms most prominent in accounting for the absence of research on extreme forms of giftedness may well have been Terman, a pioneer in the use of intelligence tests and the foremost figure in the study of the gifted.[5] Although it is difficult to fathom in retrospect, Terman believed that his high-IQ subjects were the geniuses of the future. He believed that an IQ higher than 135 or so was a prerequisite to remarkable achievement in any field.[6] Terman's subjects did indeed turn out to be remarkable, both for their intellectual accomplishments as well as their mental stability and health. Yet, with hindsight we can see that an IQ of 150 is not necessarily indicative of "genius," as Terman had implied in his writing. Only in 1954, did Terman realize that the label "genius" could not be justifiably applied to his subjects.

The acceptance of the IQ as the metric for giftedness became

4. Kathleen Montour, "William James Sidis, the Broken Twig," *American Psychologist* 32 (1977): 265-79.

5. Lewis M. Terman et al., *Genetic Studies of Genius*, vols. I-V (Stanford, Calif.: Stanford University Press, 1925-1959).

6. Paul Witty and Harvey Lehman, "Nervous Instability and Genius: Poetry and Fiction," in *Psychology and Education of the Gifted: Selected Readings*, ed. Walter B. Barbe (New York: Appleton-Century-Crofts, 1965).

clearly visible during a search of the literature on topics related to prodigious achievement. A thorough search of volumes 1 through 51 of *Psychological Abstracts* (1927-1974) used such terms as "ability, superior"; "child, gifted"; "precocious, superior"; "precocious, prodigy"; "student, gifted, superior, talented." Not all terms were present at all times. They had a disconcerting tendency to disappear for awhile and then to reappear with a new connotation or as a synonym for a term that seemed formerly to have been only distantly related. Most striking was the ever greater tendency for terms that had been separate entries to be subsumed under the heading "intelligence." From 1936 to 1941, the term "genius" alternated between being listed with other "special mental conditions" and being part of the category "intelligence." Apparently this was a transition period. The year 1941 marked the last separate classification of "genius." Before 1936, it had always appeared under the category "special mental conditions." After 1941, it appeared *only* in the category "intelligence."

It became clear that no empirical studies had been done in this country (at least none that actually studied child prodigies while they were children) to document the phenomenon of early prodigious achievement. There were a few case studies, the most notable of which was Baumgarten's study of nine children whose achievements had brought most of them to public attention before the age of twelve. The cases include "two piano virtuosi, two violinists, one orchestra leader, one girl dancer, one girl artist, one geographer, (and) one boy chess wonder." With the children's extraordinary accomplishments so clearly established, the purpose of the study was not so much to document and verify the fact of precocity but rather to investigate in what other ways these children differed "in regard to their relation to the art practiced, their relation to their parents, their contemporaries, and their environment."[7]

A reflection of the change in the meaning of the term "genius" brought about as a consequence of Terman's efforts may be seen in a comparison of the eleventh edition (1910) of *Encyclopedia Britannica* with the fourteenth edition (1972). The earlier version referred to "genius" as:

A degree of original greatness which is beyond ordinary powers or

7. Baumgarten, *Wunderkinder psychologische Untersuchungen*, p. 4.

explanations, that is, far beyond the capacity of the normal human being in creative work: and it is a convenient term (like Nietzsche's "superman") for application to those rare individuals who in the course of evolution reveal from time to time the heights to which humanity may develop, in literature, art, science, or administrative life.[8]

The later version defines the modern English usage of the term "genius" as follows:

The word genius is used in two closely related but somewhat different senses. In the first sense, as popularized by Lewis M. Terman, genius refers to high intellectual ability as measured by performance on a standardized intelligence test. The exact intelligence quotient designating genius varies. Terman set the intelligence quotient for "potential genius" at 140 or over, a level reached by about 1 in 250 of the general population. . . . In the second and more popular sense, as derived from Sir Francis Galton, "genius" is used to designate creative ability of an exceptionally high order as demonstrated by actual achievement. In this sense, men of genius are identified by the eminence of their accomplishment.[9]

The word "genius" now carries the combined meanings of high intelligence and achieved eminence. When applied to children, the first meaning, high intellectual ability, is of course the only one relevant, since achievement is years into the future. Genius in the IQ sense is a predictor of later success, an early sign of the mark of eminence. The idea of the IQ index was to be able to know in advance who among the nation's children was likely to go on to achieve eminence.

The meaning of the term "genius," therefore, has been enlarged over the years, chiefly as a consequence of the redefinition of intelligence by Terman and others in the IQ movement. High IQ became almost synonymous with genius, particularly when referring to children. We have not yet, however, come to grips with the actual phenomena that have eluded modern inquiry, namely precociousness and prodigiousness, to which we now direct our attention.

PRECOCIOUSNESS AND PRODIGIOUSNESS

Put simply, the intelligence quotient is a measure of precociousness. A high IQ means that a child is able to perform certain mental

8. *Encyclopedia Britannica*, 11th ed., s.v. "genius."
9. Ibid., 14th ed., s.v. "genius."

tasks that are ordinarily performed only by older children. A high IQ, of course, is only one of several possible ways to conceptualize rapid progress or great power in the intellectual domain. Unusual ability in a specific area, such as logic, would be another way. Curiosity about unusual topics, facile use of technologies, demonstrated achievement in a complex field, and so forth, are other ways. For better or worse, however, precociousness became part of the concept of intelligence as we know it. It follows that research on high-IQ children is by definition research on highly precocious children, precocious in whatever IQ tests measure. Virtually no studies of mental precociousness other than high IQ are to be found in the literature of the last thirty years, indicating the degree to which precocity in the IQ sense preoccupied the field. The concept of precociousness has come to be inextricably linked with the concept of intelligence, with the effect that precociousness of a certain sort was already measured by virtue of the measurement of IQ. Precociousness, then, like the concept of genius, tended to be subsumed under the IQ notion of intelligence. But what of the idea of a prodigy? From its earlier definition as "something out of the usual course of nature (as an eclipse or meteor) that is a portent" and "something extraordinary or inexplicable" (again quoting Webster's 1961 edition), a prodigy became defined as "a highly gifted or academically talented child."

The meaning of the term "prodigy" has been camouflaged by a concept of intelligence that seems to include it but really does not. Thus, prodigy came to mean the same as precocious but to an even greater degree.[10] The meanings of the terms "precocious," "prodigy," and "genius" all seem to have been subsumed under the general concept of intelligence as reflected in the IQ index. Prodigies were made part of everyday life, not taken as different in kind from the rest of humanity. Perhaps for this reason it did not seem as necessary to study prodigies as a separate, unique variant of nature.

Piaget and the Developmental View of Intelligence

Fascination with extreme forms of intellectual expression is part of another general shift in point of view about intelligence, a shift that has come about largely because of the influence of Jean Piaget.

10. Cox, The Early Mental Traits of Three Hundred Geniuses.

Piaget views intelligence as an ongoing process of transformation and change. This is in contrast to the psychometric view, which sees intelligence as a relatively unchanging trait of the individual.[11] By emphasizing the universal set of changes in thinking that all children experience, Piaget has drawn attention to intellectual development as a growth process that has certain universal milestones and processes through which these milestones are invariably achieved.

An ironic twist is that although Piaget has helped to transcend the IQ view of intelligence, he has not himself been interested in the problem of giftedness at all. Perhaps the reason is that Piaget sees all intellectual accomplishments as caused fundamentally by the same *developmental* processes, just as Terman had believed that all intellectual differences were caused by different amounts of the trait of IQ.

Thus, as Terman did earlier, Piaget has proposed a set of unifying principles for all intellectual development. These principles, to be sure, are very different from those of Terman's psychometric view. In our work on extreme forms of giftedness the Piagetian framework has been used as a guide. We have extended the framework to incorporate child prodigies, although the theory itself must be modified in some respects to do this.

EARLY PRODIGIOUS ACHIEVEMENT AS COINCIDENCE

The key difference between the Piaget-inspired view and the IQ-based view is that the IQ view locates the cause of phenomenal achievement primarily *within the child*. Prodigious achievement is better conceptualized as a remarkable *coincidence*. The coincidence consists of a human organism with a set of powerful predispositions or qualities that interact in a human environment over a segment of time during which it becomes possible for that individual to express the potential he possesses.

An individual must work *at* something or *in* some field, however loosely defined, to demonstrate his or her prodigiousness. Suppose, for example, that Albert Einstein had been born fifty thousand

11. David Feldman, "Universal to Unique," in *Essays in Creativity*, ed. Stanley Rosner and L. E. Abt (Croton-on-Hudson, N.Y.: North River Press, 1974).

years ago, five thousand years ago, or even five hundred years ago, which could well have happened.[12] Is it reasonable to suppose that Einstein would have achieved his remarkable insights into the workings of the universe if he had been born before the era of science, or for that matter, of history? Perhaps Einstein would have done something remarkable regardless of the age in which he was born, perhaps not. The point is that the transcendent quality of Einstein's achievement was as critically a function of the state of a field of knowledge at a particular point in its own history as it was a function of that talent itself.

Those familiar with Einstein's earliest years may be thinking that he was no child prodigy. Einstein apparently did not speak until he was four or five years of age. But I am not dealing here with all aspects of prodigious achievement. Rather, I wish to draw attention to the crucial importance of the state of a body of knowledge, including its codability and communicability at a given moment in historical time. Of note in this connection is the fact that Einstein's field was physics, in which truly prodigious early achievements, at least as I define them, have not occurred. Einstein was no prodigy, but his field is one in which early prodigious achievement is unheard of. Nonetheless, Einstein's achievements in physics were built upon existing theory and existing facts. Thus, *the occurrence of remarkable achievement within a field by a young child depends in part on the existence and transmission of a highly evolved and economically communicable domain of knowledge.*

Taking chess as an illustration, the amount, abstractness, and complexity of knowledge required to play adult-level chess is enormous. The probability that an individual would be able to learn enough to play sophisticated chess games by the age of six or seven years, as was the case, for example, with Bobby Fischer and for some of the children in our study, is virtually nil. The chess players in this study, for example, picked up the game with little instruction and achieved considerable skill before the age of six. To deny the obvious gifts of such early achievers requires massive distortion of the facts. But to ignore the importance of a highly dis-

12. Sherwood L. Washburn and F. Clark Howell, "Human Evolution and Culture," in *The Evolution of Man*, ed. Sol Tax (Chicago: University of Chicago Press, 1960), vol. 2, pp. 33-56.

tilled and efficiently communicable body of knowledge is equally partsighted. Bobby Fischer learned to play chess when he was about six. From that year on, however, Fischer read hundreds of books about chess, had intensive formal instruction during his teens, and reached the rank of Grandmaster when he was fifteen—a remarkable achievement to be sure, but one which took more than nine years to accomplish.

Thus, early prodigious achievement should be seen as the occurrence in time and space of a remarkably preorganized human being, born during perhaps the optimal period and educated in the precise manner most likely to enable the individual to interact optimally with a highly evolved field of knowledge. In other words, a coincidence occurs, more remarkable even than the awesome talents that make it possible. The subtle, delicate coordination of elements of human potential and cultural tradition is to me even more dazzling than the achievements attributed to various individuals. It is more dazzling because *the same processes* that are responsible for all human development are responsible for early prodigious achievement, as we shall see in later sections of this chapter.

If it is true that an optimal match of individual talent to specialized environment is highly improbable, then over evolutionary time there are likely to have been many other individuals, preorganized for one purpose but born at a moment in time or in a place where their unique organization had no appropriate environment through which to express itself. Therefore, when we see a natural experiment of the sort we typically refer to as a "child prodigy," what we are actually seeing is an astonishing but predictable coincidence. As with any random process, early prodigious achievement is no more nor less probable than any other combination of human and cultural factors interacting across a few moments of evolutionary time.

Early Prodigious Achievement: A Research Study

For the past two years, three individuals have been studied in our research. All were under the age of ten at the beginning of the study and are without question extremely gifted. These three children meet the demanding criterion of early prodigious achievement set for the study, namely, that each child performs in his chosen field at the level of an adult professional before the age of ten. The study has two aspects: one is educational, the other psychological. The educational aspect deals with the process through which a child prodigy is prepared to practice his craft. As mentioned earlier, even in the most extreme cases on record, intensive education over several years is required in bringing the talented child to full bloom as a master practitioner. To glimpse this process, considerable amounts of time have been spent with the teachers of chess and music composition who guide the three subjects in the study. More than thirty lessons have been observed; about a dozen sessions have been recorded on tape; tournaments, recitals, and concerts have been attended; and the families and teachers of the young subjects have been interviewed.

Although it is too early to report many findings from the educational phase of the project, a few things stand out strikingly:

1. The children are taught by remarkable teachers, each a master of his field and a master teacher.

2. Each teacher has a distinctive style; the styles are different, but there is a coherence to how each teacher carries out his plan of instruction.

3. All curricula (in chess, music, and I believe in mathematics as well, although I have had less experience in the latter field) recapitulate in some sense the history of the field. For example, in chess both masters guide their students through the games of all the world champions of chess, often going back 150 years.

4. The teachers are at least as passionate and committed to the field in which they work as are their pupils; they are also enormously dedicated teachers, reflective and vigilant about their instruction.

5. None of the teachers was a child prodigy himself.

There is much that these highly specialized teaching situations can tell us about teaching in general.

The psychological aspect of the research is intended to shed light on early prodigious achievement as a developmental phenomenon, while at the same time illuminating certain aspects of developmental processes in general. For this purpose, it is necessary first to show that early prodigious achievement is indeed developmental, sharing certain attributes with other developmental phenomena. The research project illustrates the point that early prodigious achievement is a developmental phenomenon, but not quite the kind of phenomenon that Piagetian theory would tend to suggest.

Some years ago Kluckhohn and Murray wrote: "Everyone is in certain respects (a) like all other men, (b) like some other men, and (c) like no other man."[13] These observations can be used as a point of departure from which to show how early prodigious achievement is (a) like all other developmental phenomena, (b) like some other developmental phenomena, and (c) like no other developmental phenomenon.

WAYS IN WHICH EARLY PRODIGIOUS ACHIEVEMENT IS LIKE ALL OTHER DEVELOPMENTAL PHENOMENA

The main way in which early prodigious achievement is akin to the Piagetian stages of intellectual development— and therefore like all other developmental changes—is that both are achieved through a sequence of broad levels of mastery. Piaget uses the term "development" (in contrast to "learning") to refer to those aspects of psychological change that occur spontaneously and take place in a universal sequence of hierarchically ordered stages or levels. The first two qualities—spontaneousness and universal achievement —are not necessary for bestowing the label "developmental," but these are two of the qualities that are central to Piaget's formulation.

The Piagetian universal sequences of developmental change are but one set of developmental phenomena, although a crucial set to be sure. There are numerous others. All regions of developmental change share certain properties with the Piagetian sequences but are distinct in some ways as well.

Things that are typically referred to as "developmental" are things that all of us eventually acquire. One of the real contributions of developmental theory and research, in particular that of Piaget, has been to draw attention to those qualities that all human

13. Clyde Kluckhohn and Henry Murray, "Personality Formation: The Determinants," in *Personality: In Nature, Society, and Culture*, ed. Clyde Kluckhohn and Henry Murray (New York: Alfred A. Knopf, 1948), p. 53.

beings share. The central premise of my way qf viewing early prodigious achievement is that it, too, is developmental, despite the fact that few persons will experience the incredible rapidity of achievement that is the hallmark of the prodigy.

The assumption that early prodigious achievement is developmental rests on the belief that the processes of transformation and change in early prodigious achievement are analogous to processes of transformation and change in more universal and inevitable aspects of human behavior. That is, in early prodigious achievement all the qualities of the more usual developmental changes are seen except for these two. As noted above, there is nothing universal about early prodigious achievement. (This is obvious enough, since the phenomenon is so strikingly different from more typical trajectories of mastery in a field.) And, the achievement of precocious mastery is not "spontaneous" in the sense that Piaget tends to use the term. Early prodigious achievement will not occur in the absence of specialized resources and intensive efforts on the part of master instructors in the field, that is, without education.

WAYS IN WHICH EARLY PRODIGIOUS ACHIEVEMENT IS LIKE SOME DEVELOPMENTAL PHENOMENA

Early prodigious achievement is not inevitable, to say the least, nor does it occur spontaneously. Perhaps some would want to dispute the second point; Mozart is often cited as a case of genius without instruction. To see a child of nine or ten years composing pieces that defy formal distinction from a mature composer's works is indeed awe inspiring. But these works did not spring from the mind of the child without extensive preparation and intensive instruction; even Mozart grew up in a home where music was played, discussed, and perhaps even composed.

After many hours of observation with prodigious children and their teachers, one is struck by the tireless efforts that go into the acquisition of one's craft. To draw attention to the lack of spontaneousness in the achievements is not in any way to dilute the impressiveness of the talents of the children; they are staggering. But to attribute the achievements of these children solely to the natural gifts they possess is to ignore a crucial part of the process. Early prodigious achievement is therefore distinguished from more

universal developmental acquisitions in being a relatively rare occurrence that requires the catalytic efforts of specialized, more experienced individuals and the availability of a body of knowledge in
a form that can be readily communicated. Early prodigious achievement is most distinguished from other phenomena by how well
education works.

Developmental phenomena that are not universal and that require instruction can be given the label "cultural."[14] Examples are
map understanding, mathematics, music, art, and so forth. Early
prodigious achievement may be seen as a special occurrence within
a certain cultural developmental domain. It is cultural because early
prodigious achievement depends upon the existence of a culturally
evolved set of techniques for transmitting the principles and practices of the domain. It would have been unfortunate, for example,
for a chess player of Bobby Fischer's stature to have been born
before there were chess boards, chess pieces, and chess books. The
existence of a body of knowledge and a technology to transmit it
made possible Fischer's achievements in chess.

Thus, early prodigious achievement shares features with other
cultural developmental phenomena. It is certainly not universal,
yet it is an accomplishment that is not altogether unique either.
The level of mastery of the field is not unprecedented; it is the
speed of mastery that is so remarkable. Early prodigious achievement is also not spontaneous, and this too it shares with other cultural and developmental phenomena. The rapidity of accomplishment is indeed striking, and we shall consider this quality next, but
no matter how astounding the *relative* speed, it is still the case that
years of intense preparation are required for even the most talented
individuals to achieve distinction in their respective fields; creative
works, of course, generally take longer.

With regard to prodigious individuals themselves, those few
cases where psychological measures have been taken reveal that
even in extraordinary instances of early prodigious mastery, individuals share general developmental qualities with their age peers.
Early prodigious achievement, then, is like some other developmental achievements, namely cultural ones; likewise, individuals
who achieve remarkable mastery are in some respects develop-
mentally similar to other children their age.

14. Feldman, "Universal to Unique."

In 1976, a battery of four general developmental measures was administered to our three subjects—two eight-year-old chess players and a student of music composition who had just turned ten years of age. Our aim in this facet of the research was to assess the general developmental progress in cognition of each of these children in relation to his age peers. One other aspect, which is also pertinent to the "stage" notion, is the extent to which remarkable precocity generalizes across developmental domains. As with other aspects of the phenomenon, there is little empirical precedent to guide us. Most of the available information is anecdotal. The evidence from Baumgarten's research, while unsystematic by today's standards, seems to support the notion that early prodigious achievement represents a *reductio ad absurdum* of Piaget's notion of décalage: why this is the case is made clear by the pattern of our results.

The four measures given were (a) Piaget's five chemicals task, a test of the level of acquisition of various concrete and formal logical operations;[15] (b) a role-taking test devised by Flavell and associates at the University of Minnesota, the aim of which is to test social/cognitive development by assessing the level of ability to take another's point of view;[16] (c) a map-drawing exercise (an adaptation of Piaget and Inhelder's layout diagram task), which gives a general estimate of the level of the coordination of spatial/logical reasoning;[17] and (d) a psychometric measure of level of moral judgment and reasoning, prepared by Rest and based on Kohlberg's stages of moral development.[18] A summary of the results is given in table 1.

15. Barbel Inhelder and Jean Piaget, *The Growth of Logical Thinking from Childhood to Adolescence* (New York: Basic Books, 1958), pp. 105-122.

16. John H. Flavell, *The Development of Role-taking and Communication Skills in Children* (New York: John Wiley and Sons, 1968), 42-55.

17. Jean Piaget and Barbel Inhelder, *The Child's Conception of Space* (London: Routledge and Kegan Paul, 1956), first published in 1948; Samuel Snyder, David Feldman, and Cheryl LaRossa, "A Manual for the Administration and Scoring of a Piaget-based Map-drawing Exercise," in *Tests and Measurements in Child Development: A Handbook (II)*, ed. Orval Johnson (San Francisco: Jossey-Bass, 1976), pp. 268-69.

18. James Rest, "Manual for the Defining Issues Test: An Objective Test of Moral Judgment Development," mimeographed (Minneapolis, Minn.: University of Minnesota, 1974).

TABLE 1

SUMMARY OF DATA ON THREE PRODIGIOUS ACHIEVERS

TASK	COMPOSER AGE 10 YRS., 3 MO.	CHESS PLAYER AGE 8 YRS., 7 MO.	CHESS PLAYER AGE 8 YRS., 9 MO.
Map-drawing task: six levels between ages 7 and 19; 10- to 11-year-olds typically achieve Level 3.[a]	Modal Level, 3-4	Modal Level, 2-3	Modal Level, 2-3
Moral judgment task: six levels from age 10 to adult; Level 1-2 typically achieved by 10-year-olds and Level 3-4 typically achieved by 13-year-olds.[b]	Modal Level, 3	Modal Level, 3	Modal Level, 4
Role-taking task: three scorable levels and one nonscorable category (N). Level 1 typically achieved by 7- to 9-year-olds; Level 1-2 by 10- to 12-year-olds; Level 2-3 by 13- to 16-year-olds.[c]	Level 2	Level 1	Category N
Five chemicals task: Four levels from age 7 to adult. Level 1 typically achieved by 7- to 9-year-olds; Level 2 by 9- to 12-year-olds; Level 3 by 12- to 14-year olds; Level 4 by 14-year-olds and up.[d]	Early Level 3	Level 2	Early Level 2

NOTES:

a. Jean Piaget and Barbel Inhelder, *The Child's Conception of Space* (London: Routledge and Kegan Paul, 1956), first published in 1948; Samuel Snyder, David Feldman, and Cheryl LaRossa, "A Manual for the Administration and Scoring of a Piaget-based Map-drawing Exercise," in *Tests and Measurements in Child Development: A Handbook (II)*, ed. Orval Johnson (San Francisco, Calif.: Jossey-Bass, 1976), pp. 268-69.

b. James Rest, "Manual for the Defining Issues Test: An Objective Test of Moral Judgment Development," mimeographed (Minneapolis: University of Minnesota, 1974). This instrument was not designed for use with children younger than thirteen to fourteen years of age. It typically yields higher scores than are obtained from Kohlberg interviews.

c. John H. Flavell, *The Development of Role-taking and Communication Skills in Children* (New York: John Wiley and Sons, 1968), pp. 42-55.

d. Barbel Inhelder and Jean Piaget, *The Growth of Logical Thinking from Childhood to Adolescence* (New York: Basic Books, 1958), pp. 105-122.

Table 1 indicates that the three subjects all fell well within the usual range of performance for their age on each of the four measures. To be sure, these children are all very bright and do well in school; likewise, they do relatively well on the developmental measures we have administered. But in none of the general developmental regions was their progress remarkable in comparison with the extraordinary levels they have achieved in chess and music. In this respect, then, these individuals, who have shown extreme early prodigious achievement in the fields of chess and music composition, fall within the typical range of variation in general developmental levels of logic, role taking, spatial reasoning, and moral judgment.

Either the children were accelerated in their mental structures such that their thinking was generally advanced beyond their years, or their performance was remarkable in their fields through the un-usually facile use of, say, concrete operations. Otherwise, we are left to explain how acceleration could occur within a relatively limited region of thought while the child's general level of thinking seemed to remain age-appropriate.

From our preliminary results to date, it appears that the rate of transformation of structures for our subjects is highly domain-specific, yet it is hard to argue that the children were not using adult formal thought in their fields of accomplishment. Indeed, we chose these fields in part because there seemed to be as little ques-tion about the demands they make as any other fields we could think of. One problem, then, is to determine if early prodigious achievement represents a simple acceleration through the *same* levels of achievement in a field that any other individual would pass, or alternatively, if the child literally *skips* levels and enters at a more advanced point in the sequence. Indeed, is the sequence itself really as similar to the more typical sequence as it appears to be?

It should be noted that the cases described were chosen for their special talents in specific domains. This was done primarily to show that there are instances of precocity within a domain that are difficult, if not impossible, to explain within existing cognitive-developmental theories such as Piaget's. If a child's performance at chess, for example, is at a level that clearly utilizes formal opera-tional logic (Piaget's most advanced stage), then theory would require that the child have these mental processes available to solve at least some other problems. Furthermore, the theory posits that certain domains are more "resistant" to the application of various mental structures than others. If so, it follows that less resistant tasks should be solved earlier. Yet we know that our prodigies violate these principles. They perform in a highly resistant domain at an advanced level long before they do so in any other domain; also, their performance in general developmental domains is not markedly different from their age peers. Thus, they "violate" Piagetian theory by moving rapidly within a single domain that should be very resistant to mastery.

Although not looking for such individuals, we have encountered two or perhaps three cases of what are best labeled "all-purpose" prodigies. These individuals seem to be remarkably precocious across several domains. One child of eight is extremely advanced for his age in all natural sciences (including science fiction), music, geography, mathematics, and has vast general knowledge. Clearly this sort of child is much different from the "special purpose" prodigies who make up the bulk of our cases. The intellectual power of these all-purpose cases seems omnibus, and their presence is also characteristically more aversive to others. Such individuals are often perceived as arrogant, mechanical, technocratic, intense, erratic, peculiar, or bizarre. They represent a fascinating form of intelligence in their own right, but for the present purpose of our research, which is to examine developmental theory in terms of certain selected extreme cases, the all-purpose prodigy is of less interest because he is less discrepant from what theory would predict. These cases would not, for example, have caused sufficient problems with existing theory to require me to invent the idea of coincidence. Once invented, however, coincidence seems to account for both special and all-purpose prodigies more adequately than other available explanations.

EARLY PRODIGIOUS ACHIEVEMENT AS A UNIQUE DEVELOPMENTAL PHENOMENON

Whatever the resolutions to the above sorts of issues turn out to be, it should be clear that they are uniquely expressed in early prodigious achievement. For in no other phenomenon does the fact of the achievement itself seem to run so counter to our notions of general psychological transformation. How could it be that a child can not only comprehend and discuss, but can *produce* original compositions of the subtlety and complexity of a mature composer, yet find Piaget's five chemicals problem to be difficult to solve? And how can a chess player who regularly wins tournaments against mature adult players show moral judgment and reasoning typical for that of an eight- or nine-year-old child? It should be abundantly clear that early prodigious achievement represents a developmental phenomenon that has distinctive and unique qualities, qualities that may lead to some new insights about developmental processes in general.

We have taken so much care in showing how early prodigious

achievement bears resemblance to other developmental phenomena because these aspects of the phenomenon are less obvious. The folklore surrounding such legendary prodigies as Mozart, Francis Galton, and Norbert Weiner derives much of its impact from their ability to master a field and produce works of quality at a very early age. This is, to be sure, what is so compelling about prodigiousness. Now we turn to look at its full force, without trying to dilute the uniqueness of the achievement by drawing parallels and analogies to other developmental regions.

Our conceptualization of early prodigious achievement as coincidence points to the need to understand the reciprocal relations among intrinsic human talents, culturally evolved qualities of a field or craft or discipline, and traditions pertaining to the formal transmission of knowledge. To ignore one set of these factors is like watching a player piano: despite what it looks like, the piano does not play itself. Reciprocally, every great performer at the piano is playing *music*, which has a history of its own, and that performer is playing his music on an *instrument*, which has a history too. To understand achievement one must understand the joint histories of all the participants, and this is especially true where really remarkable achievement occurs.

Perhaps the most striking quality in the children in our study as well as other cases is the *passion* with which excellence is pursued. Commitment and tenacity and joy in achievement are perhaps the best signs that a coincidence has occurred among child, field, and moment in evolutionary time. No event is more likely to predict that a truly remarkable, creative contribution will eventually occur. Early prodigious achievement thus is related to creativity if in no other way than because precocious mastery provides more time and more opportunity for an individual to reach the limits of his craft, to confront the unknowns, to go beyond the frontiers of the discipline he has mastered. But one thing is clear. No matter how remarkable are the feats of child prodigies, these feats are not achieved without intensive, prolonged, *educational* assistance.

CHAPTER XXII

Unique Needs of the Creative Child and Adult

E. PAUL TORRANCE

Introduction

IMPORTANCE OF MEETING NEEDS OF CREATIVE PEOPLE

At the 1967 annual meeting of the National Association for Gifted Children, it was proposed that the creative gifted be designated as a new category in the field of Special Education or Exceptional Children.[1] In the light of developments since that time, this proposal will not seem as wild now as it did then. In the intervening years, the objectives of education, teaching methods, textbooks and other instructional materials, and the attitudes of society have all become more favorable to the creative child and adult.[2] The "creatively gifted" has become one of the categories of giftedness recognized by the Office of the Gifted and Talented of the U.S. Office of Education.[3] Several state departments of education have approved the use of creativity tests as one instrument for identifying gifted children for special programs supported by state funds.

In spite of this improved climate for creative children and adults, additional educational policies and practices are needed to meet the unique needs of creative people and many important problems

1. E. Paul Torrance, "Creativity Research and Its Implications for the Gifted," *Gifted Child Quarterly* 12 (1968): 67-68.

2. E. Paul Torrance, *What Research Says to the Classroom Teacher: Classroom Creativity* (Washington, D.C.: National Education Association, 1977).

3. Sidney Marland, Jr., *Education of the Gifted and Talented*, Report to the Congress of the United States by the U.S. Commissioner of Education. (Washington, D.C.: U.S. Government Printing Office, 1972), p. 2.

remain unsolved. Many educators still deny the existence of crea-tively gifted children and others continue to ignore altogether the creative functioning of the human mind. Some educators who iden-tify themselves as experts in the education of gifted children still believe that intelligence tests identify those who are potentially creative and that skills in creative thinking are not different from the rational and logical processes of high-IQ children. These issues will be dealt with later in this chapter.

The importance of giving a fair chance to creative children and adults has been emphasized by numerous eminent historians and other scholars. For example, Toynbee expressed alarm concerning the loss of creative talent. In 1964, he wrote: "To give a fair chance to creativity is a matter of life and death for any society." Further, Toynbee observed that creativity in a child can be discouraged easily and under hostile public opinion the creative child is ready to "purchase at almost any price the toleration that is an egalitarian-minded society's alluring reward for poor-spirited conformity." [4] He warned also that when creative ability is thwarted, it will not be extinguished but will take an antisocial turn. Seaborg, an eminent scientist, has also warned, "The success with which the United States meets the challenge of the future depends upon the extent to which exceptional talent is discovered and developed today."[5]

Some critics have contended that the ideas of Toynbee and Seaborg are elitist and cannot be tolerated in a democracy. In response to this criticism, Polak has maintained that throughout history, advances in civilization have been guided and spurred by the images of the future of its gifted and talented members. Our creatively gifted people, Polak has argued, will have to write in advance a considerable part of the history of the future. According to his studies, these images of the future have always been aristo-cratic in origin.[6]

4. Arnold Toynbee, "Is America Neglecting Her Creative Minority?" in *Widening Horizons in Creativity*, ed. C. W. Taylor (New York: John Wiley and Sons, 1964), p. 4.

5. Glenn T. Seaborg, "Training the Creative Scientist," *Science News Letter*, 83 (1963): 314.

6. Fred Polak, *The Image of the Future* (New York: Elsevier Scientific Publishing Co., 1973).

Educators have long been aware that throughout history the common characteristic of those who have made outstanding scientific breakthroughs, great artistic contributions, and social improvements has been their creativity. Today, however, there are additional reasons why it is necessary to give a fair chance to creative children and adults, even elderly adults. We are living in an age of increasing rates of change. Old and tested ways of solving problems are no longer adequate. Many of our natural resources have been exhausted and cannot be replaced. We have moved into a postindustrial society characterized by increased heterogeneity, interdependence, interaction, and destandardization.[7] All these changes will require increased use of creative problem solving and wise use of the special abilities of creative children and adults.

RATIONALE FOR ATTENDING TO THE UNIQUE NEEDS OF CREATIVE PEOPLE

The logic of making the creatively gifted a recognized category of exceptionality is clear and the existing supporting evidence is fairly strong. There are many creative children whose behavior problems stem from the differences between them and other children and between them and their teachers. We have just completed a study of alternative methods of administering the verbal creativity tests to children classified as behavior disordered, learning disabled, and/or emotionally disturbed. Under both the experimental and control conditions, these children in grades one through five scored significantly higher than the national or the local norms for children at their respective grade levels. Their learning difficulties arise from the incompatibility between their abilities and learning styles on one hand, and the teaching methods and system of rewards of the school on the other. If brought together with other creatively gifted youngsters and given a chance to use their unique abilities, they would no longer be misfits. If taught in ways compatible with their abilities and interests, their school achievement might soar and their behavior problems disappear.

Many educators have argued that the creatively gifted child and adult are well endowed and no additional policies and practices are

7. Daniel Bell, *The Coming of Post-Industrial Society* (New York: Basic Books, 1973).

needed. They have generally believed that creative children and adults who do not succeed are morally delinquent and should be punished. Apparently, such people have been blinded to the countless tragedies of highly creative children and adults who have been completely powerless to help themselves and are the objects of hate and aggression. It is true that we should not give creative children and adults "something for nothing," but it is important to "give them a chance to work for it."

Evidence concerning this problem is quite varied. My correspondence files are loaded with letters from creative adolescents and adults and parents of creative children. Some of them are still pleading for "a chance to work for it," while others have surrendered hope for such a chance. I have learned a great deal from encounters with creative children and adults. The evidence from the biographies and autobiographies of eminent creative persons is rich and emotionally moving. Hard-nosed scientists, however, reject such evidence.

There is considerable evidence that in present-day schools and colleges, the creative child and adult *are* handicapped. For example, Dever found that fourth-grade pupils on the honor roll achieved lower scores on tests of creativity than did their peers not on the honor roll.[8] Anderson found that freshmen in honors programs scored lower than their peers on tests of creative thinking ability.[9] Gotkin and Massa found that creatively gifted fourth- and fifth-grade children were handicapped in learning certain types of programmed materials in language arts.[10] Macdonald and Raths and Stolurow showed that certain kinds of curriculum tasks, instructional procedures, and/or programmed instruction facilitate the

8. Wayman T. Dever, "The Relationship between the Creative Thinking Ability of Selected Fourth Graders and Parental Attitudes" (Doct. diss., North Texas State University, 1964).

9. Rodney E. Anderson, "A Comparison of the Performance of College Freshman Participants and Nonparticipants in an Honors Program on Four Psychological Measures" (Doct. diss., Colorado State University, Greeley, 1963).

10. Lassar G. Gotkin and Nicholas Massa, "Programmed Instruction and the Academically Gifted: The Effects of Creativity and Teacher Behavior on Programmed Instruction with Younger Learners" (Unpublished report, Center for Programmed Instruction, New York, 1963).

learning of creatively gifted youngsters more than that of their less creative peers, as identified by performances on creativity tests.[11] Curiously, the most commonly used procedures are just the opposite of the ones these investigators studied. Among black children in the third grade, Burke found a coefficient of correlation of −.20 between measures of self-concept and total scores on a battery of creativity tests.[12] Heist found that creative students tended to drop out of college at a higher rate than their less creative peers.[13]

ARE CHANGES IN POLICIES AND PRACTICES POSSIBLE?

The idea of changes in policies and practices to serve the unique needs of creative children and adults will probably seem too fantastic to most educators to be given support and implementation at the present time. Initially, support and implementation will have to come from individuals or agencies with the courage to take risks. Most educators will place the idea in the category of science fiction. In fact, a story that appeared in *Analog Science Fiction* magazine a few years ago gave an excellent picture of how a school for creatively gifted children might be established and operate with private funds and government approval.[14] The children in the school described in the *Analog* story were gifted in extrasensory perception(ESP). The teachers were also gifted and further trained in ESP. This was not known to the public, however, and the school was privately endowed. Public school psychologists and counselors referred to this school the children they could not "get through to," especially the kindergarteners they did not even wish to "get through to."

11. James B. Macdonald and James D. Raths, "Should We Group by Creative Abilities?" *Elementary School Journal* 65 (1964): 137-42; Lawrence M. Stolurow, "Social Impact of Programmed Instruction: Aptitudes and Abilities Revisited," in *Educational Technology*, ed. John P. DeCecco (New York: Holt, Rinehart and Winston, 1964), pp. 348-55.

12. Barbara P. Burke, "An Exploratory Study of the Relationships among Third-grade Negro Children's Self-Concepts, Creativity, and Intelligence and Teachers' Perceptions of Those Relationships," (Doct. diss., Wayne State University, 1968).

13. *The Creative College Student: An Unmet Challenge*, ed. Paul Heist (San Francisco, Calif.: Jossey-Bass, 1970).

14. Victor Foray, "Practice!" *Analog Science Fiction* 80 (February, 1968): 139-60.

The school for ESP-gifted children examined and accepted some of the children who were referred and rejected others. When pressed to explain the school's criteria for acceptance, the principal explained, "We take the children we can help." The children the school could help, of course, were the ESP-gifted. Their behavior problems usually came from the differences their ESP abilities created between them and other children. There were, of course, problems of accreditation and the *Analog* story revolves about a visit from the accrediting board appointed by the State Department of Education. All of the children cooperated to conceal the fact that the school was for ESP-gifted and used their ESP abilities to do so. One new pupil, however, slipped up and the faculty and other students were afraid that the visitors would "catch on." The visitors were completely blind to the display of ESP, and the children concluded that people lacking this sensitivity were so unaware of the ESP abilities of others that no efforts are necessary to hide such abilities.

While schools for creative children and adults similar to the school for ESP-gifted described in *Analog* may be in the realm of science fiction, a number of the needed policies and practices are entirely within the realm of reality. Some of these will now be identified.

Suggested Policies and Practices

IDENTIFYING CREATIVE CHILDREN AND ADULTS

Combining tests and observations. In the *Analog* story just mentioned, the ESP-gifted children were identified through a variety of tests and behavior observations. The analogy between the identification of ESP-giftedness and creative giftedness appears quite accurate. An occasional teacher is quite accurate in the identification of creatively gifted children. Statistically, such teachers are rare. Frequently the creatively gifted children of a classroom are relegated to a circle of "hopeless" children in the rear of the classroom to keep them out of the way and to prevent their disrupting things with their unusual ideas and questions. Or, such children may be found seated next to the teacher's desk for proximity control, standing in the corner, or waiting in the principal's office because of some imagined or real offense. More recently, we have found them in special programs for children with learning or behavior disorders. In numerous instances, identification of such children as creatively gifted through tests has changed a teacher's perception of them and consequently relationships to them. In some cases, this has been a turning point in a child's educational career. While tests of creative thinking abilities can be useful in helping teachers become aware of potentialities that might otherwise be ignored or even punished, a teacher need not be dependent upon tests for this purpose. At all educational levels, there are observable behaviors that mark a child as highly creative.

If a school's program provides learning activities that call for creative expression and creative problem solving, it is easy for the alert and sensitive teacher to observe behavior like the behavior identified by tests of creative thinking. For example, examine the following list of criteria used in evaluating responses to the figural battery of the *Torrance Tests of Creative Thinking:*

Fluency, the production of a large number of ideas
Originality, unusualness or uniqueness of ideas
Elaboration, making ideas communicate by working out the details
Abstractness of titles, verbally synthesizing elaborated drawings
Resistance to quick closure, maintaining an openness to new information and ideas to permit the emergence of original solutions
Expression of feelings and emotions through both verbal and nonverbal means
Articulateness in telling a story, communicating effectively
Movement and action communicated in drawings
Expressiveness of titles and labels
Synthesis of two or more elements
Unusual visual perspective
Internal visual perspective
Extending or breaking the boundaries of a completed form
Humor in titles, captions, and drawings
Richness of imagery (variety, vividness, strength, and so forth)
Colorfulness of imagery (excitingness, earthiness, strangeness).[15]

All of these characteristics tend to exist to a rather high degree in

15. E. Paul Torrance et al., *Research Edition: Streamlined Scoring and Interpretation Guide and Norms Manual for the Figural Forms of the Torrance Tests of Creative Thinking* (Athens, Ga.: Georgia Studies of Creative Behavior, Department of Educational Psychology, University of Georgia, 1977).

creative children and adults. All of them are important in outstanding creative achievements. All of them may be observed in school activities in almost any subject if the activities call for or permit creative expression and creative problem solving.

Most commonly used tests. Besides the *Torrance Tests of Creative Thinking* (TTCT),[16] *Thinking Creatively with Sounds and Words* (TCSW),[17] the *Thinking Creatively with Action and Movement* (TCAM),[18] the *Khatena-Torrance Creative Perception Inventory* (KTCPT),[19] and other instruments developed by the author and his associates, there are a variety of additional tests useful in helping teachers, psychologists, counselors, and parents become aware of creative talents that might otherwise be missed. These include Guilford's tests for children[20] and for adults,[21] Flanagan's *Ingenuity Test*,[22] Mednick's *Remote Associates Test*,[23] Wallach and Kogan's measures,[24] Starkweather's tests for young children,[25] and the like. These and other similar measures are described in a recent compendium by Biondi and Parnes.[26]

16. E. Paul Torrance, *Torrance Tests of Creative Thinking: Norms-Technical Manual* (Lexington, Mass.: Personnel Press, 1974).

17. Joe Khatena and E. Paul Torrance, *Thinking Creatively with Sounds and Words: Norms-Technical Manual* (Lexington, Mass.: Personnel Press, 1973).

18. E. Paul Torrance and Suzann Gibbs, *Thinking Creatively with Action and Movement* (Athens, Ga.: Georgia Studies of Creative Behavior, Department of Educational Psychology, University of Georgia, 1977).

19. Joe Khatena and E. Paul Torrance, *Manual for Khatena-Torrance Creative Perception Inventory* (Chicago, Ill.: Stoelting Co., 1976).

20. Joy P. Guilford, *Creativity Tests for Children: A Manual of Interpretation* (Orange, Calif.: Sheridan Psychological Services, 1971).

21. Joy P. Guilford et al., *Structure of Intellect Tests.* (Orange, Calif.: Sheridan Psychological Services, 1971).

22. John Flanagan, *Ingenuity Test* (Chicago: Science Research Associates, 1957).

23. Sarnoff A. Mednick, *The Remote Associates Test* (Boston: Houghton Mifflin, 1967).

24. Michael A. Wallach and Nathan Kogan, *Modes of Thinking in Young Children* (New York: Holt, Rinehart and Winston, 1965).

25. Elizabeth K. Starkweather, "Creativity Research Instruments Designed for Use with Preschool Children," in *Assessing Creative Growth: The Tests—Book One,* ed. Angelo M. Biondi and Sidney J. Parnes (Great Neck, N.Y.: Creative Synergetic Associates, 1976).

26. *Assessing Creative Growth,* ed. Biondi and Parnes.

"Creativity tests" tend to be of two types—those that involve cognitive-affective skills such as the *Torrance Tests of Creative Thinking*, Guilford's tests, and the *Remote Associates Test* and those that attempt to tap a personality syndrome such as the *Alpha Biographical Inventory*,[27] Welsh's *Figure Preference Test*,[28] and the *Khatena-Torrance Creative Perception Inventory*. Some educators and psychologists have tried to make an issue of whether creativity is essentially a personality syndrome that includes openness to experience, adventuresomeness, and self-confidence and whether the cognitive processes of rational and logical thinking in creative thinking are precisely the same as those used by high-IQ children.

The research evidence and my experience strongly indicate that neither of these arguments is entirely true. Of course, creativity involves personality characteristics such as openness to experience, adventuresomeness, and self-confidence. But it involves more than this. There must also be the necessary skills, motivations, facilitating conditions, and the like. One of our studies attests to this in a small measure.[29] When I found that the women in one of my long-range prediction studies were less predictable than the men, we obtained responses to the *Alpha Biographical Inventory* from the women. We combined a creativity index derived in 1959 with the creativity index obtained from the *Alpha Biographical* and the canonical correlation rose to .60. Using the *Alpha* score alone, the mean validity coefficient for this sample (N = 45) was .15; the mean validity coefficient for the creativity test was .38.

There are usually statistically significant relationships between the "ability" and "personality" or "motivation" variables, since people are motivated most to do the things they do best. It is erroneous, however, to assume that they are "the same thing." For example, the correlation between the creativity score of the *Alpha Biographical* creativity score and scores derived from the *Torrance*

27. Calvin W. Taylor and Robert L. Ellison, *Alpha Biographical Inventory* (Salt Lake City, Utah: Institute for Behavioral Research, 1966).

28. George S. Welsh, *Creativity and Intelligence: A Personality Approach* (Chapel Hill, N.C.: Institute for Research in Social Science, 1975).

29. E. Paul Torrance, Catherine B. Bruch, and Jean A. Morse, "Improving Predictions of the Adult Creative Achievement of Gifted Girls by Using Autobiographical Information," *Gifted Child Quarterly* 17 (1973): 91-95.

Tests of Creative Thinking is only .16. Yet they combine to yield a coefficient of .60 to predict the real-life creative achievements of this sample of women tested for creative thinking twelve years earlier.

A failure to accept the multivariate nature of the TTCT and distinctions between "creative thinking abilities" and "creative personality" characteristics has produced needless confusion. For example, the most frequently quoted study to invalidate the TTCT is one by Harvey et al.[30] First, they found that the TTCT was not univariate. They failed to note that the test tasks of these batteries were selected for their factorial differences rather than their factorial similarities. It was required only that they be significantly related to the criteria of creative behavior. They sought to invalidate the TTCT with a group of sixty-four educators (male and female) against criterion measures of such personality variables as supernaturalism, moral relativism, dictation of classroom procedures, need for structure-order, dogmatism, authoritarianism, curricular traditionalism, disciplinarianism, encouragement of student exploration, concreteness-abstractness of beliefs, and belief system classification. Even though this involved the correlation of ability and personality variables, some of which are theoretically unrelated to creativity, they obtained significant positive relationships between the creativity measures and moral relativism, fostering student independence, and fostering exploration, and significant negative relationships between the creativity measures and supernaturalism, dictation of classroom procedures, and need for structure-order. This is precisely what I would predict, yet this study is cited frequently as evidence of the invalidity of the TTCT.

It also seems obvious that the rational and logical processes involved in intelligence tests are called into play in the process of creative thinking, especially in evaluating alternatives, making decisions, and the like. The accumulated evidence, however, indicates that creative thinking requires much more than this. In fact, the emotional and nonrational or suprarational seem to be more important than the rational and logical in the essentially creative act of producing breakthrough ideas. Of course, once the "break-

30. O. J. Harvey et al., "A Partial Evaluation of Torrance's Tests of Creativity," *American Educational Research Journal* 7 (1970): 359-72.

through" has occurred, the ideas must stand the tests of rational and logical thinking. The work of Gordon, of de Bono, and of Silvano Arieti, among others, argues strongly for this position.[31]

The creativity-intelligence distinction. Numerous writers have created confusion in attempts to distinguish clearly between intelligence and creativity. Since it takes some intelligence to behave creatively and it takes some creativity to behave intelligently, this is a futile task. There are, however, important differences. Wallach has made an issue of the fact that the *Torrance Tests of Creative Thinking* are not clearly distinguished from intelligence tests and asserts that the TTCT is only another intelligence test.[32] I have never tried to make a clear-cut distinction between intelligence and creativity, as separate variables. Rather, I have insisted that they are interacting variables and that trying to force clear distinctions would create false distinctions that do not exist in real life. Almost every description of the creative problem-solving process emphasizes the necessity for both kinds of thinking processes.[33]

Although thousands of coefficients of correlation have been reported between measures derived from the TTCT and measures of intelligence, many critics select only those correlation coefficients that satisfy their biases, rather than looking at the larger picture. In 1967, I summarized a total of 388 such correlations from dissertations and published studies. The median of 114 coefficients of correlation involving figural measures was .06; for the 88 correlations involving verbal measures, the median was .21; and for the 178 correlations involving both verbal and figural measures combined, the median was .20.[34]

31. William J. J. Gordon, *Synectics* (New York: Harper and Row, 1961); Edward de Bono, *Lateral Thinking: Creativity Step by Step* (New York: Harper and Row, 1970); Silvano Arieti, *Creativity: The Magic Synthesis* (New York: Basic Books, 1976).

32. Michael A. Wallach, "Review of Torrance Tests of Creative Thinking," *American Educational Research Journal* 5 (1968): 272-81.

33. Joy P. Guilford, *Way beyond the IQ* (Buffalo, N.Y.: Creative Education Foundation, 1977); Sidney J. Parnes, Ruth B. Noller, and Angelo M. Biondi, *Guide to Creative Action* (New York: Charles Scribner's 1977).

34. E. Paul Torrance, "The Minnesota Studies of Creative Behavior: National and International Extensions," *Journal of Creative Behavior* 1 (1967): 137-54.

The degree of differentiation between the TTCT and measures of intelligence is best described by a generalization of mine that was criticized by McNemar in his 1965 presidential address before the American Psychological Association in the following terms:

The argument against the IQ is now being reinforced by the claim that the selection of the top 20 percent on IQ would mean the exclusion of 70 percent of the top 20 percent on tested creativity. This startling statistic, which implies a correlation of only .24 between IQ and creativity, is being used to advocate the use of creativity tests for identifying the gifted.[35]

The correlations in the samples from which this generalization was derived were in fact somewhat less than .24. In none of these discussions back in the early 1960s was there any advocacy on my part for replacing measures of intelligence with measures of creativity. The plea was to consider a wider range of abilities both in identification and in program development.

Perhaps the most serious oversight of those critics who maintain that there is no distinction between creativity and intelligence or between the abilities assessed by the TTCT and measures of intelligence is a failure to recognize the differences in the ways scores on the two kinds of measures behave. A few of these will be reviewed here.

Lack of racial and socioeconomic bias. Whether one agrees or disagrees with the conclusions of Jensen and others on matters of intelligence, race, and socioeconomic status, the fact remains that there are racial and socioeconomic differences in measured intelligence.[36] Elsewhere I have summarized the results of twenty studies conducted in different sections of the United States to study racial and/or socioeconomic status differences on the TTCT.[37] In some of these studies, there were no racial or socioeconomic differences on either the verbal or figural test (TTCT). In others, blacks ex-

35. Quinn McNemar, "Lost: Our Intelligence? Why?" *American Psychologist* 19 (1964): 871-82.

36. Arthur R. Jensen, "How Much Can We Boost IQ and Scholastic Achievement?" *Harvard Educational Review* 39 (1969): 1-123.

37. E. Paul Torrance, *Discovery and Nurturance of Giftedness in the Culturally Different* (Reston, Va.: Council for Exceptional Children, 1977).

celled whites on certain tasks and whites excelled blacks on others. The same was true where socioeconomic differences were studied. Overall, there were no racial nor socioeconomic differences on the TTCT. This is not true of intelligence tests.

Heritability of creative thinking abilities. A study by Pezzullo, Thorsen, and Madaus found no evidence of hereditary variation in either the figural or verbal forms of the TTCT. Their carefully tested subjects were thirty-seven pairs of fraternal and twenty-eight pairs of identical twins. These investigators found that short-term memory (Jensen's Level I abilities) has only a moderate index of heritability, .54; the general intellective factor (Jensen's Level II abilities) has a relatively high index of heritability, .85. The heritability index for the figural and verbal measures of the TTCT approached zero.[38] Another twin study by Richmond similarly found no evidence of heritability for the abilities assessed by the TTCT.[39] Using the Getzels and Jackson measures, Davenport did not find weak evidence for heritability on most of these measures of creativity.[40] The indications were so weak, however, that Davenport concluded that there was a wide margin in which experience could influence the creative thinking abilities.

Validity of creativity tests. Despite enormous amounts of validity evidence produced during the past twenty years, educators and psychologists still debate the validity of creativity tests. The most recent bibliography on the *Torrance Tests of Creative Thinking* lists 984 items, a majority of which bear upon the validity of this one set of tests.[41]

38. Thomas R. Pezzullo, Eric E. Thorsen, and George F. Madaus, "The Heritability of Jensen's Level I and II and Divergent Thinking," *American Educational Research Journal* 9 (1972): 539-46.

39. Bert O. Richmond, "Creativity in Monozygotic and Dizygotic Twins" (Paper presented at the annual meeting of the American Personnel and Guidance Association, Detroit, Mich., April, 1968.)

40. John D. Davenport, "A Study of Monozygotic and Dizygotic Twins and Siblings on Measures of Scholastic Aptitude, Creativity, Achievement Motivation, and Academic Achievement" (Doct. diss., University of Maryland, 1968); Jacob W. Getzels and Philip W. Jackson, *Creativity and Intelligence* (New York: John Wiley and Sons, 1962).

41. Suzann Gibbs, E. Paul Torrance, and Orlow Ball, *Cumulative Bibliography on the Torrance Tests of Creative Thinking* (Athens, Ga.: Georgia Studies of Creative Behavior, University of Georgia, 1977).

Wallach has contended that "tests tell us little about talent." He and others have argued that although measures of academic skills are widely used to determine access to contested educational opportunities, they lack utility, especially in their upper ranges, for predicting real-life professional achievement. This has perhaps been the most persistent criticism of creativity tests, that is, that there is no evidence of a link between performance on test tasks and real-life achievement.[42] In 1972, I reviewed thirteen predictive validity studies of the TTCT that link test performance with real-life creative achievements. In a long-range predictive validity study involving 256 high school students (grades seven to twelve) tested in 1959 and followed up in 1971, the following canonical correlations were found: for men, .59; for women, .46; and for the total group, .51.[43] From the results of this twelve-year follow-up study and an earlier seven-year follow-up study of the class of 1960, the following conclusions seem justified:

1. Young people identified as creative on the basis of creativity tests during the high-school years tend to become productive, creative adults.

2. At least twelve years after graduation from high school appears to be a more advantageous time than seven years as the time for a follow-up of creative adults.

3. The unusual occupations expressed as choices by highly creative high-school students tend to become realities.

4. Highly creative high-school students tend to develop careers that involve detours for relevant but unusual combinations of training and/or experience. A larger proportion of them include study or work in foreign countries as a part of their career development than do their less creative peers.

5. Creative achievements in writing, science, medicine, and leadership are more easily predicted by creativity tests administered in high school than are creative achievements in music, the visual arts, business, and industry.

6. More frequently than their less creative peers, young adults

42. Michael A. Wallach, "Tests Tell Us Little about Talent," *American Scientist* 64 (1976): 57-63.

43. E. Paul Torrance, "Predictive Validity of the Torrance Tests of Creative Thinking," *Journal of Creative Behavior* 6 (1972): 236-52.

identified as highly creative in high school attained peak creative achievements in writing, medical and surgical discovery, dissertation research, musical composition, style of teaching, human relations and organization.[44]

Trends in the use of creativity tests in gifted education. As creative giftedness is beginning to be accepted by a few educators as a legitimate category of giftedness and as validity evidence has accumulated, educators are beginning to feel more comfortable with policies and practices involving creativity tests. Tests should never replace alert and sensitive observation of creative behavior and awareness of creative products and other creative achievements as indicators of creative giftedness. Tests *can* help, however, in making educators aware of creative potentialities that might otherwise go unrecognized and unacknowledged.

A variety of procedures are being used regarding the function of the *Torrance Tests of Creative Thinking* in the selection of students for participation in special programs for gifted and talented students. Some programs have relied entirely upon measures derived from the TTCT to select participants. Most programs, however, seem to use multiple criteria and use the TTCT along with measures of intelligence, achievement on tests, life achievements, demonstrations of special talents in the arts, and the like. For example, one very large school system used the figural form of the TTCT to supplement the use of a group intelligence test. Students in grades three through eight were administered a group intelligence test. Those who achieved an IQ in excess of 130 were placed in the special program. Those with an IQ between 115 and 130 were then administered the figural form of the TTCT. The new streamlined scoring procedure yields a Creativity Index in addition to a variety of indicators of creative strength. These data were then used to select an additional number of gifted and talented students.

PROVIDING A REFUGE SOMEWHERE IN THE SYSTEM

Creative children and adults are under a great deal of stress. The very fact that an original idea always places the originator in a

44. E. Paul Torrance, "Career Patterns and Peak Creative Achievements of Creative High School Students 12 Years Later," *Gifted Child Quarterly* 16 (1972): 75-88.

minority of one, at least for a time, is itself stressful. Creative children and adults must be able to find a refuge from these stresses somewhere in the system. Because of the teacher's social role, teachers may not be able to supply such a refuge. To survive, however, the creative child or adult must have such a refuge. Society is still harsh in its treatment of creative persons, especially children. Almost inescapably, the creative child will come into conflict with the "authorities" in the system or establishment. He will experience frustration and must have a source of encouragement and support. He must have a right to fail without being ostracized or ruined. Even though teachers may be unable to provide this refuge, they can listen and they can help the creative child find such a refuge. There is a need in our society for identified agents who can serve this function. Perhaps it will have to start with volunteers.

PROVIDING SPONSORS OR PATRONS

Policies and practices should be developed to help creative children and adults find sponsors and patrons. Such help is particularly critical if the creative person's family does not understand and encourage his creativity. It has been noted frequently that wherever creativity has occurred and has persisted, there has always been some sponsor or patron who had arranged for the creative person to "get a chance." Providing such sponsors and patrons seems to be especially critical in helping creative gifted persons in disadvantaged and culturally different groups.[45] It has been demonstrated that it is possible to mobilize community resources to provide this kind of sponsorship in the development of creative talents.

RECOGNIZING AND ACKNOWLEDGING CREATIVE GIFTEDNESS

There is a critical need for policies and practices that provide for the recognition and acknowledgement of creative giftedness. This conviction has been important in my pioneering interscholastic competition in Future Problem Solving,[46] scenario writing con-

45. E. Paul Torrance, *Discovering and Using the Strengths of the Disadvantaged and Culturally Different in Career Education* (Athens, Ga.: Career Education Project, College of Education, University of Georgia, 1976).

46. E. Paul Torrance, Catherine B. Bruch, and J. Pansy Torrance, "Interscholastic Futuristic Problem-Solving," *Journal of Creative Behavior* 10 (1976): 117-125.

tests,[47] and the like. Many of the creative children who have won recognition through these activities had never gained recognition for excellence previously. Such recognition does not have to be public, however. It may be much more subtle and still have a powerful influence, as illustrated in the account of John, a notorious vandal in one elementary school.[48]

John was a muscular, overgrown boy in the sixth grade. Everyone knew that he was the ringleader of the vandals who left the school building a wreck every weekend and sometimes more frequently. His sixth-grade teacher recognized that John was a veritable genius at things mechanical, in art, and in organizing other boys to accomplish some rather remarkable things, many of which were rather undesirable. This teacher believed that John misbehaved because he was rejected and ridiculed and he felt that he did not belong. She believed that somehow his giftedness should be recognized and used. She arranged with the student council to have John appointed as chairman of the lunchroom committee. John organized his committee of boys to help the janitor move tables, clean up, and manage the lunchroom.

Soon John and "his boys" noticed other things about the school that needed improving, like the trash that collected in certain corners. They managed without a hitch the parking for "Back to School Night" and did many other excellent things that served the entire school. It was rumored that John had threatened to "take care of" anyone who destroyed or damaged school property. The vandalism ceased. More important, John began liking school, learned to read, and excelled in art work. All of this occurred because a teacher was able to see this boy's creative talents through the smokescreen of his vandalism, misbehavior, and inability to read.

It is possible to recognize and acknowledge creative excellence in writing, dance, art, music, science, school improvement, and many other ways. There is also a need to search for other, more

47. E. Paul Torrance, "Career Education and the Gifted and Talented: Images of the Future" (Paper presented at the Commissioner's National Conference on Career Education, Houston, Texas, November 9, 1976).

48. E. Paul Torrance and Robert E. Myers, *Creative Learning and Teaching* (New York: Harper and Row, 1971).

deliberate and widespread ways such as our Future Problem Solving Bowls, scenario contests, and the like.

HELPING CREATIVE PEOPLE UNDERSTAND THEIR CREATIVITY

Perhaps one of the most important ways that creative children and adults can be helped is in understanding and accepting their divergence—their sensitivity, their capacity to be disturbed, their tendency to become involved and committed, and their tendency to seek new and original solutions. This is especially important with creative people who tend to get into difficulties because of some nonconformity. As Menninger points out in *The Crime of Punishment*, all of us suffer more or less from infringement upon our personal freedom.[49] No one truly has complete freedom, but restrictions irk us. Since the creative person experiences more of these restrictions than his less creative counterparts, he is also likely to feel irked more frequently and intensely than others. Since engaging in active behavior to change a situation helps him to feel less helpless, he engages more frequently than others in this behavior. The creative person needs help in recognizing that his actions aggravate rather than relieve his actual state of helplessness.

Teachers and school psychologists must recognize that certain kinds of misbehavior are exciting to creative children. For example, humor is one of their favorite outlets and one of their favorite weapons. Under restrictive and dull teaching, misbehavior of various kinds, as well as humor, offers possibilities for excitement in an otherwise dull, monotonous, dreary, and despairing existence. The challenge is to engage creative people in difficult, exciting, and worthwhile undertakings.

COMMUNICATING IN ACCEPTABLE WAYS

Policies and practices in dealing with creative children and adults should provide opportunities for them to express themselves and communicate their ideas in legitimate, acceptable ways. If teachers and community workers at all levels were more practiced and skilled in listening to people, it might not be necessary for them

49. Karl Menninger, *The Crime of Punishment* (New York: Viking Press, 1968).

to riot, protest, destroy, or alienate themselves from society. In his *Psychiatry and the Dilemmas of Crime*, Halleck maintained that the future criminal is usually a person who has little chance to use his creative abilities in socially acceptable ways and that planning an illegal act provides a way of using this potentiality.[50] The curriculum at any educational level or in any subject has possibilities for providing creative persons exciting and rewarding outlets. The need to communicate creative ideas and discoveries seems to be a natural and strong need and is especially powerful in creative children and adults. If our institutions stress only the receptive nature of mankind and not his self-acting nature, opportunities for communicating creative ideas and discoveries will not be available.

MAKING RESOURCES AVAILABLE

Schools cannot provide all of the needed resources for creative children and adults. Frequently, the needed resources may not even be available in the community. Thus policies and practices are needed at all levels—community, city, county, regional, national, and international—that facilitate access to the resources needed by creative children and adults.

It is important that creative children be able to hold onto their motivations for learning the rest of their lives. Librarians in the school and the public library can be helpful in developing skills for finding out and in sustaining motivation. The motivations of creative children are such that they easily acquire sophisticated skills and concepts for doing research. Teachers not possessing these skills and concepts need to help such children find someone who can teach them how to do research. The generosity of outstanding scholars, business men, industrial researchers, and others in teaching children how to do research is generally amazing.

Some of the needs of creative children in regular school programs may be met by organizing creative writing clubs, creative dramatics groups, science clubs, Junior Great Books Clubs, and other special interest groups initiated by children. Similar kinds of needs may be met by communities by providing the facilities wherein such activities can be organized by elderly creative per-

50. Seymour Halleck, *Psychiatry and the Dilemmas of Crime* (New York: Harper and Row, 1967).

sons. Furthermore, creative senior citizen groups are a rich resource for teaching creative children. Policies and practices, however, must be such that the mobilization of resources is possible.

Conclusion

An obvious but powerful guiding principle in designing policies and practices to meet the unique needs of creative children and adults is that people are motivated most to do the things that they do best. Since creative people have their greatest strength in their creative abilities, they are motivated to learn in creative ways, to solve problems in creative ways, and to live in creative ways. Whatever policies and practices are developed should facilitate such creative ways of behaving.

CHAPTER XXIII

From Art Student to Fine Artist: Potential, Problem Finding, and Performance

JACOB W. GETZELS

Thousands of gifted young people aspire to become graphic artists; they enroll in hundreds of specialized schools of art, to say nothing of departments of art in colleges and universities. In many ways, these are the most disregarded students. Little is known about their demographic or psychological characteristics. Even less is known about their motivation for entering the field of art. Almost nothing is known about the grounds on which they choose to apply their talent to one specialization as against another—more specifically, to fine art, with its strenuous demands and uncertain rewards, as against, say, advertising or industrial art, or art education.

Since most students of fine art never become professional fine artists, they raise in concrete terms the most critical issues regarding gifted potential and gifted performance. What are the social circumstances that stand between the possession of a talent and its successful expression, and what are the personal characteristics of the students who succeed in becoming fine artists as compared with those who fail?

There is the related issue. Advertising and industrial artists typically work on problems that are assigned to them, problems often as specific as making an illustration for a cornflake box, for example. Fine artists typically work on problems of their own choosing, problems they themselves must find and formulate. What, then, are the sources of the problems they work on, and what is the relation between the quality of the problems and the quality of the solutions?

Despite its neglect, the finding and formulating of problems may be the most crucial aspect of creative performance.[1] As Einstein said regarding creative achievement in science, and, as Henle pointed out,[2] the same principle may hold in art: "The formulation of a problem is often more essential than its solution. . . . To raise new questions, new possibilities, to regard old questions from a new angle, requires creative imagination and marks real advance in science."[3] Indeed, Wertheimer generalized the principle to all thinking. "The function of thinking," he wrote, "is not just solving an actual problem but discovering, envisaging, going into deeper questions. Often in great discoveries the most important thing is that a certain question is found."[4]

To raise issues of this sort is not to promise the answers. Yet such issues must be raised and pondered if understanding is to be gained regarding how superior potential—in this case, graphic talent—eventuates, or fails to eventuate, in superior performance.

In this chapter, these issues are considered by reference to a study of talented individuals from the time they enrolled in one of America's preeminent art schools to a half-dozen years after they were graduated.[5] The reference to one school carries with it the unavoidable disadvantage of possible lack of generalizability; it carries with it the counterbalancing advantage of the opportunity to observe the students in depth while they were in the school and

1. For a discussion of types of problems and their role in creative thinking and problem solving, see Jacob W. Getzels, "Creative Thinking, Problem Solving, and Instruction," in *Theories of Learning and Instruction*, ed. Ernest R. Hilgard, Sixty-third Yearbook of the National Society for the Study of Education, Part I (Chicago: University of Chicago Press, 1964), pp. 240-67; and Jacob W. Getzels and Mihaly Csikszentmihalyi, "Scientific Creativity," *Science Journal* 3 (1976): 80-84.

2. Mary Henle, "Fishing for Ideas," *American Psychologist* 30 (1975): 795-99.

3. Albert Einstein and Leopold Infeld, *The Evolution of Physics* (New York: Simon and Schuster, 1938), p. 92.

4. Max Wertheimer, *Productive Thinking* (New York: Harper and Row, 1945), p. 123.

5. Most of the citations will be to Jacob W. Getzels and Mihaly Csikszentmihalyi, *The Creative Vision: A Longitudinal Study of Problem Finding in Art* (New York: John Wiley and Sons, 1976), which is the fullest report of the work. Some of the data, however, are contained in journal articles, and citation will be to them where appropriate.

to continue the observations longitudinally—something that had not been attempted before—over a period of years after they left the school.

Cognitive, Perceptual, Personality, and Value Characteristics of Art Students

The setting for the initial observations, that is, before the longitudinal inquiry, was one of the most selective degree-granting art schools in the nation. The investigators obtained the cooperation of several hundred talented young artists preparing for careers in fine art, advertising art, industrial art, and art education. Of the 321 second and third year students, who were the target population, 266 took at least one of the three batteries of demographic and psychological instruments, and 179 (86 males, 93 females), who then formed the "core sample," completed all instruments. The school records containing course grades and teacher ratings of each student in originality and artistic potential were also available. The core sample did not vary from the total population in age, sex, field of specialization, course grades, or any other measures where comparison was possible.

The first notable set of observations was the performance of the art students compared with other students of the same age and sex on the intelligence, perceptual ability, values, and personality measures.[6] The art students were within the range of college norms on the two speed and power tests of intelligence that were given. Although there were some differences, it seemed clear that the abilities tapped by the usual cognitive measures were not a crucial factor distinguishing the students involved in artistic pursuits.

A characteristic that on a priori grounds ought to show a substantial difference between art students and others is perceptual ability, and in fact large differences in favor of the art students were observed on two instruments that were given—one a spatial visualization measure and the other not so much a measure of perceptual skill as of aesthetic perception or taste.

But the most striking observations were in the realm of values

6. The complete data from which the sample observations in this section are drawn are given in Getzels and Csikszentmihalyi, *The Creative Vision,* pp. 29-42.

and personality. The male and female art students differed significantly from the norms on four of the six values of the Allport-Vernon-Lindzey *Study of Values* and on ten of sixteen personality factors on Cattell's *Sixteen Personality Factors Questionnaire* (16 PF). On three of the values and six of the personality factors, the male and female art students differed from the norms in the same direction. That is, they had higher aesthetic and lower economic and social values, and they were more aloof, introspective, alienated, imaginative, self-sufficient, and experimental in outlook. These nine characteristics seemed to be a consistent dispositional pattern of both the male and female art students.

In addition to this general pattern, an important set of differences between the male and female future artists also appeared. The latter were significantly more dominant (said to be a "masculine" trait) than other women their age, while the former were significantly more sensitive (said to be a "feminine" trait) than other men their age. That is, future artists possess traits that our culture traditionally associates with the opposite sex. This is not the place to enter into the ramifications of these observations. But it seems clear that artists, who must be able to express the broadest range of experience, tend to possess a fuller spectrum of human feelings and emotions than other individuals of the same age and sex.

Value and Personality Determinants of Artistic Specialization

Art schools, responsive to developments in technology and the demands of the market place, have institutionalized specialized training for different career lines. Students could enroll in the school serving as the locus of these observations in four curricula: fine art, advertising art, industrial art, and art education.[7]

The admissions officers, administrators, and teachers said that the students in the several curricula did not differ in graphic skills when they were admitted or during the first year of compulsory

7. Jacob W. Getzels and Mihaly Csikszentmihalyi, "The Value Orientations of Art Students as Determinants of Artistic Specialization and Creative Performance," *Studies in Art Education* 10 (1968): 5-16; idem, "On the Roles, Values, and Performance of Future Artists: A Conceptual and Empirical Exploration," *Sociological Quarterly* 9 (1968): 516-30; idem, *The Creative Vision*, pp. 46-53.

common courses. They further insisted that although they did not know the grounds on which the students differentiated themselves into the four curricula, it was not on the basis of technical skill or early training. But if the difference among the students in fine art, advertising art, industrial art, and art education did not lie in technical skill, achievement in the first-year common courses, or earlier training, in what did it lie?

When the performance of the four groups of students on the standard tests was compared, two salient results appeared. There were no differences on the cognitive or perceptual tests; there were profound differences on the values and personality tests.

Especially noteworthy was that despite the already extreme scores in aesthetic, economic, and social values, which differentiated the entire sample of art students from other students, these values also tended to differentiate the four groups of art students. Relative to the other groups, the fine art students had higher aesthetic and lower economic values, the advertising and industrial art students had higher economic and lower aesthetic values, and the art education students had lower economic and aesthetic values but higher social values.

The personality data provided a similar pattern.[8] Again, the between-group differences were all the more notable in view of the already extreme scores of the entire sample. Six of the 16PF personality factors showed significant variation by field of specialization. The difference between the fine art group and the other groups was especially notable. The mean scores of the fine art students were significantly different from at least one of the other groups in Factors A (sociability), G (super-ego strength), I (sensitivity), M (imaginativeness), N (shrewdness), and Q3 (self-sentiment). In other words, the future fine artists were less sociable, less conscientious, more imaginative, less worldly, and less conforming than other art students. In most cases, the advertising artists were at the other extreme on these traits for the sample as a whole.

Here, then, is one element—it is surely not the only one—in

8. Mihaly Csikszentmihalyi and Jacob W. Getzels, "The Personality of Young Artists: An Empirical and Theoretical Exploration," *British Journal of Psychology* 64 (1973): 91-104; see also Getzels and Csikszentmihalyi, *The Creative Vision*, pp. 46-53.

what might be involved in the choice of one artistic career over another. Personality dispositions and values affect how the young persons will choose to apply their graphic talent. Those who value social goals will tend to use their talent in a teaching capacity; those who value material and worldly goals will tend to use their talent in the more remunerative and conventional advertising and industrial capacities. Students who are characterized by the highest aesthetic values and imaginative dispositions will have the courage— or be driven by their values and dispositions—to risk specialization in fine art, where creativity is more encouraged for its own sake, but where material and social rewards are unpredictable and rare.

Student Characteristics and
Achievement in Art School

The first real test of whether an art student will become a professional artist is confronted in art school. To be sure, one can become a brilliant artist without a brilliant school record, or even without attending art school at all. Nevertheless, the hopes and prospects of those who do enroll in art school depend at least in part on their achievement there.[9]

The school records contained two measures of artistic achievement. One was the grade point average in studio courses. The other was a rating in overall originality and artistic potential. These ratings were made seriously, since they become part of the student's permanent record; they were not made merely for the purposes of the study. The intercorrelations among the measures were: between the first- and second-year ratings, .32 ($p < .001$) and between the cumulative studio grades and the ratings for each of the two years, .41 and .31 ($p < .001$)—relationships that were statistically reliable but indicative that the measures were far from redundant.

The relationships between the student characteristics and the criteria of achievement varied in the most striking ways depending on the sex and field of specialization of the students. For example, for the male students, twelve of the forty-five possible relationships between the 16PF personality factors (excluding Factor B, intelligence) and the three criteria of achievement were significant at

9. Getzels and Csikszentmihalyi, *The Creative Vision*, pp. 58-74.

the .05 level; for the females, not a single one was. Conversely, for the female students, five of the six possible relationships between the two main perceptual ability tests and the criteria of achievement were significant; for the males, none was. For the female students, six of a possible eighteen relationships between values and the three criteria of achievement were significant, three at the .05 level, two at the .01 level, one at the .001 level; for the female students, only two were significant, both at the .05 level.

A specific instance or two will illustrate the point concretely. For male students, the correlation between economic values and the three criteria of achievement were $-.32$ $(p < .01)$, $-.23$ $(p < .05)$, and $-.40$ $(p < .001)$; for female students the respective correlations were $-.03$, $.02$, and $-.04$. Conversely, for female students the correlation between perceptual memory (error) and the three criteria of achievement were $-.25$ $(p < .05)$, $-.36$ $(p < .01)$, and $-.33$ $(p < .01)$; for male students the respective correlations were $-.09$, $-.07$, and $.03$.

When the sample was further divided by field of specialization as well as by sex, additional significant relationships emerged and the magnitude of a number of the preceding relationships was increased. For example, the correlation between spatial visualization and studio grades for female advertising and industrial artists was now $.52$ $(p < .01)$; the correlation between economic values and studio grades for male fine art students was $-.47$ $(p < .01)$.[10]

It is not feasible within the limitations of space to enter here into any extended discussion of these observations. Suffice it to make the obvious comment: There are systematic relationships between the perceptual, value, and personality characteristics of art students and their achievement in art school—relationships, however, that vary by sex of the student and by field of specialization.

Problem Finding and Creative Performance

The preceding observations seemed to yield a reasonably consistent picture of how the personal characteristics of future artists differed from other individuals of the same age and sex, how their

10. Jacob W. Getzels and Mihaly Csikszentmihalyi, "The Study of Creativity in Future Artists: The Criterion Problem," in *Experience, Structure, and Adaptability*, ed. O. J. Harvey (New York: Springer, 1966), pp. 362-63.

characteristics were associated with the pursuit of different specializations in art, and how the characteristics were related to achievement in art school.

Yet, this was also true: the results had not provided much, if any, direct means of understanding, or even describing, creative production. Something more was known about the *correlates* of creative performance. But nothing much more was revealed about the *processes* of creative performance. There was the .47 correlation between certain values and creative performance, for example —a correlation almost as high as between intelligence and academic performance. But what does this say about the way in which the creative achievement was attained?

Instead of attempting to provide observations into how a work of art is created, which was the truly important issue, the work had conformed to the safer and more traditional paradigm of calculating correlations between personal characteristics and creative products. If one was to come to grips with the process of creativity in art, it was necessary to observe how an art object—say, a drawing or painting—was produced.[11]

The initial observations and conversations with the art students as they worked at their easels were fascinating; they were also bewildering. Some artists worked rapidly, others haltingly; one artist said he painted because it was the only thing he could do, another because he wanted to develop a new image of universal man. And nothing that was seen or heard was related to the quality of the product.

But this was also observed: A student in advertising or industrial art usually began with a specific assignment—a problem as specific as drawing an illustration for a cornflake box, for example; the student in fine art usually began with only a blank canvas before him—*he himself had to find or create the problem he was to work on.*

---

11. A detailed account of the procedures and results is given in Getzels and Csikszentmihalyi, *The Creative Vision*, pp. 83-137. See also Mihaly Csikszentmihalyi and Jacob W. Getzels, "Discovery-oriented Behavior and the Originality of Creative Products: A Study with Artists," *Journal of Personality and Social Psychology* 19 (1971): 47-52; Jacob W. Getzels and Mihaly Csikszentmihalyi, "Aesthetic Opinion: An Empirical Study," *Public Opinion Quarterly* 33 (1969): 34-45.

It became evident phenomenally as it had been averred conceptually—recall the statements by Einstein and Wertheimer—that problem finding was a crucial phase in the creative process, and that it was necessary to observe not only how an artistic problem is worked on, but, perhaps even more importantly, how the problem was, to use Wertheimer's term, *found*.

Methods for observing how a problem is solved are readily available. Typically, one administers one or more of the numerous problem-instruments devised for this purpose and draws inferences regarding the problem-solving process and ability from what the subject does and says. But suppose one wanted to observe how a problem is found—how an individual discovers, creates, formulates a problem? A way had to be devised to observe the phenomena of problem finding just as ways had been devised to observe the phenomena of problem solving.

Once this issue was formulated in these terms, the procedure that suggested itself was relatively straightforward. A studio at the art school was furnished with two tables, an easel, drawing board, paper, and a variety of dry media. On one table were placed twenty-seven still life objects collected from the studio classrooms. The thirty-one male fine art students were asked, one at a time, to compose a still-life problem on the second table, using as many objects from the first table as they needed, and then to make any drawing they wished of the still life. Despite the apparent artificiality of the situation, in the interview following the experiment, 72 percent stated that once they began working they felt no different than in the free-creative setting to which they were accustomed; 14 percent said they felt more like in the usual studio classroom setting; 14 percent said they felt some unusual constraint.

During the course of the work, an observer took notes of each artist's behavior—from composing the still-life problem to completing the actual drawing. It soon became evident that there were three readily identifiable categories of individual differences in the way the artists proceeded, even before they turned to the drawing.

One category was the number of objects handled; some artists handled as few as two of the twenty-seven objects, others as many as nineteen. The presumption then was that in order to discover an original problem rather than merely set up an already known or "canned" design, one had to consider a great number of possible stimuli. A second category was what the artists did with the objects. Some simply picked up the objects, took them to the second table, and began to draw. Other artists explored the objects; they rolled them in their hands, felt their texture, turned them upside down, and so on. The presumption was that in order to discover a more original problem, one not only had to consider more objects but to explore each object in greater depth. The third category was the uniqueness of the objects that were selected. Some artists seemed to seek out original objects, that is, objects few others chose; other artists seemed drawn only to the most popular objects, that is, objects many of the others also chose. An artist can, of course, create an original work with the most hackneyed of objects. But the presumption was that, other things equal, the more uncommon the objects, the more unique the problem was likely to be.

These three variables seemed to reflect, at least within the limits of the experiment, characteristic ways in which an artist approaches an unstructured aesthetic task. In normal practice, the artist does not touch and move objects about, but he still has to weigh visual stimuli, emotions, or ideas in his mind. The experimental assumption was that behavior, like handling, exploring, and choosing objects in this problem-finding situation, reflected mental operations in considering inner stimuli, just as the manifest behavior on the Vygotsky test, for example, is similarly taken to reflect mental operations in a problem-solving situation.

The procedure for examining the central issue, that is, the relation between the quality of the problem finding and the quality of the ensuing solution, the completed drawings, was quite simple. The ranking of the thirty-one artists on the quality of their problem finding was a composite of the three experimental measures—the relative number, depth of exploration, and uniqueness of objects. Needed next was a criterion for judging the quality of the drawings. No contemporary criterion for assessing a work of art is foolproof; only time is the ultimate arbiter, and even this verdict varies from generation to generation. Accordingly, the same procedure that galleries and museums use in the same circumstances was applied—recourse to an "expert jury."

The thirty-one experimental drawings were displayed as at an exhibit, and five artist-critics ranked the drawings on three dimensions: graphic skill or craftsmanship, originality, and overall aesthetic value. If a judge asked for a definition of the dimensions, he was told to define them as he would if he were judging an art show.

The composite ranking of the students in problem finding was correlated with the composite ranking of the drawings by the artist-critics on each of the dimensions. The results were as follows: for craftsmanship, the correlation was .28, not significant; for originality, it was .54, significant at the .005 level; for overall aesthetic value, it was .40, significant at the .025 level.

A word more needs to be said regarding the problem-finding variables in possible explanation of the results. The experimental conditions seem to have brought into the open a process that normally goes on undetected in the creative endeavor—a process described by Henry Moore in these words: "I sometimes begin drawing with no preconceived problem to solve, with only a desire to use pencil on paper and only make lines, tones and styles with no conscious aim. But as my mind takes in what is so produced a point arrives where some idea becomes conscious and crystallizes, and then a control and ordering begin to take place." [12]

What Moore is describing is the birth of a creative problem. Prior to its emergence there is no structure and no task. After the problem emerges, the skills of the artist take over; control and ordering begin. The crucial step is how the formless situation where there is no problem to resolve—for Moore only the idle lines, in the experiment only a bunch of objects—is transformed into a situation where a creative problem for solution emerges. For the formulation of a creative problem is the forerunner of a creative solution; it is perhaps not too much to say that from this point of view a creative solution is the response to a creative problem.[13]

The Social and Personal Context of Becoming a Fine Artist

After leaving school, the former students face the same task as other young people; they have to find a place for themselves in an

---

12. Henry Moore, "Notes on Sculpture," in *The Creative Process*, ed. Brewster Ghiselin (New York: Mentor, 1955), 73-78.

13. Getzels and Csikszentmihalyi, *The Creative Vision*, p. 4.

occupation. Other occupations provide more or less formalized ways of doing this. The steps to becoming a physician or engineer, or even plumber or bricklayer, are well marked. For other workers, there are hiring halls, employment agencies, civil service tests, help-wanted advertisements. There are institutions that not only facilitate entry into an occupation but also protect the interests of those already in it: professional associations, trade unions, political lobbies, and so on.

But what institutions can the young fine artist count on to help him establish and maintain occupational status? The obvious answer seems to be: none. It is absurd to think of a fine artist applying for a job. Indeed, can one think of a fine artist being out of work? He need only paint to be an artist.

In reality it is not as simple as that, for to become a professional artist it is not enough to paint for one's own delectation. One also wishes to "show" his work and has hopes that society will recognize and reward what he is doing. The ambiguity, if not absence, of the formal institutions does not mean that the artist is free of societal evaluation and legitimation.[14]

It may seem at first that the art school is a formal legitimizing institution. But it is so for a fine artist only in the most restricted sense. A degree in fine arts has little effect on the holder as a fine artist. The art school may increase artistic skills, but the certification it gives does not bestow artistic status in the sense that a school of law or medicine bestows legal or medical status.

A number of informal institutions have emerged that a would-be artist must ordinarily negotiate almost as rites of passage if he is to be recognized as an independent artist. There is the "loft," the various types of shows, acceptance by a gallery, notice by art critics, perhaps consistent patronage by a group of customers, and, who knows, finally with a break or two even purchase by a museum. From the vantage of the aspiring artist, these mechanisms for "making it" as an artist often engender the deepest contradictions and conflicts.

Take the first of the mechanisms—the loft—as an instance. The loft is a large room, often in a vacated factory. The stated purpose

14. See ibid., pp. 184-207, for a full discussion of the social and cultural dilemmas facing the young artist, on which the brief sketch here is based.

of the loft is to have plenty of space in which to work. But it has outgrown its initial utilitarian purpose and has become an important symbolic institution for launching young artists on their career.

When a person rents a loft, he is communicating the message that he is in earnest about becoming an artist. Since he cannot put an advertisement in a trade paper or hang out a shingle, for the message to be effective the young artist must spread the word himself; he invites to his loft other artists, prospective customers, art dealers, and anyone else who may be willing to come. The main need is for exposure, to be recognized as one who has committed himself to being an artist and is seriously at work. The loft is not just a physical space; it is an informal institution that allows the artist to get in touch with the public. A loft without parties and visitors, a loft that is not known in artistic circles, is not a *loft* in the institutional sense.

Although the loft, or its equivalent, has become almost an essential first step to certify the former art student's commitment as a fine artist, the requirement entails serious difficulties for the young artist. He is temperamentally withdrawn, introverted, sensitive, self-sufficient, and he holds the conventional economic and social values in low esteem. These values and traits are functional, since they make for tolerance and even enjoyment of the solitary and subjective condition under which works of art are created. But a loft requires the artist to be entrepreneurial and sociable, a salesman and master of ceremonies. It often demands behavior that is at odds with the most basic aspect of his character. And so, too, do many of the other modes that have evolved presumably to help art students become artists. Some of the students negotiate the difficulties, while others do not.

Virtually all developmental studies of artists have been retrospective, that is, carried out only after the artist has become worthy of biographical attention. But this method cannot answer such crucial questions as: Which, if any, of the art students would succeed or fail in their aspiration to become fine artists? Would their psychological characteristics and school performance be related to success or failure? Needed to answer questions of this order was what had hitherto been unavailable—a *longitudinal* study.[15]

15. Ibid., pp. 159-70.

Accordingly, five to six years after their graduation, an attempt was made to seek out the thirty-one former fine art students. It was impossible to locate seven of them, who may be considered no longer pursuing a career in art or at least are not visibly successful in it. Of the twenty-four former students who were located, eight had completely abandoned art as a career, seven were marginally involved, and nine had achieved various levels of success as fine artists. Several had shown their work in reputable galleries and competitive shows in Chicago and New York, and one, whose work had been bought by a leading museum, was by almost any contemporary criterion an eminent young artist. A relative success scale was constructed on the basis of ratings given by an art dealer with galleries in New York and Chicago, who knew eight of the artists, and a newspaper art critic, who knew seven (of whom four overlapped with those known by the art dealer), as well as the students' accomplishments as manifested by gallery shows, purchase by a museum, and the like.

There were idiosyncratic accidents and exigencies determining each artist's life and achievement that could not be reflected in the group data—for example, a personal event that turned one highly talented student from art to social action, a move in residence from one part of the country to another that unexpectedly caused a disconcerting change in another artist's palette.

But there were also a number of systematic relationships between the data collected while the artists were in school and their subsequent status. Several family background characteristics were related to success or failure. The successful artists came from families of higher socioeconomic position, where the father had higher education and the mother was employed outside the home; 62 percent of the mothers in the successful group as against 20 percent in the unsuccessful group ($p < .01$) were so employed. The largest difference was in sibling position—a difference at once remarkable and inexplicable. Thirteen, or 81 percent, of the successful artists were eldest sons; only five, or 33 percent, of the unsuccessful artists were eldest sons ($p < .01$). Fifty percent of the unsuccessful artists were middle sons; none of the successful ones was ($p < .001$).

Although the overall grade-point average in school was not related to subsequent status, when the grades were divided by studio courses and academic courses, significant relationships emerged. Students who had the best grades in studio courses tended to be the more successful artists ($p < .01$), but good grades in academic courses were related to failure rather than success as an artist ($p < .05$). The teacher ratings in originality and artistic potential given during the first year of school were also related to success ($p < .05$). The fit between the teachers' judgment in school and the students' accomplishment after school is surprising; in general, less of a relationship has typically been found between college grades and later occupational performance.[16]

But the most noteworthy observation was the relation between the problem-finding scores of the students in the pre-drawing stage of the experiment and their status as artists seven years after the experiment and five to six years after graduation. The correlation was .30, significant at the .05 level.[17] When the other two ratings of problem finding that were collected—that is, at the actual drawing stage and by interview—were added to the ratings at the pre-drawing stage, the correlation rose to .41, significant at the .01 level.[18]

Conclusion

Before turning to a concluding comment regarding the most provocative of the observations, that is, the apparent mediating role of what has been called "problem finding" between talented potential and creative performance, it is necessary to emphasize three caveats that may have been glossed over. First, problem finding and problem solving in creative thought are not as discontinuous as any necessarily schematic account may suggest. They meld into one another and the problem may be altered in the very act of its solution. Second, under ordinary circumstances, the artist does not manipulate and order objects; he manipulates and orders feelings and perceptions. In observing how a problem is found, it was assumed, as it had been in observing how a problem is solved, that

16. W. W. Willingham, "Predicting Success in Graduate Education," *Science* 183 (1974): 273-78.

17. Getzels and Csikszentmihalyi, *The Creative Vision*, p. 173.

18. *Ibid.*, p. 179.

the latent and manifest processes reflect one another to some degree. One should not extrapolate any implication that touching many objects, choosing unique objects, and so on "causes" originality. Third, despite the assurance of the majority of the artists that the experimental situation did not differ markedly from the usual situation in which they worked, it must not be forgotten that it was an experiment with unavoidable constraints.

Nonetheless, and despite these caveats, a number of tentative conclusions may be ventured, if only as hypotheses for further examination. Problem finding can be studied objectively; there are individual differences in problem finding as there are in problem solving; there is a positive relation between the quality of the problem finding and the quality of the ensuing solution.

More generally, finding and formulating a problem is an important aspect of creative performance in art as in science. Indeed, the orientation toward problems may be the essential difference between the scientist and the technician, the artist and the copyist. Surely, the difference between the scientist and the technician is not that the one is more technically proficient or better informed than the other, and the difference between the original artist and the copyist is not in raw graphic talent or craftsmanship per se. Rather, it seems that the one is content to apply his skill or talent in situations where the problem for solution is presented to him and the other is impelled to apply his skill and talent in situations where he himself discovers or creates the problem for solution; the latter's success depends not only on his craftsmanship but on the quality of the problems he "finds."

CHAPTER XXIV

Unique Needs of a Special Population

GWENDOLYN J. COOKE AND ALEXINIA Y. BALDWIN

While there is a dearth of research and writing on the gifted of the black population, black Americans have historically asserted that there are among them those whose talents and gifts should be identified and nurtured. Foremost among twentieth century advocates of this persuasion was W. E. B. DuBois. Although he articulated an educational philosophy proposing that all blacks should receive an education that would permit them to make their daily bread at an honest skilled job, DuBois's theory of the "Talented Tenth" more accurately became the heart of his philosophy. This theory in large measure establishes him as father of gifted education for blacks.

The theory posits that in the black race, as in all other races, there is a hereditarily controlled elite whose potential would blossom within the proper educational context.[1] The task then, as it is now, was to identify these talented persons and give them the best education available. It followed from the "Talented Tenth" theory that identifying and nurturing this talent would result in educated black leaders with the intellectual tools to set political, economic, and social goals of black liberation from poverty, social malaise, and educational deficit.

Several decades following DuBois's formal exposition of his theory, writings by various scholars noted the lack of development of black talent in communities throughout the country.[2] The

1. William E. B. DuBois, "The Talented Tenth," *The Negro Problem: A Series of Articles by Representative American Negroes of Today* (New York: James Pott Co., 1903), pp. 33-75.

2. Jonathan Kozol, *Death at an Early Age* (Boston: Houghton Mifflin, 1967); A. Harry Passow, "The Talented among the Disadvantaged," *Accent on Talent* 1, no. 1 (1966): 3, 7; Benjamin S. Bloom et al., *Compensatory*

documentation of this need resulted in a comprehensive attack on the problems at the local, state, and federal levels. As a result of these activities, a deficit model surfaced and the cult of the disadvantaged and the culturally deprived became the contemporary nomenclature. Meanwhile, societal pressures prevailed and federal dollars flowed to compensate for the deficiencies of the blacks. Two early programs designed to give motivation and preparation to potential black scholars were the National Scholarship and Service Fund for Negro Students and the National Achievement Scholarship Program for Negroes. A report on the latter program can be found in a follow-up study by Burgdorf, who found that youth selected by the National Achievement program did well in college.[3]

A spate of literature has discussed the deficit model in an attempt to explain the deviation of blacks from the norms set by whites on standardized tests.[4] In the meantime, however, a wealth of talent has been neglected because scores on conventional intelligence and achievement tests, which correlate with measures of abilities deemed important by schools, have seriously underestimated the potential or intellectual ability of blacks to process information. This dilemma presents a great challenge and leads to the recommendation that a kaleidoscopic approach is necessary in order to identify the gifted children who are culturally different and to plan a suitable curriculum for such children.

Research by Bruch and Torrance has revealed that black children in their sample seemed to excel in the following areas: high nonverbal fluency and originality; high creative productivity in small groups; adeptness in visual activities; high creativity in movement, dance, and other physical activities; ability to be highly moti-

---

Education for Cultural Deprivation (New York: Holt, Rinehart and Winston, 1965).

3. Kenneth Burgdorf, *Outstanding Negro High School Students: A One-year Follow-up* (Evanston, Ill.: National Merit Scholarship Corp., 1969).

4. Frank Reissman, *The Culturally Deprived Child* (New York: Harper and Row, 1962); James B. Conant, *Slums and Suburbs* (Hightstown, N.J.: McGraw-Hill, 1961); Jerome S. Kagan et al., "Discussion: How Much Can We Boost IQ and Scholastic Achievement?" *Harvard Educational Review* 39 (1969): 273-356.

vated by games, music, sports, humor, and concrete objects; and use of language rich in imagery.[5]

Using Guilford's structure of intellect model as a reference point,[6] Bruch noted that blacks possess superior social intelligence, exhibit figural strengths (visual, auditory, and kinesthetic), diverge creatively in their thinking patterns, and transform products at a superior level. The language of blacks is described as being colorful while at the same time giving evidence of subtle nuances and double meanings. Purcell and Hillson have added to this array of unique abilities by noting that blacks possess tough, pragmatic problem-solving abilities, are loyal to the group, and show unusual resiliency in the face of hardships.[7]

In spite of this large array of abilities, it is difficult, as Gallagher has pointed out, to specify characteristics that can be generalized to all gifted children and we feel that it is equally difficult to formulate a composite that specifies the black gifted child.[8] This is especially true since the only common characteristic among the people of this culture is a familial structure of genes that designates darker skin pigment, different hair texture, and a self-concept that has been affected negatively by societal attitudes originating centuries ago. As the Meekers have pointed out in their pleas for profiles for individual students, careful attention should be given to individuals within the group, because the experiential groupings within the black ethnic social structure are as diverse as the various ethnic groupings outside the black groupings.[9]

5. Catherine Bruch, "Pro-Cultural Measurement: The Use of the Abbreviated Binet for the Disadvantaged (ABDA)," in *First National Conference on the Disadvantaged Gifted* (Ventura, Calif.: Office of the Ventura County Superintendent of Schools, 1975), pp. 18-19; E. Paul Torrance, "Finding Hidden Talents among Disadvantaged Children," *Gifted Child Quarterly* 12 (1968): 131-37.

6. Joy P. Guilford and Ralph Hoepfner, *The Analysis of Intelligence* (New York: McGraw-Hill, 1971).

7. Francis P. Purcell and Maurie Hillson, "The Disadvantaged Child," in *Education and the Urban Community*, ed. Maurie Hillson (New York: American Book Co., 1969), pp. 129-37.

8. James J. Gallagher, *Teaching the Gifted Child* (Boston: Allyn and Bacon, 1975).

9. Mary Meeker and Robert J. Meeker, *Strategies for Assessing Intellectual Patterns in Black, Anglo, and Mexican-American Boys or Any Other Children —and Implications for Education* (Los Angeles: Structure of Intellect Institute, 1975).

In using the kaleidoscopic approach, as illustrated in the Baldwin Identification Matrix (BIM) shown in figure 1, the child is not penalized because of social deprivation and is not stigmatized condescendingly by generalizations about groups. In using this approach, the first step is to accept the traits included in the definition of giftedness of the United States Office of Education as constants. These include: general intellectual ability, creative and productive thinking ability, psychomotor ability, leadership ability,

ASSESSMENT ITEMS	BALDWIN IDENTIFICATION MATRIX					
STUDENT	SCHOOL					
AGE GRADE	SEX	DATE	SCHOOL DISTRICT			
	SCORES					
	5	4	3	2	1	BA/NA*
Standardized intelligence test	140+ ( )	130–139 ( )	120–129 ( )	110–119 ( )	100–109 ( )	( )
Achievement test, composite score	95%ile ( )	90–94%ile ( )	85–89%ile ( )	80–84%ile ( )	75–79%ile ( )	( )
Achievement test, reading score	Stanine 9 ( )	Stanine 8 ( )	Stanine 7 ( )	Stanine 6 ( )	Stanine 5 ( )	( )
Achievement test, mathematics score	95%ile ( )	90–94%ile ( )	85–89%ile ( )	80–84%ile ( )	75–79%ile ( )	( )
Learning scale score	32 ( )	28–31 ( )	24–27 ( )	20–23 ( )	16–19 ( )	( )
Motivational scale score	34–36 ( )	30–33 ( )	26–29 ( )	22–25 ( )	18–21 ( )	( )
Creativity scale score	40 ( )	35–39 ( )	30–34 ( )	25–29 ( )	20–24 ( )	( )
Leadership scale score	40 ( ) Without reservation	35–39 ( ) Yes	30–34 ( ) Perhaps	25–29 ( ) Questionable	20–24 ( ) No	( )
Various teacher recommendations	( )	( )	( )	( )	( )	( )
Psychomotor ability	( )	( )	( )	( )	( )	( )
Peer nominations	( )	( )	( )	( )	( )	( )
Other items	( )	( )	( )	( )	( )	( )
Total number of checks						
Weight	×5	×4	×3	×2	×1	
Add across	+	+	+	+	=	
Total score						

FIG. 1. The Baldwin Identification Matrix

* BA/NA. Below average/Information not available
Note: A similar version of this matrix appears in the *N/S-LTI-G/T Bulletin* 4 (March 1977): 3.

specific academic aptitudes, and special talent (visual and performing arts) abilities.

The second step would be to select an array of techniques for
establishing exceptional strengths in the particular "constant." For
example, for leadership ability one would select an instrument or
observation procedure that assesses leadership ability generic for
leadership in any culture. The vertical axis of the matrix would
show the assessment techniques used. The scale from 1 to 5 on the
horizontal axis represents a ranking of scores that are average or
above in any or all of the areas listed under the definition of the
Office of Education.

Upon completion of the matrix, the researcher totals the points
made on all variables, with "5" being the highest received on any
one assessment item. The number of items on the vertical axis times
five equals the highest possible score. The sum of points received
by each child on the horizontal axis equals the total score of the
individual. According to the plan for a community, children can
be selected from the gross screening for particular program
emphases, that is, mathematics, science, general intellectual ability,
creative development, and so forth. The evidence from the matrix
produces a total score that gives the black child, or any child from
a different culture, an opportunity to compete for recognition in
a specialized program. It also gives the researcher a picture of the
strengths and weaknesses of the particular child. The BIM Matrix
concept has been used successfully in Minnesota school districts to
pull together a variety of assessment techniques into a profile that
allows a child equal access to programs for the gifted.

A curriculum/instructional rationale must be devised to accommodate deficit in stimuli and nourish innate abilities. Such a
rationale should accommodate a vertical and/or horizontal movement for the child. The research of Guilford and others indicates
that an individual can have the ability to process information at a
very high level but lack the stimulus for developing the skills
necessary for product development.[10] For children who show
weaknesses in the kaleidoscopic matrix in areas considered crucial
for success in the specified program of the community, a threshold
program might be necessary. Evidence of the change in IQ as well

10. Guilford and Hoepfner, *The Analysis of Intelligence.*

as the change in academic abilities of black children is reported
by Baldwin.[11] A profile chart can be made for each child using
information taken from the identification matrix. For example, the
profile chart shown in figure 2 for a seventh-grade student indicates that the student is underachieving in reading and requires
"vertical" emphasis on basic skills and concepts in that area, but
is developing satisfactorily in mathematics and should have "horizontal" enrichment in that area. The vertical emphasis in reading
should help the child achieve at a level commensurate with his
abilities, while the horizontal emphasis in mathematics would involve in-depth analyses and problem solving.

ASSESSMENT AREA	NEEDED EMPHASIS	
	VERTICAL	HORIZONTAL
Reading...............	X	
Mathematics...........		X
Leadership.............		X
Creativity.............	X	
Name of Student:	Grade:	Date:

FIG. 2. Sample profile chart showing areas of skill development (vertical)
or of enrichment (horizontal) appropriate for a seventh-grade student

In summary, attention to the cultivation of talents among blacks
has historical precedents in the writings of W. E. B. DuBois. Subsequent research and social pressures have brought to the fore the
need to examine unique paradigms for discovering and developing
this talent, because behaviors often considered aberrant in the
dominant culture belie the rough diamond of intellect and talent
waiting to be polished to the brilliance it is capable of exhibiting.
As Brazziel states,

Hopefully, the nation can rally its resources to work with the 1.5
million or so black children and youth with special gifts and talents.
About one-half of these young people are poor. Full development of
their abilities and full benefits of their talents to the black community

11. Alexinia Young Baldwin, "Tests Can Underpredict: A Case Study,"
Phi Delta Kappan 58 (1977): 620-21.

and the nation depend heavily on the abilities of educators to spot unusual talent in poor settings, celebrate the unique expressions and manifestations of this talent, and organize programs to develop it.[12]

12. William F. Brazziel, *Quality Education for All Americans* (Washington, D.C.: Howard University Press, 1974), p. 61.

CHAPTER XXV

The Education of the Culturally Different Gifted

ERNEST M. BERNAL, JR.

In recent times, the leadership of what may be called the gifted movement in education has responded to the educational needs of nondominant ethnic minorities.[1] Some of these concerns are discussed in this chapter, and illustrations are given of the practices in the field of gifted education that meet the needs of minority children as well as other practices that do not. Many of the views expressed here can be documented; others are based on firsthand experience with gifted minority youth, particularly Mexican Americans, and the school personnel and school systems (to distinguish individual persons from institutions) in whose care they are placed. Both facts and experience are offered here, because the concern for the education of the culturally different gifted is relatively new.

The juxtaposition of minority and gifted still produces dissonance in the minds of many educators.[2] Words like "underprivileged," "culturally deprived," or, more recently, "disadvantaged" have acquired a more comfortable acceptability. Indeed, "compensatory education," "bilingual education," and "limited English-speaking ability" are all highly interrelated terms that militate against educators' practical understanding that a child with limited ability to speak English may be verbally gifted (albeit in a language other than English), that many children in the *barrio* exhibit higher-order cognitive processes only in the service of survival (not in taking standardized tests or in making good grades),

---

1. Irving S. Sato, "The Culturally Different Gifted Child—the Dawning of His Day?" *Exceptional Children* 40 (1974): 572-76.

2. Ernest M. Bernal, Jr., "Gifted Programs for the Culturally Different," *Bulletin of the National Association of Secondary School Principals* 60 (1976): 67-76.

and that being culturally *different* does not mean culturally inferior (although it does imply a somewhat different set of values and behavioral repertoires). Most important of all, however, educators have not realized that programs for the culturally different also need to accommodate gifted students in a systematic way. If gifted children from the dominant ethnic group have not in general fared well at the hands of the schools, imagine the plight of gifted children from the nondominant groups.

This is not to say, however, that the schools have always failed to identify gifted minority children. Many of the gifted Mexican-American adults interviewed in a previous study acknowledged that the schools, and particularly certain teachers, had a strong influence on their development.[3] But many educators fail to realize that a great percentage of these extraordinary Mexican Americans are no longer functioning members of *La Raza*, that they have forsaken their ethnic ties in the pursuit of the American Dream and have largely eschewed any meaningful involvement with the very people who could most benefit from their leadership. Many were straightforwardly shaped by their educational environments to dissociate themselves from other Mexican Americans; some were coaxed away ("You're not like the other Mexicans. Why don't you become . . ."); and yet a few others admitted upon reflecting that they were wooed away in the most nefarious manner, by creating a conflict of values ("Think how much you could do for your family if . . ."). Neither they nor their sponsors understood the risk to mental health that they ran, a risk that has been noted by several scholars who discuss the acculturational process.

One such scholar, Arciniega, has developed a highly useful model for following the consequences not only of acculturation but also of biculturation, that is, the process by which members of a nondominant ethnic group—Mexican Americans, specifically—achieve higher social status without having to betray their cultural background.[4] But upwardly mobile persons risk failure at the hands of the dominant ethnic group, and persons who fail face the psy-

3. Ernest M. Bernal, Jr., "Gifted Mexican-American Children: An Ethnoscientific Perspective," *California Journal of Educational Research* 25 (1974): 261-63.

4. Tomas A. Arciniega, *Public Education's Response to the Mexican-American Student* (El Paso, Texas: Innovative Resources, 1971).

chological dangers of falling into "deviant" or "reject" categories. Deviants are characterized by the pursuit of illegal or illegitimate activities; they have accepted the goals of the American Dream, but, having failed to achieve them through societally acceptable means, select unacceptable ways to satisfy their ambitions. Rejects, on the other hand, are more akin to marginal persons,[5] people who, having failed in their quest for improved socioeconomic status, reject both the goals and the means of the dominant society, yet cannot readjust to a previous style of life. Societally, they are in limbo; personally, they are in hell.

But Arciniega's model is also optimistic. It demonstrates how those Mexican Americans who achieve mainstream status as assimilates or biculturates can exercise interesting personal options. Biculturates, for example, can function usefully in both worlds, and by implication can thus provide leadership and facilitate mutual understanding and cooperation. This is what is happening among a growing percentage of young Mexican Americans, the Chicano generation.[6] They are achieving upward social mobility without sacrificing their cultural integrity. Assimilates, by virtue of their having achieved a secure status, also have the option of entering the ranks of the biculturates, of "coming back" to their roots.

One of the first needs is for educators to recognize (after having admitted that gifted students need to be identified and deliberately nurtured) that gifted programs for culturally different youngsters must be suited to them,[7] not merely offered on a take-it-or-leave-it basis, and not designed and implemented with only little deliberation about their psychological, cultural, and linguistic characteristics.[8]

5. See Robert E. Park, *Race and Culture* (Glencoe, Ill.: Free Press, 1950) and Arnold W. Green, "A Reexamination of the Marginal Man Concept," *Social Forces* 26 (1947-48): 167-71.

6. Rodolfo Alvarez, "The Psycho-historical and Socioeconomic Development of the Chicano Community in the United States," in *Chicanos: Social and Psychological Perspectives,* ed. Carrol A. Hernandez, Marsha J. Haug, and Nathaniel N. Wagner (St. Louis, Mo.: C. V. Mosby, 1976), pp. 38-54.

7. Bernal, "Gifted Programs for Culturally Different."

8. Jose A. Cardenas and Blandina Cardenas, *The Theory of Incompatibilities: A Conceptual Framework for Responding to the Educational Needs of Mexican-American Children* (San Antonio, Texas: Intercultural Development Research Association, 1977).

If one considers the 120 abilities represented in Guilford's Structure of Intellect model[9] (and the fact that not all 120 have been clearly delineated by empirical studies), is it so difficult to believe that no society is able to develop all of them to any great degree in all or most of its citizens? It is more reasonable to believe that every culture selectively reinforces a more limited number, thus producing in its members some specialization of cognitive abilities, leaving others to happenstance. While Meeker has analyzed responses of culturally different children according to the Guilford model,[10] diverse cognitive strengths in black populations have been identified by Bruch[11] and by Torrance.[12] We can well understand why so few youngsters from minority groups are identified as gifted when tested with instruments designed for children from the dominant ethnic group, since the validity of these tests in these circumstances is questionable.[13]

A previous study, based on extensive surveys in Texas, indicates that Mexican Americans value those cognitive and linguistic abilities in children that are manifested in pragmatic alertness, sensitivity to others, leadership, related interpersonal skills (for example, maturity, expressive style, charm, humor), and bilingual fluency.[14] Children with such abilities are *our* best and brightest, yet these abilities are only partially tapped by most screening or selection instruments. Unless these children also have developed the English prerequisites and the cognitive abilities measured by traditional tests, they may never be identified.

9. Joy P. Guilford, *The Nature of Human Intelligence* (New York: McGraw-Hill, 1967).

10. Mary N. Meeker, "Identifying Potential Giftedness," *Bulletin of the National Association of Secondary School Principals* 55 (1971): 92-95.

11. Catherine B. Bruch, "Modifications of Procedures for Identification of the Disadvantaged Gifted," *Gifted Child Quarterly* 15 (1971): 267-72.

12. E. Paul Torrance, "Issues in the Identification and Encouragement of Gifted Disadvantaged Children," *TAG Gifted Children Newsletter* 11 (March 1969): 48-55.

13. Ernest M. Bernal, Jr., "A Response to 'Educational Uses of Tests with Disadvantaged Subjects'," *American Psychologist* 30 (1975): 93-95.

14. Ernest M. Bernal, Jr. and Josephine Reyna, *Analysis of Giftedness in Mexican-American Children and Design of a Prototype Identification Instrument*, Final Report, Contract DEC-4-7-062113-307, USOE (Austin, Texas: Southwest Educational Development Laboratory, 1974).

When well-intentioned educators first contemplate the issue of minority gifted students, they frequently make one of two mistakes: they either adopt a supercompensatory approach or seek a simple ethnic integration of the program. The former accepts the minority children's intelligence but reacts overzealously to their not being like the "other" gifted children. In such a program the minority children are to be exposed to a compressed richness of experience and otherwise recreated in the image and likeness of the touchstone group of white children. The compensatory approach, however, is based on the false premise that a great deal of cognitive homogeneity exists among the gifted from the dominant ethnic culture. Also, it runs the risk of becoming an acculturation program that respects only a select few modes of thought.

The simple integration of gifted minority children into an established gifted curriculum may not be successful either, for it places the burden of accommodation on the minority children instead of on the institution. Such a program may inadvertently also select— or, worse, retain—only the more acculturated children. The result is, of course, that a great deal of ethnic talent will go by under-educated or alienated while much of the rest will be acculturated.

Successful programs for the gifted seem to have two important qualities: they provide children with the opportunity to learn not only receptively but productively as well. In such programs gifted youngsters are encouraged not only to study, but also to venture, risk, dream, reflect, and become involved in projects that they themselves consider meaningful. Programs for the culturally different children should do this also.

It is for this reason that the argument is advanced for a versatile procedure for identification based on the principle of inclusion, such that if a child qualifies as gifted on at least one count, the child is admitted to the program. Once such a diverse group of students comes together under the guidance of skillful teachers who implement a meaningful curriculum, particularly one that gives individual students opportunities to produce as well as to learn, then there will be ample opportunities for these students to master a more encompassing set of skills and abilities and to learn them from one another as well as from their tutors.

It is a sad commentary on our educational system to find gifted Chicano adults who are literate only in their second language,

English. Transitional bilingual programs, in which children with limited ability to speak English are educated in their native language only until they have learned to understand and speak enough English to benefit from the traditional, monolingual English curriculum, are senseless for gifted children who natively speak a language other than English. Instead, so-called maintenance (or, preferably "developmental")[15] bilingual programs are in order, programs that teach *in* the culture, as well as *about* it, thus capitalizing on the interpersonal, cognitive, and motivational styles of the minority learners to broaden their experience and repertoires without necessarily compromising their ethnic loyalties.[16] Conversely, native speakers of English, whatever their ethnicity, could learn as a second language the native language of the children with limited English-speaking ability (for example, in a Spanish as a Second Language program).

As a rule, then, a program for culturally different gifted students should build on their assets, foster interethnic understanding, and widen the style-of-life options for all students, including, of course, students from the dominant ethnic groups.

An ethnically and linguistically integrated gifted program would be the result, one that could utilize the best of two or more cultures and provide tomorrow's leaders with an extraordinary opportunity to understand and appreciate the meaning of cultural diversity in our pluralistic society.

15. Ernest M. Bernal, Jr., "Dimensions of Bilingual Education: A Look at the Real World" (Paper presented at the National Institute of Education Conference on Dimensions of Bilingual Programs, Washington, D.C., February 1977).

16. Manuel Ramirez III, "Cognitive Styles and Cultural Democracy in Education," *Social Science Quarterly* 53 (1973): 895-904.

CHAPTER XXVI

The Gifted and Talented Woman

CAROLYN M. CALLAHAN

The underlying impetus giving rise to a consideration of gifted women as a topic separate from the discussion of gifted children or gifted people in general is the fact that the number of men recognized as gifted, creative, or talented in our society far exceeds the number of women who have achieved the same level of success. A perusal of the literature on the achievements and characteristics of gifted and talented adults demonstrates the emphasis and attention historically given to the study and description of the successful male.[1]

This emphasis on the gifted and creative male was not unjustified or unreasonable in light of the overwhelming proportion of men who had achieved outstanding status and recognition and the prevailing biases of our society regarding the roles of women. Important questions are now being raised, however, about the sources of inequality in the achievement of males and females. Are there basic differences in the intellectual abilities or personality structures of men and women that might account for this phenomenon? If such differences exist, are these differences a result of innate structures or of cultural influences? Are the programs for the identifica-

1. Francis Galton, *Hereditary Genius* (London: Macmillan, 1869); James M. Cattell, "A Statistical Study of American Men of Science," *Science* 24 (1906): 732-42; *The Creative Process*, ed. Brewster Ghiselin (New York: Mentor, 1952); Anne Roe, *The Making of a Scientist* (New York: Dodd, Mead, 1952); Lewis M. Terman and Melita Oden, *Genetic Studies of Genius*, vol. 5, *The Gifted Group at Mid-life: Thirty-five Years' Follow-up of the Superior Child* (Stanford, Calif.: Stanford University Press, 1959); Frank Barron, *Creativity and Psychological Health* (Princeton, N.J.: Van Nostrand, 1963); Donald N. MacKinnon, "The Study of Creative Persons: A Method and Some Results," in *Creativity and Learning*, ed. Jerome Kagan (Boston: Beacon Press, 1967), pp. 20-35.

tion and education of gifted children based on findings that are appropriate for boys but not for girls in our society? What other factors might account for the discrepant numbers of gifted men and women? Are there models of differential education that are more appropriate for the education of gifted and talented women? What do we know about the unique characteristics of gifted females that can guide us in the development of effective programs for the education of this population? Answers to these questions may help explain the observation that girls earn higher grades in school, yet men write more books, earn more degrees, produce more works of art, and make more contributions in all professional fields.

Intellectual Abilities and Achievements

A prevailing stereotype of the intellectual differences between males and females that is particularly pervasive among educators is the notion that girls excel in English, foreign languages, and the arts, while boys are better in mathematics and science. If, in fact, girls do excel in particular aspects of intellectual ability, the realization of their potential is severely limited as evidenced by the overwhelming preponderance of successful males in every endeavor—literature, music, art, history, and government, as well as in mathematics and science. If the basis for the stereotype is a well-founded distinction, the origins of these differences must be considered. If the basis for the stereotype is only myth and folklore, then the failure of women to capitalize on their special talents must be considered. In considering the nature of intellectual differences between gifted males and females, several precautions are necessary. There is limited literature that systematically considers the intellectual differences between gifted males and females, and one must be cautious in generalizing from the intellectual characteristics of the general population to the gifted. Physiological variables interact with psychological variables in a complicated and unclear fashion. Furthermore, the results of studies done in the past may not be relevant to the children reared in today's culture.

The current and comprehensive review of sex differences by Maccoby and Jacklin extensively examines the way in which the sexes differ in general ability to learn, achievement, specific aptitudes, and cognitive styles.[2] Pointing out that the Stanford-Binet and other standardized measures of general intelligence were constructed in such a way that any sex differences are minimized, the authors dismiss the lack of sex differences on this variable as due to psychometric rather than psychological differences. It is thus necessary to examine specific abilities in order to ascertain the extent of sex differences in intellectual ability. The basic findings of the Maccoby and Jacklin review may be summarized as follows:

1. There does not appear to be any difference in *how* the two sexes learn. That is, there is great similarity in the basic intellectual processes of perception, learning, and memory.

2. Up to age ten or eleven, girls and boys do equally well on measures of verbal performance.

3. After age eleven, girls frequently outscore boys on tests of verbal performance by .1 to .5 standard deviations. It is important to note that this difference exists on tests requiring more than simple tasks such as spelling. The differences are also noted on measures of comprehension of complex text, measures of understanding of logical relations expressed in verbal terms, and some measures of verbal creativity.

4. There do not seem to be any differences in measures of quantitative ability until about age nine to thirteen, when boys begin to do better. These differences still favor boys when the number of mathematics courses completed is equal.

5. Differences in quantitative ability seem to be accompanied by differences in science achievement.

6. On tests of spatial ability, an advantage for boys appears at the beginning of adolescence and increases through high school.

7. No difference is found in the problem-solving tasks of response inhibition or problem restructuring.

8. No differences are found on tests of concept mastery and reasoning and measures of nonverbal creativity. Girls are superior on measures of verbal creativity after age seven.[3]

Thus, it appears that the only areas where boys in the general

2. Eleanor E. Maccoby and Carol Jacklin, *The Psychology of Sex Differences* (Stanford, Calif.: Stanford University Press, 1974), p. 68.

3. Ibid., pp. 63-133.

population seem clearly and consistently superior to girls are visual-spatial ability and achievement in mathematics and science. Further, these differences are only apparent after the onset of adolescence.[4]

An examination of the literature on the gifted that does attend to sex differences would tend to support many of these conclusions. The superior ability of boys in arithmetic was also noted among Terman's sample of gifted children.[5] However, the most dramatic support for differences in quantitative abilities, especially among adolescents, is derived from the recent studies of mathematically precocious youths at Johns Hopkins University (Study of Mathematically Precocious Youth—SMPY). During the first three years that this program identified gifted youth in the area of mathematics, 167 boys but only 19 girls in the seventh and eighth grades scored 640 or above on the mathematics section of the *Scholastic Aptitude Test*.[6] Mathematical ability and visual-spatial ability are often closely associated. The relationship between the superior achievement of males in tests of mathematical ability and tests of spatial relations, however, is not clearly understood. Initial hypotheses that visual-spatial abilities were necessary for outstanding mathematics achievement have not been clearly documented. In a limited exploration of this theory, Fox found that among girls and boys who were identified as mathematically precocious, sex differences in visual-spatial abilities did not occur,[7] and Daniel and Guay found a variety of such measures to be correlated to mathematical abilities in young children.[8] This evidence is very sketchy, however, and even though some have regarded visual-spatial abilities to be innate

4. Ernest D. Daniel and Roland B. Guay, "Spatial Abilities, Mathematics Achievement, and the Sexes" (Paper presented at the annual meeting of the American Educational Research Association in San Francisco, 1976). This paper suggests that even though girls have equivalent scores on tests of lower-level spatial abilities, males score higher on tests of the higher-level spatial abilities as early as the second grade.

5. Lewis M. Terman, *Genetic Studies of Genius*, vol. 1, *Mental and Physical Traits of a Thousand Gifted Children* (Stanford, Calif.: Stanford University Press, 1925).

6. Lynn H. Fox, "Sex Differences: Implications for Program Planning for the Academically Gifted" (Paper presented at the Lewis M. Terman Memorial Symposium on Intellectual Talent, Baltimore, Md., November, 1975), p. 3.

7. Ibid., p. 4.

8. Daniel and Guay, "Spatial Abilities, Mathematics Achievement, and the Sexes."

characteristics, there is still reason to be hesitant in making any strong causal connections between the two abilities or in concluding that males are innately superior to females in mathematical aptitude. In fact, one interpretation of the origins of the relationship between mathematics and visual-spatial abilities includes a consideration of cognitive styles and environmental influences on these styles. Maccoby and Jacklin suggest that visual-spatial ability appears to be closely connected to field independence on visual tasks and field independence is positively related to cultural conditions that allow one to be more assertive and less restricted. Because girls are not encouraged to be assertive and are restricted in play and exploration of their environment, they are at a disadvantage in developing field independence and, thus, in visual-spatial abilities and mathematical abilities.[9] Another cognitive style that has been linked to mathematics and visual-spatial ability is the global/analytic dimension of perception. It has been suggested that girls learn a more global style of problem solving, while boys learn analytic approaches and thus become more skilled at quantitative tasks.[10] This global approach to processing information is attributed to a tendency for parents to overprotect and discourage independent problem solving among females.

Evidence regarding the degree to which sex differences found in the normal population in language arts or verbal skills hold up among the gifted is somewhat contradictory. Although Terman's sample of gifted girls was characterized as having greater ability in reading and other language arts skills, and Hitchfield found similar results among a group of intellectually gifted children in England,[11] results of the Study of Verbally Gifted Youth (SVGY) and testing of students in the SMPY program indicate equal verbal abilities across sexes.[12] Other differences or lack of differences

9. Maccoby and Jacklin, *The Psychology of Sex Differences*, p. 133; Eleanor E. Maccoby, "Woman's Intellect," in *The Potential of Women*, ed. Seymour M. Farber and Roger H. L. Wilson (New York: McGraw-Hill, 1963), pp. 24-39.

10. Fox, "Sex Differences: Implications for Program Planning for the Academically Gifted," pp. 5-6.

11. Elizabeth M. Hitchfield, *In Search of Promise* (London: Longman, 1973); Terman, *Mental and Physical Traits of a Thousand Gifted Children.*

12. Peter V. McGinn, "Verbally Gifted Youth: Selection and Description," in *Intellectual Talent: Research and Development*, ed. Daniel P. Keating (Baltimore, Md.: Johns Hopkins University Press, 1976), pp. 160-82.

noted in Hitchfield's study include: higher scores for boys on tests of general knowledge at ages seven and eleven, higher scores for boys on tests of science and geography information, and no differences on tests of logical thinking.[13] Terman found higher scores for boys on tests of musical aptitude, drawing, and manual dexterity, and higher scores for girls on tests of mechanical ingenuity, general information, and science.[14] Thus, results of studies examining gifted children seem inconclusive about the extent of intellectual differences among gifted children in areas other than mathematics. Further, there is little to account for the overwhelming dominance of males among those identified as gifted among the adult population or to help identify those characteristics that distinguish the females who realize their potential from those who do not.

Personality, Interests, and Values

Although differences between boys and girls in one presumably innate intellectual ability (visual-spatial) have been used to explain differences in particular intellectual achievements (in mathematics), many more of the explanations offered for the differences between males and females in intellectual ability and achievement are based on differences in personality and the interaction between personality and cognitive variables. In many instances, environmental and cultural influences on the development of personality characteristics are integral parts of the hypotheses examined in exploring reasons for the failure of females to realize their potential. Therefore, such cultural influences will be discussed here in conjunction with descriptions of the personality characteristics of the gifted and talented female.

One aspect of the literature relevant to the personality traits of gifted women is derived from male/female comparisons in characteristics considered to be associated with success. As previously mentioned, one must be cautious in generalizing from the general population to the gifted; these studies, however, provide some useful clues for understanding the gifted female. Other studies comparing the successful female to less successful peers add con-

13. Hitchfield, *In Search of Promise.*

14. Terman, *Mental and Physical Traits of a Thousand Gifted Children.*

siderable information about the personality characteristics of the successful, talented female.

One personality characteristic that has often been considered as an influence on the success of women is achievement motivation. In their analysis, Maccoby and Jacklin concluded that there is no demonstrated difference by sex among school-age children in achievement motivation, although males show more arousal of this motivation under directly competitive conditions.[15] No direct comparisons of gifted male and female students are available, but studies that compare more accomplished gifted females to their less successful peers seem to indicate that achievement motivation has a differential effect on achievement among gifted women. For example, a group of high-ability college women identified as "achievers" scored significantly higher than their underachieving peers on the "Achievement via Conformity" and "Achievement via Independence" scales of the *California Psychological Inventory* (CPI).[16] On the *Adjective Check List,* these groups responded similarly, with the achieving group checking conscientious, capable, and industrious significantly more often than the underachieving group, and the underachieving group checking lazy, leisurely, dreamy, and easygoing more often. In a similar study of academically gifted women college students, scores on the *Minnesota Multiphasic Personality Inventory* of those who completed their programs were compared with scores of those who had not completed their programs. Those who had completed their programs were characterized as more persevering and as having more achievement motivation than those who did not complete their programs.[17] In Helson's comparison of creative and noncreative female mathematicians, the more creative females scored higher than their less creative female peers on the "Achievement via Independence" scale of the CPI.[18]

15. Maccoby and Jacklin, *The Psychology of Sex Differences,* p. 149.

16. Mary Ann Warburton Norfleet, "Personality Characteristics of Achieving and Underachieving High-ability Senior Women," *Personnel and Guidance Journal* 46 (1968): 976-80.

17. Patricia S. Faunce, "Personality Characteristics and Vocational Interests Related to the College Persistence of Academically Gifted Women," *Journal of Counseling Psychology* 15 (1968): 31-40.

18. Ravenna Helson, "Women Mathematicians and the Creative Personality," *Journal of Consulting and Clinical Psychology* 36 (1971): 210-20.

The "fear of success" variable investigated initially by Horner seems closely related to achievement motivation and particularly relevant to this discussion. Data collected with a projective situational instrument suggest that women may develop a "fear of success motive" that acts to inhibit achievement motivation.[19] This phenomenon may account for the lowered arousal of achievement motivation for females in competitive situations. The origins of the "fear of success" are not clear. It appears, however, that many young girls and women have been enculturated to the extent that they fear they will be rejected socially or be considered unfeminine if they appear to be too bright or too competent. It is postulated that the motive to avoid success is greatest for those women of high ability and the conflicts between achievement motivation and fear of success may create anxiety, which reduces the likelihood that these women will pursue success.[20] High levels of anxiety may also be detrimental to learning and creativity. It thus appears that achievement motivation must be strong with a concomitant absence of motives to avoid success in order for women to seek actualization of their potential.

Another personality variable that may have an impact on the relative achievement of females is locus of control. Maccoby and Jacklin report that throughout the elementary- and high-school years, both sexes are likely to believe that they can determine their own destinies. Yet, during college, men exhibit greater internal locus of control and greater confidence in their ability to succeed at school-related tasks.[21] Studies of gifted achieving college women would indicate that, related to gifted peers who have not been as successful, they had greater self-confidence, good ego strength, greater rebellious independence, and greater rejection of outside influence.[22] Gifted and creative girls also score significantly higher

19. Matina S. Horner, "Femininity and Successful Achievement: Basic Inconsistency," in *Feminine Personality and Conflict*, ed. Judith M. Bardwick et al. (Belmont, Calif.: Brooks/Cole, 1970), pp. 45-74.

20. Matina S. Horner, "Toward an Understanding of Achievement-related Conflicts in Women," *Journal of Social Issues* 28 (1972): 157-75.

21. Maccoby and Jacklin, *The Psychology of Sex Differences*, p. 350.

22. Faunce, "Personality Characteristics and Vocational Interests Related to the College Persistence of Academically Gifted Women"; Helson, "Women Mathematicians and the Creative Personality"; Norfleet, "Personality Characteristics of Achieving and Underachieving High-ability Senior Women."

on measures of such traits than do their normal peers.[23] One might hypothesize from the data presented above that gifted women must be encouraged to develop a strong locus of control and gain confidence in their own ability to control their fates if maximum potential is to be realized.

One of the most striking findings in the literature that focuses on differences between gifted males and females and/or differences between gifted persons and the normal population is the greater homogeneity of females as a group. Gifted boys and men appear to differ from normal males on many more traits than gifted girls and women differ from normal females. In addition, the variability of scores among males seems to be greater than among females across many cognitive and personality variables. In a study of creative women (mathematicians, architects, and college students), Helson found that, in general, there was less variability among this group on most personality traits than among men.[24] Torrance found less variability among girls than among men on measures of fluency, flexibility, inventive level, originality, and on the *Iowa Test of Basic Ability*; and Werner and Bachtold, in comparing creative males and females, found fewer personality traits distinguishing gifted females from normal peers.[25] More recently, the results of testing in the Study of Mathematically Precocious Youth indicate much greater variability in mathematics ability among gifted males.[26] The lack of variability among females may be cautiously interpreted as a manifestation of desire for conformity among gifted women in order to avoid being labeled as abnormal and the risk of social rejection.

23. Charles E. Schaefer, "A Psychological Study of Ten Exceptionally Creative Adolescent Girls," *Exceptional Children* 36 (1970): 431-41; Emmy E. Werner and Louise M. Bachtold, "Personality Factors of Gifted Boys and Girls in Middle Childhood and Adolescence," *Psychology in the Schools* 2 (1969): 177-82.

24. Ravenna Helson, "Generality of Sex Differences in Creative Style," *Journal of Personality* 36 (1968): 33-48.

25. E. Paul Torrance, "Creative Young Women in Today's World," *Exceptional Children* 38 (1972): 597-603; Werner and Bachtold, "Personality Factors of Gifted Boys and Girls in Middle Childhood and Adolescence."

26. Lynn H. Fox, "Identification and Program Planning: Models and Methods," in *Intellectual Talent: Research and Development*, ed. Keating, pp. 32-54.

Other personality traits that the literature suggests distinguish the more successful gifted female from her less successful gifted peers include: psychological mindedness, intellectual efficiency, tolerance, conscientiousness, flexibility, independence and autonomy, narcissism, modesty, originality, exactitude, and aloofness.[27] Comparisons of successful women psychologists with men psychologists show higher scores for women psychologists on intelligence, superego strength, and unconventionality.[28] These findings would seem to indicate that gifted women must have much more distinct personalities and inner strength in order to succeed.

Several background and familial variables seem to influence the development of the personality of the gifted and talented girl. One of these variables, identity with a father or masculine model, has been noted in studies of creative female mathematicians and creative adolescent girls.[29] Greater masculine interests among mathematically precocious girls than among normal females, greater problem-solving ability among youth with male sex-role identity, and strong attachments to fathers noted in autobiographies of gifted women would support claims that strong maternal figures or female sex-role identification could be inhibiting.[30] Of course, the relevance of this variable depends on the cultural biases operating at the time of the investigations. It is quite likely that expanding concepts of feminine roles may make sex-role identification less influential in the choice of career or the development of potential. Other family or background variables that may reflect the influence of cultural phe-

27. Norfleet, "Personality Characteristics of Achieving and Underachieving High-ability Senior Women"; Faunce, "Personality Characteristics and Vocational Interests Related to the College Persistence of Academically Gifted Women"; Helson, "Women Mathematicians and the Creative Personality"; Louise M. Bachtold and Emmy E. Werner, "Personality Profiles of Gifted Women," *American Psychologist* 25 (1970): 234-43.

28. Bachtold and Werner, "Personality Profiles of Gifted Women."

29. Schaefer, "A Psychological Study of Ten Exceptionally Creative Adolescent Girls"; Helson, "Women Mathematicians and the Creative Personality."

30. Herbert J. Walberg, "Physics, Femininity, and Creativity," *Developmental Psychology* 1 (1969): 47-54; Fox, "Sex Differences: Implications for Program Planning for the Academically Gifted"; G. A. Milton, "The Effects of Sex-role Identification upon Problem-solving Skill," *Journal of Abnormal and Social Psychology* 55 (1975): 208-212.

nomena focus on the position of the child in the family, number of brothers, and cultural heritage. Helson, for example, found that the most creative mathematicians grew up outside the United States or had at least one parent who was European, suggesting that these girls would not be as influenced by traditional feelings of antiintellectualism in the American culture. These women usually grew up in families where there were no male siblings and little financial security.[31] A group of creative adolescent females who, incidentally, did not like mathematics did not share these characteristics.[32] It may be that interests, background, and family have differential influences on gifts and talents according to the area of potential.

The interests and values of gifted women have been used as indicators of motivation to succeed in given academic pursuits. The assumptions that academic and professional success is predicated on interest as well as ability is supported by findings that intellectually gifted women are more successful in completing degrees if they demonstrate interests characteristic of professional or academic careers.[33] Even though gifted females do seem to exhibit scores that are significantly greater in masculine areas than normal peers, these same girls also score high on feminine interests, thus presenting potential conflicts in interests when making career choices.[34] Similar findings for value orientations are noted by Fox and Denham. Although gifted females tend to score higher than normals on the theoretical, economic, and political scales, they still are lower than males in those scales, and higher than males on the social, aesthetic, and religious values.[35]

31. Helson, "Women Mathematicians and the Creative Personality"; Schaefer, "A Psychological Study of Ten Exceptionally Creative Adolescent Girls."

32. Schaefer, "A Psychological Study of Ten Exceptionally Creative Adolescent Girls."

33. Faunce, "Personality Characteristics and Vocational Interests Related to the College Persistence of Academically Gifted Women."

34. Fox, "Sex Differences: Implications for Program Planning for the Academically Gifted."

35. Lynn H. Fox and Susanne Denham, "Values and Career Interests of Mathematically and Scientifically Precocious Youth," in Mathematical Talent: Discovery, Description, and Development, ed. Julian C. Stanley, Daniel P. Keating, and Lynn H. Fox (Baltimore, Md.: Johns Hopkins University Press, 1974), pp. 140-75.

Environmental Factors Impinging on the Success
of the Gifted Female

Underlying the problems of achievement and motivation of gifted and talented females lie hypotheses yet to be tested and perhaps untestable in the experimental tradition. As in all questions focusing on the relative impact of heredity and environment, it is impossible to control completely the hereditary and environmental factors influencing the development of males and females. Yet, there are certain factors within the environment that would seem logically to have an impact on the development of girls and young women. Until cultural or environmental factors are altered considerably to neutralize the potential effects, there will be no way of assessing how great that impact is.

It has been hypothesized that one of the reasons females do not attain higher levels of success is a lack of motivation to seek careers in certain professions. Traditionally, school programs fail to provide examples of females who have succeeded and have been rewarded for achievement in professions not typically judged female. Even in the study of literature, where it would seem there is ample opportunity to explore the lives and writings of both men and women, it is common practice to choose books that boys will enjoy with the rationale that girls will usually read anything assigned anyway.[36] Thus, literature written by men and about men predominates. Further, textbooks, beginning with the reading primers, have portrayed females as wives and mothers, weaker sisters, and dependent and helpless minor characters.[37] Standardized educational achievement test batteries also contribute to the general bias presented in classrooms through both content bias (a greater number of male nouns and pronouns—excluding generic nouns and pronouns) and sex-role stereotyping.[38] Of course, all females may

36. Millicent Rutherford, "Reinforced Concrete," *English Journal* 63 (1974): 25-33.

37. Marjorie B. U'Ren, "The Image of Woman in Textbooks," in *Woman in a Sexist Society*, ed. Vivian Gornick and Barbara K. Moran (New York: Signet, 1972), pp. 318-28.

38. Carol K. Tittle, Karen McCarthy, and Jane F. Stickler, *Women in Educational Testing* (Princeton, N.J.: Educational Testing Service, 1974).

be influenced by these pervasive biases in texts, tests, and other instructional materials, but it is perhaps the gifted female who will be stunted the most because her potential is the greatest for fulfilling a wide variety of roles and careers. Hopefully, greater emphasis in the general curriculum on nontraditional role possibilities and greater acceptance of female achievement in a variety of careers will affect the gifted girl in positive ways.

The sociological literature has offered a variety of explanations for the failure of women to ascend to the same levels of success as men. In addition to providing evidence of the cultural factors that have been discussed as influential in the development of the intellectual capabilities and personalities of females, this literature suggests that even when bright females have attained educational levels indicative of the aptitude and achievement necessary for success in a given profession, additional circumstances within job settings may mitigate against equal levels of accomplishment. For example, Epstein has pointed out that success within professional groups is most often under the influence of a general system of social control by those within the profession. This system promotes those who are considered potential candidates for elite membership and excludes those not considered as desirable candidates. Because women generally fall into the latter category (due to cultural biases), they are left to flounder and/or perish.

Epstein also suggests that for males the reward system is made clear and rational, but that for females it is often left cloudy and unclear. More importantly, when rewards are doled out to women, they are often given on the bases of irrelevant performance criteria or on the basis of judgments made against a set of standards not comparable to the standards set for males. Thus, women do not receive adequate feedback to improve their performance. Rewards for males and females are often differential in their nature, with males receiving an increase in salary or a promotion while females receive attention and affection. Furthermore, women are often left out of the relationships that allow one to learn the secret know-how of a profession or that provide for equivalent supervised "on-the-job training." Thus, women are often perceived by themselves and others as standing at the periphery of a profession. Such perceptions may result in a feeling of insignificance and a concomitant lack of motivation to make significant contributions to a profession that has no vested interest in them.[39]

Although data relative to the effect that marriage has on the productivity of female professionals are unclear,[40] an analysis of the prevailing attitudes of women toward their role and status within the professions indicates that married women professionals do not expect full equality in the profession and do not expect to accept the same responsibility for achieving career success. In a sample of families where wives were physicians, college professors, and attorneys, the careers of the women were generally regarded as a hobby, the primary role of the women was viewed as wife and mother, and the women expressed greater satisfaction with their family role than with their professional role. Women twenty-three to thirty years of age did not differ from women fifty years of age and older in these perceptions.[41]

Other barriers faced by the gifted women are a result of general stereotyping by both males and females. Even though boys and girls in elementary school believe their respective sex group to be superior in all subject fields, by the time they reach high school both sexes believe girls will excel in literature and males will excel in science.[42] If the self-fulfilling prophecy is a viable construct, its implications are far-reaching in this case. Stereotypic judgments that influence the evaluation of work produced by females have also been noted in the literature. Presenting identical paintings while altering only male and female artists' names resulted in differentially higher ratings for males regardless of the sex of rater, and ratings

39. Cynthia F. Epstein, "Successful Women in the Sciences," *Chemtech* (1973): 8-13.

40. Radcliffe Committee on Graduate Education for Women, *Graduate Education for Women* (Cambridge, Mass.: Harvard University Press, 1956); Margaret M. Paloma and T. Neal Garland, "The Married Professional Woman: A Study in Tolerance of Domestication," *Journal of Marriage and the Family* 33 (1971): 531-40; Marianne A. Ferber and Jane W. Loeb, "Performance, Rewards, and the Perceptions of Sex Discrimination among Male and Female Faculty," *American Journal of Sociology* 78 (1973): 233-40.

41. Paloma and Garland, "The Married Professional Woman."

42. John Ernest, *Mathematics and Sex* (Santa Barbara, Calif.: University of California, 1975).

of identical articles by college students were consistently higher if the article was attributed to a male. Only if paintings had been described as "award winning" were females accorded the same ratings as males.[43] This may be indicative of a feeling that only if a female has already proven her worth to someone else, she might be considered seriously by others. The barrier becomes one of making the first hurdle one of initial recognition.

Other, more subtle barriers to the achievement of gifted and talented females may be found in the literature on discrimination against women. Two others noted here are test bias and reinforcement of inappropriate behavior. Ironically, even behaviors that earn gifted females good grades in school may act against them in competitive professional situations. Walberg, for example, found girls in physics classes to be more conforming, dependent, and docile; Gallagher, Aschner, and Jenne found that girls expressed themselves less often while boys were eight times as likely to quarrel with teachers in biology classes.[44] These same females are rewarded with high grades and are, therefore, likely to interpret their in-class behaviors as contributing to high grades and, thus, appropriate for success. Test bias has been offered as one explanation for differences in measured achievement in mathematics and science. Walberg noted that on a physics test with predominantly visual-spatial items boys did better, while on a physics test with primarily verbal items girls did better. Another study indicated that women improved their mathematical performance (even on abstract reasoning problems) if problems are worded so as to involve feminine tasks rather than masculine tasks, even though the solution to the problem requires exactly the same process.[45] Potential discrimination in other areas of testing has not been explored, but must not be discounted.

43. Margaret M. Clifford and Elaine Walster, "The Effect of Sex on College Admission, Work Evaluation, and Job Interviews," *Journal of Experimental Education* 41 (1972): 1-5; Philip Goldberg, "Are Women Prejudiced against Women?" *Transaction* 5 (1968): 28-30.

44. Walberg, "Physics, Femininity, and Creativity"; James J. Gallagher, Mary Jane Aschner, and William Jenne, *Thinking of Gifted Children in Classroom Interaction*, Council for Exceptional Children Research Monograph No. B5 (Arlington, Va.: Council for Exceptional Children, 1967).

45. Walberg, "Physics, Femininity, and Creativity"; G. A. Milton, "Sex Differences in Problem Solving as a Function of Role Appropriateness of the Problem Content," *Psychological Reports* 5 (1959): 705-708.

Administrative Programming for the Gifted and Talented Female

The literature and research on the appropriateness of models for administrative adaptations in programs for the gifted and talented have generally failed to consider systematically the differential effects of those models on males and females.[46] The conclusions of most reviews of the literature on the effects of various administrative options such as enrichment, acceleration (including early admission), homogeneous ability grouping, and independent study include statements that favor acceleration as a preferred alternative based on research findings regarding the impact of such programs. The potential for varied effects that these types of programs might have on the intellectual, social, or emotional adjustment of males or females as subgroups of gifted children, however, is not noted.[47] This lack of consideration of sex as a relevant variable may be a result of an assumption that the learning characteristics of gifted students are generalizable to both sexes, and, therefore, that a given administrative change would be equally beneficial or nonbeneficial to all gifted and talented children. Whether this assumption has been made in these studies, or whether nonsignificant sex differences were simply not noted, cannot be known. The lack of attention to sex as a relevant variable in studying the efficacy of various programs for the gifted lends further credence to the statement of Passow that "no single adaptation has yet proven to be *the* conclusive method for providing adequately for all kinds and degrees of giftedness," and to the conclusion of Passow et al. that

46. Virgil S. Ward, "Program Organization and Implementation," in *Psychology and Education of the Gifted*, ed. Walter B. Barbe (New York: Appleton-Century-Crofts, 1965), pp. 382-89; Sidney L. Pressey, "A New Look at 'Acceleration'," ibid., 413-48; Jack W. Birch, "Early School Achievement for Mentally Advanced Children," *Exceptional Children* 21 (1954): 84-87; Judie B. Sklarsky and Merle R. Baxter, "Science Study with a Community Accent," *Elementary School Journal* 61 (1961): 301-7; Virginia P. Ryder, "A Docent Program in Science for Gifted Elementary Pupils," *Exceptional Children* 38 (1972): 629-31.

47. Paul A. Witty and Leroy W. Wilkins, "The Status of Acceleration or Grade Skipping as an Administrative Practice," in *Psychology and Education of the Gifted*, ed. Barbe, pp. 390-441; James J. Gallagher, *Teaching the Gifted Child*, 2d ed. (Boston: Allyn and Bacon, 1975); idem, *Research Summary on Gifted Education* (Springfield, Ill.: Office of the Superintendent of Public Instruction, 1966).

research has not clearly suggested "for whom and under what circumstances one kind of plan is more desirable than another."[48]

Recent research on mathematically talented young women would suggest that perhaps there is a great need to attend to the differing effects that certain strategies for dealing with the gifted may have on young adolescent women and men.[49] Although these studies have focused primarily on programs that are accelerative in nature and include only mathematically precocious children, the findings would appear to suggest that closer attention must be paid to the possibility that young gifted girls may self-select themselves out of potentially valuable educational experiences simply because the structure of the program is unattractive to females. In assessing the attitudes of mathematically gifted seventh- and eighth-grade boys and girls, Fox found that girls had significantly less favorable attitudes than boys toward acceleration for themselves. Further, these same girls felt that their parents would not approve of acceleration.[50] These findings were supported by earlier observations that gifted girls in the Study of Mathematically Precocious Youth appeared to be more fearful than boys of being rejected by peers if they participated in programs that included academic acceleration and that fear of failure among adolescent girls seems to inhibit them from taking part in new and different academic activities. It was also noted that there was no correlation between willingness to participate in accelerative type programs and actual ability level.[51] Even when gifted adolescent females are offered the option of taking part in a subject-specific acceleration program in mathemat-

48. A. Harry Passow, "Enrichment of Education for the Gifted," in *Education for the Gifted*, Fifty-seventh Yearbook of the National Society for the Study of Education, Part II, ed. Nelson B. Henry (Chicago: University of Chicago Press, 1958), p. 201; A. Harry Passow et al., *Planning for Talented Youth* (New York: Bureau Publications, Teachers College, Columbia University, 1955), p. 35.

49. Fox, "Sex Differences: Implications for Program Planning for the Academically Gifted."

50. Lynn H. Fox, "Career Interests and Mathematical Acceleration for Girls" (Paper presented at the annual meeting of the Amercian Psychological Association, Chicago, August, 1975).

51. Lynn H. Fox, "Facilitating the Educational Development of Mathematically Precocious Youth," in *Mathematical Talent: Discovery, Description, and Development*, ed. Stanley, Keating, and Fox, pp. 47-69.

ics, which simply involves being in accelerated classes in one specific subject area, girls are less likely to take part in these activities.[52]

Fox has suggested that willingness to participate in subject-specific acceleration may be a function of a sex-by-subject-area interaction.[53] In fact, it may be a three-way interaction of sex, age, and subject area. The suggestion that sex and subject matter interact is based on the observation that greater numbers of boys elect to take optional mathematics courses, that few girls expressed an interest in participating in the SMPY program at Johns Hopkins, and that data from the Advanced Placement Program show that participation by females in nonmathematical or nonscience programs is far greater than participation in the mathematics and science programs. Males also outnumber females in mathematics and science Advanced Placement Programs. In fact, of the nineteen different *Advanced Placement* tests, female students examined outnumber boys in only six areas: Art History, Studio Art, English, French Language, French Literature, and Spanish. Those examinations where the number of males exceed the number of females are in American History, European History, the classics, German, and in all the science and mathematics fields.[54] Age may also be an interacting variable influencing the receptivity of females to accelerative programs, as is suggested by the studies of children who enter school early. In most of these studies, girls have outnumbered boys, and yet the programs have been judged highly successful with positive intellectual and social adjustments.[55] It would seem that if girls become actively involved in accelerative programs at an age where social pressures are minimal and if they are not forced to be sepa-

52. Fox, "Sex Differences: Implications for Program Planning for the Academically Gifted."

53. Ibid.

54. Ibid.

55. Dean A. Worchester, *The Education of Children of Above-average Mentality* (Lincoln, Neb.: University of Nebraska Press, 1956); Joseph L. Braga, "Early Admission as Evidence," *Elementary School Journal* 72 (1972): 35-46; Maynard Reynolds, John Buck, and Alice Tuseth, "Review of Research on Early Admission," in *Early Admission for Mentally Advanced Children*, ed. Maynard Reynolds (Reston, Va.: Council for Exceptional Children, 1962); Witty and Wilkins, "The Status of Acceleration or Grade Skipping as an Administrative Practice."

rated from established peer groups in adolescence, the chances of positive and greater involvement are increased. Quite obviously, these statements are based largely on observations of female reactions to mathematics and must be cautiously interpreted. Fear of social rejection may not be as big a factor in accelerative programs in language arts or art or music. The literature gives us no evidence that similar feelings might influence these areas. Further research in comparing the differential effects of acceleration on boys and girls in other subject or talent areas is needed. Furthermore, these studies do not investigate the achievement of students, but rather their willingness to participate and their attitudes toward the program.

The research on other administrative program possibilities does not allow one to draw any conclusions about their sociological or affective effects on gifted or talented females. Flesher and Pressey did not find that early admission to college inhibited the academic success of females.[56] Few data are available, however, regarding the willingness of gifted females to participate in such programs.[57] Enrichment programs as a general class of programs have not been systematically studied to yield evidence of their effects on females, nor have mentor programs, internship programs, or independent study programs. Further research on all of these programs is needed before any firm conclusions can be drawn about the gifted student and interactions of age, subject area, type of program, and sex.

Other variables also seem to be influential in the willingness of young adolescent girls to take part in accelerative mathematics classes. If those classes take place during the regular school day, females are more likely to attend than if the classes are held on Saturday. Girls are also more likely to achieve on a par with boys if the classes are predominantly female and taught by women.[58] The differences reflected here are quite likely to be a result of cultural biases. The identity with other gifted females in the classroom probably serves to make the gifted girl feel much less "different" or

56. Marie A. Flesher and Sidney L. Pressey, "War-time Accelerates Ten Years After," *Journal of Educational Psychology* 46 (1955): 228-38.

57. Fox, "Sex Differences: Implications for Program Planning for the Academically Gifted."

58. Ibid.

"abnormal." Certainly, mathematics and science classes would seem to be the most likely classes to be impacted by these variables since they are areas generally regarded as part of the male domain.

In planning for other types of classes or programs, however, these observations made about mathematics and science may provide some useful guidelines for consideration. For example, are the most effective mentor relationships based on a consideration of the sex of the mentor? Are gifted females placed in internships where there are more females in nonprofessional, subordinate roles than in leadership or professional roles? What impact does this have on the goals of female interns? Answers to these questions are not known at this time and may depend on many cultural factors that may or may not change over the next ten years. As Fox has suggested, the purpose of these observations is not to guide in the construction of gifted programs that will reinforce existing stereotypes, but rather to guide in the construction of programs that will attend to the existing values, needs, and interests of females and work to broaden those values, needs, and interests within nonthreatening structures.[59]

Counseling the Gifted and Talented Female

In conjunction with providing for the academic and social needs of the gifted females as discussed previously, it is important to consider the counseling needs of this group. The more obvious components of a satisfactory counseling program for gifted females include exposure to a wide variety of career options, provision of models of women in varied careers and professions, consideration of alternative learning programs that allow the girl to develop intellectually while not sacrificing social development, and encouragement of career aspirations that may be nontraditional. There are, however, more subtle components of a counseling program that may have a significant impact on the gifted female. One of these elements having the potential for biasing the choices of females is the testing of interests. Many interest inventories contain considerable test bias and restrict the range of career options for women. Interest inventories that have not been sex-balanced (constructed

59. Ibid.

to provide item pools reflecting activities and experiences equally familiar and attractive to males and females) may tend to have a negative, limiting effect on the career choices of young women and discourage by omission interests that might have been viable career options. A recent study of sex-balanced inventories found no significant difference in the predictive validity or discriminative ability of these instruments, suggesting no loss of utility as a result of balancing the instrument.[60] Achievement or aptitude tests should also be examined for potential stereotyping through the role models presented or possible discrimination as a result of types of problems presented.

Other counseling activities, such as academic program planning, should not be neglected in considering the needs of gifted and talented women. There is some evidence that counselors have not always been supportive of programs that could be beneficial to this group. Casserly, for example, did not find counseling to be a factor in positively influencing young women to enroll in Advanced Placement Program courses. In fact, both male and female high school counselors were found to discourage girls from taking such courses in mathematics and science even in schools where teachers were actively recruiting female students for these classes and students had been enrolled in homogeneously grouped courses since elementary school.[61] Reasons for discouraging girls from these courses differed by sex of counselor. Female counselors often generalized their own negative attitudes toward mathematics and science to the students, said that girls needed more time for social activities, or claimed that they did not wish to put girls in classes where they might get low grades. Incidentally, girls enrolled in Advanced Placement Program courses in the schools where these counselors worked were seldom in danger of making poor grades. Male counselors tended to regard the job market in the physical sciences as very limited and concluded that it would be unfair to

60. Gary R. Hanson and Jack Rayman, "Validity of Sex-balanced Interest Inventories" (Paper presented at the annual meeting of the American Educational Research Association, San Francisco, April, 1976).

61. Patricia L. Casserly, "An Assessment of Factors Affecting Female Participation in Advanced Placement Programs in Mathematics, Chemistry, and Physics," Report of National Science Foundation Grant GY-11325 (Princeton, N.J.: Educational Testing Service, 1975).

encourage females to enter professions where the jobs should go to men first.

One final area in which counselors may have an impact in encouraging gifted and talented women is through family advising, teacher contacts, and individual counseling. Encouragement from parents, female role models, teachers, and peers has been shown to be a factor influencing creative women mathematicians and women who have achieved doctorates.[62] The counselor should be prepared to advise parents of gifted children of their role in encouraging their daughter to pursue development of her talent, to seek out and provide contacts with appropriate female role models, and to encourage teachers to view all students as equally competent, regardless of sex and subject area. In short, counselors should attempt to provide opportunities for the gifted and talented female to see a wide variety of options for career and life-style and encourage her choices regardless of the sex-role stereotyping of those choices. Through the efforts of all of those around the gifted and talented female, perhaps the barriers to success and achievements can be broken down. Certainly, society stands to gain from the contribution of this largely untapped resource.

Summary

The research on the intellectual ability of gifted females as compared to gifted males is inconclusive except in the area of mathematics, where there is a definitely greater proportion of males identified as gifted. The degree of cultural and hereditary influence on this ability is not apparent. Studies of other areas of intellectual abilities reveal no consistent difference between males and females. Given the lack of evidence of aptitude differences, personality variables are examined as a source of variation that affects the disproportionate numbers of men and women who achieve success. Achievement motivation and locus of control have been suggested as traits that influence the degree of success of professional women. Family variables have also been suggested as influencing the gifted woman's success. Identification with a father or masculine model,

62. Ibid. See also Helen S. Astin, *The Woman Doctorate in America* (New York: Russell Sage Foundation, 1969) and Helson, "Women Mathematicians and the Creative Personality."

for example, has been characteristic of successful professional women. The research literature has also suggested many cultural barriers to the gifted woman, and although environment and heredity cannot be studied within controlled experimental designs, the studies examining teacher behavior, organizational reward systems, test bias, and social biases suggest many cultural handicaps for the gifted woman.

The research in the area of administrative programming for the gifted woman has suffered by little attention to the effect of sex on the impact of various administrative options. There is some indication, at least within the area of mathematics, that enrichment programs are unattractive for adolescent females. The degree of social influence on other programs has not been fully explored. Other questions regarding models, sex of instructor, and the timing of enrichment activities are also relevant to considerations of programming for gifted women.

Finally, special consideration should be given to the counseling of gifted women. Test biases should be identified, occupational counseling needs to be broadened, and counselors need to be sensitized to the needs of gifted females.

The era of the women's movement is yet new and may perhaps have a profound influence on the gifted woman. At this time, the impact of this movement is an unknown factor. Hopefully, however, it will at least allow the potential of young women to be identified and realized without the constraints that have been imposed by society in the past.

CHAPTER XXVII

Counseling and Guidance Needs of the Gifted and Talented

MARSHALL P. SANBORN

Twenty-one years ago, an interdisciplinary committee was formed at the University of Wisconsin to develop a program whereby the University could help schools meet needs of gifted and talented students. Members of the faculties of Education, Engineering, Medicine, Letters and Science, Agriculture, Law, Business, and University Extension worked together over the ensuing years to design and finance a center for advanced study of pupils who showed superior promise in any field. The Research and Guidance Laboratory was established as an official unit of the University, and its services were offered to school districts throughout the state.

Since 1958, the Laboratory has carried on direct longitudinal counseling and guidance work with gifted and talented students in some ninety cooperating school systems. It has utilized a research-through-service format to help local schools develop procedures for the identification, education, and guidance of the gifted. Nearly 4,000 young people, their parents, and their teachers have taken part in the program. Data regarding students' development during school and postschool years have been systematically collected and analyzed. Cumulative case records on each participating student have been maintained, and follow-up surveys have been used to trace their progress through higher education and into their developing career and life-styles.

Schools involved in the Laboratory program have provided an excellent cross section of school communities in Wisconsin. They range in size from those with fewer than ten teachers (grades nine through twelve) to those with more than 100 teachers, and they represent most socioeconomic environments in the state. There is perhaps no other agency that has sustained direct counseling and guidance contacts with so many gifted and talented young people and their "significant others" over so long a period of time.

Observations discussed below have been drawn mainly from research and clinical experiences at the Laboratory. Case-by-case experience has taught us to make very few sweeping statements about the gifted and talented. A counseling and guidance approach calls for highly individualized contacts and interpretations. We have been interested in uniqueness, and we have found uniqueness. Although Laboratory activities generate gross data, those of us who try to interpret the data do so in the light of many case contacts, and we have become aware of many limitations in our attempts to generalize.

Gifted and talented individuals differ from each other in more ways than they resemble each other. This is perhaps the only generalization that can be safely made. It is also perhaps the most important principle to consider in a discussion of the counseling and guidance needs of the gifted. One of the main purposes of counseling and guidance in schools is to discover unique patterns of individual characteristics—interests, aptitudes, abilities, values, motives —and to assist the individual to determine the meaning of these characteristics in relation to educational, career, and life-style opportunities. A corollary purpose is to assist the teaching staff in utilizing individual characteristics in generating appropriate developmental experiences.

Identification and Description

It seems axiomatic that a primary need of the gifted is to be recognized as individuals who, by virtue of superior performances and/or hypothesized potentialities, will require special attention of the school. Educational literature already contains a large amount of material to this effect, and a variety of schemes for identification of the gifted have been developed. It must be stressed, however, that whatever identification process is used can at best provide only a beginning point in the total process of appraisal and description that is needed.

Unfortunately it is too often the case that once a group of gifted and talented children has been identified, further efforts to describe them do not occur. The process used to identify them, once accomplished, marks the end of attempts to know and understand their unique individual qualities. Even when fairly adequate individual data are used in the identification process, these data are seldom considered seriously in the later challenge of planning and delivering an appropriate set of educational experiences for each child. Instead, those who have been classified as "gifted," no matter how they may vary, are put into programs that appear to be based on the assumption that if they are gifted they must be alike.

The fact that they are not alike, however, has been demonstrated many times. In Terman's original study, for example, he noted a range in IQ from 140-200 among 643 gifted youngsters.[1] Although his subjects were all in the top 2 percent of the general population in terms of performance on an intelligence test, they nevertheless revealed a range of at least sixty points on the IQ scale. Sumption and Luecking observed that a range as large as this is as great as the difference between "the moron and the bright child."[2] While there is no reason to believe that equal IQ differences represent equal differences in learning ability all along the IQ scale, it does appear that the full range of IQs found among the gifted reflect wide variations in intelligence even among this "homogeneous" group.

Criteria in current use are much broader and entail more sources of variation than did the IQ criterion used by Terman. A recent list of the U.S. Office of Education includes, in addition to assessment of general intelligence, consideration of specific aptitudes, creativity, leadership, and artistic and psychomotor performances.[3] This list is designed, in part, to encourage those who identify the gifted to include factors that are not as culturally biased as are measures of intelligence. The list includes, however, factors not necessarily associated with performance on an intelligence test even when cultural background is held constant. Hence, we may expect

1. Lewis M. Terman et al., *Genetic Studies of Genius*, vol. 1, *Mental and Physical Traits of a Thousand Gifted Children* (Stanford, Calif.: Stanford University Press, 1925).

2. Merle R. Sumption and Evelyn M. Luecking, *Education of the Gifted* (New York: Ronald Press, 1960), p. 111.

3. Sidney Marland, Jr., *Education of the Gifted and Talented*, Report to the Congress of the United States by the U.S. Commissioner of Education (Washington, D.C.: U.S. Government Printing Office, 1972), p. 2.

to find wider variations among present groups of gifted youngsters than were found in the past.

Another source of variation among the gifted, "cognitive style," has been the subject of research for many years but has received only scanty attention from practitioners who design programs for the gifted. Sundberg declares cognitive style to be "in the border-land between ability and personality."[4] The possibility that variations in cognitive style may be related to personality differences has been shown by a number of researchers.[5] Recent work by Piechowski leads to the inference that differences in cognitive style may at least in part be functions of constitutional traits that can be assessed independent of context of development and that represent sensual, psychomotor, emotional, imaginational, and intellectual channels through which information is processed.[6]

Studies at the Research and Guidance Laboratory have demonstrated that although gifted children may perform alike in terms of product quality, they may vary significantly in terms of processes whereby products are achieved.[7] Thus it appears that atten-

4. Norman D. Sundberg, *Assessment of Persons* (Englewood Cliffs, N.J.: Prentice-Hall, 1977), p. 236.

5. See, for example, Herman A. Witkin and J. W. Berry, "Psychological Differentiation in Cross-Cultural Perspective," *Journal of Cross-Cultural Psychology* 6 (1975): 4-87; Jerome Kagan, Howard A. Moss, and Irving E. Sigel, "Psychological Significance of Styles of Conceptualization," in *Basic Cognitive Processes in Children*, ed. John C. Wright and Jerome Kagan *Monographs of the Society for Research in Child Development* 28, no. 2 (1963): 73-124; *Perspectives in Personal Construct Theory*, ed. David Bannister (London: Academic Press, 1970); Leon H. Levy and Robert D. Dugan, "A Factorial Study of Personal Constructs," *Journal of Consulting Psychology* 20 (1956): 53-57; Julian B. Rotter, "Generalized Expectancies for Internal versus External Control of Reinforcement," *Psychological Monographs* 80, no. 1 (1966): entire issue.

6. Michael M. Piechowski, "Two Developmental Concepts: Multilevelness and Developmental Potential," *Counseling and Values* 18 (1974): 86-93.

7. John J. Cody and John W. M. Rothney, "Oral Problem-Solving Performances of Superior High School Students," *Personnel and Guidance Journal* 41 (1963): 425-29; Patricia M. Harrington, "The Use of Free-Response Analogy Items to Assess Verbal Performances of Superior High School Students" (Master's Seminar Paper, University of Wisconsin-Madison, 1965); Norbert E. Koopman, "Evaluations by Superior High School Students of their Problem-Solving Performances" (Ph.D. diss., University of Wisconsin-Madison, 1964); John W. M. Rothney and Marshall P. Sanborn, "Verbal Skills of Superior Students," Final Report, Cooperative Research Project S-036, (Washington, D.C.: U.S. Office of Education, 1965).

tion to style should be given importance in planning developmental experiences for the gifted. More accurate description of learner individuality on dimensions of style will tend to emphasize the need for ideographic approaches to programming. It is on these kinds of characteristics that they are most likely to show both inter- and intra-individual profiles.

Recognizing Uniqueness

Anyone who has worked with the gifted is almost certain to have encountered the fact that many of them (perhaps the vast majority) do not like to be called "gifted." Sometimes this fact is explained by the assertion that gifted individuals are outcasts in an egalitarian society, or that they are sensitive to attitudes of anti-intellectualism held by most of the people with whom they must live. This kind of an explanation may have some truth in it, but it may also be simplistic in the sense that it tends to fix blame only on others and never on advocates of the gifted.

If attitudes of egalitarianism and antiintellectualism actually lead to discrimination against the gifted and talented, it would appear that they do so mainly in schools. Outside of schools, society seems to recognize and reward many gifted and talented persons who, for one reason or another, have been motivated to develop their potentialities and exercise them. In the arts, in science, in business and industry, in athletics, in entertainment, in the professions, and occasionally even in politics, pure excellence of performance is recognized and rewarded.

This is true, of course, only with regard to those who have not been discriminated against for some reason other than their "giftedness." It is likely that many gifted women, blacks, native Americans, or members of other groups who have been treated categorically would argue that it is not always true. It seems that whenever we attempt to characterize individuals on the basis of generalized beliefs we have about the category to which those individuals have been assigned, we risk making inappropriate judgments.

The terms "gifted" and "talented" are also categorical terms. They are not very descriptive. They tell us no more about an individual than do such words as "black" or "female" or "Caucasian."

An alert and sensitive young person may know this, and may be keenly aware that being classified as "gifted" can be associated with unpleasant and unproductive consequences from any source where stereotyping occurs. In many cases, these consequences may go undiscovered, and we may enjoy the illusion that we are making appropriate adjustments for a gifted child even when we are not. This fact was aptly illustrated recently during a conversation with a fourteen-year-old boy from a northern Wisconsin community. "My teachers think I'm bright," he said, "and they give me a lot of 'extra' work to do. To keep up my image, I do it. The result of this is that none of us—not even me myself—really knows who I am."

A major outcome of the identification and description process should be that it helps gifted children *learn about their own unique qualities.* If they differ from other children in their need for self-discovery, it is likely that the difference is usually in degree of complexity of the problem. Gifted and talented children usually have multiple "gifts." They perform well in a variety of areas, and they reveal wide ranges of interests and concerns. Laboratory data have illustrated this "multipotentiality" again and again. Performances of Laboratory participants cluster around the 95th-97th percentiles on most standardized tests.[8] Furthermore, individuals tend to perform evenly across a variety of verbal, quantitative, and special aptitude or subject-matter tasks, with sharp profiles of performance either on tests or in school courses being relatively rare.[9] Contrary to the "egghead" stereotype often applied to the gifted, Laboratory data reveal a group of young people who display during school and postschool years rich patterns of interest and involvement in a wide variety of activities. A summary of activities of 350 school-age boys and girls and a follow-up study of 497 young men and women who were four years beyond high school both demonstrated that the Laboratory group tends to achieve high levels of

8. John W. M. Rothney and Marshall P. Sanborn, "Wisconsin's Research-through-Service Program for Superior Students," *Personnel and Guidance Journal* 44 (1966): 694-99.

9. Ronald Fredrickson and John W. M. Rothney, *Recognizing and Assisting Multipotential Youth* (Columbus, Ohio: Charles Merrill Publishing Co., 1972), pp. 80-81.

performance in academic, athletic, religious, political, social, solitary, and creative pursuits.[10]

The following statement written at the Laboratory by a twelfth-grade boy illustrates the guidance problem associated with multipotentiality:

> I have found that if I apply myself I can do almost anything. I don't seem to have a serious lack of aptitude in any field. I find an English assignment equally as difficult as a physics problem. I find them also to be equally as challenging and equally as interesting. The same goes for mathematics, social studies, music, speech, or any other subject area. . . . Nothing is so simple for me that I can do a perfect job without effort, but nothing is so hard that I cannot do it. This is why I find it so difficult to decide my place in the future. Many people wouldn't consider this much of a problem; but to me, this lack of one area to stand out in is a very grave problem indeed.[11]

How do we assist gifted young people to learn how to set life goals and to pursue valid life-styles for themselves? When abilities and interests are determined to be high in a variety of things, what other facets should be considered? What criteria should we encourage them to use in determining how, or whether, to focus themselves on particular pursuits? How, within the school program, can we learn to respond to the unique factors individual students show us? How can we respond so as to assist the young person to know, value, and utilize valid personal traits in personal decision making? How can we learn to recognize and capitalize not only on their "gifts," but also on their other developmental potentialities and needs?

Several years ago I visited a special summer program for gifted and talented children at San Fernando Valley State College in California. I became especially interested in observing the work of one mathematics teacher who appeared to exemplify teaching at its best. The teacher was developing some concepts in probability

10. *Career Education for Gifted and Talented Students*, ed., Kenneth B. Hoyt and Jean Hebeler (Salt Lake City: Olympus Publishing Co., 1974), pp. 110-13; Charles W. Lewis, Richard L. Bradley, and John W. M. Rothney "Assessment of Accomplishments of College Students Four Years after High School Graduation," *Personnel and Guidance Journal* 47 (1969): 745-52.

11. *Career Education for Gifted and Talented Students*, ed. Hoyt and Hebeler, p. 121.

theory with a group of about twenty young boys and girls. After two or three class sessions in which probability events were predicted theoretically, he suggested that members of the class bring dice, decks of playing cards, and other paraphernalia on the following day, so that empirical checks could be made to see whether things actually happened according to theory.

At the next class session, the children gathered about the room in small groups and began to throw the dice, deal the cards, and record results of repeated events. That is, all the children did this except one boy who sat in a vacant part of the room, brought out a music book and a small harmonica, and began to play.

"Why isn't that boy working with the others?" I asked the teacher.

"Well," he replied, "he's a theoretical guy. Once he understands the theory, he's quite content that it tells the story. He doesn't care much for the empirical part, so when we get to sessions like this one, I let him practice his harmonica."

In this instance, a perceptive teacher recognized and responded to an important difference in developmental styles between one gifted student and the others. One is impressed by the possibility that this teacher not only made an appropriate classroom adjustment for a unique individual, but also helped this young person to explore and perhaps to validate one of his own unique characteristics.

Two Cases in Point

In schools, counseling and guidance activities ought to be designed to help children learn about their own qualities and to attempt to relate these qualities to opportunities open to them both in the present and in the future. Concomitant with this self-discovery objective, guidance activities ought to help the school learn about the student, so that appropriate educational opportunities can be generated for the particular style and needs of the student. A satisfactory guidance experience for a gifted child will probably depend on achievement of both these objectives. If both are achieved, results will be visible not only in better awareness by the students of their own pattern of developmental characteristics, but also in more appropriate responses to individual students in the classroom, where the real impact of a good guidance program is most likely to be felt.

Most gifted students like school. Even those who are frustrated by shortcomings of the school usually sense the potentialities of education. Even severe anger and frustration with school is likely to be an indication that the student cares about school. Therefore the possibilities for implementing meaningful guidance activities through the curriculum are very strong. In most cases adequate mastery of subject matter is a relatively minor challenge for both the teacher and the student. It is also a relatively minor challenge to proceed on to other subject matter once current topics have been mastered. The real challenge is to know the student's unique needs that can be met through curriculum strategies, and then to meet them.

Guidance people can use appraisal and counseling skills to help identify developmental characteristics and needs, but it is unlikely that they will have a strong impact unless they can enlist teachers to work together with them and the student to meet those needs. This point can be illustrated with case data drawn from Laboratory records of two gifted boys who attended the same school in the early 1960s. More complete case reports of each of these boys can be found elsewhere.[12] The focus here is on data pertaining to differences in guidance needs these two boys displayed—differences that were recognized by their teachers and counselors but were ignored in classroom planning. We shall call these boys "John" and "Mark".

Both John and Mark were high performers. A summary of selected test and school performances in table 1 reveals almost identical productivity on verbal, quantitative, and critical thinking tests, as well as in school and college grades.

On the above criteria, no meaningful differences between John and Mark appear. Nor do any appear on a number of other criteria. Both boys, for example, were very fine athletes. Both were on state

12. Marshall P. Sanborn, "School Counseling: Emphatically Not a Therapy Service," in *The Counselor's Handbook*, ed., Gail Farwell, Neal Gamsky, and Philippa Mathieu-Coughlan (New York: Intext Educational Publishers, 1974), pp. 27-52; Charles J. Pulvino, Nick Colangelo, and Ronald T. Zaffran, *Laboratory Counseling Programs* (Madison, Wisc.: Research and Guidance Laboratory, University of Wisconsin, 1976), pp. 30-35.

TABLE 1

SUMMARY OF PERFORMANCE OF TWO HIGH-PERFORMING BOYS

PERFORMANCE INDICATORS	JOHN	MARK

School and College Ability Test
    Verbal percentile rank
    Quantitative percentile rank
	96–99
	99
		96–99
		97

Differential Aptitude Tests Verbal percentile rank	96	99
Watson-Glaser Critical Thinking Appraisal Percentile rank	99	99
Henmon-Nelson Test of Mental Ability Percentile rank	97	95
Terman Concept Mastery Test Twelfth-grade raw score	100	105
High school grade-point average	3.91	3.87
College undergraduate grade-point average	3.94	3.81

championship debate teams. Both elected to attend high prestige colleges, and both graduated *cum laude* with majors in social studies.

Differences were noted, however, by their classroom teachers in grade nine. The teacher remarks shown in table 2 were solicited at the time students were being selected for participation in the Laboratory program. They reveal sharp contrasts in the two boys as viewed by the teachers who had them in an "accelerated" program in their school.

It might appear that these teachers are describing an "over-achiever" and an "underachiever" but very little other evidence on the two boys would bear this out. Both achieved very well, and there appeared to be no serious inconsistency between aptitude and achievement. It might appear that the teachers were describing one boy who was highly motivated and one who was not. But this is not true either. If there was a difference in motivation, it was in the source more than in the amount.

It might also appear that the ninth-grade teachers were less satisfied with John than they were with Mark. This is probably true. Throughout high school, Mark did his best to meet and surpass teacher and peer expectations, but John did not. Mark's record

TABLE 2

TEACHER REMARKS ABOUT TWO HIGH-PERFORMING BOYS

TEACHER OF	JOHN	MARK
Biology	John often becomes interested in things on his own and carries them out to satisfy his own curiosity.	Mark is one of the hardest workers I have ever encountered. Very meticulous, and tries hard to overcome his "weak" points. Too much concern for little things may hamper his overall progress.
History	John has an excellent, sharp mind. Tremendous potential. Things come almost too easy for him. He depends on getting by on his quick wit. Does very excellent work when he puts his mind to it.	Mark tries hard and succeeds.
French	John is a superior student, but seems to come by this without too much effort. He is content to do what is required of him and stop there. Does not take on additional work unless prodded.	Mark is a superior student in all ways.
Mathematics	John has a lot of ability going to waste. If he ever finds a purpose in life, he will be a powerhouse. Right now he is content to get by without too much exertion.	Mark could be good, but he's spread too thin. Does not possess the keen analytical mind needed in math. If he would concentrate, however, it could be easily developed.
English	John is very capable but inclined to rely on the ease and quickness with which he can work. Definitely superior to most people in his class.	Mark's ideas and opinions are valued by his classmates, (partly because) he never loses his consideration for others. He is quick to analyze situations in literature, and to grasp ideas and concepts. He is a thinker, and an excellent writer.
Physical Education	John does not think before he acts.	Mark has to learn to lose along with winning.
Music	John's energy seems to run about parallel with his interest in a topic.	

shows that he achieved virtually the highest possible levels in athletics, student government, debate and forensics, Boy Scouts, and in his academic work. On a rating scale completed by his teachers, Mark received top ratings from all his instructors on initiative, dependability, leadership, popularity, study habits, and concern for others. John, on the other hand, often disappointed his teachers even though he received good marks in his classes. He was characterized by his teachers as "lazy," "cocky," "immature," and "lacking in responsibility." Teacher responses on a rating scale for John reflected their attitudes. He received low ratings on initiative, responsibility, dependability, and study habits. The cumulative records for all four years of high school reflected high satisfaction with Mark's progress, and considerable dissatisfaction with John's, even though both boys performed almost equally well insofar as school grades are concerned.

It was only after graduation from college that differences their teachers had noted as early as grade nine began to show in terms of educational, vocational, and personal development. Laboratory follow-up records tell the story.

John, who breezed through the accelerated program on his quick wit, who did not seem to his teachers to be willing to take on challenges they set up for him, and who did his best work only on things that happened to interest him, went on to study at a prestigious state university. He began with a major in physics, but after his sophomore year he switched to social studies. "Physics," he said, "was too narrow." After graduation he went directly on to a theological seminary. On completion of seminary work he took a position as an associate clergyman in a large church, where his duties included personal counseling, preaching and leading in worship, and programming of Christian education for adults.

Now, more than ten years after high school, John's intention is to gain a few more years of experience as a clergyman and then aim for a Ph.D. in philosophy and a teaching position in a theological seminary. He has been married since 1967. He is a highly regarded member of his church staff, and by his own report is happy in his work and his life-style. He looks forward to his future and believes it promises to be interesting and enjoyable. At the same time, he describes the present as an "extremely satisfying and challenging life, with plenty of opportunity for continuing learning and development."

When asked to look back at his high school, John said, "There was some solid work . . . in sciences. Debate, athletics, music helped me gain confidence. Humanities and social sciences were not very good, and some people were overzealous about pushing me in science fields. The school's abominable personality rating program . . . was more destructive than anything."

Mark's postcollege history is quite different from John's. After graduating from an Ivy League school, he enlisted in the Navy and served for a period of time as a naval officer. He left the Navy because he did not see how he could ever make a career of it. Although his early plan had been to enter a law school, by the time he left the Navy he had decided against a law career. He said that he would like to do something to "improve the quality of life" in the country, but had no ideas about what to do to achieve this goal. Mark is presently enrolled in a graduate school program in social studies. He has thought of a number of alternative careers, but has settled on none. He has never married and lives alone. He has no plans for the future and says that right now he is trying to keep his options "as open as possible, at least until sufficiently confident to make a choice."

About his high school and college education he said he felt an "empty sense of achievement." He compared his own developmental progress to the problem of Sysyphus, who was condemned forever to roll a heavy stone toward the top of the mountain only to have it slip from his grasp and roll to the bottom again. This analogy seems appropriate. In school, he found that completing a task sooner or better than teachers expected resulted only in another, more difficult task. "My problem," he said, "is to attempt to plan my time and set goals for myself. This is something that I did not have to do in high school or college. It was more or less done for me by my instructors."

At the time of this writing, Mark and John are each about thirty years of age. It seems ironic that many of the descriptive statements made about Mark by his high school teachers now could be made about John, and vice versa. It is John who works hard and enjoys success. It is John who enjoys learning, whose opinions are highly valued, who shows strong social concern in his daily activities, and who seems to be "a thinker." Mark, on the other hand, seems to lack a purpose in life, to be "immature" in his career and life-style development, and to represent "a lot of ability going to waste." At the moment he seems to be stalled and it is very difficult to find any basis for predicting what direction he will take in the future.

Actually in terms of the personal qualities noted by their teachers during high school—qualities that would logically be of concern in the guidance program—neither of these young men seems to have changed much over the past fifteen years. If the guidance program should have had any significant impact on these qualities, it did not. John, who went according to his own values and interests during high school, has continued to do so since. Mark, who was "other-directed" during his schooling, seems to have no self-direction now.

Fortunately for John, by the time he entered the high school accelerated program he had developed enough inner strength to maintain himself even in the face of considerable teacher disapproval. Unfortunately for Mark, he did not have such strength. He needed the approval he worked so effectively to get. Unfortunately for everyone concerned, John's very great personal strength was observed but never systematically utilized by his teachers in his education; and Mark's very significant personal need, although recognized by some teachers (see the comments of teachers of biology, mathematics, and physical education, for example), was never systematically attacked. Instead, John's independence was a source of frustration and Mark's dependence was reinforced. Both of these errors were committed in the interest of the boys' intellectual development.

Conclusion

Gifted children, like other children, need someone in their school whose primary objective is to generate sound and useful information pertaining to their unique and important individual qualities. They need someone who has the professional skill to assist them and their teachers in making sound interpretations of individual appraisal data and wise decisions concerning developmental activities to undertake. They need teachers who, with the assistance of competent guidance personnel, are willing and able to recognize and adjust to developmental strengths and needs that are not strictly intellectual and who see the curriculum as the strongest potentiality the school has for meeting guidance needs of children. They need a school in which openness and accuracy of communication among the teaching-counseling-parenting team is taught and encouraged, and where people work together to develop sound guidance strategies, child by child when necessary. In these respects, gifted and talented children do not differ much from children in general.

In one respect, however, they may be different from many children; for no matter how poorly we do, they are likely to behave tolerably well and to do well on the kinds of things we customarily use to assess progress in school. Therefore, it is often difficult for them to command attention and concern on matters of importance. Those who counsel regularly with the gifted know this; but those who do the counseling cannot change it by themselves. The teaching staff has the real control over the experience of a pupil in school. And because gifted and talented children are interested in and concerned about subjects taught in school, it is the curriculum that has the greatest potential as a delivery system for meeting their guidance needs. The guidance personnel can provide resources for both the teacher and the child, but the teacher guides the child. Once this fact is recognized, the question becomes, "Toward what?" This question can only be answered for one child at a time.

A Look Around and a Look Ahead

A. HARRY PASSOW

"The idea of providing special educational facilities for children of superior intelligence is by no means a novel one."[1] This statement appeared more than a half century ago in the opening chapter of the Twenty-third Yearbook of the National Society for the Study of Education. The editor of that volume noted that the rise of various plans for more effective education of gifted pupils had been a natural consequence "of the recognition of individual differences in their relation to the mechanizing tendency of the graded school system."[2] A number of plans, beginning in 1868 with one plan in St. Louis for acceleration through promotion at short intervals, were described very briefly, most of them having been initiated in city school systems. Most of the plans involved some form of acceleration (usually special promotion or grade skipping) or segregated groupings (usually special classes or sections), or a combination of the two. Enrichment classes were operated in some school systems as an alternative to rapid promotion where that practice was seen as undesirable.

Most of the Twenty-third Yearbook was devoted to special studies of the gifted, including studies of their physical and mental traits and their educational attainments as well as "experimental and statistical studies" of plans for ability grouping or for acceleration. Horn presented some general principles that he thought should control curricula for gifted pupils, focusing specifically on adjust-

---

1. Guy M. Whipple, "Historical and Introductory," in *The Education of Gifted Children,* Twenty-third Yearbook on the National Society for the Study of Education, Part I, ed. Guy M. Whipple (Bloomington, Ill.: Public School Publishing Co., 1924), p. 1.

2. Ibid., p. 8.

ing instruction in spelling.[3] Rugg wrote on the curriculum for gifted children, calling attention to "four chief divisions of our army of gifted youth . . . : the verbally intelligent, the socially intelligent, the mechanically intelligent, the esthetically intelligent." Rugg was one of the earliest advocates for broadening "our notion of talent, of 'giftedness,' to include many aspects of culture, for the school is responsible for the development of all the abilities in a child." He also pointed to the graduation in ability from the level of the true genius (perhaps one in a million) down to those of less conspicuous ability or talent (perhaps one in a hundred) and suggested that the actual number depended on one's definition of "giftedness."[4]

More than two decades ago, Tannenbaum traced the ups and downs in special provisions for the gifted, observing that although such provisions "were never widespread, the end of World War II found interest in the gifted in the public schools at a low ebb."[5] He found a heightened concern in the early 1950s which he ascribed to the cold war struggle for scientific and technological leadership, to the shortage of resources in high-level manpower, and to the critical reappraisals of public school programs. This concern, which was intensified by the launching of the Russian Sputnik in 1957, resulted in a loosening of some of the rigid thinking that had guided educational planning for the gifted.

The Fifty-seventh Yearbook included chapters on the motivation, creativity, and social leadership of gifted children. Williams presented thirteen characteristics of a program for the gifted.[6] Programs in elementary schools, in secondary schools, in colleges and universities, and in nonschool community agencies were discussed in detail, with contributors drawing from ongoing programs for

3. Ernest Horn, "The Curriculum for the Gifted: Some Principles and an Illustration," in *The Education of Gifted Children*, ed. Whipple, pp. 73-89.

4. Harold Rugg, "The Curriculum for Gifted Children," in *The Education of Gifted Children*, ed. Whipple, p. 93.

5. Abraham J. Tannenbaum, "History of Interest in the Gifted," in *Education for the Gifted*, Fifty-seventh Yearbook of the National Society for the Study of Education, Part II, ed. Nelson B. Henry (Chicago: University of Chicago Press, 1958), p. 34.

6. Clifford W. Williams, "Characteristics and Objectives of a Program for the Gifted," in *Education for the Gifted*, ed. Henry, pp. 147-65.

content and illustrations. The tenor of the writing, reflecting the climate of education at the time, was essentially upbeat. In the introductory chapter it was argued that:

the ideas and proposals for education for gifted children in this yearbook have a validity which is independent of particular arguments based on present-day scarcities and needs. The programs described in the following chapters are good in themselves for education in the United States, for reasons of American values.[7]

By the early 1960s, however, a decline had begun in the attention to the education of the gifted, a decline that Tannenbaum attributed to a number of factors. In his view, the idea of special provisions for such students "never really entered the bloodstream of American education"; rather, "gifted children were considered ornaments to be detached and discarded when the cost of upkeep became prohibitive."[8] National concern with education of the disadvantaged, with civil rights, and with equality of educational opportunity resulted in a shift in school priorities.

The dilemma posed by Gardner concerning the simultaneous pursuit of excellence and equality,[9] was restated by Tannenbaum as follows:

by leaning too far in the direction of excellence, the country is in danger of creating a special kind of elitism out of meritocracy; by leaning heavily in the direction of equality, it easily loses sight of real human differences and ignores outstanding potential rather than offering special privileges for its cultivation. At this point in history, any neglect of the principle of equality can tear the nation apart from within; neglect of our need to build the largest possible reservoir of excellent human resources can make us vulnerable to attack from without. There is always the danger that the pursuit of excellence can only be accomplished by a retreat from equality and vice versa. . . . The most serious task facing us today is to place both goals in the same direction so that they can be pursued with equal vigor at the same time.[10]

7. Robert J. Havighurst et al., "The Importance of Education for the Gifted," in *Education for the Gifted*, ed. Henry, p. 4.

8. Abraham J. Tannenbaum, "A Backward and Forward Glance at the Gifted," *National Elementary Principal* 51 (February 1972): 18.

9. John W. Gardner, *Can We Be Equal and Excellent Too?* (New York: Harper and Row, 1961).

10. Tannenbaum, "A Backward and Forward Glance at the Gifted," pp. 18-19.

A most significant event was the passage of the addition to the Elementary and Secondary Education Amendments of 1969 (Public Law 91-230), which not only made clear the congressional intent that the gifted and talented should benefit from existing federal legislation on education, but also mandated a study by the U.S. Commissioner of Education to determine the extent to which the special educational needs of this population were being met, to assess how existing federal programs for educational assistance could be made more effective in meeting those needs, and to recommend what new programs were needed. In transmitting his report to the Congress, Sidney P. Marland, Jr., the Commissioner of Education, observed that the study had "confirmed our impression of inadequate provisions for these students and widespread misunderstanding about their needs."[11]

The second volume of the Commissioner's report contained seven appendixes, which provided the basic data for the findings and gave direction to the recommendations. Martinson reviewed the relevant research, selecting studies that seemed to respond directly to the pertinent questions that had been raised, and suggesting the implications of the studies for education. She observed that "the United States has been inconsistent in seeking out these [gifted and talented] students, finding them early in their lives, and individualizing their education."[12] Moreover, the research indicated that:

special programs have produced ample evidence of their merits. Widely varying arrangements have been found successful, and indicate clearly that excellence for the gifted can become a universal practice with less expenditure than in programs for other children with special learning needs.[13]

Some 204 leaders and influential professionals in the field of education for gifted and talented students completed an Advocate

11. Sidney P. Marland, Jr., *Education of the Gifted and Talented: Report to the Congress of the United States by the U.S. Commissioner of Education* (Washington, D.C.: U.S. Government Printing Office, 1972), vol. 1, p. ix.

12. Ruth A. Martinson, "Research on the Gifted and Talented: Its Implications for Education," in Marland, *Education of the Gifted and Talented: Background Papers*, vol. 2, p. 110.

13. Ibid.

Survey questionnaire. Their view of the adequacy of existing programs and provisions was a dismal one: "Nearly all communities are described as having very few provisions, or none at all. The neglect is greatest at the early school years, but even at the high school level, little is done."[14]

The Marland report provided a benchmark concerning the education of the gifted and talented programmatically at the federal, state, and local levels and politically as well. Marland proposed ten major activities to be initiated in 1971 which, although never fully implemented, did serve to establish the United States Office of Education as the agency taking responsibility for leadership in the field. An Office of Gifted and Talented was established within the Bureau of Education for the Handicapped in the Office of Education.

Federal leadership has been growing and has ranged from advocacy and raising the nation's level of consciousness concerning the educational needs of the gifted and talented to program development through categorical funding. Among its earliest efforts was the creation of the National/State Leadership Training Institute on the Gifted and Talented (N/S-LTI-G/T), which has focused on developing awareness and advocacy, on training state and local leadership, and on enhancing the program-planning competencies of both teams and individuals. All fifty states have been involved at one time or another with LTI workshops and conferences at which product development, usually in the form of a plan to be implemented, is required of all participants.

Section 404 of Public Law 93-380, passed in 1975, provided for "grants and contracts to State and local educational agencies, institutions of higher education, and other agencies and organizations for exemplary programs and projects to meet the educational needs of gifted and talented children and youth." The appropriation for Section 404 was small by most standards of federal funding for education (well under $3 million), but the competition for the grants, which ranged from $10,000 to $190,000, has been very keen, with sizeable numbers of state and local educational agencies submitting proposals each year. The existence of an approved state

14. Ibid., vol. 1, p. 30.

plan was an important consideration in the evaluation of applications.

In 1978, both houses of Congress were considering legislation that would dramatically expand federal involvement. In addition to providing other authorizations, the House version ("Gifted and Talented Children's Act of 1978") would enable the Commissioner of Education

to make grants to State educational agencies in order to assist them in planning, development, operation, and improvement of programs, including the in-service training of personnel designed to meet the special educational needs of gifted and talented children at the preschool, elementary, and secondary levels.

The Senate version, know as "Part E: Education of Gifted and Talented Children," would authorize grants to states that are to be expended solely

to plan, establish, and operate programs and projects which (1) are designed to identify and to meet the special education and related needs of gifted and talented children and (2) are of sufficient size, scope, and quality as to hold reasonable promise of making substantial progress toward meeting those needs.

In October 1975, the Commissioner of Education issued a policy statement declaring that the "United States Office of Education recognizes the education of the gifted and talented as being an integral part of our educational system and supports the endeavors of all those who are involved in providing increased educational opportunities for these students." The Commissioner pledged the resources of the Office of Education to provide technical and supportive services to state and local institutions and persons in developing special programs. One significant development, then, in the 1970s has been the growing federal commitment to encourage an awareness of the need and to assist the development and implementation of programs at the local, regional, and state levels.

Typical of development at the state level is the statement of policy and proposed action by the Board of Regents of the University of the State of New York (State Education Department), which contains ten recommendations that the Board believed would "promote more equitable opportunity for the State's gifted and talented pupils."[15] The recommendations urged that local boards develop policy statements and administrative guidelines to assure that these pupils are provided an appropriate education; that early screening and identification procedures are developed; that special strategies for identification and nurturance of the disadvantaged gifted are included in the plans; that plans for educational programming take into account the intellectual and social needs of the gifted; that competent and concerned staff are selected as teachers of the gifted; that statewide and regional resource development and demonstration centers are organized; and that cooperation among various agencies and institutions (schools, industry, universities, parent groups, and so forth) is increased in order to create a variety of optional learning environments for the gifted and talented. The position paper also recommended a review of provisions of federally funded programs to ascertain what amounts of those funds can be used to support statewide programs for the gifted and talented. A long-range state plan to implement the policies was to be developed.

With support from the federal and state educational agencies, local educational authorities appear to be designing programs that are integrally related to the educational system rather than peripheral appendages. Such programs and provisions for the gifted are likely to be more durable, even though subject to modification and adaptation, as should be the case with all educational programs.

A Look Around

A survey of programs, including a review of the prototype programs discussed in earlier chapters in this volume, indicates a wide variety of curricular, instructional, and organizational strategies. There is no simple formula for appropriate education for gifted and talented students. Earlier literature discussed three approaches: acceleration, segregation or ability grouping, and enrichment in the regular classroom. In fact, each of these administrative adaptations has its own variations. Special grouping, for

15. Regents of the University of the State of New York, *Educating the Gifted and Talented in New York State* (Albany: State Education Department, 1976), p. 15.

example, may involve a special school, complete multiple-tracks, partial multiple tracks (for example, honors classes), and extraclass groups. Students may be grouped for all or part of the school day. Consequently, the trinity of adaptations for the gifted and talented actually refers to some aspects of a program for such students.

Commissioner Marland's report noted that the gifted and talented "require differentiated educational programs and/or services beyond those normally provided by the regular school program in order to realize their contribution to self and society."[16] The development of plans for such programs will require attention to the following elements: the nature and needs of gifted and talented students; philosophies of education and special goals and objectives; strategies and procedures for identification; curricular differentiation; appropriate instructional strategies; personnel resources, including teachers, mentors, and role models; material resources in school and community; administrative and organizational adaptations; ancillary services for socioemotional support; evaluation and assessment procedures; linkages with other institutions and agencies, including other schools, colleges, and nonschool establishments; legislation and judicial decisions.

A comprehensive program that attends to these elements can provide an appropriate total educational environment. All aspects of such a program are interrelated and it is the interactions among them that yield educational experiences that contribute to the nurturing of giftedness and talent. As Kaplan put it:

A program for the gifted and talented provides multidimensional and appropriate learning experiences and environments which incorporate the academic, psychological, and social needs of these students. The implementation of administrative procedures and instructional strategies which afford intellectual acquisition, thinking practice, and self-understanding characterize a program for the gifted and talented. A program assures each student of alternatives which teach, challenge, and expand his knowledge while simultaneously stressing the development of an independent learner who can continuously question, apply, and generate information.[17]

16. Marland, *Education of the Gifted and Talented*, vol. 1, p. 2.

17. Sandra N. Kaplan, *Providing Programs for the Gifted and Talented: A Handbook* (Ventura, Calif.: Office of the Ventura County Superintendent of Schools, 1974), p. 8.

As one looks around at various programs and practices and studies the continuously growing body of research and literature, some generalizations or principles emerge that can help in the design of differentiated education for the very diverse population of gifted and talented students.

1. *In designing differentiated education for the gifted and talented, both the special characteristics that apply to the gifted generally and the specific individual differences existing within a gifted group must be taken into account.* The special characteristics of the gifted and talented have been identified through various studies over the years, the most notable of which have been the investigations reported in the series of volumes entitled *Genetic Studies of Genius* by Lewis M. Terman and others. These special characteristics clearly support the concept that giftedness is a multidimensional phenomenon. The range of individual differences among gifted and talented persons can be as great or greater than those existing between the gifted and the nongifted.

2. *The specific goals and objectives that delineate educational imperatives for the gifted and talented should be stated to guide program planning.* As with any students, the basic educational goal for the gifted and talented individuals is to develop their potential in ways consonant with their self-fulfillment and with the interests of society. There are specific objectives, however, that delineate educational imperatives for the gifted population. To the extent that these objectives are made explicit, the appropriate educational experiences and opportunities can be more effectively provided. Sumption, Norris, and Terman have suggested that objectives for the gifted differ from those of other children in the relatively "greater emphasis placed on creative effort, intellectual initiative, critical thinking, social adjustment, and the development of unselfish qualities of leadership."[18]

3. *A design for a curriculum for the gifted and talented should provide for differentiation of goals, content, instructional strategies,*

18. Merle B. Sumption, Dorothy Norris, and Lewis M. Terman, "Special Education for the Gifted Child," in *The Education of Exceptional Children,* Forty-ninth Yearbook of the National Society for the Study of Education, Part II, ed. Nelson B. Henry (Chicago: University of Chicago Press, 1950), p. 278.

resources, and evaluation. A design for curricular differentiation must consider how all of these curricular components affect the outcomes of learning and opportunities for individual development.

4. *Educational experiences for the gifted and talented can be viewed as differing in at least three ways from those of the non-gifted: (a) in breadth and/or depth, (b) in tempo or pace, or (c) in kind.*[19] It is the interaction of the special characteristics of the gifted and talented student with the substance and processes of the curriculum that results in these qualitative differences in programs. The distinctions are not always clear, however, since some experiences may be qualitatively different simply because they come at an earlier age or require less time than usual, or because greater breadth and/or depth may be made possible by acceleration or by the telescoping of content.

5. *Instructional strategies that stress independent thinking and action, the building of relationships, higher levels of abstraction, concept development, creativity, and higher levels of performance are especially appropriate for the gifted and the talented.* As Newland and other writers have observed, there are no teaching methods uniquely appropriate to the needs of the gifted. Rather, the strategies employed with them:

(1) should focus upon helping them to learn to learn, (2) should be appropriate (a) to the level of the intellectual and social development of the child and (b) to the varying kinds of demands and opportunities inherent in the different kinds of learning situations encountered by the child, (3) should reflect a dominant and consistent, though not sole, nurturance of the relatively high capacity of the gifted in the cognitive area, and (4) should reflect persistently a sensitivity to the importance of the progression from the perceptual or low conceptual level to the higher conceptual kinds of cognitive operation.[20]

Discovery learning, satisfaction of curiosity through one's own efforts, understanding of problem-solving processes, and understanding of creative and productive thinking are appropriately stressed with gifted and talented individuals. Educational activities

19. A. Harry Passow, "Enrichment of Education for the Gifted," in *Education for the Gifted*, ed. Henry, p. 197.

20. T. Ernest Newland, *The Gifted in Socioeducational Perspective* (Englewood Cliffs, N.J.: Prentice-Hall, 1976), pp. 153-54.

and provisions made for their development at ages that may be different from the ages at which it is appropriate to program for intellectual giftedness. Intellectual giftedness can be identified early, even at preschool levels. Provisions for identification and for educational programs must take into account these developmental differences. There are also so-called "morning glories" (individuals whose giftedness is apparent early but soon wanes), "late bloomers" (persons whose talents emerge somewhat later than usual), and "underachievers" (persons whose achievements are substantially below what has been predicted). Development of giftedness and talent hardly follows a linear pattern.

10. *Gifted and talented students need access to a variety of "teachers"—instructors, mentors, counselors, and role models.* Teachers of the gifted should certainly include certified classroom teachers as well as other persons who can interact with the students so as to open up educational and developmental opportunities appropriate to their special needs. Teachers must have accurate conceptions about the nature and needs of the gifted and talented, having acquired insights into the origins, qualities, potential, attitudes, drives, and behaviors of this population. The teachers must have reflected on their own attitudes toward giftedness and talent, on their ability to accept nonconformity, divergency, and unconventional attitudes and behaviors, and to allow the freest possible exchange of ideas and the widest variety of solutions to problems. The teacher must have knowledge of instructional strategies and curricular expertise. There is greater consensus on these and other requirements for those who are to work with gifted and talented students than on how individuals with the required qualities and competencies can be identified. There is as yet no clear consensus as to whether professional educators should have special certification for this work. Various approaches are needed in both pre-service and in-service training of persons who would work with the gifted and talented.

11. *Full development of the gifted and talented requires the use of a variety of resources both within and outside the school.* It is probable that the fullest development of the potential of gifted and talented persons cannot occur wholly within the confines of the school, since many of the resources needed are in the community

and family. Education and socialization take place in a variety of settings and involve a variety of resources. The range and kinds of nonformal education are potentially great. The school serves as the catalyst and the coordinator for matching the gifted and talented individuals with the persons and the resources in non-school educative settings. Sometimes these arrangements are formalized and even institutionalized (for example, with a museum, library, laboratory, governmental agency, and so forth), while at other times they are informal and on a one-to-one basis. It may well be that there are even limits to what schools can do to develop so-called "nonacademic" talents such as art, music, drama, and dance without involving the resources of the community.

12. *Parents of gifted and talented pupils must be involved in their development.* Schools can provide the counseling and education that will increase parental insights into the nature and needs of gifted and talented children and youth and into the ways parents can contribute to their development by clarifying their own attitudes and values and by participating more effectively in nurturing their children's talents.

13. *Procedures for evaluating the growth and development of gifted and talented students should take into account their special characteristics.* Evaluation procedures should take into account the higher cognitive concepts and processes, the creative and productive behavior, and the affective growth that are especially appropriate and often unique for gifted and talented persons. Reliance on standardized tests alone is a much too limited approach to evaluation for such students. Much more attention needs to be paid to their products and their performance in evaluating their development.

14. *Programs for the gifted and talented should provide (a) for a balance between mediated independent study and independent activity; (b) for small-group activities with other gifted and talented students, including some interage groupings; and (c) for activities involving interaction with both gifted and nongifted students.* Since there is concern for both cognitive and affective growth—including self-concepts, attitudes toward others who are more or less gifted and talented, values, and so forth—arrangements must be made for various kinds of experience and opportunities.

15. *In each educational unit there should be an individual designated to provide the necessary leadership and to carry responsibility for initiating, arranging, and coordinating the personnel and material resources needed for educating the gifted and talented.* While it is true that "what is good for the gifted is good for all learners," there are clearly unique aspects of a program for the gifted and talented that must be planned and implemented and not left to chance or to the possible initiative of some individual. Leadership is required at all levels of an educational system.

16. *Programs for the gifted require additional funding.* How much additional funding is required depends on the nature of the program. Some additional money is available in some states for identification or for educational programming. Additional funding from federal sources is quite limited, although there is a move to provide categorical grants.

17. *Programs for the gifted and talented must be viewed as an integral part of an ongoing educational program of the school system and not as an appendage or a luxury.* Even when special provisions are made—for instance, a seminar, a special class, an arrangement with a university or college, a special project—these opportunities should be related to the total educational experiences for the gifted and talented population.

The absence of a theory that would explain the nature of giftedness and its nurture has allowed program planners, practitioners, and researchers to operate on the basis of insights that could contribute to the development of such a theory. "Giftedness" is a multiordinal term; it has many different definitions, most of which are operational definitions that guide practice. Different conceptions of giftedness and talent lead to very diverse programs and practices. The diversity one sees in this country and abroad is a natural consequence of these varied conceptions. The generalizations or principles stated above can be grounded to some extent in research. The confidence with which they are expressed varies considerably.

A Look Ahead

As has been pointed out earlier, interest in and concern for the education of the gifted and talented has tended to be a cyclical phenomenon. From time to time, a combination of societal and educational factors has resulted in renewed activity on behalf of these students. Throughout the periods when concern has ebbed, there have, of course, been school programs that have continued and even thrived. The Cleveland Major Work Program, for example, has operated continuously since its inception in 1921. There are aspects of the current revival of interest in the education of the gifted and talented that suggest greater stability and lasting power. Some of this optimism stems from extrapolations from single events. For instance, a report of an "Olympics of the Mind," held at Glassboro State College and cosponsored by the New Jersey State Department of Education, described the event as follows: "With high spirits, sharpened wits, and a collection of gadgets designed to demonstrate their creative ingenuity in solving problems in a nonconventional way, more than 300 students from 25 schools across the state showed up at the college with their teacher-coaches."[27] For some time, it has been advocated that giftedness be developed and rewarded in the same way that athletic prowess is recognized through competitive participation. Plans are being made for an International Olympics of the Mind. While there are a number of issues surrounding such competitions, the holding of these Olympics suggests at least the beginning of some shifts in the social context for the development of talent.

The extent and nature of advocacy for education of the gifted and talented at the federal, state, and local levels involving various individuals and groups—parents, educators, legislators—differ radically from previous support. Advocates are much better organized, seem to be in better communication with one another, and are seeing the fruits of their efforts in federal and state legislation and appropriations.

The development of long-range state and local plans that encompass detailed roles and strategies for educating the gifted and the talented promise more significant institutionalization of such programs. The format of one plan suggests a development that provides a "framework upon which a comprehensive course of action can be built regardless of the agency in which the plan

27. "Gifted Students in an 'Olympic of the Mind'," New York *Times*, 25 May 1978, p. B-3.

originates."[28] The seven major elements of this plan include: (a) a position statement, (b) planning tasks, (c) goals, (d) objectives, (e) programs, (f) budgetary considerations, and (g) strategies for change.[29] The matrix includes details concerning the individual(s) to whom primary responsibility for accomplishing the objectives is assigned, the means for implementing the objectives, and the date of accomplishment. State and local educational authorities are being urged or required to develop long-range plans for the education of the gifted and talented, plans that take different forms, but give details of goals, means of implementation, roles and responsibilities of personnel, and funding.

Among the concerns of those in the field of education for the gifted and the talented are some that have been receiving increased attention but that should be given even more consideration in the years ahead. One of these is a concern for the highly gifted and the exceptionally talented who are not now adequately served by conventional procedures in most schools. A second is a concern for experimentation with new models for instruction that utilize settings other than the regular classroom. It is also exceedingly important that ways be found to identify and develop giftedness and talent among various ethnic and racial minorities and children of the poor. There should also be a much more systematic attempt to involve individuals in many positions, especially at the grass-roots and leadership levels, as advocates for the gifted and the talented. We need also to continue to find ways in which out-of-school community resources, both personal and material, can be used to extend educational opportunities for these students. Finally, the matter of an appropriate preparation for teachers and others who will be working with gifted and talented students must receive further study.[30]

For far too long, education of the gifted and talented has

---

28. Irving S. Sato, Martin Birnbaum, and Jane E. LoCicero, *Developing a Written Plan for the Education of Gifted and Talented Students* (Ventura, Calif.: Office of the Ventura County Superintendent of Schools, 1974), p. 3.

29. Ibid.

30. A. Harry Passow and Abraham J. Tannenbaum, "Education of the Gifted and Talented: Some Perspectives for the Mid-70s," *NASSP Bulletin* 60 (March 1976): 11.

lacked a real commitment on the part of educators and lay persons alike, with the consequence that such efforts were too often simply part of the current educational fad. The growing commitment to the development of the total range of abilities and talents because it is the right and necessary thing to do suggests that the future of education of the gifted and talented is brighter than it has been in the long history of concern for society's most able and talented individuals.

Index

Ability, differences in areas of, 189-92

Academic aptitudes, statutory definitions of, 66-67

Accelerated classes, use of, in education of the gifted, 117-19

Acceleration of learning, mode of instruction for, 107-9

Acceleration vs. enrichment, in education of the gifted, 187-89

Advanced intellectual abilities: identification of, 145; identification of, by parent information, 147-49; identification of, by test performance, 145; tests used in identification of, 145-46

Allport, G. W., 375

Anastasi, Anne, 187

Anderson, Rodney E., 355

Anthropometric measurements, projected study of, of the gifted, 94

Arciniega, Tomas A., 396, 397

Arieti, Silvano, 362

Art schools, student characteristics and achievement in, 377-78

Art students, cognitive, perceptual, personality, and value characteristics of, 374-75

Artist, social and personal context in development of, 382-86

Artistic specializations, value and personality determinants of, 375-77

Aydelotte, Frank, 225

Baccalaureate programs for the gifted, practice of shortening of, 179-80

Bachtold, Louise M., 409

Bacon, Francis, 140

Baker, Paul, 239

Baldwin, Alexinia, 333, 391, 393

Baldwin Identification Matrix (figure), 391

Baumgarten, Franziska, 335, 347

Bereiter, Carl, quoted, p. 191

Bernal, Ernest M. Jr., 333

Bestor, Arthur E., 7, 11

Binet, Alfred, 169

Biondi, Angelo, 359

Bishop, William E., 278

Black gifted population, unique needs of, 388-94

Blacks, historical precedents for cultivation of talents of, 393-94

Bloom, Benjamin S., 34

Board of Regents (N.Y.), recommendations of, for education of the gifted, 444-45

Boston, Bruce O., 275, 276

Brazziel, William F., quoted, 393-94

Brickman, William W., 103

Bridges, Sydney, 313

Briggs, Paul, quoted, 199

Bronowski, Jacob, quoted, 33

Bruch, Catherine, 389, 398

Bruner, Jerome S., 32

Burgdorf, Kenneth, 389

Burke, Barbara P., 356

Burt, Sir Cyril, 310

Bypassing bachelor's degree, practice of, in education of the gifted, 180-82

Calasanctius, Joseph, 117

Calasanctius School in Buffalo, 90, 98; outcomes of, 136-37; program and experiences of, 127-37; uniqueness of program of, 129-33

Callahan, Carolyn M., 183, 333, 334

Career, assisting gifted to make proper choices of, 248-50

Career education: assumptions underlying programs in, 246-47; programming of, for the gifted, 250-52

Carnegie Commission on Higher Education, 119; proposal of, to shorten A.B. programs, 225

Cattell, J. McK., 375

Certification of teachers of the gifted: problems of, 285-86; state action in relation to, 286-88

Cohen, Joseph W., 226

Coleman, James S., 13

College Level Examination of Proficiency (CLEP), college credit based on performance on, 224-25

457

INFORMATION CONCERNING
THE NATIONAL SOCIETY FOR THE STUDY OF EDUCATION

1. *Purpose.* The purpose of the National Society is to promote the investigation and discussion of educational questions. To this end it holds an annual meeting and publishes a series of yearbooks and a series of paperbacks on Contemporary Educational Issues.

2. *Membership.* Any person interested in the purpose of the Society and in receiving its publications may become a member by sending in name, title, address, and a check covering dues and the entrance fee (see items 4 and 5). Graduate students may become members, upon recommendation of a faculty member, at a reduced rate for the first year of membership. Dues for all subsequent years are the same as for other members.

Membership is not transferable. It is limited to individuals and may not be held by libraries, schools, or other institutions, either directly or indirectly.

3. *Period of Membership.* Membership is for the calendar year and terminates automatically on December 31, unless dues for the ensuing year are paid as indicated in item 6. Applicants for membership may not date their entrance back of the current calendar year.

4. *Categories of Membership.* The following categories of membership have been established:

Regular. Annual dues are $13.00. The member receives a clothbound copy of each part of the yearbook.

Comprehensive. Annual dues are $27.00. The member receives a clothbound copy of the yearbook *and* all volumes in the current year's paperback series on Contemporary Educational Issues.

Secial Memberships for Retired Members and Graduate Students.

Retired members. Persons who are retired or who are sixty-five years of age *and* who have been members of the Society continuously for at least ten years may retain their Regular Membership upon payment of annual dues of $10.00 or their Comprehensive Membership upon payment of annual dues of $20.00.

Graduate Students. Graduate students may pay annual dues of $10.00 for Regular Membership or $20.00 for Comprehesive Membership for their first year of membership, plus the $1.00 entrance fee in either case.

Life Memberships. Persons sixty years of age or above may become life members on payment of a fee based on the average life expectancy of their age group. Regular life members may take out a Comprehensive Membership for any year by payment of an additional fee of $10.00. For information apply to the Secretary-Treasurer.

5. *Privileges of Membership.* Members receive the publications of the Society as described above. All members are entitled to vote, to participate in meetings of the Society, and (under certain conditions) to hold office.

6. *Entrance Fee.* New members are required to pay an entrance fee of one dollar, in addition to the dues, for the first year of membership.

7. *Payment of Dues.* Statements of dues are rendered in October for the following calendar year. Any member so notified whose dues remain unpaid on January 1 thereby loses membership and can be reinstated only by paying the dues plus a reinstatement fee of fifty cents ($.50).

School warrants and vouchers from institutions must be accompanied by definite information concerning the name and address of the person for whom the membership fee is being paid. Statements of dues are rendered on our own form only. The Secretary's office cannot undertake to fill out special invoice forms of any kind or to affix a notary's affidavit to statements or receipts.

Cancelled checks serve as receipts. Members desiring an additional receipt must enclose a stamped and addressed envelope therefor.

8. *Distribution of Yearbooks to Members.* The yearbooks, normally ready prior to the February meeting of the Society, will be mailed from the office of the distributor only to members whose dues for that year have been paid.

9. *Commercial Sales.* The distribution of all yearbooks prior to the current year, and also of those of the current year not regularly mailed to members in exchange for their dues, is in the hands of the distributor, not of the Secretary. Orders may be placed with the University of Chicago Press, Chicago, Illinois 60637, which distributes the yearbooks of the Society. Orders for paperbacks in the series on Contemporary Educational Issues should be placed with the designated publisher of that series. The list of the Society's publications is printed in each yearbook.

10. *Yearbooks.* The yearbooks are issued about one month before the February meeting. Published in two volumes, each of which contains 300 to 400 pages, the yearbooks are planned to be of immediate practical value as well as representative of sound scholarship and scientific investigation.

11. *Series on Contemporary Educational Issues.* This series, in paperback format, is designed to supplement the yearbooks by timely publications on topics of current interest. There will usually be three of these volumes each year.

12. *Meetings.* The annual meeting, at which the yearbooks are presented and critiqued, is held as a rule in February at the same time and place as the meeting of the American Association of School Administrators. Members will be notified of other meetings.

Applications for membership will be handled promptly at any time. New members will receive the yearbook scheduled for publication during the calendar year in which application for Regular Membership is made. New members who elect to take out the Comprehensive membership will receive both the yearbook and the paperbacks scheduled for publication during the year in which application is made.

KENNETH J. REHAGE, Secretary-Treasurer

5835 Kimbark Avenue
Chicago, Illinois 60637

PUBLICATIONS OF THE NATIONAL SOCIETY FOR THE STUDY OF EDUCATION

1. The Yearbooks

NOTICE: Many of the early yearbooks of this series are now out of print. In the following list, those titles to which an asterisk is prefixed are not available for purchase.

*First Yearbook, 1902, Part I—*Some Principles in the Teaching of History.* Lucy M. Salmon.
*First Yearbook, 1902, Part II—*The Progress of Geography in the Schools.* W. M. Davis and H. M. Wilson.
*Second Yearbook, 1903, Part I—*The Course of Study in History in the Common School.* Isabel Lawrence, C. A. McMurray, Frank McMurry, E. C. Page, and E. J. Rice.
*Second Yearbook, 1903, Part II—*The Relation of Theory to Practice in Education.* M. J. Holmes, J. A. Keith, and Levi Seeley.
*Third Yearbook, 1904, Part I—*The Relation of Theory to Practice in the Education of Teachers.* John Dewey, Sarah C. Brooks, F. M. McMurry, et al.
*Third Yearbook, 1904, Part II—*Nature Study.* W. S. Jackman.
*Fourth Yearbook, 1905, Part I—*The Education and Training of Secondary Teachers.* E. C. Elliott, E. G. Dexter, M. J. Holmes, et al.
*Fourth Yearbook, 1905, Part II—*The Place of Vocational Subjects in the High-School Curriculum.* J. S. Brown, G. B. Morrison, and Ellen Richards.
*Fifth Yearbook, 1906, Part I—*On the Teaching of English in Elementary and High Schools.* G. P. Brown and Emerson Davis.
*Fifth Yearbook, 1906, Part II—*The Certification of Teachers.* E. P. Cubberley.
*Sixth Yearbook, 1907, Part I—*Vocational Studies for College Entrance.* C. A. Herrick, H. W. Holmes, T. deLaguna, V. Prettyman, and W. J. S. Bryan.
*Sixth Yearbook, 1907, Part II—*The Kindergarten and Its Relation to Elementary Education.* Ada Van Stone Harris, E. A. Kirkpatrick, Marie Kraus-Boelté, Patty S. Hill, Harriette M. Mills, and Nina Vandewalker.
*Seventh Yearbook, 1908, Part I—*The Relation of Superintendents and Principals to the Training and Professional Improvement of Their Teachers.* Charles D. Lowry.
*Seventh Yearbook, 1908, Part II—*The Co-ordination of the Kindergarten and the Elementary School.* B. J. Gregory, Jennie B. Merrill, Bertha Payne, and Margaret Giddings.
*Eighth Yearbook, 1909, Part I—*Education with Reference to Sex: Pathological, Economic, and Social Aspects.* C. R. Henderson.
*Eighth Yearbook, 1909, Part II—*Education with Reference to Sex: Agencies and Methods.* C. R. Henderson and Helen C. Putnam.
*Ninth Yearbook, 1910, Part I—*Health and Education.* T. D. Wood.
*Ninth Yearbook, 1910, Part II—*The Nurses in Education.* T. D. Wood, et al.
*Tenth Yearbook, 1911, Part I—*The City School as a Community Center.* H. C. Leipziger, Sarah E. Hyre, R. D. Warden, C. Ward Crampton, E. W. Stitt, E. J. Ward, Mrs. T. C. Grice, and C. A. Perry.
*Tenth Yearbook, 1911, Part II—*The Rural School as a Community Center.* B. H. Crocheron, Jessie Field, F. W. Howe, E. C. Bishop, A. B. Graham, O. J. Kern, M. T. Scudder, and B. M. Davis.
*Eleventh Yearbook, 1912, Part I—*Industrial Education: Typical Experiments Described and Interpreted.* J. F. Barker, M. Bloomfield, B. W. Johnson, P. Johnson, L. M. Leavitt, G. A. Mirick, M. W. Murray, C. F. Perry, A. L. Stafford, and H. B. Wilson.
*Eleventh Yearbook, 1912, Part II—*Agricultural Education in Secondary Schools.* A. C. Monahan, R. W. Stimson, D. J. Crosby, W. H. French, H. F. Button, F. R. Crane, W. R. Hart, and G. F. Warren.
*Twelfth Yearbook, 1913, Part I—*The Supervision of City Schools.* Franklin Bobbitt, J. W. Hall, and J. D. Wolcott.
*Twelfth Yearbook, 1913, Part II—*The Supervision of Rural Schools.* A. C. Monahan, L. J. Hanifan, J. E. Warren, Wallace Lund, U. J. Hoffman, A. S. Cook, E. M. Rapp, Jackson Davis, J. D. Wolcott.
*Thirteenth Yearbook, 1914, Part I—*Some Aspects of High-School Instruction and Administration.* H. C. Morrison, E. R. Breslich, W. A. Jessup, and L. D. Coffman.
*Thirteenth Yearbook, 1914, Part II—*Plans for Organizing School Surveys, with a Summary of Typical School Surveys.* Charles H. Judd and Henry L. Smith.
*Fourteenth Yearbook, 1915, Part I—*Minimum Essentials in Elementary School Subjects—Standards and Current Practices.* H. B. Wilson, H. W. Holmes, F. E. Thompson, R. G. Jones, S. A. Courtis, W. S. Gray, F. N. Freeman, H. C. Pryor, J. F. Hosic, W. A. Jessup, and W. C. Bagley.
*Fourteenth Yearbook, 1915, Part II—*Methods for Measuring Teachers' Efficiency.* Arthur C. Boyce.
*Fifteenth Yearbook, 1916, Part I—*Standards and Tests for the Measurement of the Efficiency of Schools and School Systems.* G. D. Strayer, Bird T. Baldwin, B. R. Buckingham, F. W. Ballou, D. C. Bliss, H. G. Childs, S. A. Courtis, E. P. Cubberley, C. H. Judd, George Melcher, E. E. Oberholtzer, J. B. Sears, Daniel Starch, M. R. Trabue, and G. M. Whipple.

*Fifteenth Yearbook, 1916, Part II—*The Relationship between Persistence in School and Home Conditions.* Charles E. Holley.
*Fifteenth Yearbook, 1916, Part III—*The Junior High School.* Aubrey A. Douglass.
*Sixteenth Yearbook, 1917, Part I—*Second Report of the Committee on Minimum Essentials in Elementary-School Subjects.* W. C. Bagley, W. W. Charters, F. N. Freeman, W. S. Gray, Ernest Horn, J. H. Hoskinson, W. S. Monroe, C. F. Munson, H. C. Pryor, L. W. Rapeer, G. M. Wilson, and H. B. Wilson.
*Sixteenth Yearbook, 1917, Part II—*The Efficiency of College Students as Conditioned by Age at Entrance and Size of High School.* B. F. Pittenger.
*Seventeenth Yearbook, 1918, Part I—*Third Report of the Committee on Economy of Time in Education.* W. C. Bagley, B. B. Bassett, M. E. Branom, Alice Camerer, J. E. Dealey, C. A. Ellwood, E. B. Greene, A. B. Hart, J. F. Hosic, E. T. Housh, W. H. Mace, L. R. Marston, H. C. McKown, H. E. Mitchell, W. V. Reavis, D. Snedden, and H. B. Wilson.
*Seventeenth Yearbook, 1918, Part II—*The Measurement of Educational Products.* E. J. Ashbaugh, W. A. Averill, L. P. Ayers, F. W. Ballou, Edna Bryner, B. R. Buckingham, S. A. Courtis, M. E. Haggerty, C. H. Judd, George Melcher, W. S. Monroe, E. A. Nifenecker, and E. L. Thorndike.
*Eighteenth Yearbook, 1919, Part I—*The Professional Preparation of High-School Teachers.* G. N. Cade, S. S. Colvin, Charles Fordyce, H. H. Foster, T. S. Gosling, W. S. Gray, L. V. Koos, A. R. Mead, H. L. Miller, F. C. Whitcomb, and Clifford Woody.
*Eighteenth Yearbook, 1919, Part II—*Fourth Report of Committee on Economy of Time in Education.* F. C. Ayer, F. N. Freeman, W. S. Gray, Ernest Horn, W. S. Monroe, and C. E. Seashore.
*Nineteenth Yearbook, 1920, Part I—*New Materials of Instruction.* Prepared by the Society's Committee on Materials of Instruction.
*Nineteenth Yearbook, 1920, Part II—*Classroom Problems in the Education of Gifted Children.* T. S. Henry.
*Twentieth Yearbook, 1921, Part I—*New Materials of Instruction.* Second Report by Society's Committee.
*Twentieth Yearbook, 1921, Part II—*Report of the Society's Committee on Silent Reading.* M. A. Burgess, S. A. Courtis, C. E. Germane, W. S. Gray, H. A. Greene, Regina R. Heller, J. H. Hoover, J. A. O'Brien, J. L. Packer, Daniel Starch, W. W. Theisen, G. A. Yoakam, and representatives of other school systems.
*Twenty-first Yearbook, 1922, Parts I and II—*Intelligence Tests and Their Use,* Part I—*The Nature, History, and General Principles of Intelligence Testing.* E. L. Thorndike, S. S. Colvin, Harold Rugg, G. M. Whipple, Part II—*The Administrative Use of Intelligence Tests.* H. W. Holmes, W. K. Layton, Helen Davis, Agnes L. Rogers, Rudolf Pintner, M. R. Trabue, W. S. Miller, Bessie L. Gambrill, and others. The two parts are bound together.
*Twenty-second Yearbook, 1923, Part I—*English Composition: Its Aims, Methods and Measurements.* Earl Hudelson.
*Twenty-second Yearbook, 1923, Part II—*The Social Studies in the Elementary and Secondary School.* A. S. Barr, J. J. Coss, Henry Harap, R. W. Hatch, H. C. Hill, Ernest Horn, C. H. Judd, L. C. Marshall, F. M. McMurry, Earle Rugg, H. O. Rugg, Emma Schweppe, Mabel Snedaker, and C. W. Washburne.
*Twenty-third Yearbook, 1924, Part I—*The Education of Gifted Children.* Report of the Society's Committee. Guy M. Whipple, Chairman.
*Twenty-third Yearbook, 1924, Part II—*Vocational Guidance and Vocational Education for Industries.* A. H. Edgerton and others.
*Twenty-fourth Yearbook, 1925, Part I—*Report of the National Committee on Reading.* W. S. Gray, Chairman, F. W. Ballou, Rose L. Hardy, Ernest Horn, Francis Jenkins, S. A. Leonard, Estaline Wilson, and Laura Zirbes.
*Twenty-fourth Yearbook, 1925, Part II—*Adapting the Schools to Individual Differences.* Report of the Society's Committee. Carleton W. Washburne, Chairman.
*Twenty-fifth Yearbook, 1926, Part I—*The Present Status of Safety Education.* Report of the Society's Committee. Guy M. Whipple, Chairman.
*Twenty-fifth Yearbook, 1926, Part II—*Extra-Curricular Activities.* Report of the Society's Committee. Leonard V. Koos, Chairman.
*Twenty-sixth Yearbook, 1927, Part I—*Curriculum-making: Past and Present.* Report of the Society's Committee. Harold O. Rugg, Chairman.
*Twenty-sixth Yearbook, 1927, Part II—*The Foundations of Curriculum-making.* Prepared by individual members of the Society's Committee. Harold O. Rugg, Chairman.
*Twenty-seventh Yearbook, 1928, Part I—*Nature and Nurture: Their Influence upon Intelligence.* Prepared by the Society's Committee. Lewis M. Terman, Chairman.
*Twenty-seventh Yearbook, 1928, Part II—*Nature and Nurture: Their Influence upon Achievement.* Prepared by the Society's Committee. Lewis M. Terman, Chairman.
Twenty-eighth Yearbook, 1929, Parts I and II—*Preschool and Parental Education,* Part I—*Organization and Development.* Part II—*Research and Method.* Prepared by the Society's Committee. Lois H. Meek, Chairman. Bound in one volume. Cloth.
*Twenty-ninth Yearbook, 1930, Parts I and II—*Report of the Society's Committee on Arithmetic.* Part I—*Some Aspects of Modern Thought on Arithmetic.* Part II—*Research in Arithmetic.* Prepared by the Society's Committee. F. B. Knight, Chairman. Bound in one volume.
*Thirtieth Yearbook, 1931—Part I—*The Status of Rural Education.* First Report of the Society's Committee on Rural Education. Orville G. Brim, Chairman.
Thirtieth Yearbook, 1931, Part II—*The Textbook in American Education.* Report of the Society's Committee on the Textbook. J. B. Edmonson, Chairman. Cloth, Paper.

*Thirty-first Yearbook, 1932, Part I—*A Program for Teaching Science.* Prepared by the Society's Committee on the Teaching of Science. S. Ralph Powers, Chairman.
*Thirty-first Yearbook, 1932, Part II—*Changes and Experiments in Liberal-Arts Education.* Prepared by Kathryn McHale, with numerous collaborators.
*Thirty-second Yearbook, 1933—*The Teaching of Geography.* Prepared by the Society's Committee on the Teaching of Geography. A. E. Parkins, Chairman.
*Thirty-third Yearbook, 1934, Part I—*The Planning and Construction of School Buildings.* Prepared by the Society's Committee on School Buildings. N. L. Engelhardt, Chairman.
*Thirty-third Yearbook, 1934, Part II—*The Activity Movement.* Prepared by the Society's Committee on the Activity Movement. Lois Coffey Mossman, Chairman.
Thirty-fourth Yearbook, 1935—*Educational Diagnosis.* Prepared by the Society's Committee on Educational Diagnosis. L. J. Brueckner, Chairman. Paper.
*Thirty-fifth Yearbook, 1936, Part I—*The Grouping of Pupils.* Prepared by the Society's Committee. W. W. Coxe, Chairman.
*Thirty-fifth Yearbook, 1936, Part II—*Music Education.* Prepared by the Society's Committee. W. L. Uhl, Chairman.
*Thirty-sixth Yearbook, 1937, Part I—*The Teaching of Reading.* Prepared by the Society's Committee. W. S. Gray, Chairman.
*Thirty-sixth Yearbook, 1937, Part II—*International Understanding through the Public-School Curriculum.* Prepared by the Society's Committee. I. L. Kandel, Chairman.
*Thirty-seventh Yearbook, 1938, Part I—*Guidance in Educational Institutions.* Prepared by the Society's Committee. G. N. Kefauver, Chairman.
*Thirty-seventh Yearbook, 1938, Part II—*The Scientific Movement in Education.* Prepared by the Society's Committee. F. N. Freeman, Chairman.
*Thirty-eighth Yearbook, 1939, Part I—*Child Development and the Curriculum.* Prepared by the Society's Committee. Carleton Washburne, Chairman.
Thirty-eighth Yearbook, 1939, Part II—*General Education in the American College.* Prepared by the Society's Committee. Alvin Eurich, Chairman. Cloth.
*Thirty-ninth Yearbook, 1940, Part I—*Intelligence: Its Nature and Nurture. Comparative and Critical Exposition.* Prepared by the Society's Committee. G. D. Stoddard, Chairman.
*Thirty-ninth Yearbook, 1940, Part II—*Intelligence: Its Nature and Nurture. Original Studies and Experiments.* Prepared by the Society's Committee. G. D. Stoddard, Chairman.
*Fortieth Yearbook, 1941—*Art in American Life and Education.* Prepared by the Society's Committee. Thomas Munro, Chairman.
Forty-first Yearbook, 1942, Part I—*Philosophies of Education.* Prepared by the Society's Committee. John S. Brubacher, Chairman. Cloth, Paper.
Forty-first Yearbook, 1942, Part II—*The Psychology of Learning.* Prepared by the Society's Committee. T. R. McConnell, Chairman. Cloth.
*Forty-second Yearbook, 1943, Part I—*Vocational Education.* Prepared by the Society's Committee. F. J. Keller, Chairman.
*Forty-second Yearbook, 1943, Part II—*The Library in General Education.* Prepared by the Society's Committee. L. R. Wilson, Chairman.
Forty-third Yearbook, 1944, Part I—*Adolescence.* Prepared by the Society's Committee. Harold E. Jones, Chairman. Paper.
*Forty-third Yearbook, 1944, Part II—*Teaching Language in the Elementary School.* Prepared by the Society's Committee. M. R. Trabue, Chairman.
*Forty-fourth Yearbook, 1945, Part I—*American Education in the Postwar Period: Curriculum Reconstruction.* Prepared by the Society's Committee. Ralph W. Tyler, Chairman.
Forty-fourth Yearbook, 1945, Part II—*American Education in the Postwar Period: Structural Reorganization.* Prepared by the Society's Committee. Bess Goodykoontz, Chairman. Paper.
*Forty-fifth Yearbook, 1946, Part I—*The Measurement of Understanding.* Prepared by the Society's Committee. William A. Brownell, Chairman.
*Forty-fifth Yearbook, 1946, Part II—*Changing Conceptions in Educational Administration.* Prepared by the Society's Committee. Alonzo G. Grace, Chairman.
*Forty-sixth Yearbook, 1947, Part I—*Science Education in American Schools.* Prepared by the Society's Committee. Victor H. Noll, Chairman.
Forty-sixth Yearbook, 1947, Part II—*Early Childhood Education.* Prepared by the Society's Committee. N. Searle Light, Chairman. Paper.
Forty-seventh Yearbook, 1948, Part I—*Juvenile Delinquency and the Schools.* Prepared by the Society's Committee. Ruth Strang, Chairman. Cloth.
Forty-seventh Yearbook, 1948, Part II—*Reading in the High School and College.* Prepared by the Society's Committee. William S. Gray, Chairman. Cloth, Paper.
Forty-eighth Yearbook, 1949, Part I—*Audio-visual Materials of Instruction.* Prepared by the Society's Committee. Stephen M. Corey, Chairman. Cloth.
*Forty-eighth Yearbook, 1949, Part II—*Reading in the Elementary School.* Prepared by the Society's Committee. Arthur I. Gates, Chairman.
*Forty-ninth Yearbook, 1950, Part I—*Learning and Instruction.* Prepared by the Society's Committee. G. Lester Anderson, Chairman.
Forty-ninth Yearbook, 1950, Part II—*The Education of Exceptional Children.* Prepared by the Society's Committee. Samuel A. Kirk, Chairman. Paper.
Fiftieth Yearbook, 1951, Part I—*Graduate Study in Education.* Prepared by the Society's Board of Directors. Ralph W. Tyler, Chairman. Paper.
Fiftieth Yearbook, 1951, Part II—*The Teaching of Arithmetic.* Prepared by the Society's Committee. G. T. Buswell, Chairman. Cloth, Paper.
Fifty-first Yearbook, 1952, Part I—*General Education.* Prepared by the Society's Committee. T. R. McConnell, Chairman. Cloth, Paper.

Fifty-first Yearbook, 1952, Part II—*Education in Rural Communities.* Prepared by the Society's Committee. Ruth Strang, Chairman. Cloth, Paper.

*Fifty-second Yearbook, 1953, Part I—*Adapting the Secondary-School Program to the Needs of Youth.* Prepared by the Society's Committee: William G. Brink, Chairman.

Fifty-second Yearbook, 1953, Part II—*The Community School.* Prepared by the Society's Committee. Maurice F. Seay, Chairman. Cloth.

Fifty-third Yearbook, 1954, Part I—*Citizen Co-operation for Better Public Schools.* Prepared by the Society's Committee. Edgar L. Morphet, Chairman. Cloth, Paper.

Fifty-third Yearbook, 1954, Part II—*Mass Media and Education.* Prepared by the Society's Committee. Edgar Dale, Chairman. Paper.

*Fifty-fourth Yearbook, 1955, Part I—*Modern Philosophies and Education.* Prepared by the Society's Committee. John S. Brubacher, Chairman.

Fifty-fourth Yearbook, 1955, Part II—*Mental Health in Modern Education.* Prepared by the Society's Committee. Paul A. Witty, Chairman. Paper.

*Fifty-fifth Yearbook, 1956, Part I—*The Public Junior College.* Prepared by the Society's Committee. B. Lamar Johnson, Chairman.

Fifty-fifth Yearbook, 1956, Part II—*Adult Reading.* Prepared by the Society's Committee. David H. Clift, Chairman. Paper.

Fifty-sixth Yearbook, 1957, Part I—*In-service Education of Teachers, Supervisors, and Administrators.* Prepared by the Society's Committee. Stephen M. Corey, Chairman. Cloth, Paper.

Fifty-sixth Yearbook, 1957, Part II—*Social Studies in the Elementary School.* Prepared by the Society's Committee. Ralph C. Preston, Chairman. Cloth, Paper.

Fifty-seventh Yearbook, 1958, Part I—*Basic Concepts in Music Education.* Prepared by the Society's Committee. Thurber H. Madison, Chairman. Cloth.

Fifty-seventh Yearbook, 1958, Part II—*Education for the Gifted.* Prepared by the Society's Committee. Robert J. Havighurst, Chairman. Cloth, Paper.

Fifty-seventh Yearbook, 1958, Part III—*The Integration of Educational Experiences.* Prepared by the Society's Committee. Paul L. Dressel, Chairman. Cloth.

Fifty-eighth Yearbook, 1959, Part I—*Community Education: Principles and Practices from World-wide Experience.* Prepared by the Society's Committee. C. O. Arndt, Chairman. Cloth, Paper.

Fifty-eighth Yearbook, 1959, Part II—*Personnel Services in Education.* Prepared by the Society's Committee. Melvene D. Hardee, Chairman. Paper.

*Fifty-ninth Yearbook, 1960, Part I—*Rethinking Science Education.* Prepared by the Society's Committee. J. Darrell Barnard, Chairman.

Fifty-ninth Yearbook, 1960, Part II—*The Dynamics of Instructional Groups.* Prepared by the Society's Committee. Gale E. Jensen, Chairman. Cloth, Paper.

Sixtieth Yearbook, 1961, Part I—*Development in and through Reading.* Prepared by the Society's Committee. Paul A. Witty, Chairman. Cloth, Paper.

Sixtieth Yearbook, 1961, Part II—*Social Forces Influencing American Education.* Prepared by the Society's Committee. Ralph W. Tyler, Chairman. Cloth.

Sixty-first Yearbook, 1962, Part I—*Individualizing Instruction.* Prepared by the Society's Committee. Fred T. Tyler, Chairman. Cloth.

Sixty-first Yearbook, 1962, Part II—*Education for the Professions.* Prepared by the Society's Committee. G. Lester Anderson, Chairman. Cloth.

Sixty-second Yearbook, 1963, Part I—*Child Psychology.* Prepared by the Society's Committee. Harold W. Stevenson, Editor. Cloth.

Sixty-second Yearbook, 1963, Part II—*The Impact and Improvement of School Testing Programs.* Prepared by the Society's Committee. Warren G. Findley, Editor. Cloth.

Sixty-third Yearbook, 1964, Part I—*Theories of Learning and Instruction.* Prepared by the Society's Committee. Ernest R. Hilgard, Editor. Paper.

Sixty-third Yearbook, 1964, Part II—*Behavioral Science and Educational Administration.* Prepared by the Society' Committee. Daniel E. Griffiths, Editor. Paper.

Sixty-fourth Yearbook, 1965, Part I—*Vocational Education.* Prepared by the Society's Committee. Melvin L. Barlow, Editor. Cloth.

Sixty-fourth Yearbook, 1965, Part II—*Art Education.* Prepared by the Society's Committee. W. Reid Hastie, Editor. Cloth.

Sixty-fifth Yearbook, 1966, Part I—*Social Deviancy among Youth.* Prepared by the Society's Committee. William W. Wattenberg, Editor. Cloth.

Sixty-fifth Yearbook, 1966, Part II—*The Changing American School.* Prepared by the Society's Committee. John I. Goodlad, Editor. Cloth.

Sixty-sixth Yearbook, 1967, Part I—*The Educationally Retarded and Disadvantaged.* Prepared by the Society's Committee. Paul A. Witty, Editor. Cloth.

Sixty-sixth Yearbook, 1967, Part II—*Programed Instruction.* Prepared by the Society's Committee. Phil C. Lange, Editor. Cloth.

Sixty-seventh Yearbook, 1968, Part I—*Metropolitanism: Its Challenge to Education.* Prepared by the Society's Committee. Robert J. Havighurst, Editor. Cloth.

Sixty-seventh Yearbook, 1968, Part II—*Innovation and Change in Reading Instruction.* Prepared by the Society's Committee. Helen M. Robinson, Editor. Cloth.

Sixty-eighth Yearbook, 1969, Part I—*The United States and International Education.* Prepared by the Society's Committee. Harold G. Shane, Editor. Cloth.

Sixty-eighth Yearbook, 1969, Part II—*Educational Evaluation: New Roles, New Means.* Prepared by the Society's Committee. Ralph W. Tyler, Editor. Cloth.

Sixty-ninth Yearbook, 1970, Part I—*Mathematics Education.* Prepared by the Society's Committee. Edward G. Begle, Editor. Cloth.

Sixty-ninth Yearbook, 1970, Part II—*Linguistics in School Programs.* Prepared by the Society's Committee. Albert H. Marckwardt, Editor. Cloth.

Seventieth Yearbook, 1971, Part I—*The Curriculum: Retrospect and Prospect.* Prepared by the Society's Committee. Robert M. McClure, Editor. Paper.

Seventieth Yearbook, 1971, Part II—*Leaders in American Education.* Prepared by the Society's Committee. Robert J. Havighurst, Editor. Cloth.

Seventy-first Yearbook, 1972, Part I—*Philosophical Redirection of Educational Research.* Prepared by the Society's Committee. Lawrence G. Thomas, Editor. Cloth.

Seventy-first Yearbook, 1972, Part II—*Early Childhood Education.* Prepared by the Society's Committee. Ira J. Gordon, Editor. Cloth, Paper.

Seventy-second Yearbook, 1973, Part I—*Behavior Modification in Education.* Prepared by the Society's Committee. Carl E. Thoresen, Editor. Cloth.

Seventy-second Yearbook, 1973, Part II—*The Elementary School in the United States.* Prepared by the Society's Committee. John I. Goodlad and Harold G. Shane, Editors. Cloth.

Seventy-third Yearbook, 1974, Part I—*Media and Symbols: The Forms of Expression, Communication, and Education.* Prepared by the Society's Committee. David R. Olson, Editor. Cloth.

Seventy-third Yearbook, 1974, Part II—*Uses of the Sociology of Education.* Prepared by the Society's Committee. C. Wayne Gordon, Editor. Cloth.

Seventy-fourth Yearbook, 1975, Part I—*Youth.* Prepared by the Society's Committee. Robert J. Havighurst and Philip H. Dreyer, Editors. Cloth.

Seventy-fourth Yearbook, 1975, Part II—*Teacher Education.* Prepared by the Society's Committee. Kevin Ryan, Editor. Cloth.

Seventy-fifth Yearbook, 1976, Part I—*Psychology of Teaching Methods.* Prepared by the Society's Committee. N. L. Gage, Editor. Cloth.

Seventy-fifth Yearbook, 1976, Part II—*Issues in Secondary Education.* Prepared by the Society's Committee. William Van Til, Editor. Cloth.

Seventy-sixth Yearbook, 1977, Part I—*The Teaching of English.* Prepared by the Society's Committee. James R. Squire, Editor. Cloth.

Seventy-sixth Yearbook, 1977, Part II—*The Politics of Education.* Prepared by the Society's Committee. Jay D. Scribner, Editor. Cloth.

Seventy-seventh Yearbook, 1978, Part I—*The Courts and Education,* Clifford P. Hooker, Editor. Cloth.

Seventy-seventh Yearbook, 1978, Part II—*Education and the Brain,* Jeanne Chall and Allan F. Mirsky, Editors. Cloth.

Seventy-eighth Yearbook, 1979, Part I—*The Gifted and the Talented: Their Education and Development,* A. Harry Passow, Editor. Cloth.

Seventy-eighth Yearbook, 1979, Part II—*Classroom Management,* Daniel L. Duke, Editor. Cloth.

Yearbooks of the National Society are distributed by

THE UNIVERSITY OF CHICAGO PRESS, CHICAGO, ILLINOIS 60637

Please direct inquiries regarding prices of volumes still available to the University of Chicago Press. Orders for these volumes should be sent to the University of Chicago Press, not to the offices of the National Society.

2. The Series on Contemporary Educational Issues

In addition to its Yearbooks the Society now publishes volumes in a series on Contemporary Educational Issues. These volumes are prepared under the supervision of the Society's Commission on an Expanded Publication Program.

The 1979 Titles

Educational Environments and Effects: Evaluation, Policy, and Productivity (Herbert J. Walberg, ed.)

Research on Teaching: Concepts, Findings, and Implications, (Penelope L. Peterson and Herbert J. Walberg, eds.)

The Principal in Metropolitan Schools (Donald A. Erickson and Theodore L. Reller, eds.)

The 1978 Titles

Aspects of Reading Education (Susanna Pflaum-Connor, ed.)

History, Education, and Public Policy: Recovering the American Educational Past (Donald R. Warren, ed.)

From Youth to Constructive Adult Life: The Role of the Public School (Ralph W. Tyler, ed.)

The 1977 Titles

Early Childhood Education: Issues and Insights (Bernard Spodek and Herbert J. Walberg, eds.)

The Future of Big City Schools: Desegregation Policies and Magnet Alternatives (Daniel U. Levine and Robert J. Havighurst, eds.)

Educational Administration: The Developing Decades (Luvern L. Cunningham, Walter G. Hack, and Raphael O. Nystrand, eds.)

The 1976 Titles

Prospects for Research and Development in Education (Ralph W. Tyler, ed.)

Public Testimony on Public Schools (Commission on Educational Governance)

Counseling Children and Adolescents (William M. Walsh, ed.)

The 1975 Titles

Schooling and the Rights of Children (Vernon Haubrich and Michael Apple, eds.)

Systems of Individualized Education (Harriet Talmage, ed.)

Educational Policy and International Assessment: Implications of the IEA Assessment of Achievement (Alan Purves and Daniel U. Levine, eds.)

The 1974 Titles

Crucial Issues in Testing (Ralph W. Tyler and Richard M. Wolf, eds.)

Conflicting Conceptions of Curriculum (Elliott Eisner and Elizabeth Vallance, eds.)

Cultural Pluralism (Edgar G. Epps, ed.)

Rethinking Educational Equality (Andrew T. Kopan and Herbert J. Walberg, eds.)

All of the above volumes may be ordered from

McCutchan Publishing Corporation
2526 Grove Street
Berkeley, California 94704

The 1972 Titles

Black Students in White Schools (Edgar G. Epps, ed.)

Flexibility in School Programs (W. J. Congreve and G. L. Rinehart, eds.)

Performance Contracting—1969-1971 (J. A. Mecklenburger)

The Potential of Educational Futures (Michael Marien and W. L. Ziegler, eds.)

Sex Differences and Discrimination in Education (Scarvia Anderson, ed.)

The 1971 Titles

Accountability in Education (Leon M. Lessinger and Ralph W. Tyler, eds.)

Farewell to Schools? ? ? (D. U. Levine and R. J. Havighurst, eds.)

Models for Integrated Education (D. U. Levine, ed.)

PYGMALION *Reconsidered* (J. D. Elashoff and R. E. Snow)

Reactions to Silberman's CRISIS IN THE CLASSROOM (A. Harry Passow, ed.)

A limited number of copies of the above titles (except PYGMALION *Reconsidered*) are still available from the Office of the Secretary, NSSE, 5835 Kimbark Avenue, Chicago, Ill. 60637.

THE ABENAKI